Introduction to AutoCAD Plant 3D 2025

Tutorial Books

This book may not be duplicated in any way without the express written consent of the publisher, except in the form of brief excerpts or quotations for review. The information contained herein is for the personal use of the reader. It may not be incorporated in any commercial programs, other books, databases, or any software without the written consent of the publisher. Making copies of this book or any portion for a purpose other than your own is a violation of copyright laws.

Limit of Liability/Disclaimer of Warranty:

The author and publisher make no representations or warranties concerning the accuracy or completeness of the contents of this work and specifically disclaim all warranties, including without limitation warranties of fitness for a particular purpose. The advice and strategies contained herein may not be suitable for every situation. Neither the publisher nor the author shall be liable for damages arising hereafter.

Trademarks:

All brand names and product names used in this book are trademarks, registered trademarks, or trade names of their respective holders. The author and publisher do not associate with any product or vendor mentioned in this book.

Copyright © 2024 Tutorial Books

All rights reserved.

Download Resource files from *www.tutorialbook.weebly.com*

Table of Contents

Introduction

This book introduces you to AutoCAD Plant 3D 2025, which is used to create Piping and Instrumentation diagrams and design a 3D Plant model quickly. AutoCAD Plant 3D is the product of Autodesk. It was first released to help the process and power industry in the year 2007. It also includes AutoCAD P&ID. This software is designed to create Piping and Instrumentation Diagrams and then design a 3D Plant model based on the P&ID. A P&ID (Piping and Instrumentation Diagram) displays the connections between the equipment of a process and the instrumentation controlling the process. A P&ID is created using standard symbols. In AutoCAD Plant 3D, you can create P&IDs using symbols related to various standards such as PIP, ISO, ISA, DIN, and JIS-ISO. You can create 3D Models using predefined and user-defined parts. You can then relate the 3D model to the corresponding P&ID. After creating the 3D models, you can use them to generate Orthographic, elevation, and section views. You can also create Isometric drawings, which can be used to manufacture.

AutoCAD Plant 3D is based on AutoCAD User-interface. However, the intelligent 2D/3D symbols and the connected Database are the main features of this application. You can use this database to generate reports, create annotations, and so on. When you change the attributes of various symbols, the annotations are updated automatically.

In AutoCAD Plant 3D, you create everything inside a project in order to make your design consistent. You can create a project on a Standalone workstation or a Network. Creating a project on a Network synchronizes your work with your team members. You can also use the validation tools to check any errors inside the project

Chapter 1: Creating P&IDs

Starting AutoCAD Plant 3D 2025

Starting AutoCAD Plant 3D 2025

- Click the AutoCAD Plant 3D 2025 icon on the Desktop.

- Alternatively, click the Windows icon (Start button) at the bottom left corner, then:

    - Click "All apps" or search for "AutoCAD Plant 3D 2025"

    - Select the AutoCAD Plant 3D 2025 folder or icon

    - Click the AutoCAD Plant 3D 2025 icon; the Autodesk AutoCAD Plant 3D 2025 window will appear.

Note: In Windows 11, the Start menu is centered, and the "All apps" list is accessible by clicking the "All apps" button or searching for the app name.

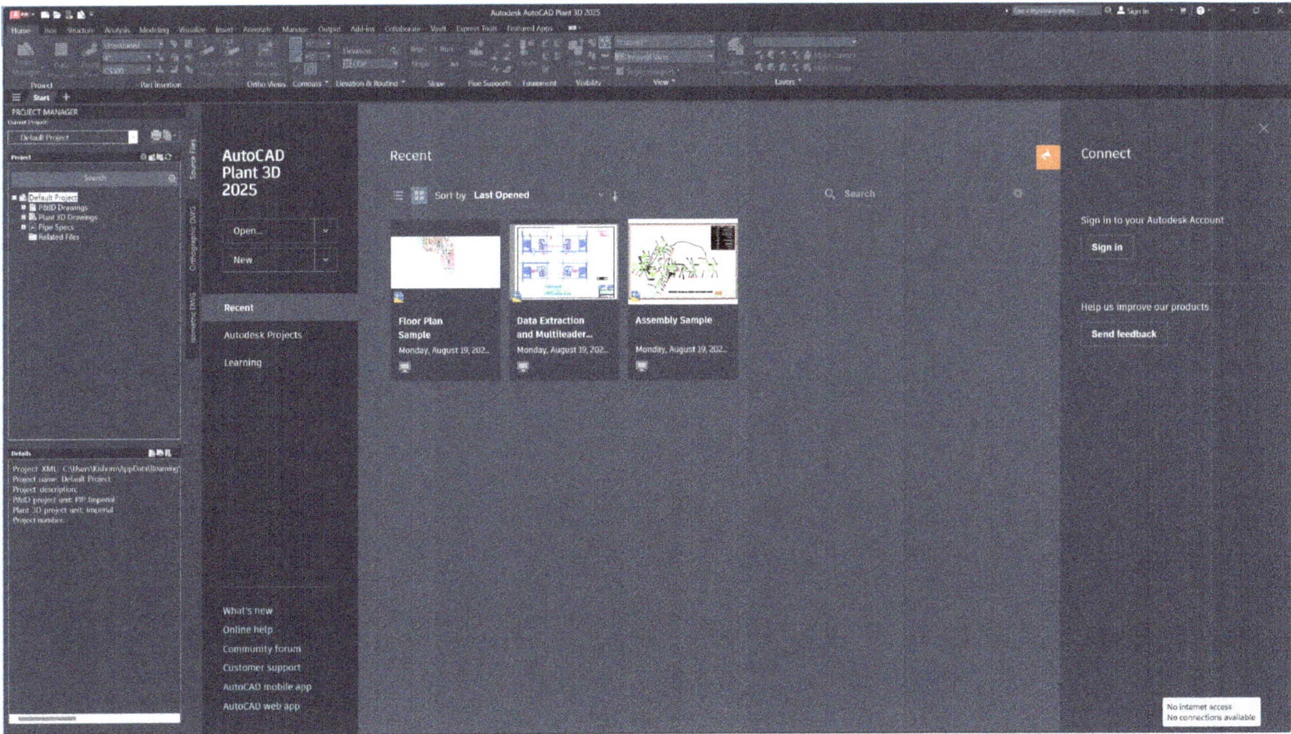

Understanding Projects in AutoCAD Plant 3D 2025

AutoCAD Plant 3D 2025 is a project-based application that stores all objects in a Project database. The Project Manager palette allows you to access and manage project files from the database. To get started, explore the Sample Project by clicking on the Current Project drop-down menu and selecting Sample Project in the Project Manager.

Project Manager Overview

The Project Manager consists of various drawing types, including:

- P&IDs
- 3D piping
- Orthographic drawings
- Isometric drawings
- Additional files like spreadsheets

These are organized into tabs:

- **Source Files:** P&IDs, Plant 3D drawings, Pipe Specs, and related files in a folder hierarchy
- **Orthographic DWG:** Plan view and elevation drawings
- **Isometric DWG:** Isometric and spool drawings in folders

Note that orthographic and isometric drawings are generated from the 3D Model.

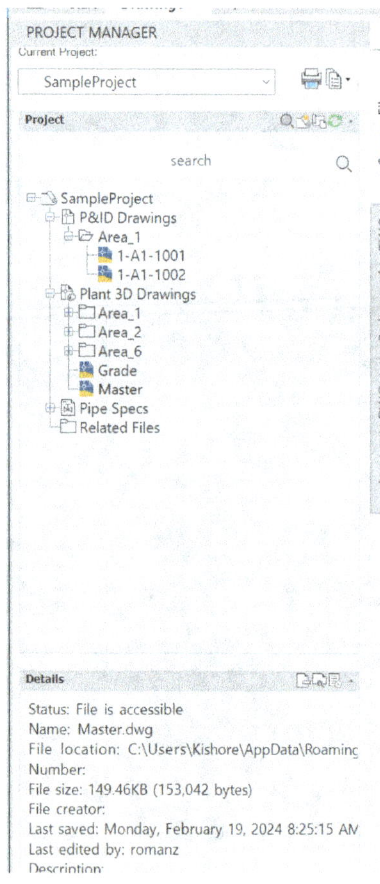

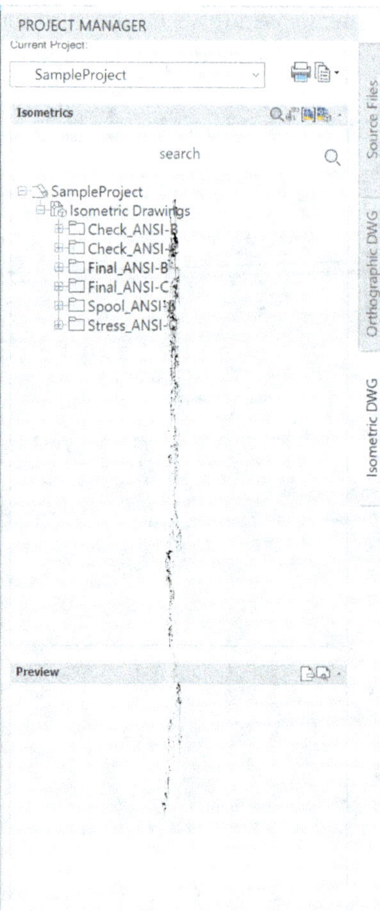

Tutorial 1

In this tutorial, you start a project and then create a P&ID (Piping and Instrumentation Diagram).

Creating a New Project

The first step in the design process is to create a project. The project has a set of files and standards.

1. Start AutoCAD Plant 3D 2025.

2. On the Start screen, click the **New > New Project**.

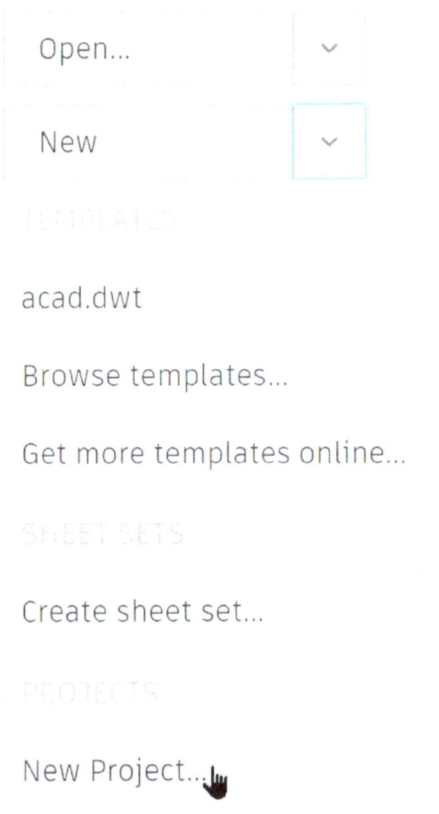

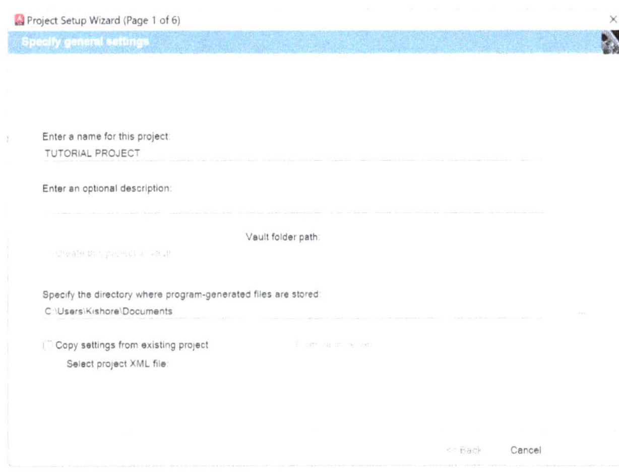

3. Enter **TUTORIAL PROJECT** in the **Enter a name for this project** field.

4. Specify the location of the program generated files and supporting files.
5. Click the **Next** button; the **Specify unit settings** page appears.
6. Select **Imperial** to define the units for project drawings.

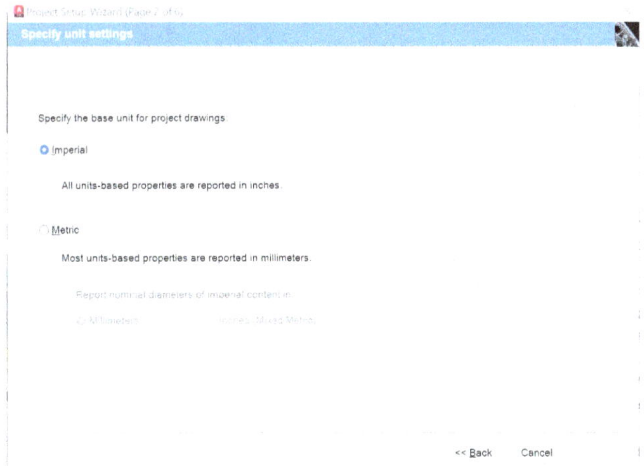

7. Click the **Next** button; the **Specify P&ID settings** page appears.
8. Specify the directory to save the P&ID files.
9. Select **PIP** as the P&ID symbology standard to be used.

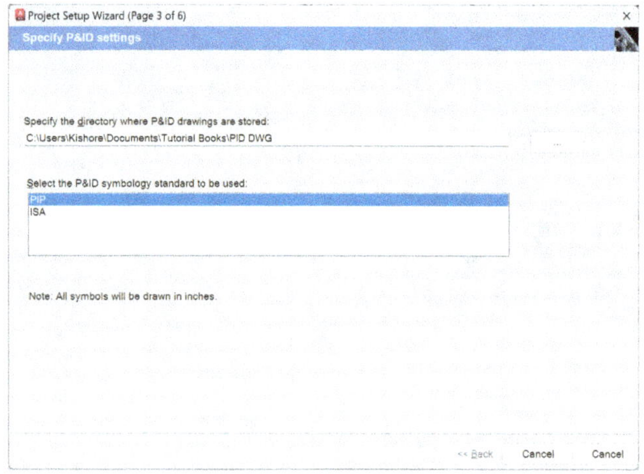

10. Click the **Next** button; the **Specify Plant 3D directory settings** page appears.

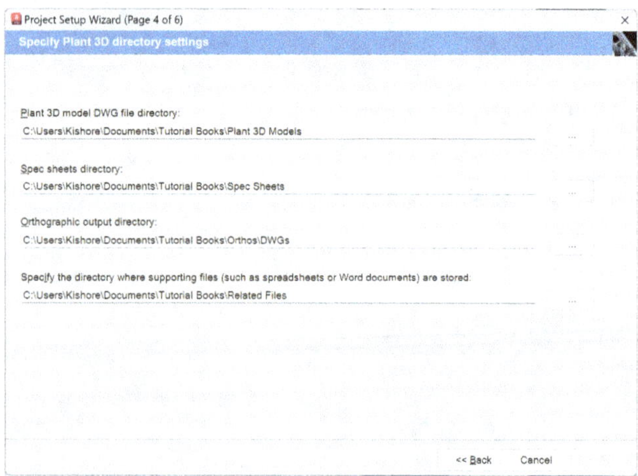

11. Click the **Next** button; the **Specify database settings** page appears.

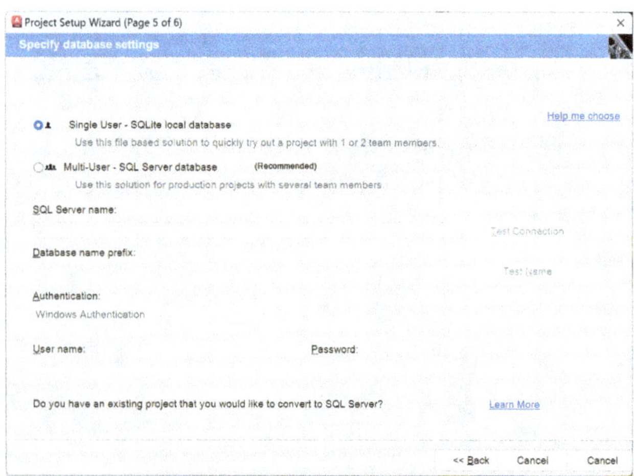

12. Select the **Single User - SQLite local database** option if you are working on a standalone workstation.

If you are working on a server, select the **Multi-User - SQL Server database** option, and configure the server settings.

13. Click the **Next** button; the **Finish** page appears.
14. Click **Finish** to create a new project.

Opening an Existing Project in AutoCAD Plant 3D

To open an existing project in AutoCAD Plant 3D:

1. Select "**Open**" from the drop-down menu in the Project Manager.
   Alternatively, click "**Home**" > "**Project**" > "**Project Manager**" > "**Open Project**" on the ribbon.

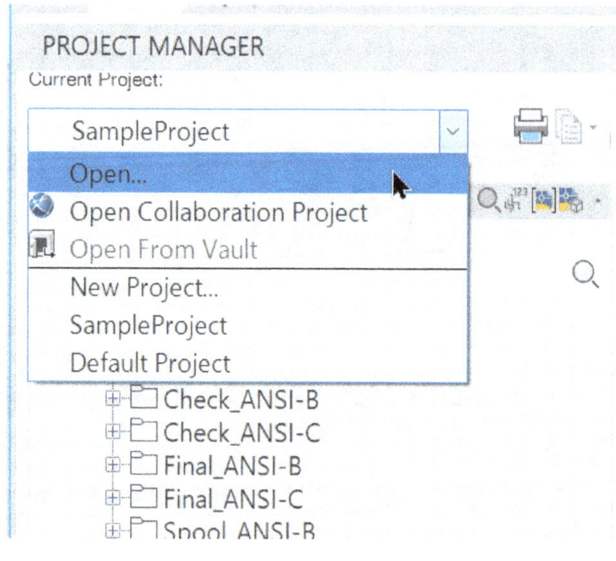

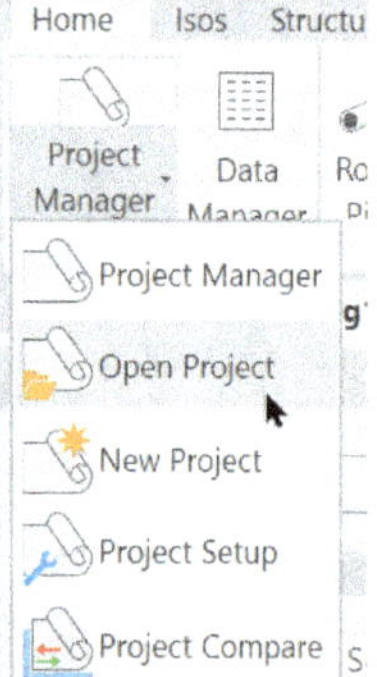

2. In the **Open** dialog, navigate to the project location.

3. Select the .xml (Extensible Markup Language) file associated with the project. This file contains all project information.

Important: Avoid editing or renaming this file, as it may cause project corruption.

Note: Only one project can be open at a time. To open another project, close all files related to the currently active project before proceeding.

Best Practice: Always use the Project Manager to open or create files in AutoCAD Plant 3D. Avoid using the New and Open icons in the AutoCAD application to ensure proper project management.

Creating a New Drawing

Once the project is created or opened, you can create new drawings using the Project Manager. The Project Manager helps you to create new drawings with all the standards built in it.

1. Right-click on **P&ID Drawings**, and then choose **New Drawing.**

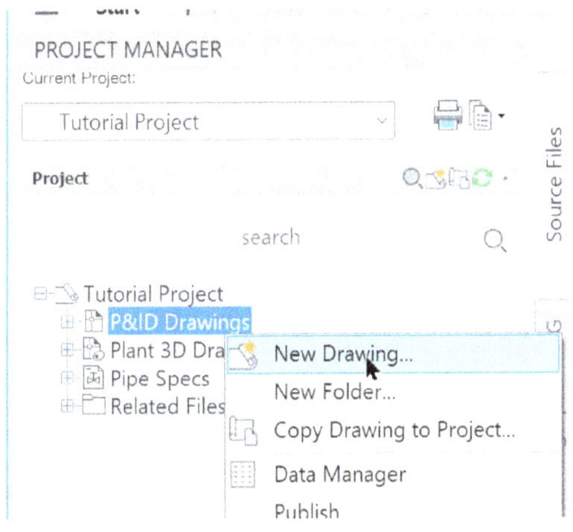

The **New DWG** dialog appears.

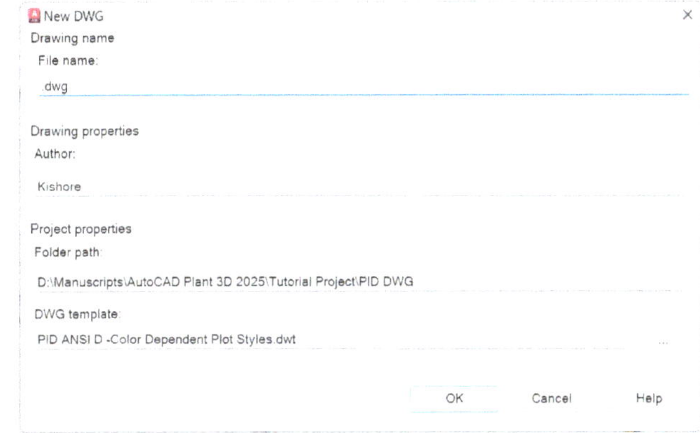

2. Enter **Tutorial1** in the **File name** field.

   The **PID ANSI D - Color Dependent Plot Styles.dwt** is the default template. You can select any other template by clicking the **Browse** button next to the **DWG template** field.

3. Click **OK** to create a new P&ID file.

The default screen of the Plant 3D file appears as shown.

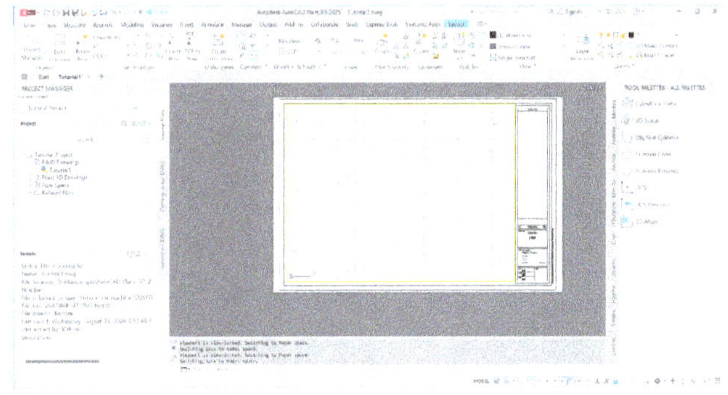

By default, the color scheme of the user interface is **Dark**. You can change it to **Light** if you prefer a bright user interface. To do so, right click and select Options. On the **Options** dialog, click the **Display** tab and select **Color theme > Light** from the **Window Elements** section. Click **OK** to change the color scheme.

See the lower section of the Project Manager. You can view the details, preview, and work history of the currently opened file.

Also, notice that the **Tool Palette** appears on the right side of the screen. You can change the tools displayed on the **Tool Palette**. Right-click on the title bar of the **Tool Palette** to display a menu.

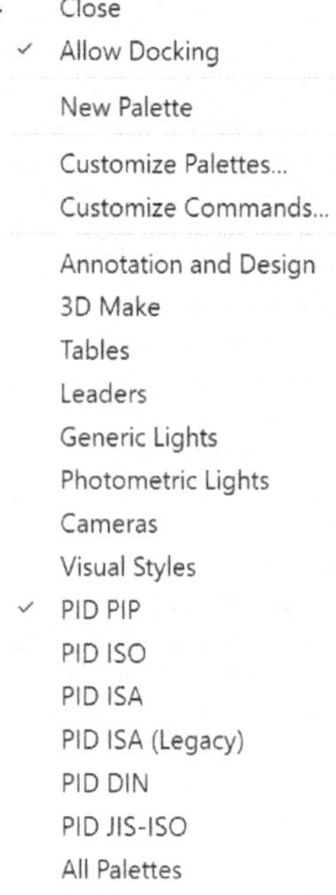

If you cannot see the P&ID PIP tool palette, click **P&ID PIP** on the menu.

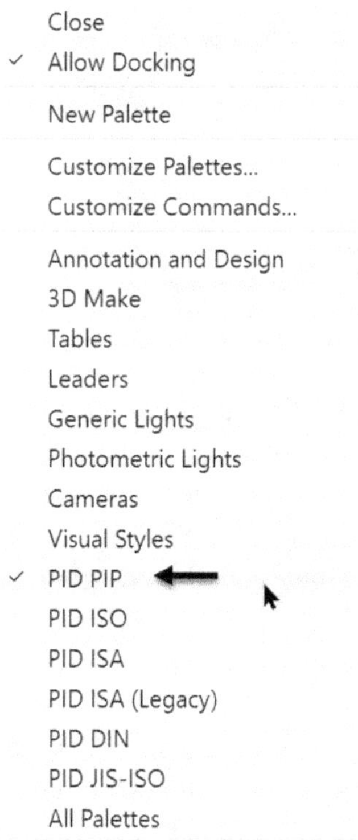

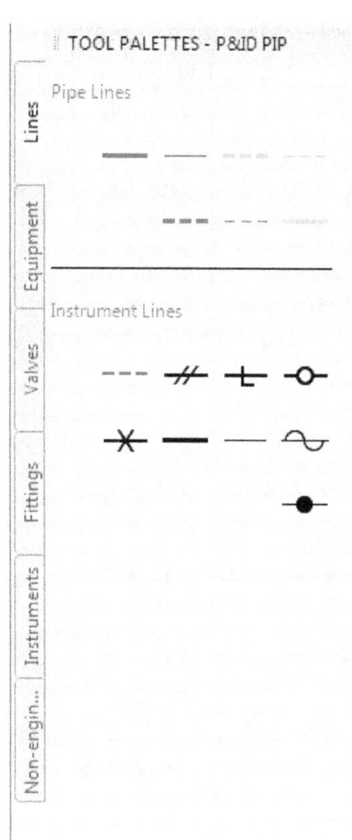

Changing the Workspace

A Workspace is the arrangement of tools and options used for a specific purpose. If a Workspace other than PID PIP is activated in AutoCAD Plant 3D, you can change it. To do this, click the **Workspace Switching** down arrow at the right-side on the Status bar, and then select PID PIP from the flyout.

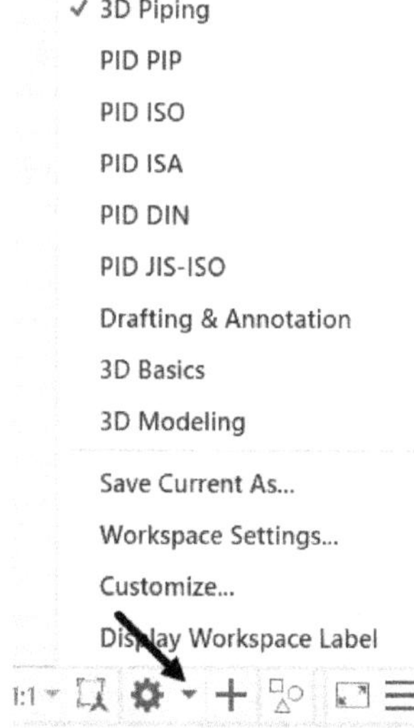

Viewing the Drawing Properties

1. To view the drawing properties, right-click
    on the drawing file, and select **Properties**;
    the **Drawing Properties** dialog appears.

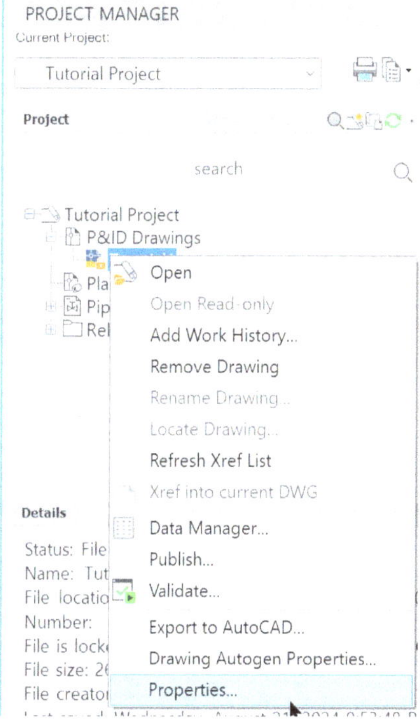

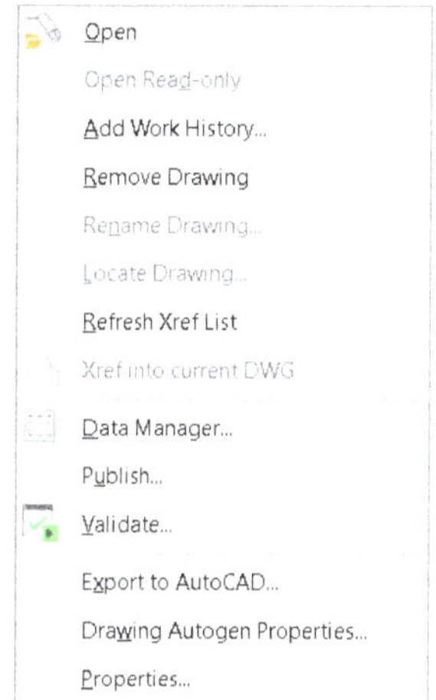

2. Change the properties on the **Drawing Properties**
    dialog, and then click **OK**.

If you want to open an already existing drawing file,
then expand the P&ID Drawings or Plant 3D
Drawings folder and double-click on the drawing file.
You can also right-click and select **Open**.

If two or more people are working on a project, then
only one person can edit the drawing file at a time. If
the other person wants to open the file open in
another workstation, then he/she can use the **Open
Read-Only** option.

P&ID Symbology Standards

The design process in AutoCAD Plant 3D begins with
a Piping and Instrumentation Diagram (P&ID), which
enables rapid understanding of the process. While
creating a P&ID, you can add data to the drawing,
which is then linked to the 3D model.

P&ID Creation in AutoCAD

In simple AutoCAD, P&IDs are created using various
symbol blocks, designed based on industry standards
specific to your country or region.

P&ID Symbology Standards in AutoCAD Plant 3D

AutoCAD Plant 3D offers different symbol libraries
based on five international standards:

1. PIP (Process Industry Practices)

2. ISO (International Organization for
    Standardization)

3. ISA (International Society of Automation)

4. DIN (Deutsches Institut für Normung)

5. JIS (Japanese Industrial Standard)

Each standard has unique symbols, such as the
Centrifugal Pump symbol, which varies across
standards.

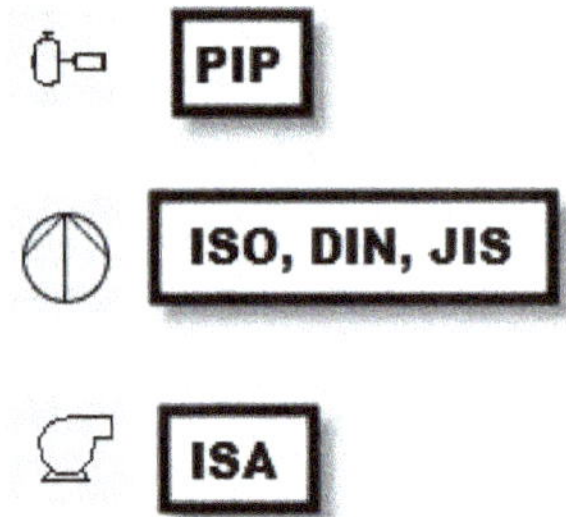

You need to choose a standard while starting a project. You can use only the selected standard throughout the project. So, select the right standard while creating a project.

Placing Equipment

You can start the process of creating a P&ID by first placing the Equipment symbols. After that, you create lines, place inline equipment, place instrumentation, and create annotations.

In this section, you learn to place equipment. AutoCAD Plant 3D provides you with the various pre-defined equipment. The **Equipment** Tool Palette contains all this equipment.

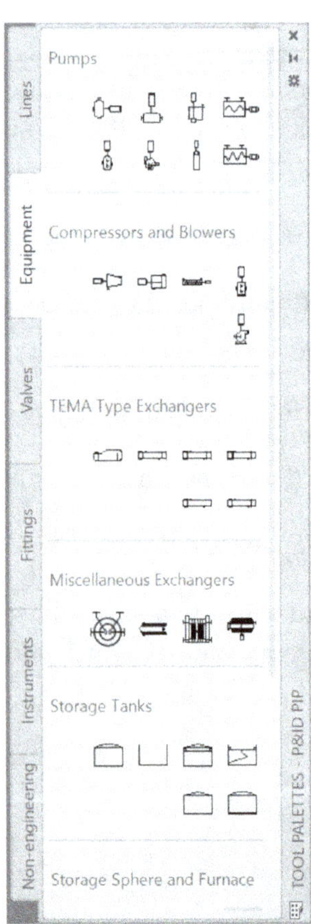

1.   On the Tool Palette, select the **Equipment** tab.

2.   Click the **Vessel** icon under **Vessels and Miscellaneous Vessel Details.**

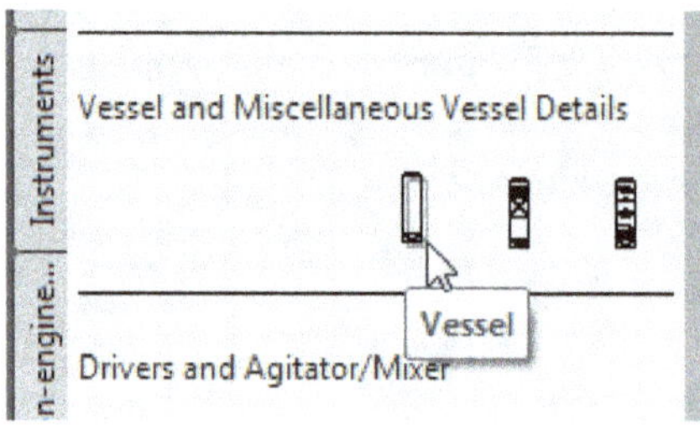

3.   Click in the middle of the drawing area to define the vessel location.

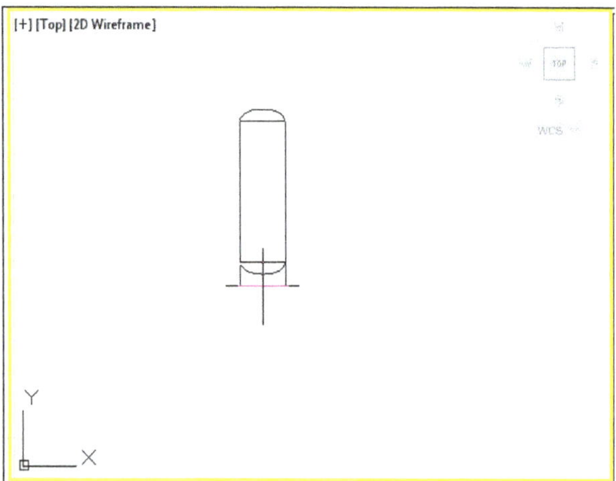

Note: You can turn ON or OFF the grid by clicking the Display grid ▦ *icon located on the Status bar.*

4.   Type 1.5 at the scale prompt and press **Enter** key to specify the scale factor.

The **Assign Tag** dialog appears.

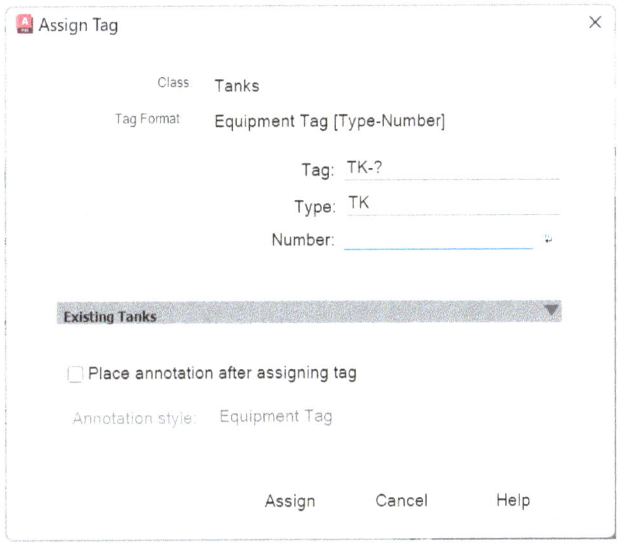

You can type in the information on this dialog, and then assign it to the P&ID component. The program stores the information in the project database. You can then use the Data Manager to view, modify, and export this information.

5.   On the **Assign Tag** dialog, click the button next to the **Number** field.

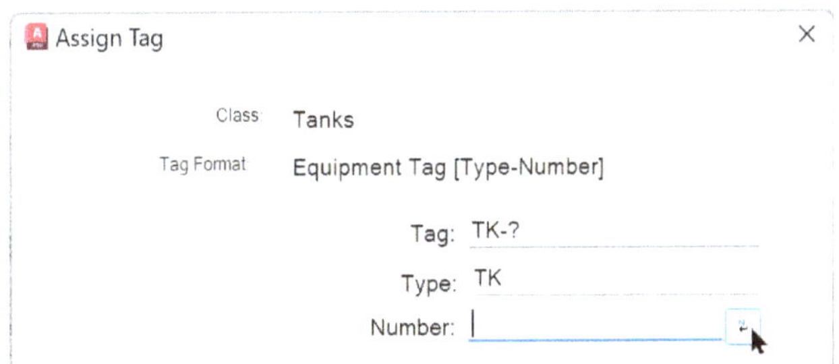

6.   Select the **Place annotation after assigning tag** option.
7.   Select **Annotation style > Equipment tag**.

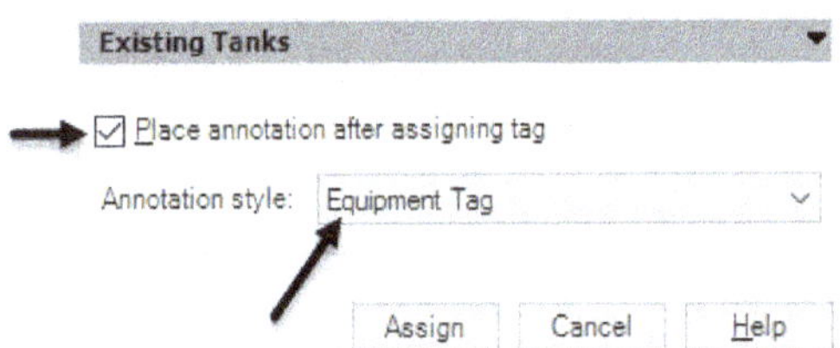

8.   Click **Assign** on the **Assign tag** dialog.
9.   Click above the vessel to place the annotation.

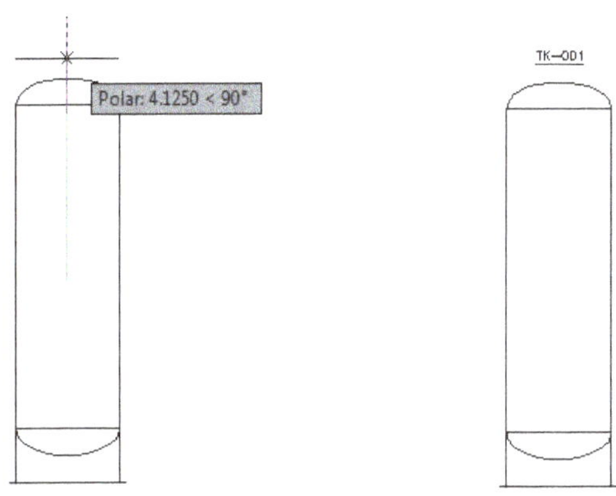

Next, place a Horizontal Centrifugal pump.

10. To place a pump, click the **Horizontal Centrifugal Pump** icon under the **Pumps** section.

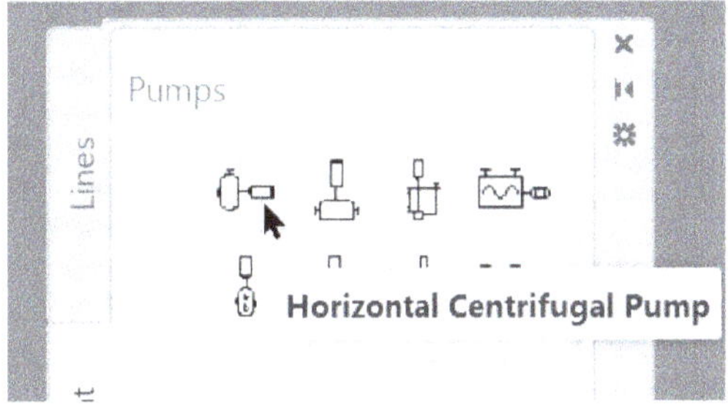

11. Click somewhere near the bottom left of the vessel.

12. Click the button next to the **Number** field.
13. Click **Assign**. The program assigns the tag information to the pump.
14. Place the tag below the pump.

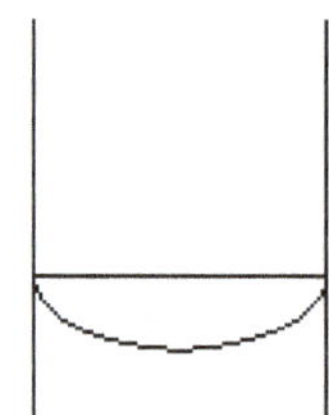

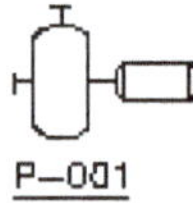

15. Select the pump and its tag by dragging a window across it.

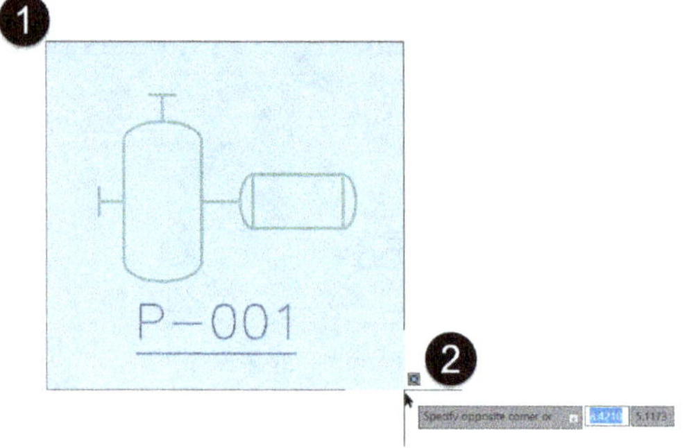

16. Type-in **COPY** in the command line and press Enter.
17. Select the node of the horizontal nozzle of the pump.
18. Move the pointer toward the left and click to copy the pump. Press **Esc**.

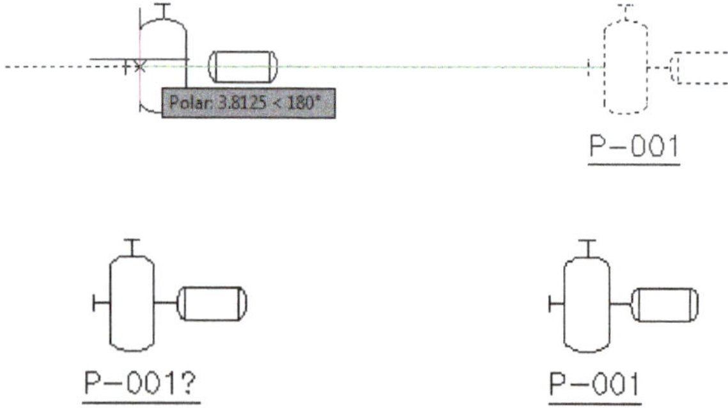

Notice the question mark on the copied tag. To solve this, you have to update the tag.

19. Right-click on the pump and select **Assign Tag**.

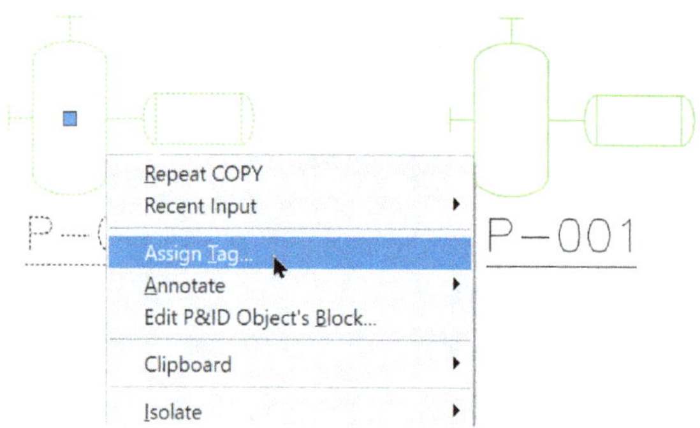

20. Click the button next to the **Number** field and clear the **Place annotation after assigning tag** option.
21. Click **Assign**.

22. Likewise, place a TEMA type BEM Exchanger on the right side of the vessel.

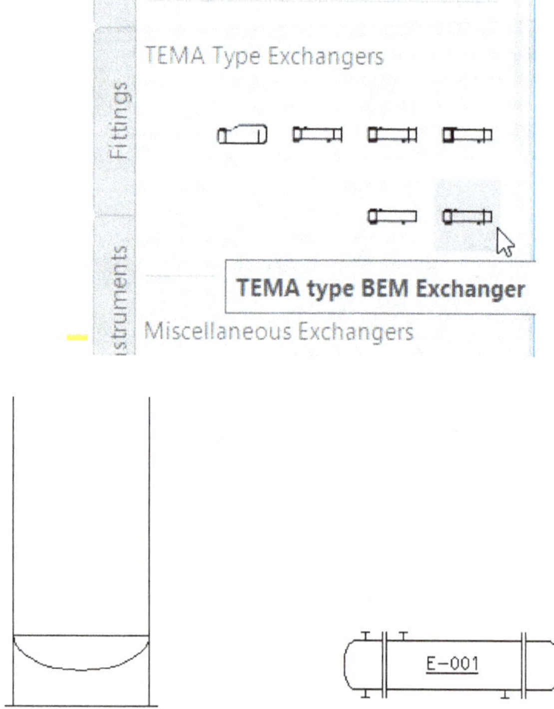

23. The P&ID, after placing all the equipment looks, as shown.

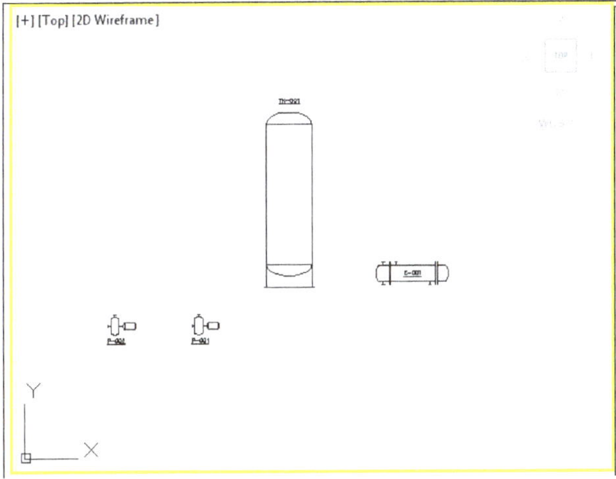

Editing the P&ID Symbols

During the design process, you may require editing the existing P&ID symbols. In this example, you modify the vertical vessel.

1. To edit the vertical vessel, right-click on it and choose **Edit P&ID Object's Block.**

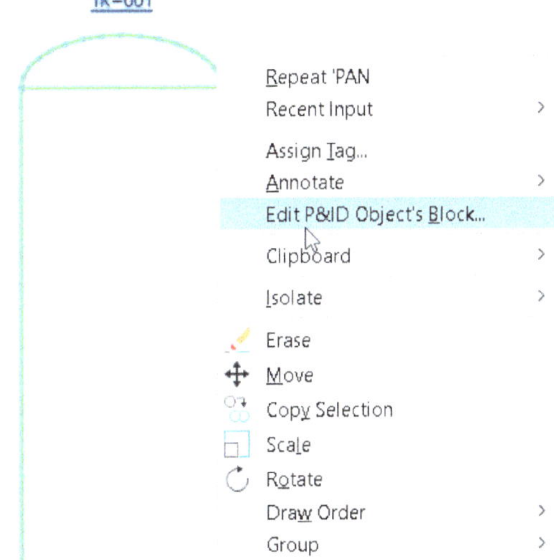

The AutoCAD Block editor appears.

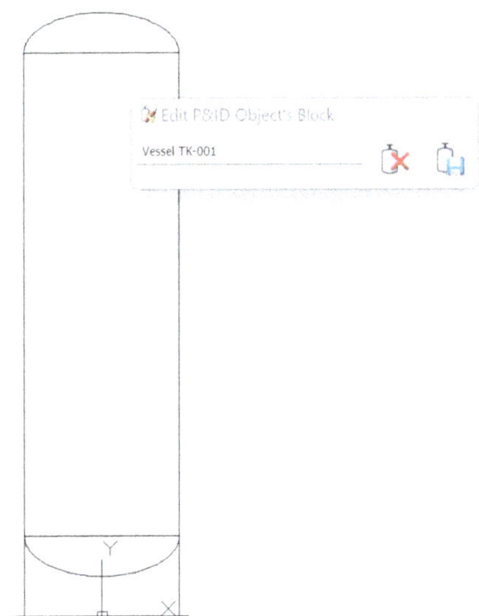

2. Create a selection box and select the dome of the vessel. Press **Delete** to delete the selection.

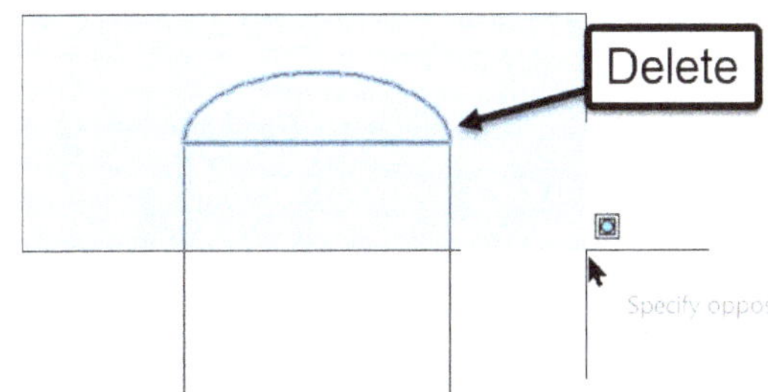

3. Select the left vertical line of the vessel.
4. Click on the top endpoint grip and drag it downwards.
5. Type **2** and press Enter to reduce the length of the line.

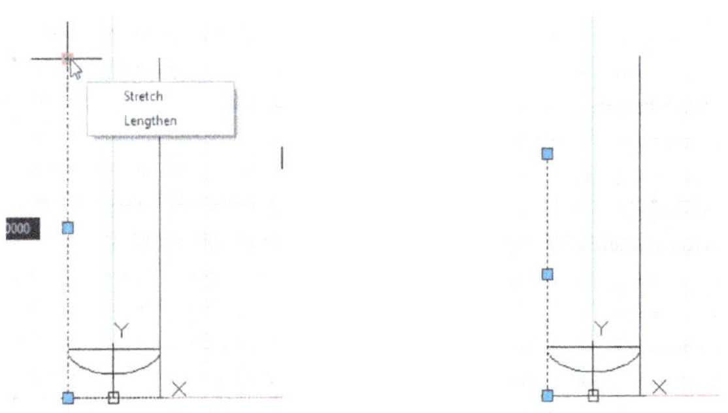

6. Likewise, reduce the length of the right vertical line.
7. Type-in **L** in the command line and press Enter. Create an inclined and vertical line on the left side.

- Activate the **Polar Tracking** ⟳ icon on the status bar.
- Click the down arrow next to the **Polar Tracking** icon and select **30** from the menu.
- Select the top endpoint of the left vertical line.
- Move the pointer and pause when a trace line appears at a 60-degree inclination.

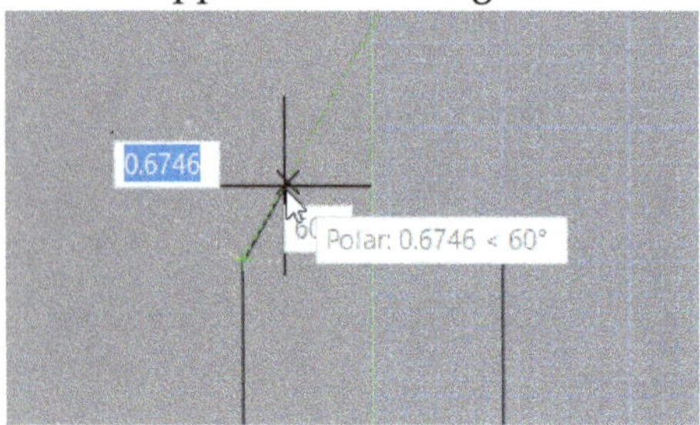

- Move the pointer along the trace line up to a short distance, and then click; an inclined line is created.
- Move the pointer vertically up, type **3,** and press Enter.
- Press Esc to deactivate the **Line** command.

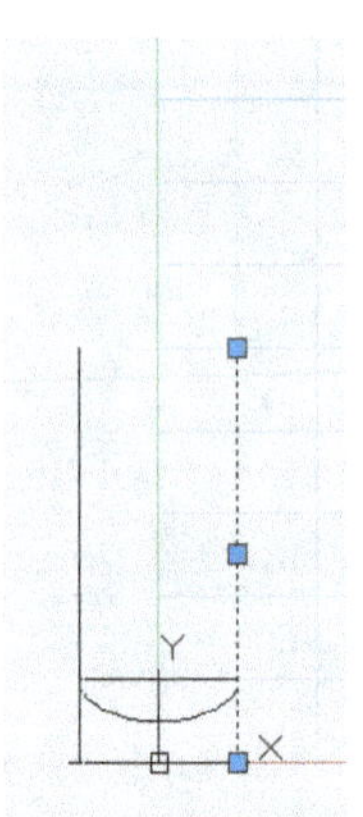

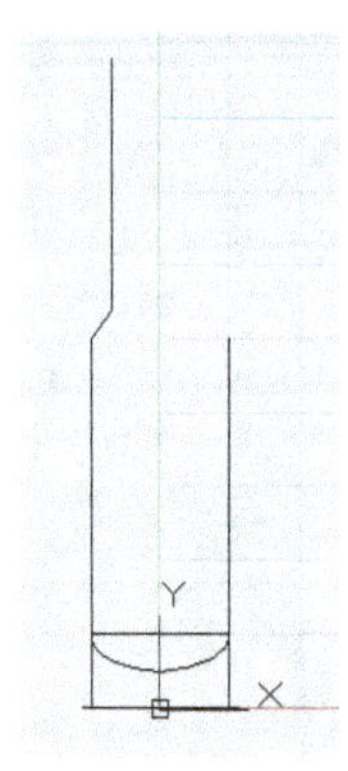

8. Type-in **MI** in the command line and press Enter.
9. Select the newly created inclined and vertical lines. Press Enter to accept the selection.
10. Select the origin point of the UCS.
11. Move the pointer upward, and then click to define the mirror line; the selected entities are mirrored about the mirror line.
12. Select **No** to keep the source objects.
13. Create a horizontal line connecting the endpoints of the top vertical lines.

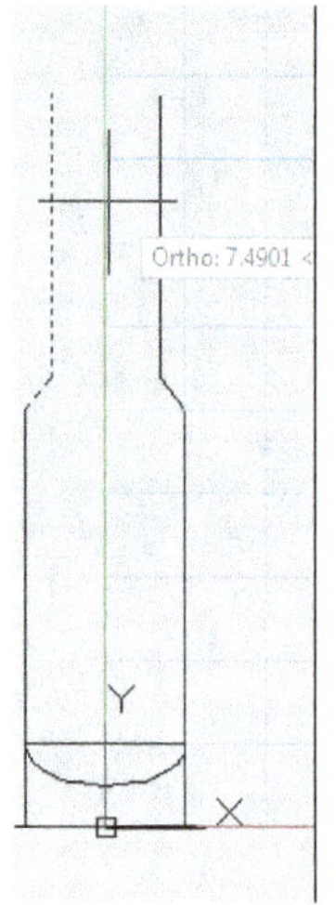

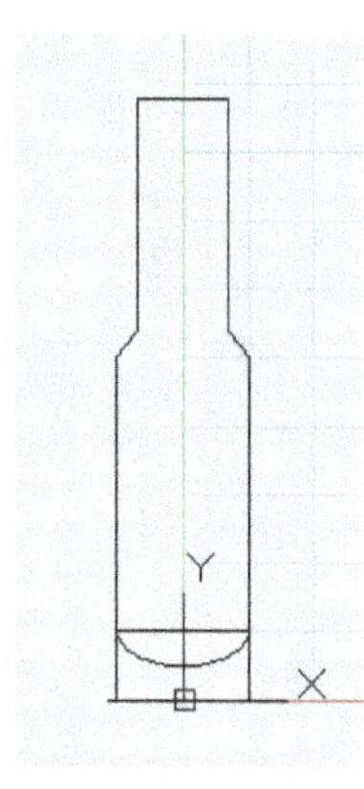

14. Draw other entities, as shown next.

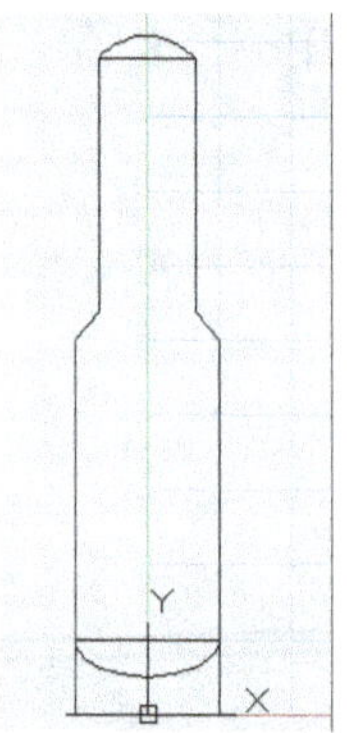

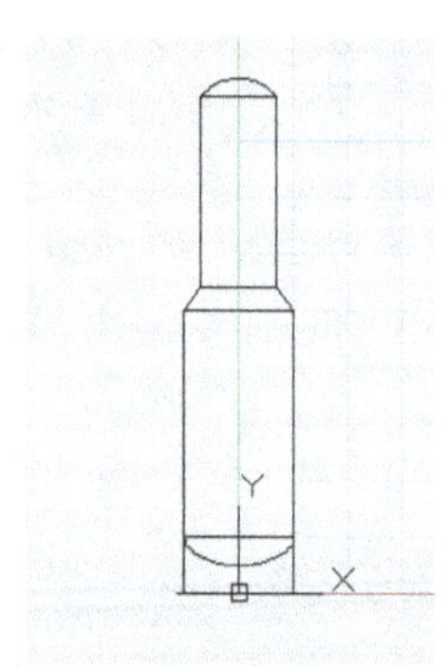

15. Click the **Save** button

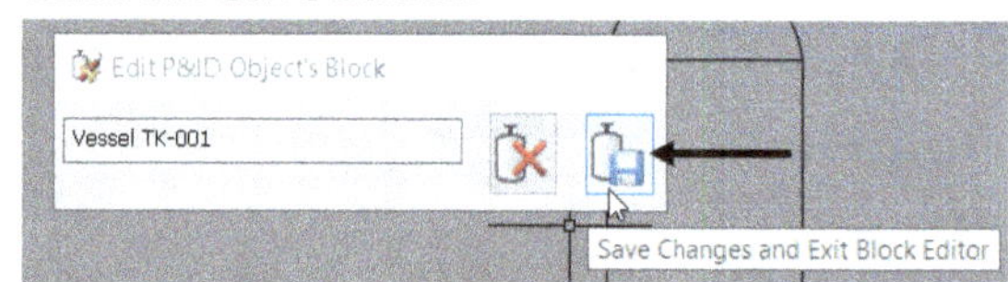

The P&ID symbol after editing is displayed next.

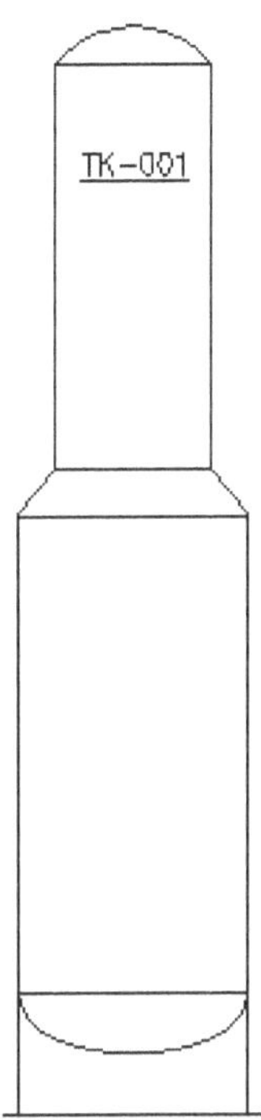

Adding Nozzles to the Equipment

Nozzles are required to connect equipment with a pipe. The program adds Most of the nozzles when you connect equipment with a pipe. Sometimes, you may need to add nozzles to equipment, manually.

1. To add nozzles to equipment, click the **Fittings** tab on the TOOL PALETTES.

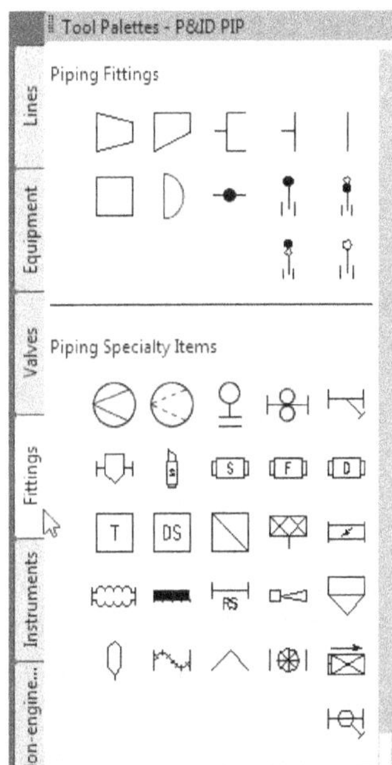

2. Click the **Flanged Nozzle** icon under the **Nozzles** section.

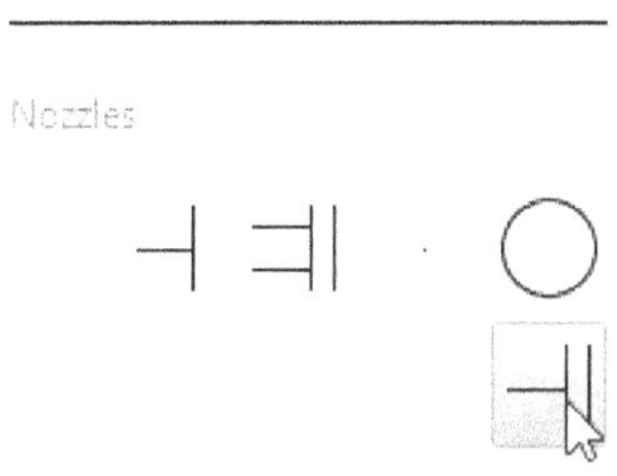

3. Click on the outline of the vertical vessel.

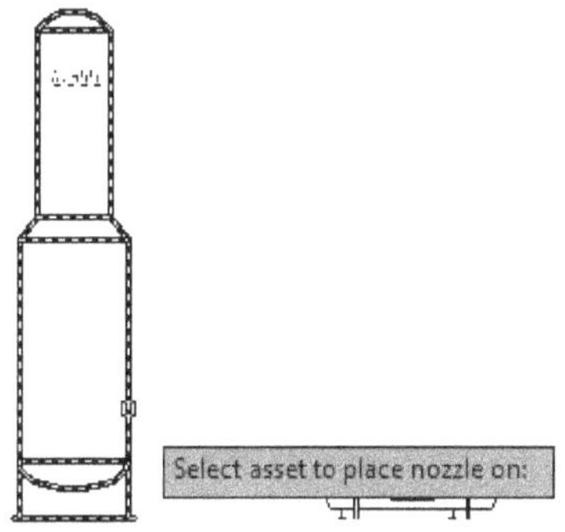

4. Define the Insertion point, as shown.

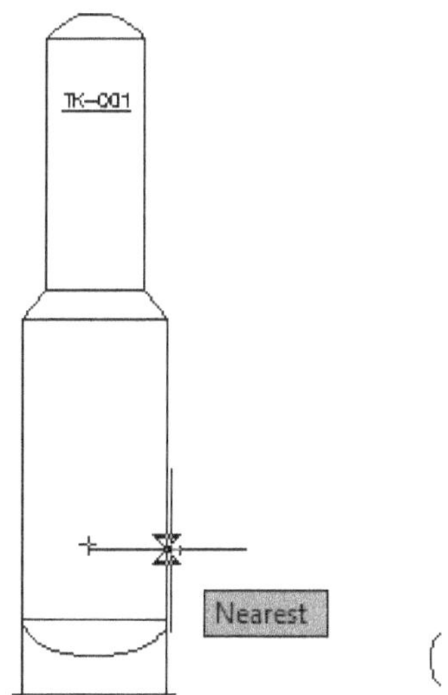

5. Type **0** as the angle of rotation, and then press Enter.
6. Likewise, place another nozzle on the vessel.

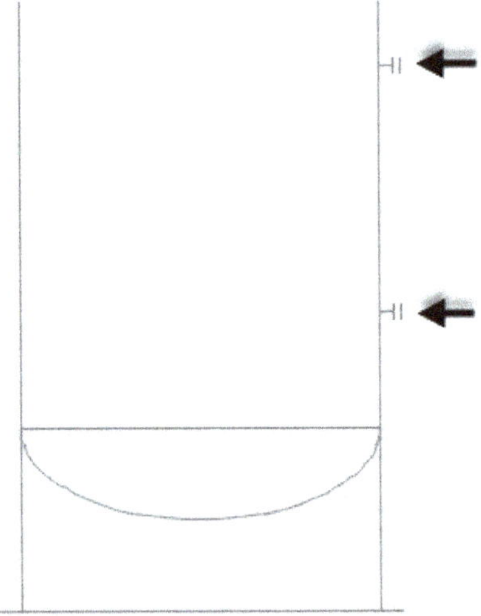

7. To add an annotation to the nozzle, select it, right-click, and then select **Assign Tag**.
8. On the **Assign Tag** dialog, check the **Place annotation after assigning tag** option.
9. Click **Assign** on the **Assign Tag** dialog, and then place it below the nozzle.
10. Likewise, add the annotation tag to the second nozzle.

Creating Schematic Lines

Schematic lines are an important part of a P&ID. They are used to connect the equipment symbols. The schematic lines, which represent actual pipelines, are very different from AutoCAD lines and polylines. They store piping data such as size, spec, line number, process, and so on. This information can be linked to the 3D pipelines. In AutoCAD Plant 3D, you can create a schematic using the tools available in the **Lines** tool palette.

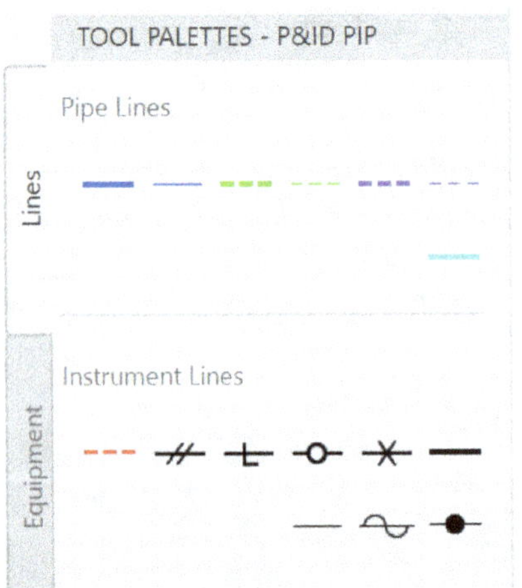

1. To create a schematic line, click the **Primary Line Segment** icon under the **Pipe Lines** section.

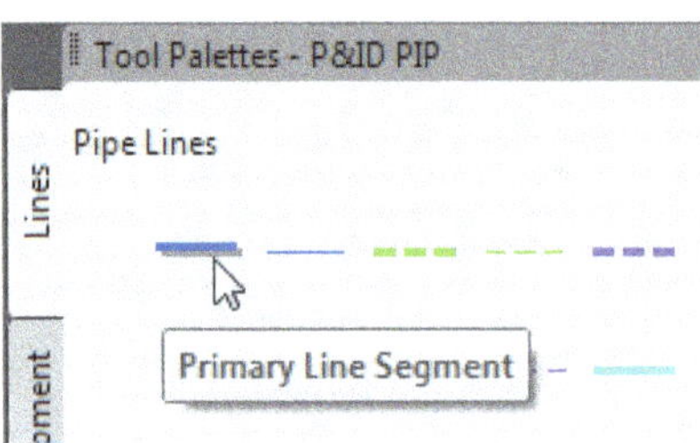

2. On the status bar, click the down-arrow next to the **2D Snap** icon and select the **Quadrant** option.

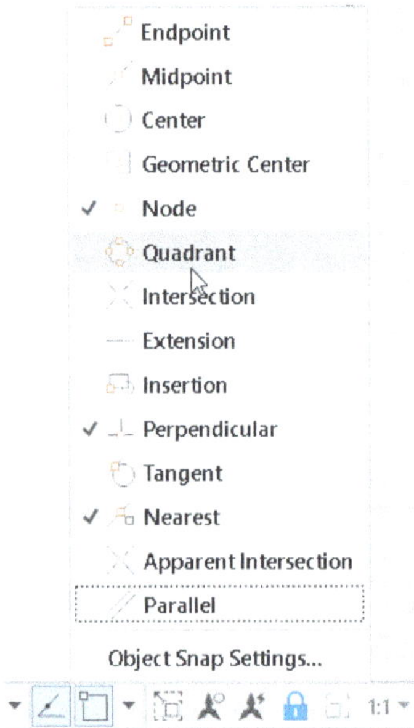

3. Click on the top portion of the vertical vessel.

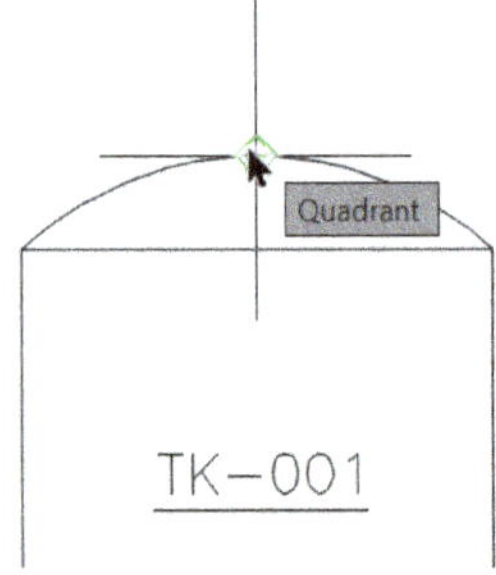

4. Move the pointer upward and click.
5. Move the pointer right-ward and click. An arrow appears at the endpoint of the line, which represents the flow direction of the pipeline.
6. Press the **Enter** key.

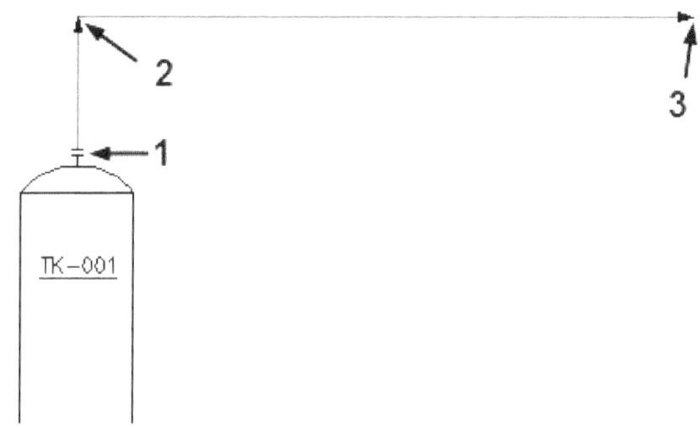

Notice that the program creates nozzles automatically.

7. Click the **Primary Line Segment** icon on the **Lines** tab of the Tool Palettes.
8. Select the nozzle of the pump, as shown in the figure.

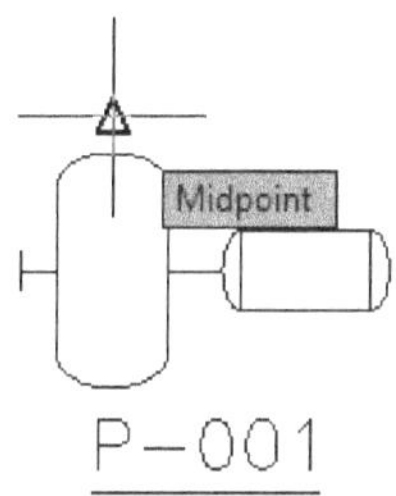

9. Move the pointer upward and click.
10. Move the pointer right-ward and click on the vessel.

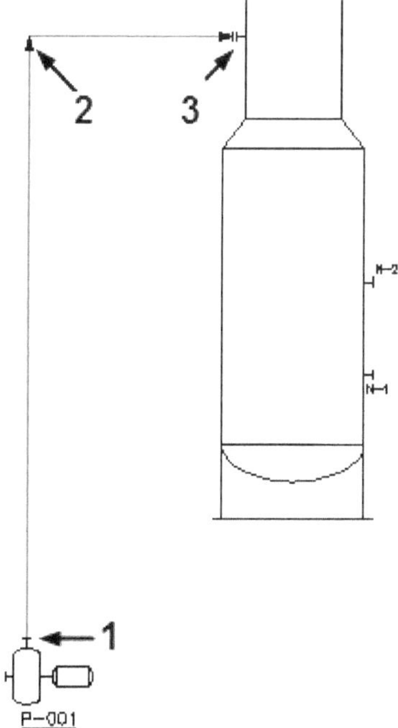

11. Likewise, create a line between the two pumps

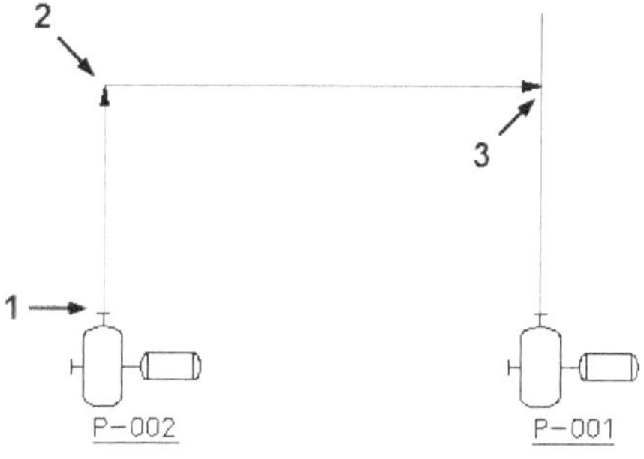

12. Create an inlet pipeline connected to the pump.
   - Click the **Primary Line Segment** icon on the Tool Palette.
   - Specify the first point, as shown.
   - Move the pointer horizontally and specify the second point, as shown.
   - Move the pointer vertically upward.
   - Place the pointer on the inlet nozzle of the pump; a trace line appears.
   - Click on the trace line to create a vertical line.
   - Move the pointer horizontally toward the right and select the node of the inlet nozzle.

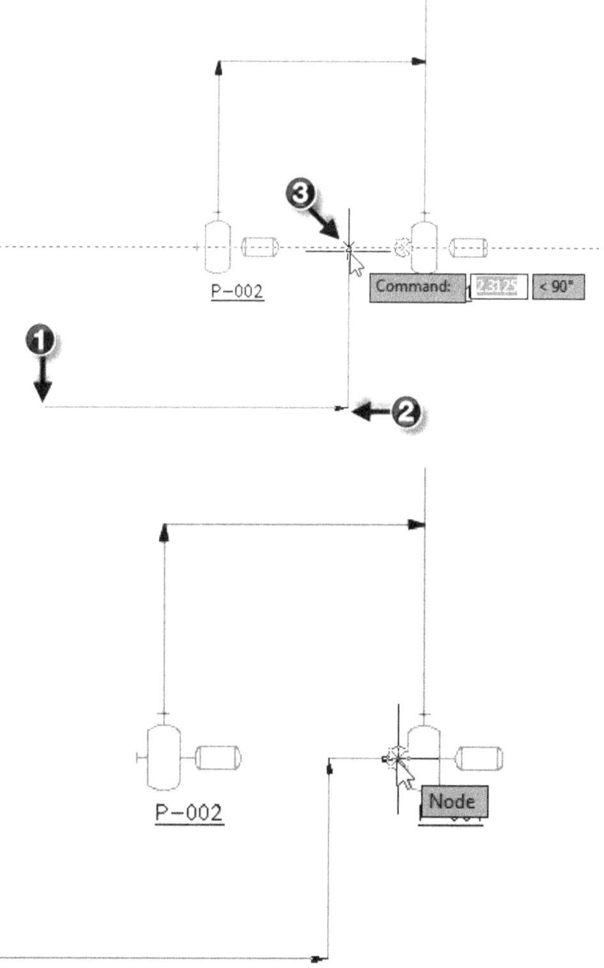

13. Create an inlet pipe connecting the other pump.

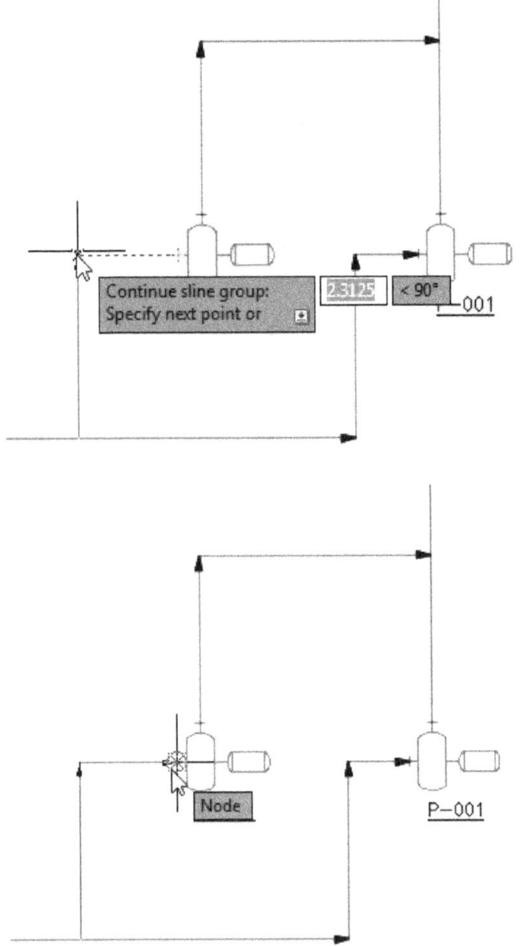

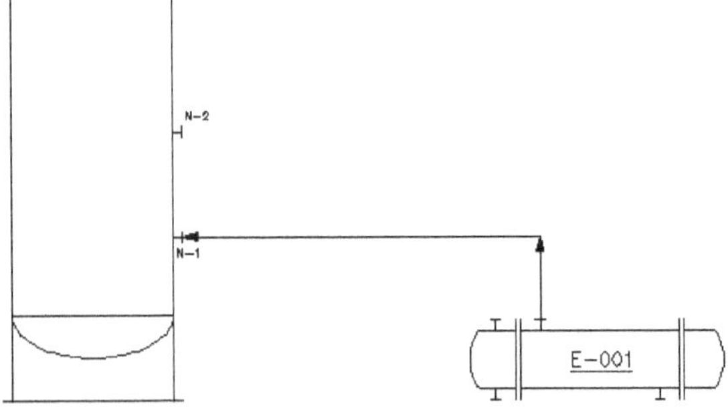

14. Create the other pipelines in the P&ID.

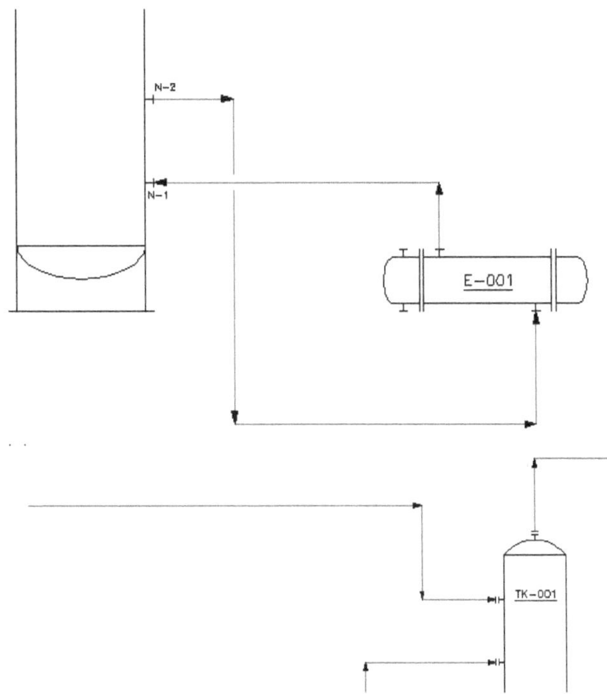

The following figure shows the P&ID after adding all the lines.

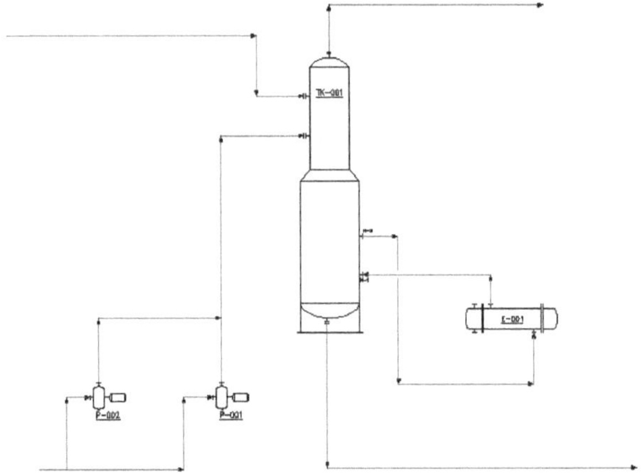

Assigning Tags to lines

In a P&ID, the lines represent the pipes in the real plant. You have to show the information related to the pipelines by assigning tags.

1. Click the **Assign Tag** button on the **P&ID** panel of the **Home** ribbon.

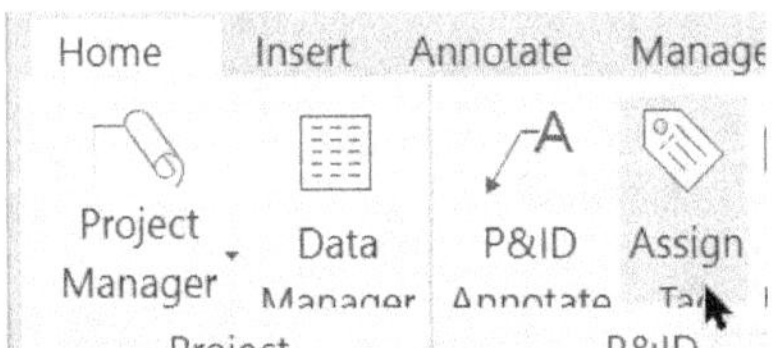

2. Select the inlet line of the pumps.

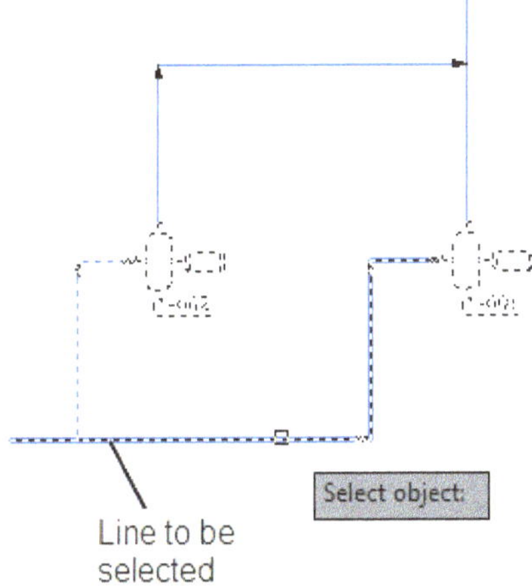

3. Press the Enter key. The **Assign Tag** dialog appears.
4. Enter the following information in the **Assign Tag** dialog.

   Size: 6"
   Spec: CS300
   Pipe Line Group Service: P
   Pipe Line Group Line Number: 001

5. Select the **Place annotation after assigning tag** option and click **Assign**.
6. Place the annotation below the line.

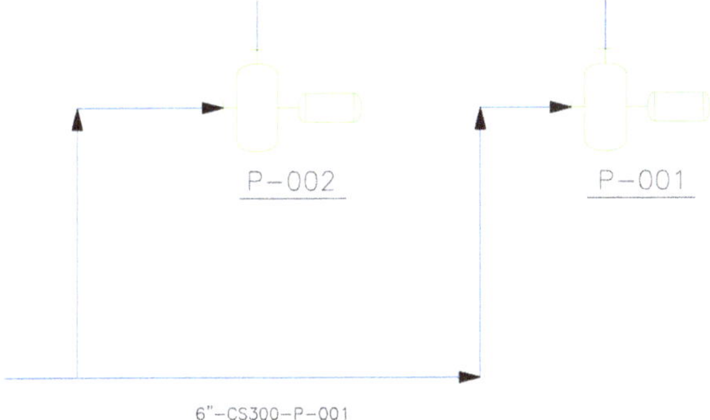

Next, you have to group two lines and assign a tag to them. By grouping lines, you create an association between different line segments. Also, the grouped line segments have the same line number.

7. To group lines, click the **Make Group** button on the **Line Group** panel of the **Home** ribbon.

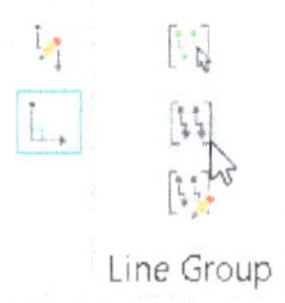

8. Select the lines connecting the vessel and the pumps.

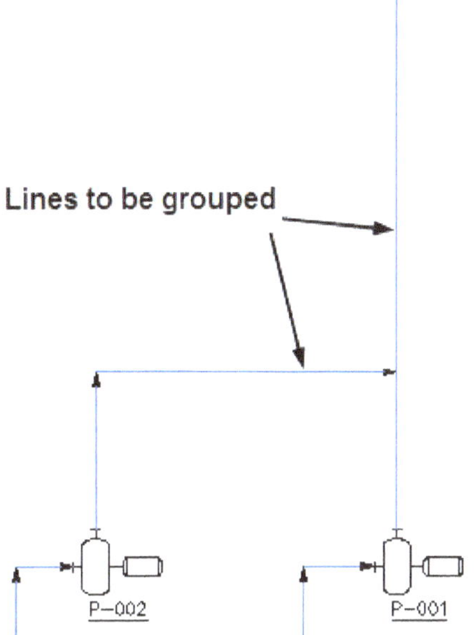

9. Press the **Enter** key to group the lines.

   You can also edit a line group using the **Edit Group** command (on the ribbon, click **Home > Line Group > Edit Group**). Activate this command and select the line group to edit. The command line provides five options (**Add**, **Remove**, **Ungroup**, **Linenumber**, and **Service**).

10. Right-click on the line connected to the pumps and the vertical vessel.

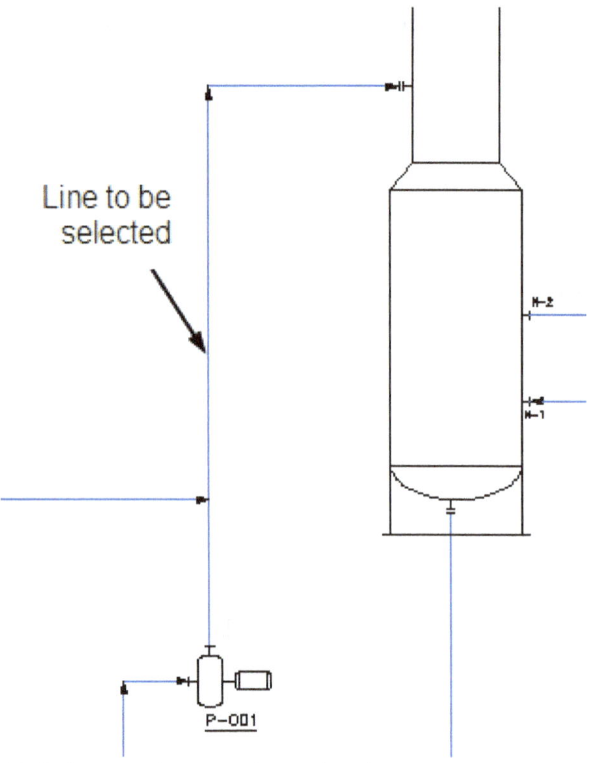

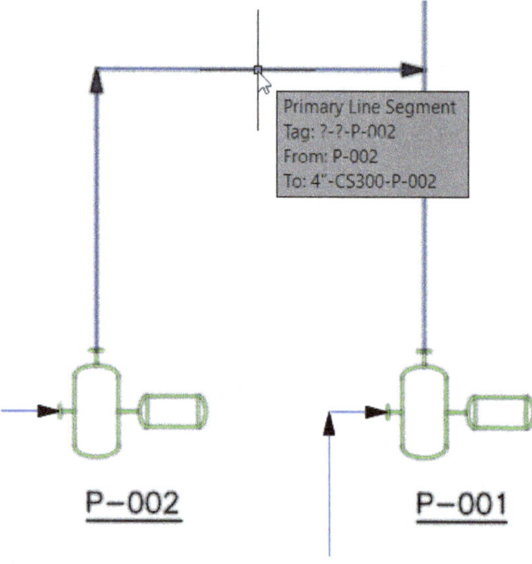

11. Select **Assign Tag** from the shortcut menu to open the **Assign Tag** dialog.
12. Enter the information in the **Assign Tag** dialog, as shown.

    Size: 4″
    Spec: CS300
    Pipe Line Group Service: P
    Pipe Line Group Line Number: 002

13. Click **Assign**.
14. Place the annotation next to the line.
15. Place the pointer on the pipe connecting the second pump. The information related to the pipe appears.

Notice that the tag information is partially applied to the line. You have to specify the line size and spec of the pipeline.

16. Right-click on the line and select **Assign Tag** from the shortcut menu.
17. Enter the **Size** and **Spec** values in the **Assign Tag** dialog.

    Size: 4″
    Spec: CS300

18. Click **Assign**.
19. Place the tag above the line.

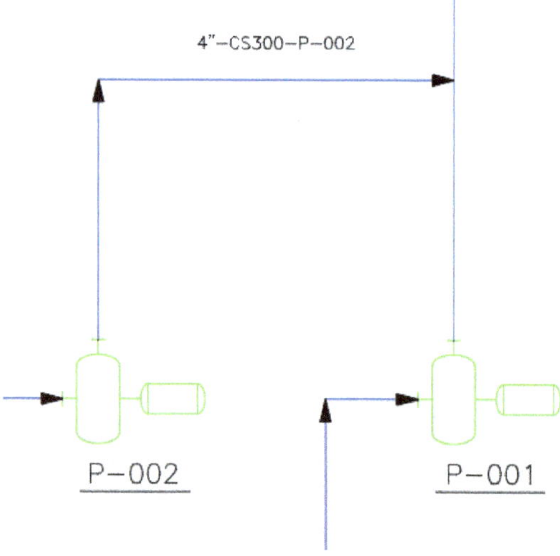

20. Likewise, add tag information to other lines in the P&ID.

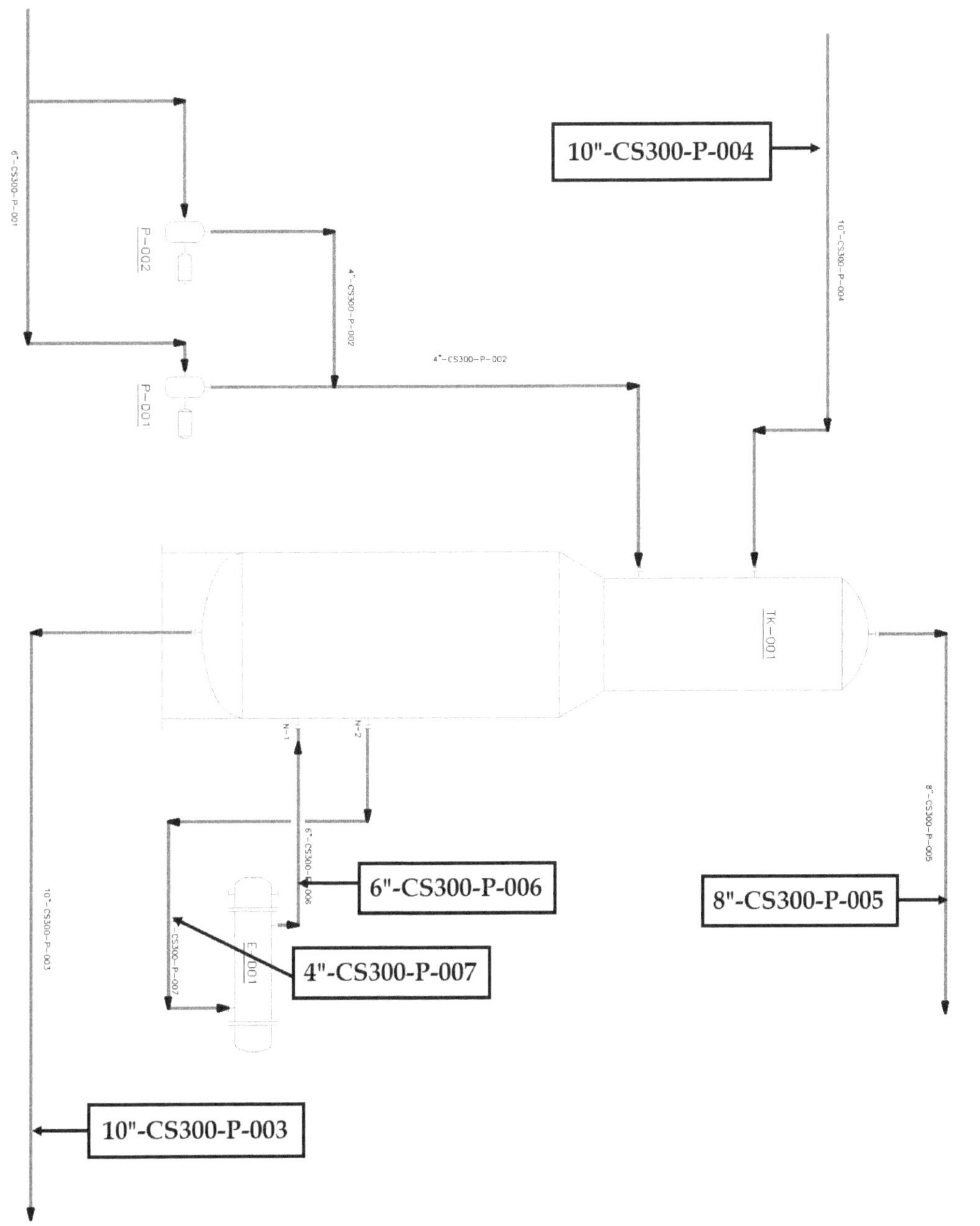

P&ID Painter

In AutoCAD Plant 3D, you can specify the color of a P&ID component based on its size or service for which it is used.

1. On the ribbon, click **Home > P&ID Painter > Paint P&ID**.

2. On the **P&ID Painter** panel of the ribbon, select **Color by Service** from the **Painter style** drop-down; the color of the P&ID components changes based on their service.

3. Likewise, select **Color by Size** from the **Painter style** drop-down to change the color based on size.

Placing Valves and Fittings

After creating schematic lines, you can add inline equipment such as valves and fittings. You place inline symbols on a schematic line. When you move the line, the inline symbols move along with it. You can find the valve and fitting symbols on the **Valves** and **Fittings** tabs, respectively.

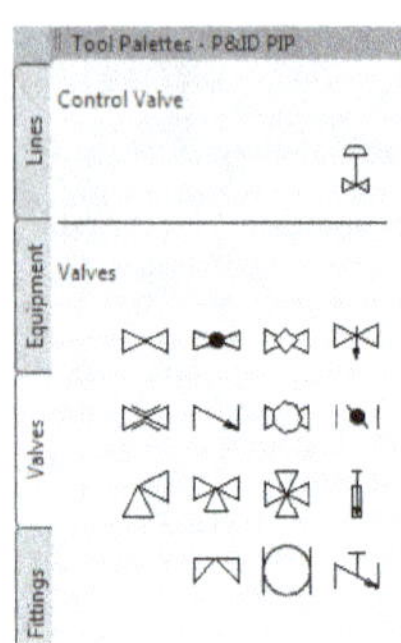

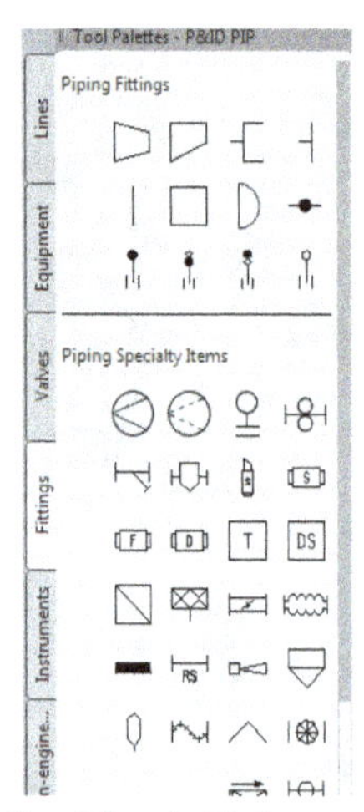

1. To place a check valve, click the **Check Valve** icon on the **Valves** tool palette.

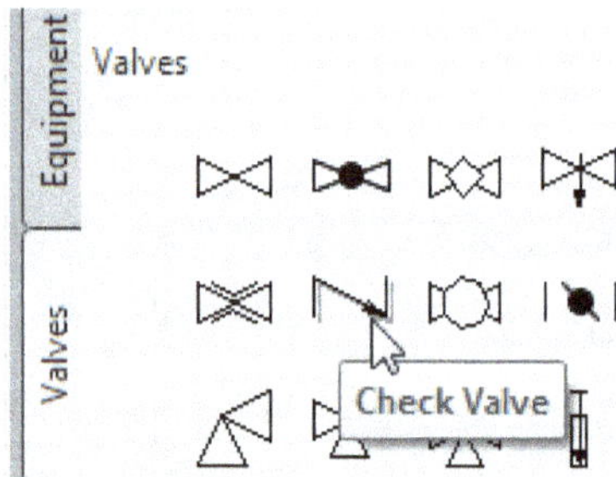

2. Move the pointer on a line, and you notice that the valve is aligned with the line.
3. Place the valve on the line connecting the pump. You notice that the valve is attached to the line. Also, the tag is added to the valve and placed beneath it.

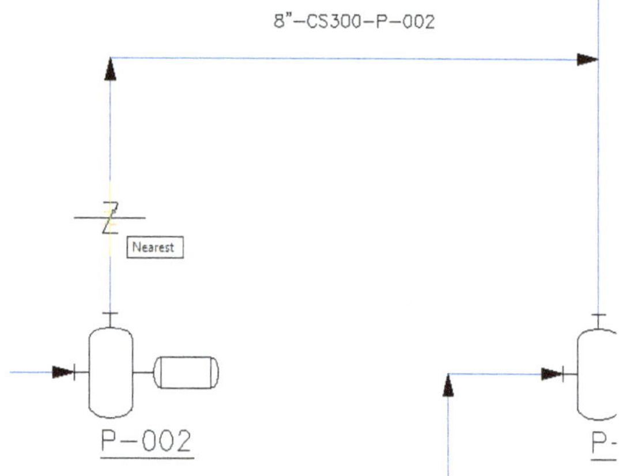

4. Place another check valve.

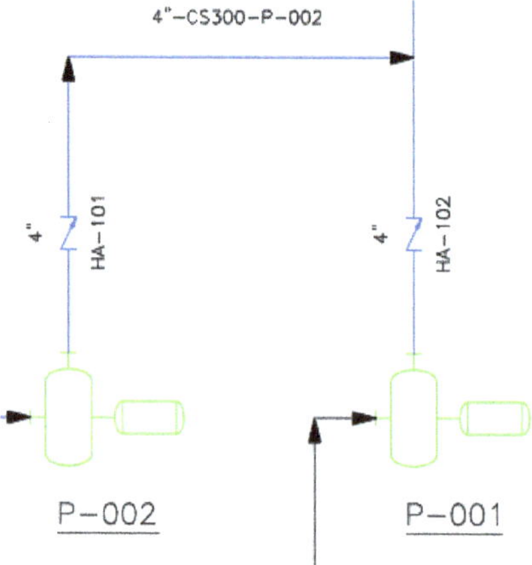

Now, you have to place reducers.

5. To place a reducer, click the **Fittings** tab on Tool Palettes.
6. Click the **Concentric Reducer** icon under the **Pipe Fittings** section.

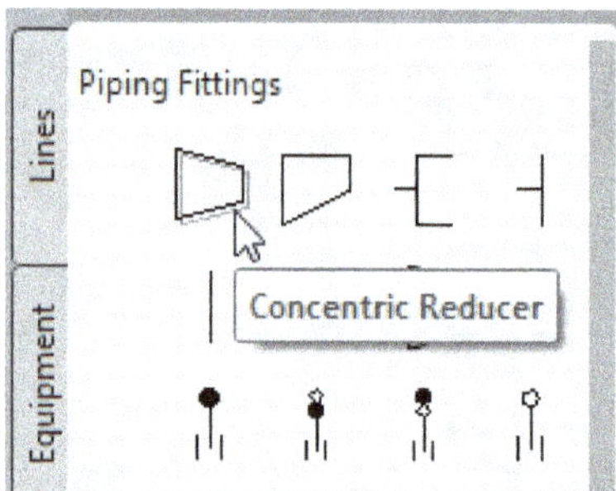

7. Place it on the line connecting the bottom of the vessel.

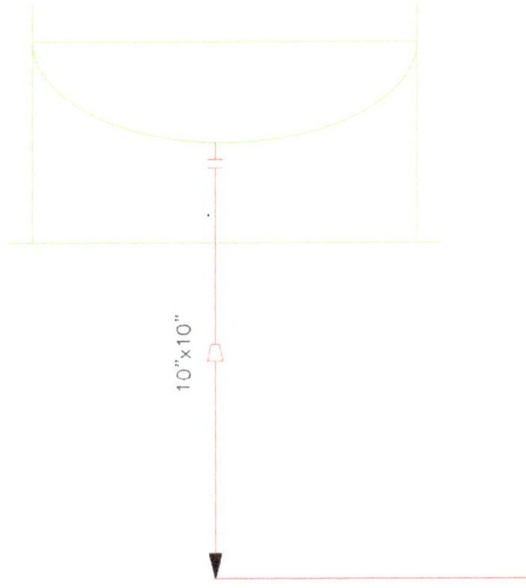

8. Click the **Assign Tag** button on the **P&ID** panel of the **Home** ribbon.
9. Select the line segment below the reducer.

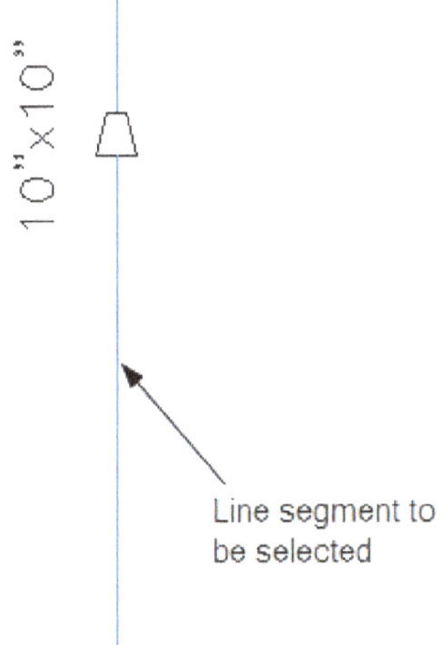

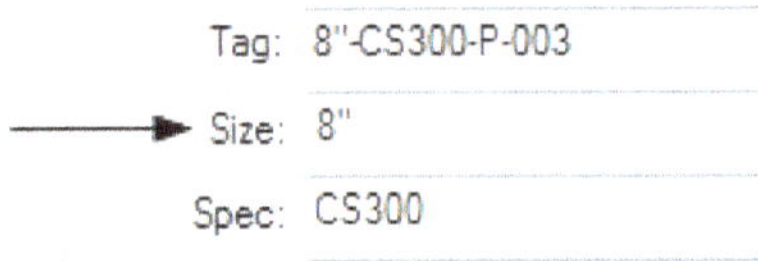

10. Press the **Enter** key.
11. In the **Assign Tag** dialog, change the **Size** to 8″.

12. Clear the **Place annotation after assigning tag** option.
13. Click **Assign**.

The orientation of the reducer changes.

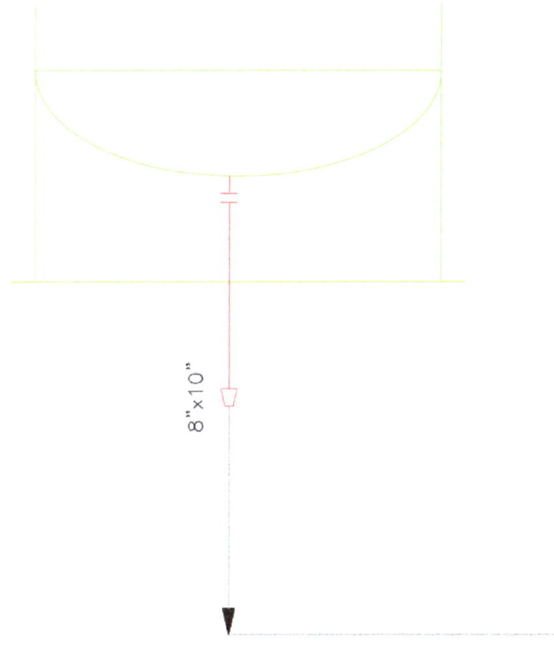

14. Place another concentric reducer at the location shown below.

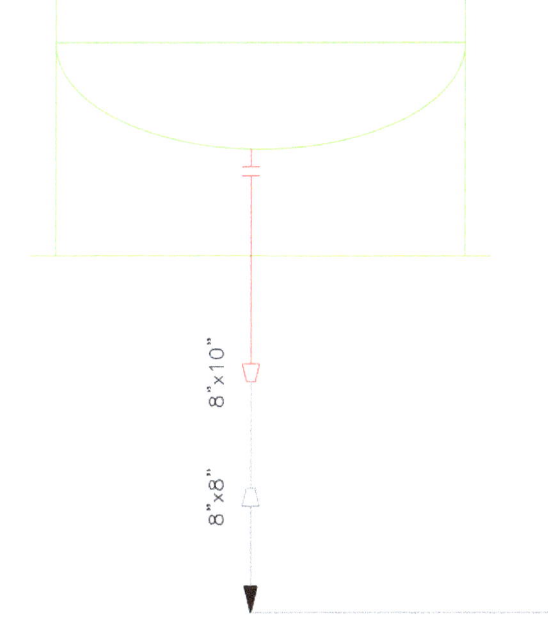

15. Click the **Assign Tag** button on the **P&ID** panel of the **Home** ribbon.
16. Select the line segment below the reducer.
17. Press Enter.
18. Clear the **Place annotation after assigning tag** option.
19. Click **Assign**.

The orientation of the reducer changes.

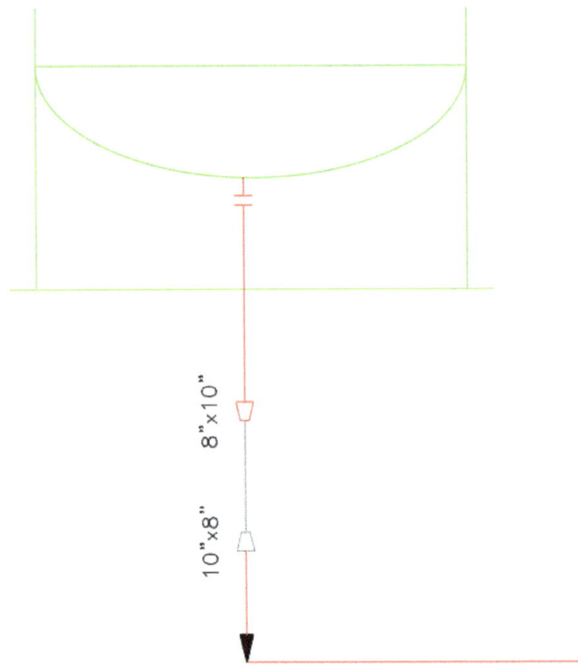

Next, you have to place a gate valve.

20. To place a gate valve, click the **Gate Valve** icon on the **Valves** tool palette.

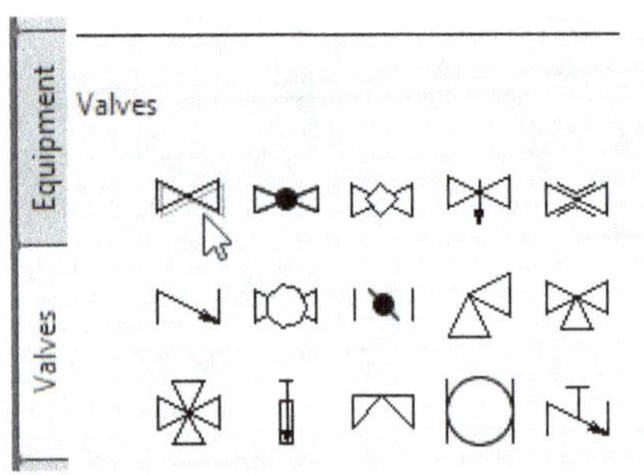

21. Place it at the location shown in the figure.

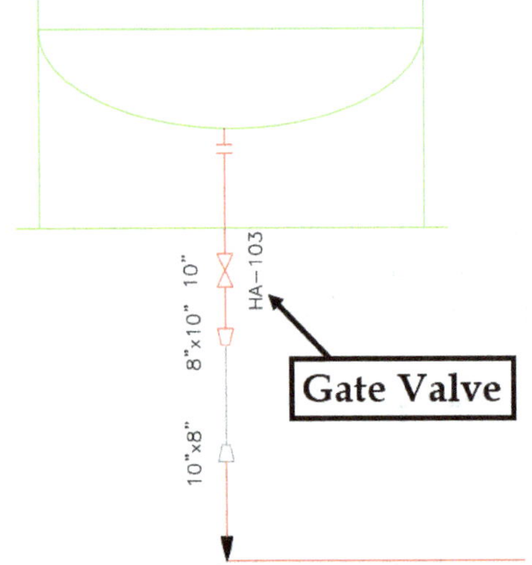

22. Likewise, place valves on lines connecting the pumps.

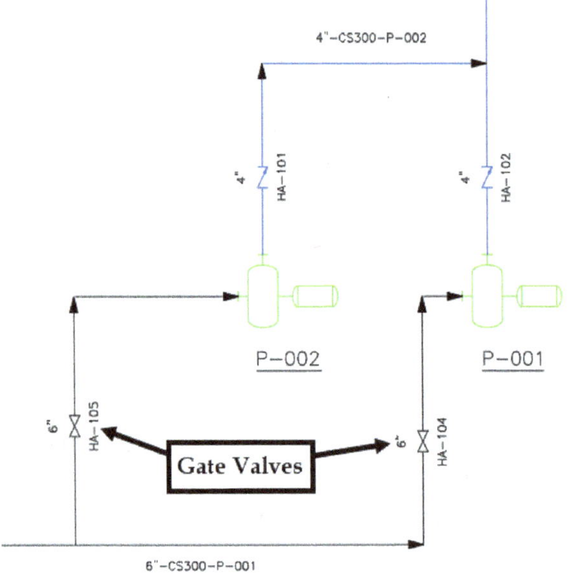

Placing Instruments

In a P&ID, the instrumentation that controls the operation of the plant equipment is represented by the instrument symbols. You can find these symbols on the **Instruments** tool palette. There are many sections on this tool palette, which are based on the use of the instrument symbols.

The **Control Valve** section contains the control valve symbol.

The **Relief Valves** section contains the symbols of various pressure relief valves.

The **Primary Element Symbols (Flow)** section contains the symbols related to flow measuring instruments.

The **General Instruments** section contains the instrument symbols related to the process control instruments.

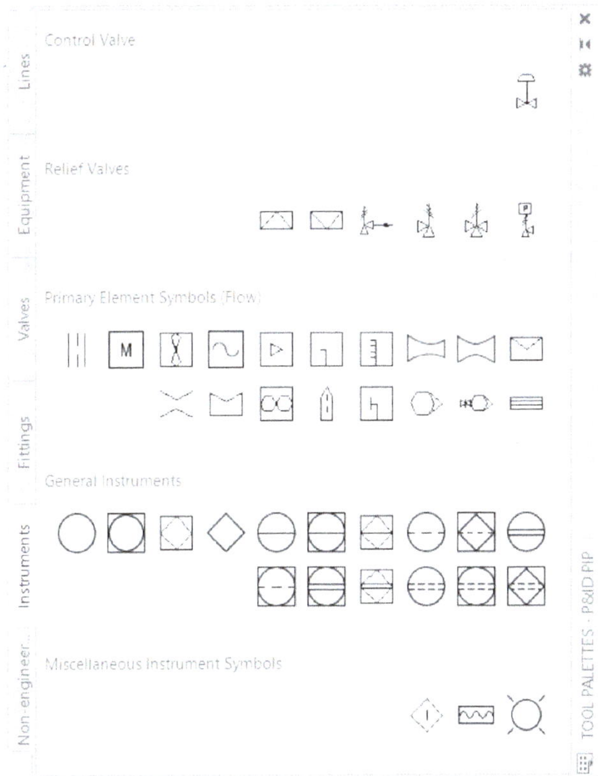

1. To place a control valve, click the **Control Valve** icon on the **Valves** tool palette.

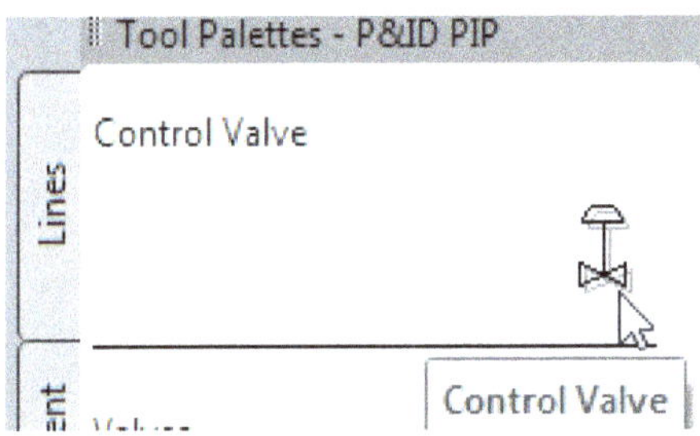

The **Control Valve Browser** appears.

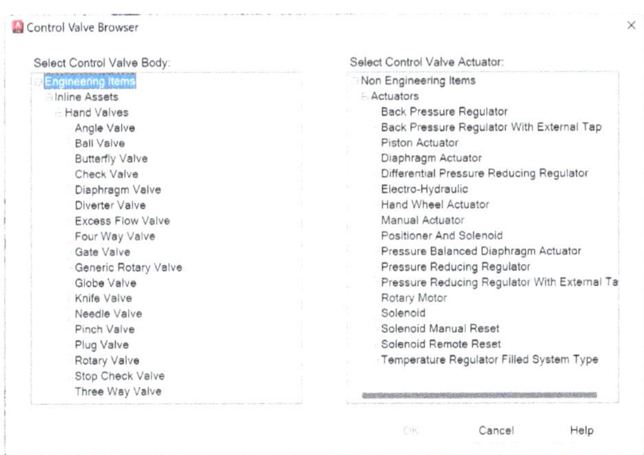

If the **Control Valve Browser** does not appear, select the **Change body or actuator** option from the command line.

2. In the **Control Valve Browser**, select **Gate Valve** as the **Control Valve Body**.

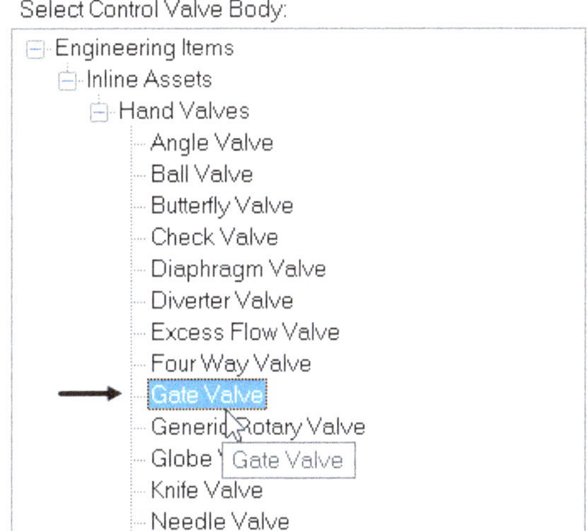

3. On the dialog, click **Non Engineering Items > Actuators > Piston Actuator** under the **Select Control Valve Actuator** section.

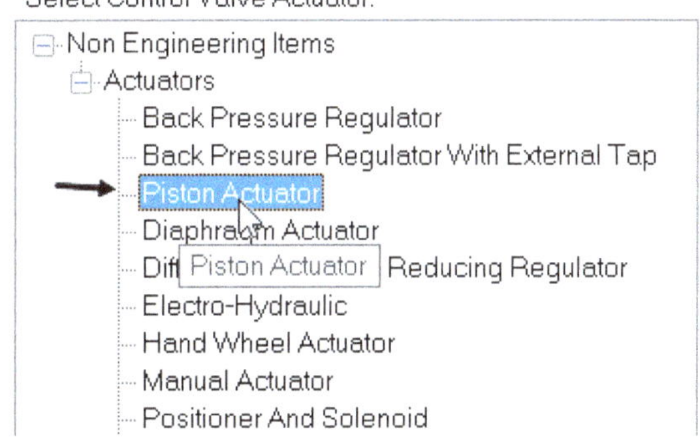

4. Click the **OK** button.
5. Place the control valve at the location shown in the figure.

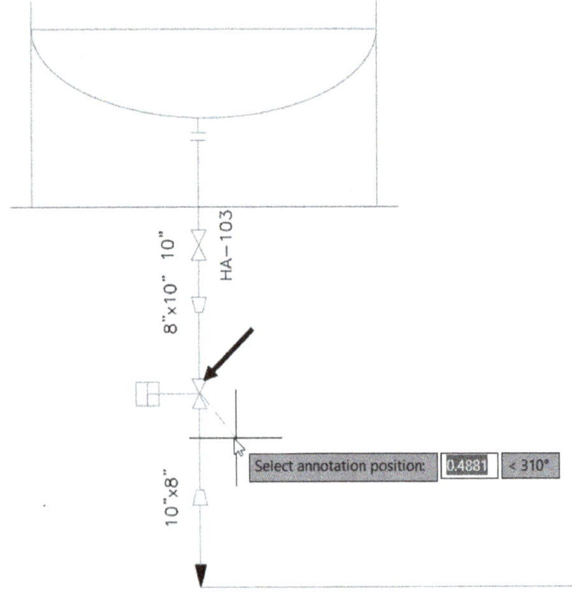

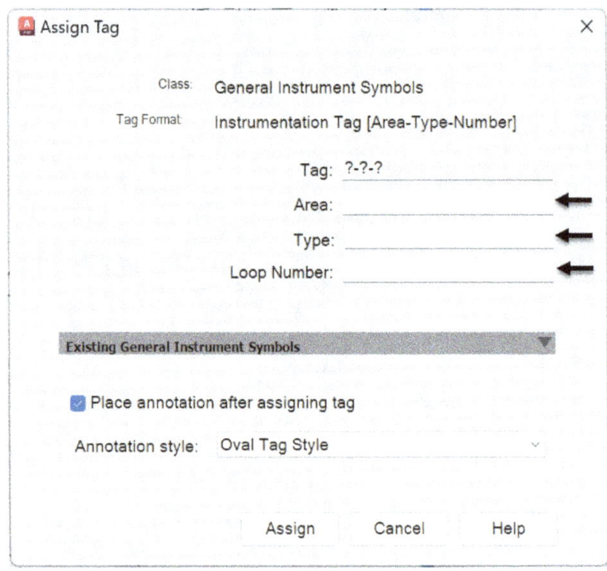

6. Place the annotation balloon.
   The **Assign Tag** dialog appears.
7. On the dialog, uncheck **Place annotation after assigning tag**.
8. On the **Assign Tag** dialog, type in the values, as shown.

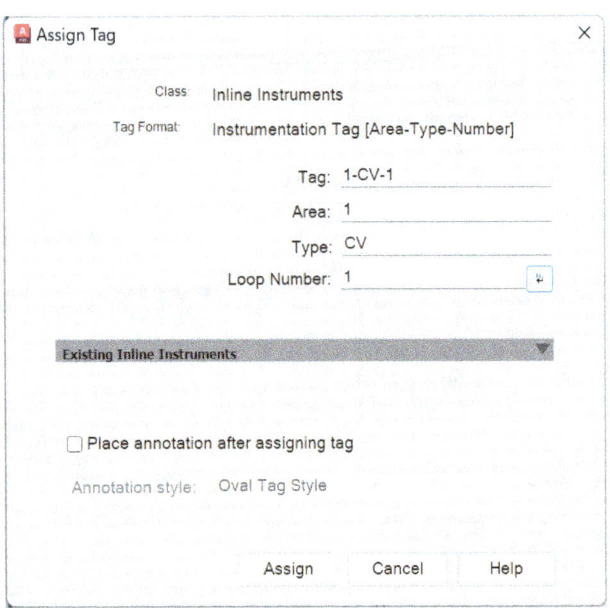

Follow the steps given next, if the **Area**, **Type**, and **Loop Number** fields are disabled on the **Assign Tag** dialog.

- On the ribbon, click **Home > Project > Project Manager > Project Setup**.

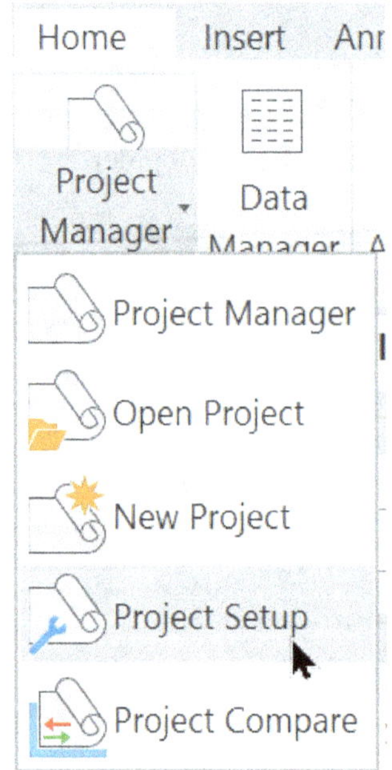

- On the **Project Setup** dialog, click **P&ID DWG Settings > PID Class Definitions > Engineering Items > Instrumentation**.
- On the **Class Settings: Instrumentation** page, under the **Properties** section, uncheck the **Area**, **Type**, **Loop Number** boxes in the **Read Only** column.

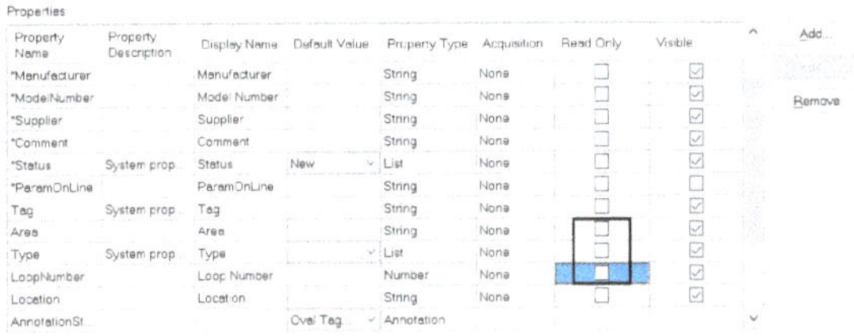

- Click **OK**.

9. Click the **Assign** button, and place the tag below the control valve.

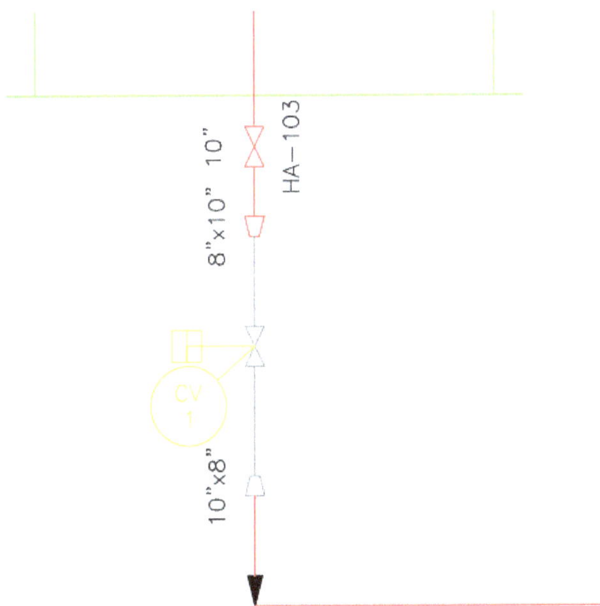

Creating Instrumentation Lines

Instrumentation lines are used to connect the instrument symbols with the P&ID equipment and pipelines. You can create instrumentation lines by picking them from the **Instrument Lines** section on the **Lines** tool palette.

1. To create an electric signal line, click the **Electric Signal** line from the **Instrument Lines** section on the **Lines** tool palette.

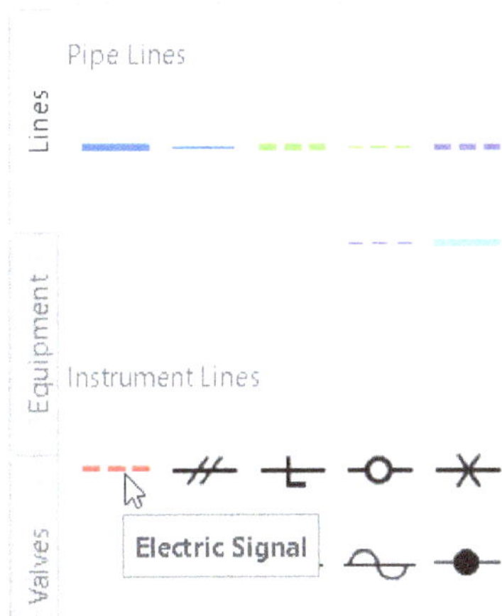

2. Select a point on the lower-left portion of the vessel.
3. Move the pointer toward the left and select the second point.
4. Move the pointer downward and select the third point.
5. Move the pointer toward the right and select a point on the vessel.

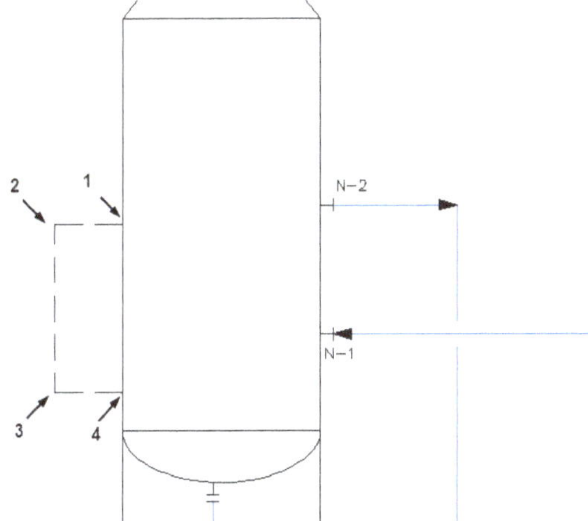

Placing the Field Discrete instrument symbol

1. To place a field discrete instrument symbol, click the **Field Discrete Instrument** icon from the **General Instruments** section on the **Instruments** tool palette.

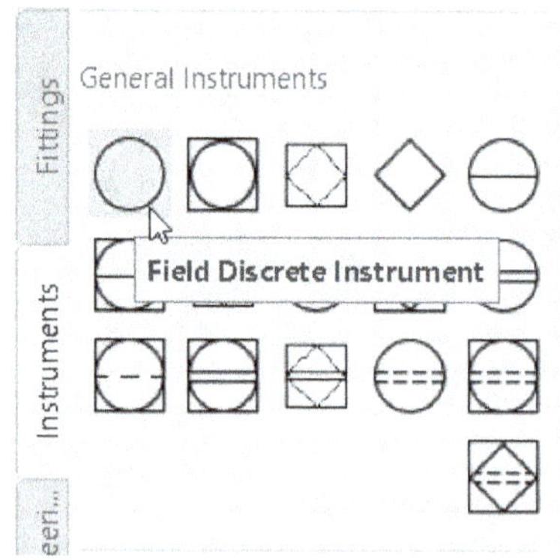

2. Place it on the electric signal line.

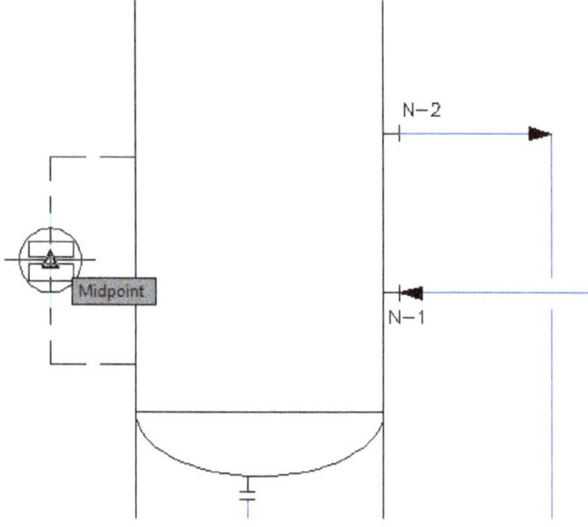

The **Assign Tag** dialog appears.

3. Enter the tag information, as shown in the figure.

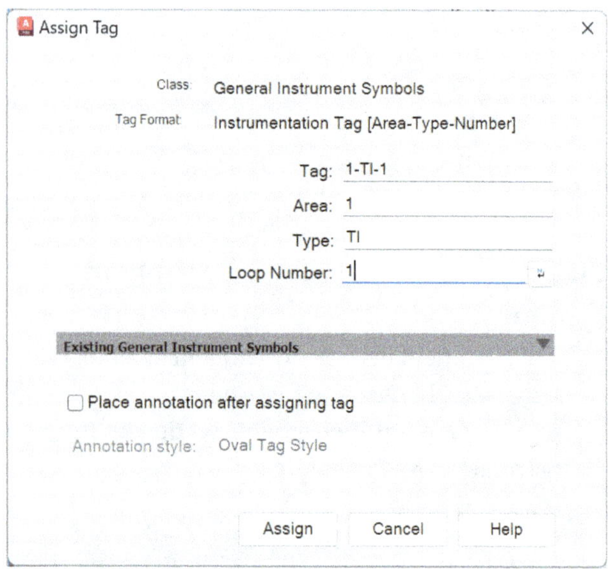

4. Click the **Assign** button.

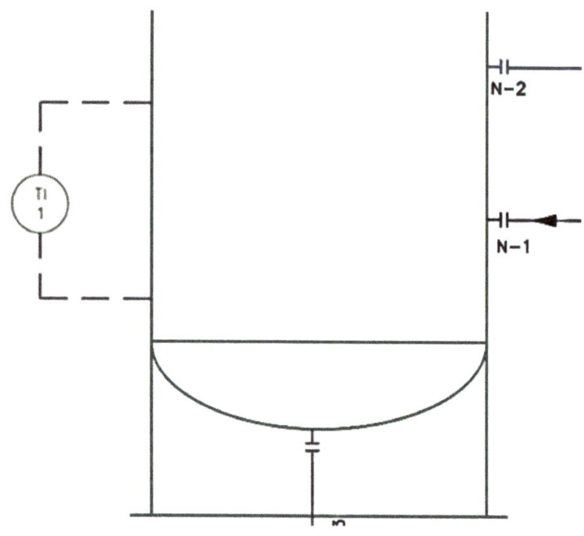

Creating the Pneumatic Signal lines

1. On the **Lines** tool palette, under the **Instrument Lines** section, click the **Pneumatic Signal** icon to create pneumatic lines.

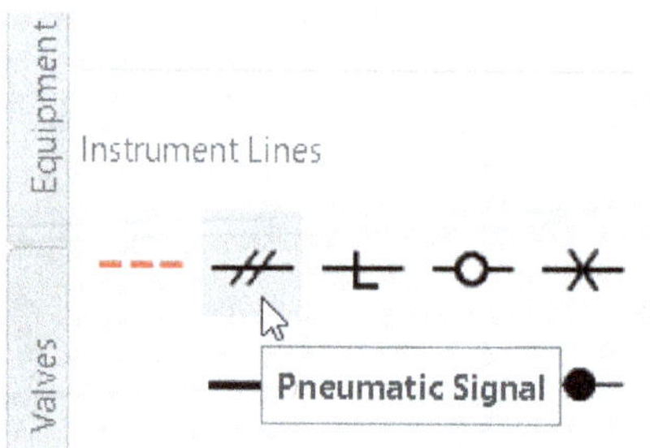

2. Select a point on the **Temperature Indicator** symbol.

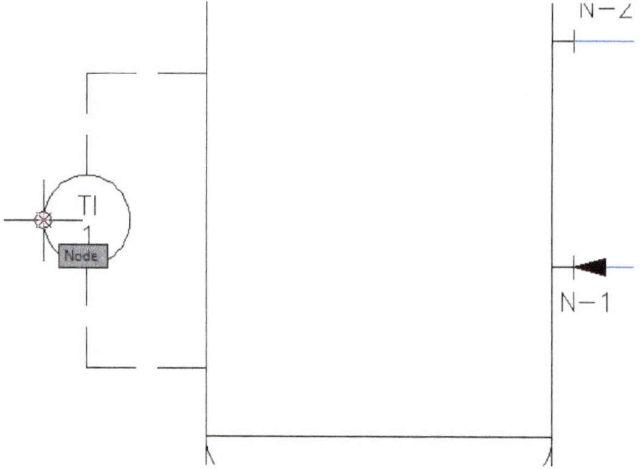

3. Connect the signal line with the control valve.

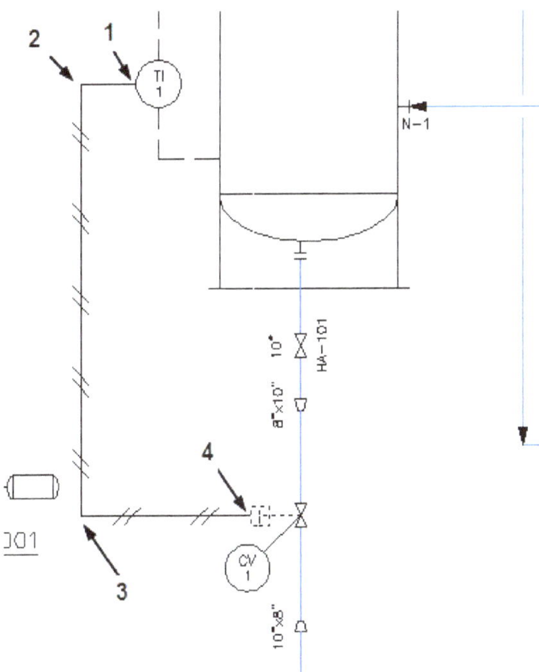

Adding Off-page connectors

In this section, you add off-page connectors. Usually, the P&ID of a project is divided into multiple P&IDs. Therefore, you should maintain a connection between the P&IDs. Off-page connectors are used to connect the P&IDs.

1. To add an off page connector, click the **Non-engineering** tab on the Tool palette.
2. Click the **Off Page connector** icon on the **Non-engineering** tool palette.

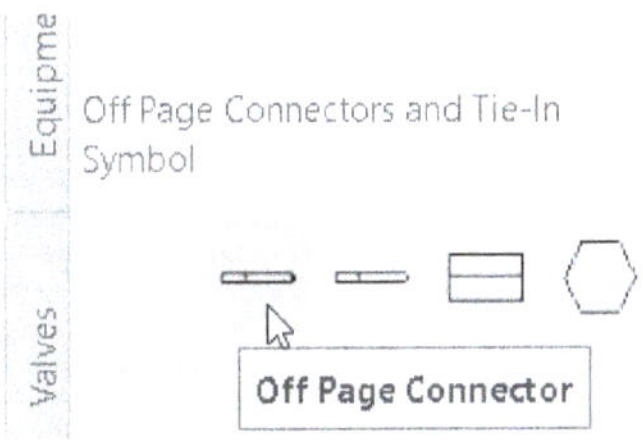

3. Zoom into the drawing.
4. Select the endpoint of the line connecting the top portion of the vessel, as shown.

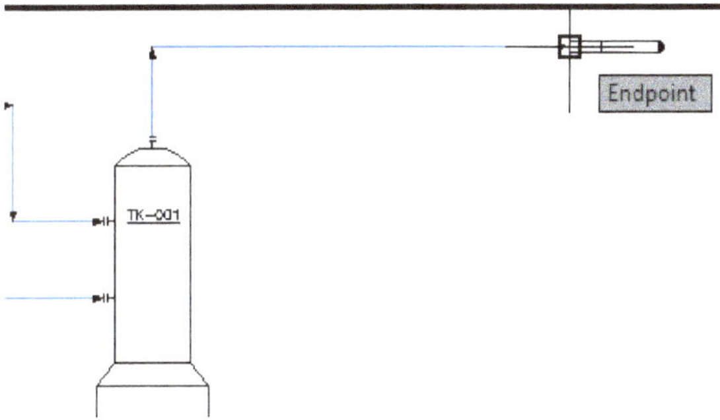

The off page connectors can be used to open the drawing file connected to the currently opened file, quickly. You will learn how to connect two off page connectors in the next tutorial.

Checking the Drawing

1. Click the **Drawing Checker** button on the **Validate** panel of the **Home** Ribbon.

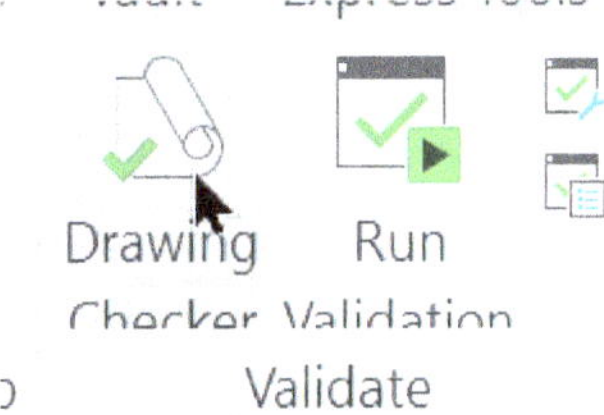

The program checks the drawing for any inconsistencies with the project.

2. Click the **Save** button on the **Quick Access Toolbar**.

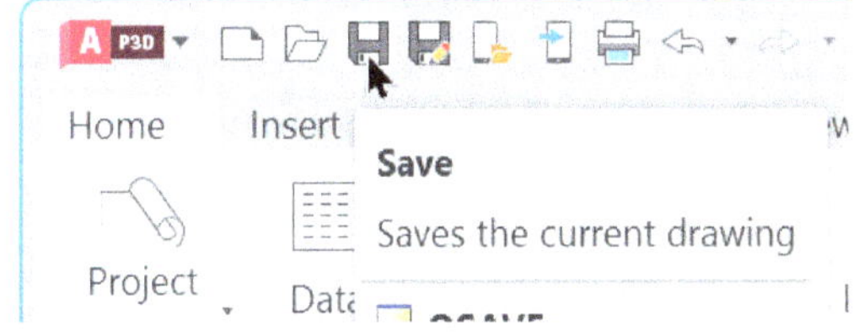

Tutorial 2

In this tutorial, you create a P&ID shown in figure.

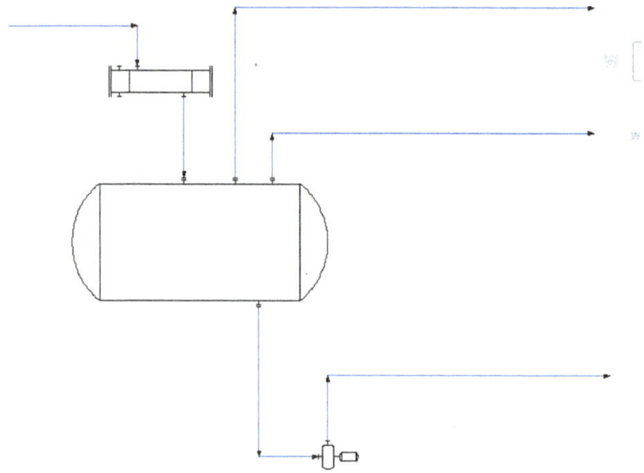

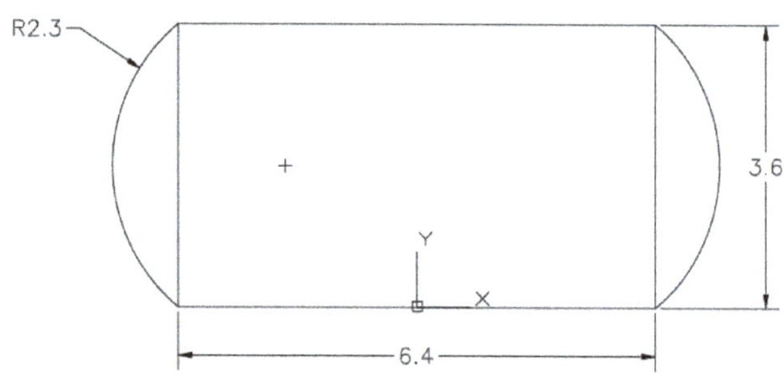

1. To create a new P&ID drawing, select the **P&ID Drawings** node in the **Project Manager** and click the **New Drawing** button.

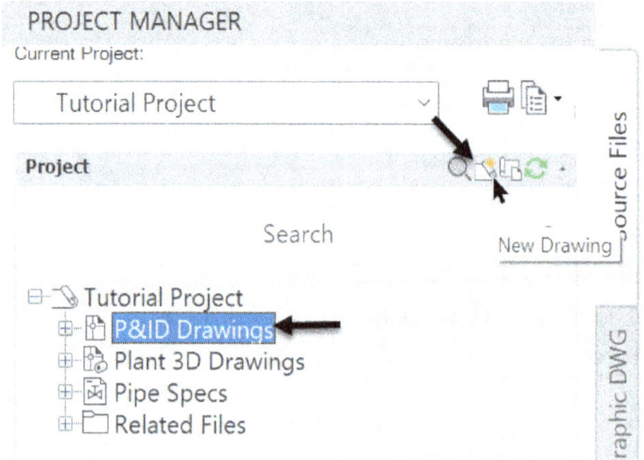

The **New DWG** dialog appears.

2. Enter **Tutorial 2** in the **File name** field and click **OK**.

Creating a Custom symbol and converting it into a P&ID symbol

1. Create the symbol shown in the below figure using the **Line** and **Arc** command. Do not apply the dimensions. Dimensions are for your reference only.

2. Select all the entities of the symbol by dragging a window.

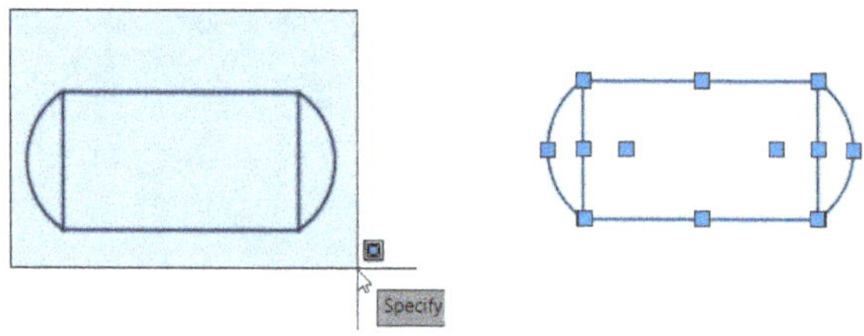

3. Right-click and select **Convert to P&ID Object**.

The **Convert to P&ID Object** dialog appears.

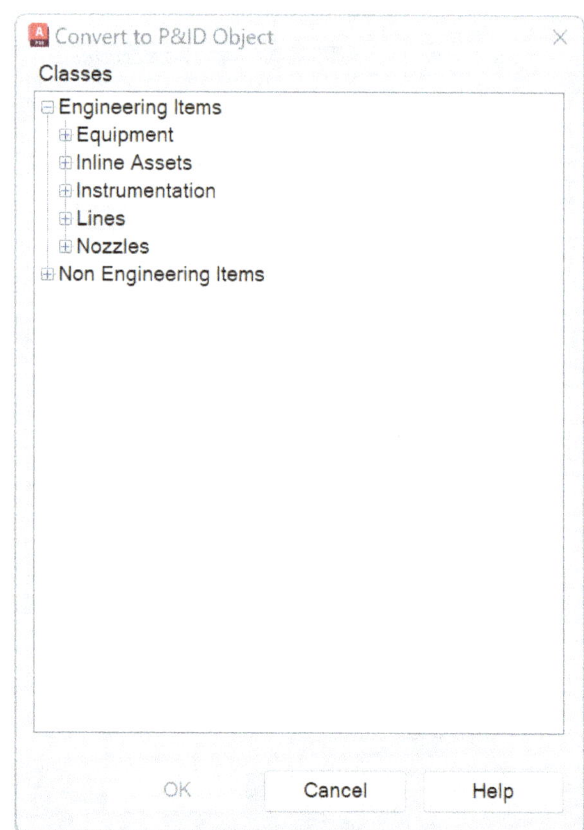

4. Expand the **Equipment** class and select **Tank > Vessel**.

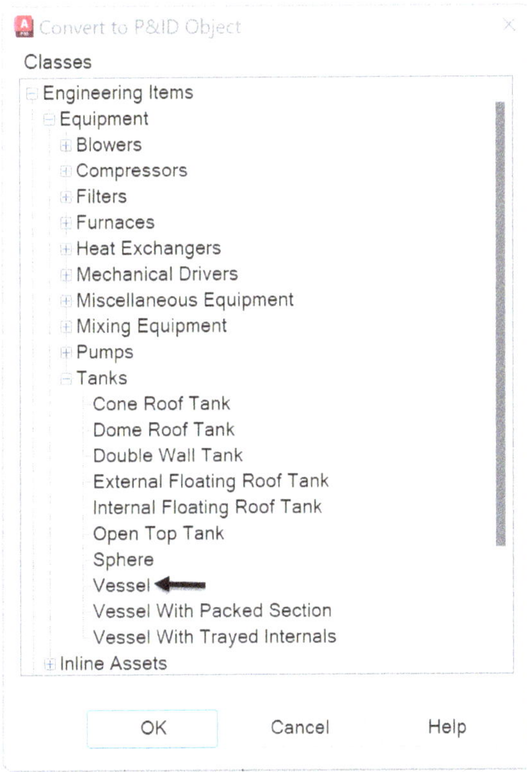

5. Click **OK**.

Next, you have to select the insertion base point.

6. Press and hold the SHIFT key and right-click.
7. Select **Midpoint** from the shortcut menu.
8. Select the midpoint of the lower horizontal line.

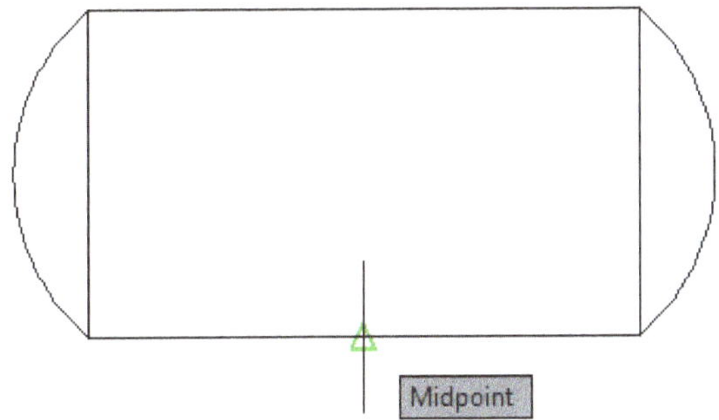

The custom symbol is converted into a P&ID object.

9. Select the symbol and move it to the left side of the drawing sheet.

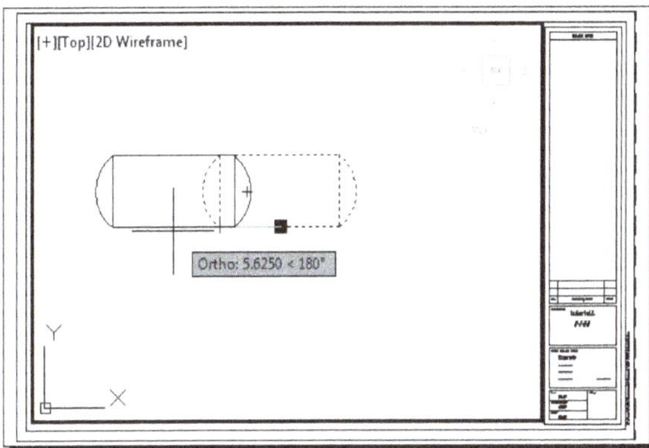

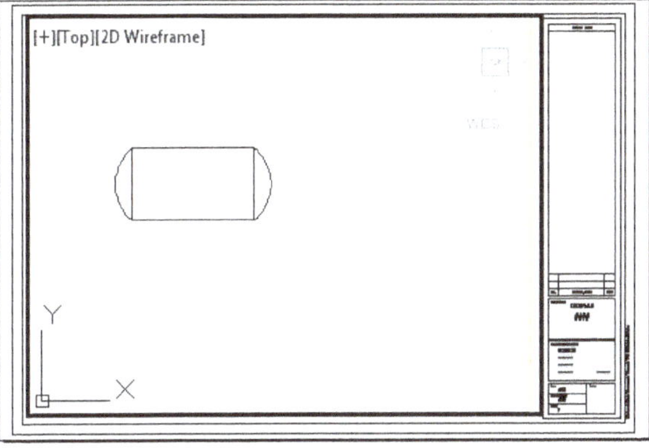

You can also convert regular lines or polylines into P&ID Schematic lines. For example, create lines and arcs using the LINE and ARC command. Next, join them using the **JOIN** command. You can also use the POLYLINE command to create continuous lines and arcs.

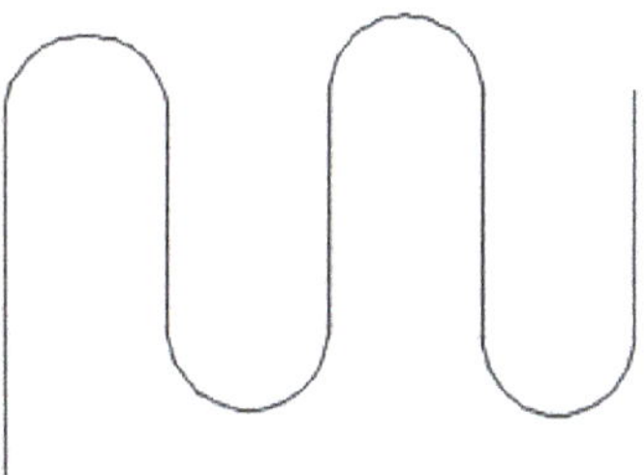

- Select the continuous line and click the right mouse button.
- Select the **Convert to P&ID Object** option.
- On the dialog, select **Engineering Items > Lines > Pipe Line Segments > Primary Line Segment** and click **OK**.

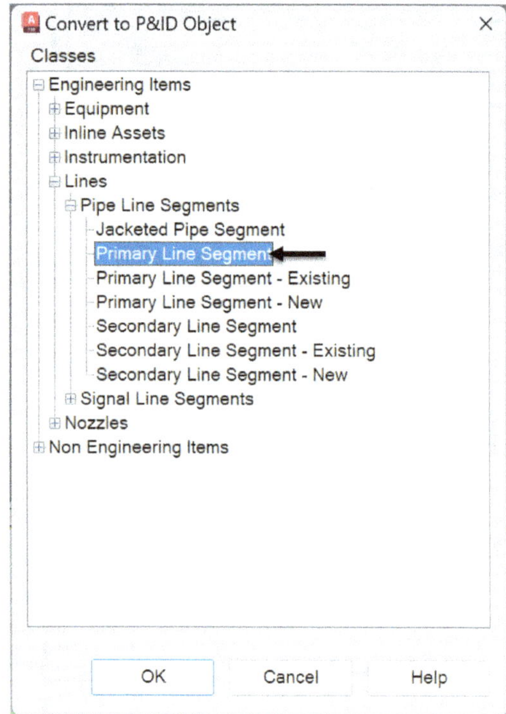

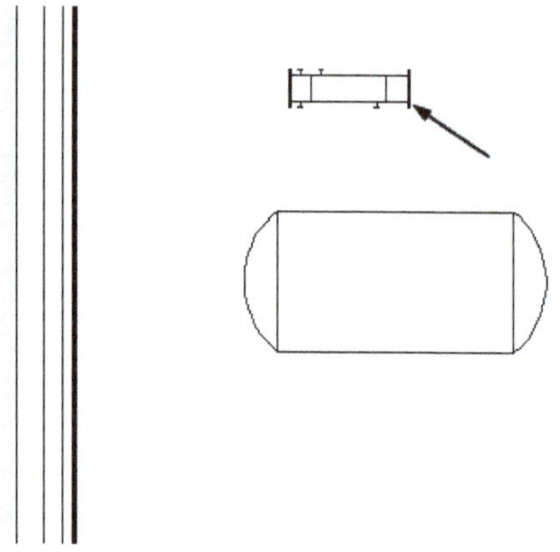

12. On the **Assign Tag** dialog, click the button next to the **Number** box.
13. Click the **Assign** button on the **Assign Tag** dialog, and then place the annotation below the heat exchanger.
14. Place a Horizontal Centrifugal pump.

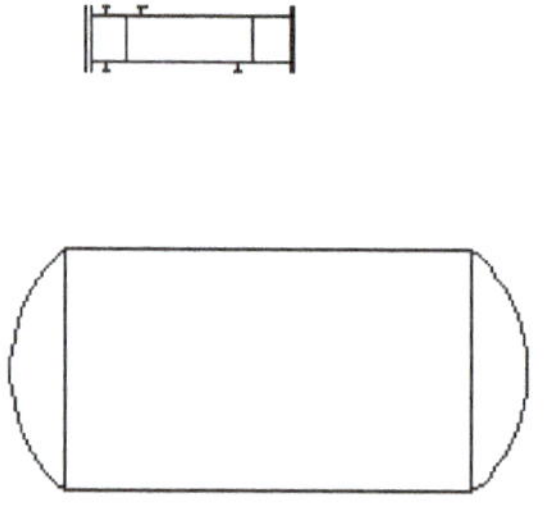

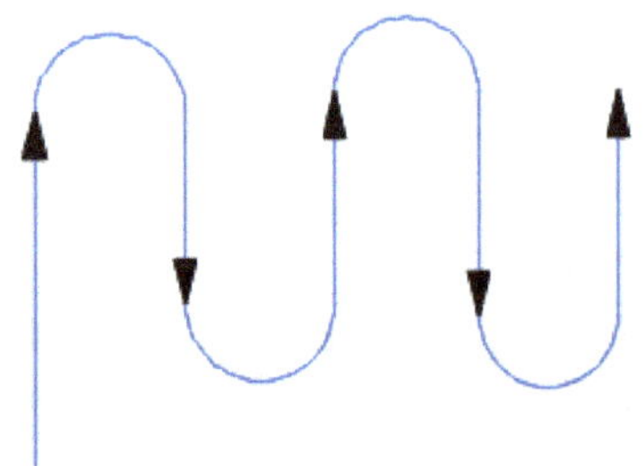

10. Select the **TEMA Type NEN Exchanger** from the **TEMA Type Exchangers** section on the **Equipment** tab.

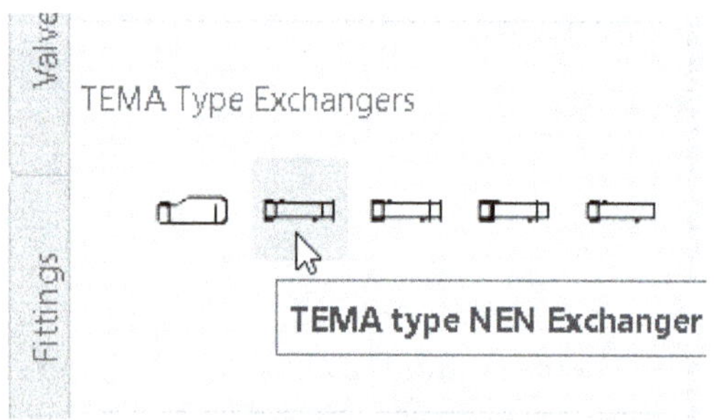

11. Click to place the heat exchanger, as shown.

Next, you have to draw the pipelines.

15. Click the **Primary Line Segment** icon under the **Pipe Lines** section of the **Lines** tool palettes.

16. Draw the pipeline connecting the equipment symbols.

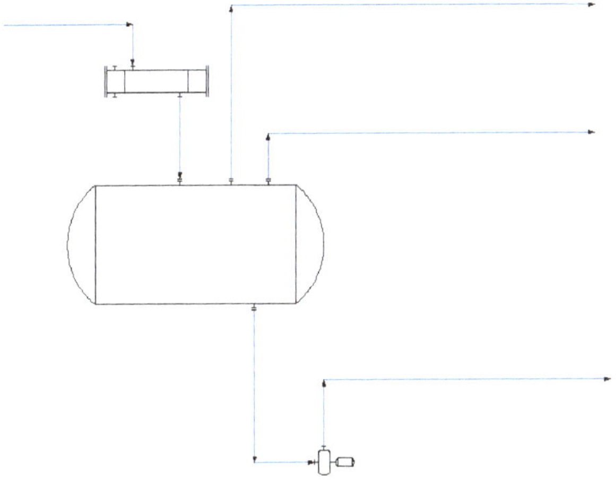

Creating the Secondary Line Segments

1. Click the **Secondary Line Segments** icon on the **Lines** tool palette and create the secondary line segments, as shown next.

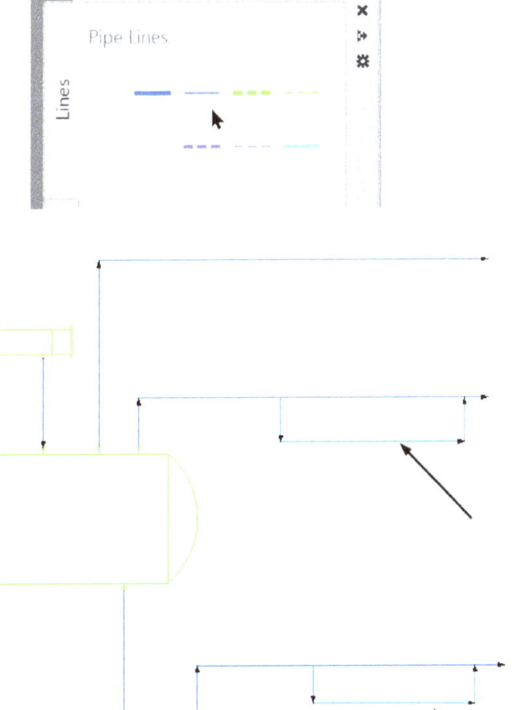

2. Click the **Off Page connector** icon on the **Non-engineering** tool palette.

3. Select the endpoint of the line connecting the heat exchanger, as shown.

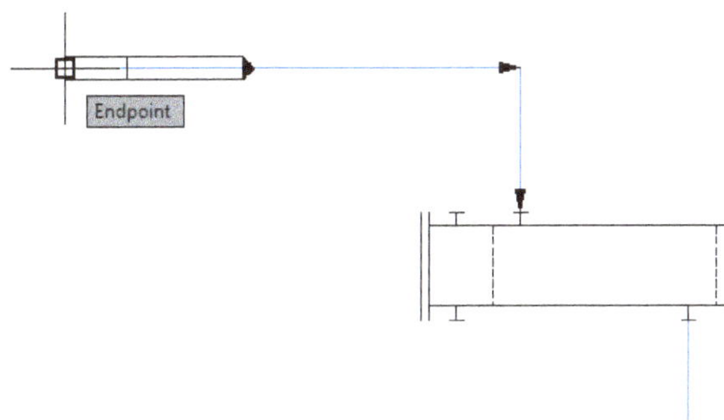

Connecting the Off page connectors

1. To connect off page connectors, select the off page connector located at the top left corner.

2. Click on the (+) plus symbol displayed on the off page connector and select **Connect To**.

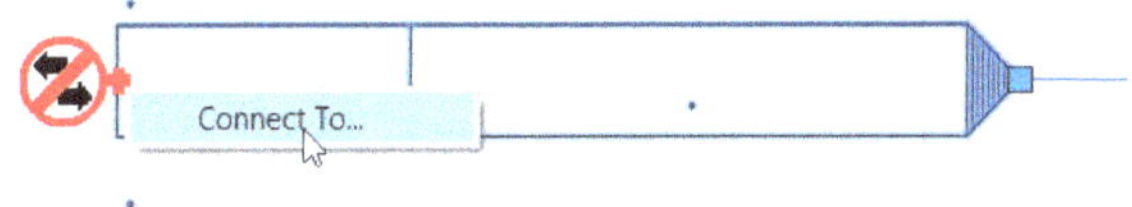

The **Create Connection** window appears.

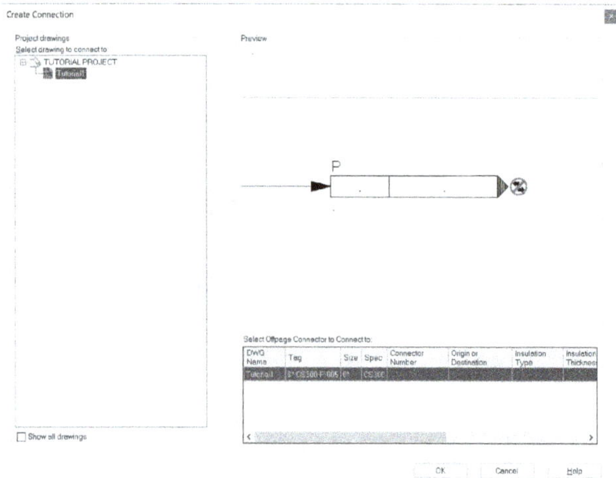

You will notice that the off page connector located in the **Tutorial1.dwg** is selected, by default.

3. Click **OK**.

In AutoCAD Plant 3D, you can use the Off page connectors to connect the instrumentation lines, as well. You can also connect the lines within the same drawing.

4. Click the **Save** button on the **Application Menu**.

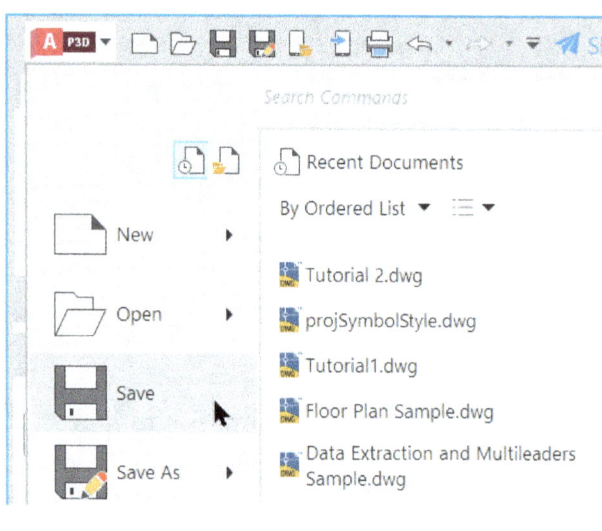

Exercise 1

In this exercise, open the Tutorial2 P&ID and add valves, fittings, instruments and instrumentation lines, and tags. Various regions of the P&ID are given in the following figures.

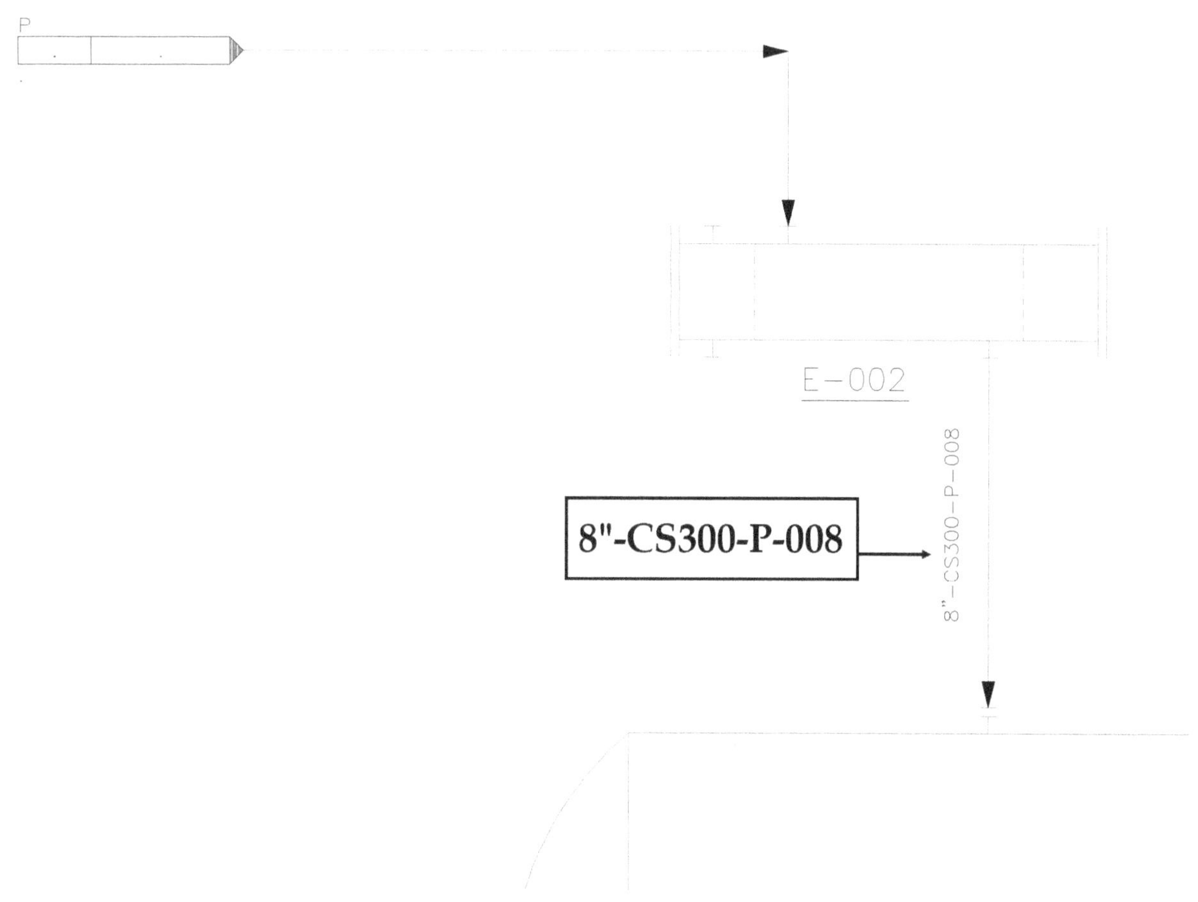

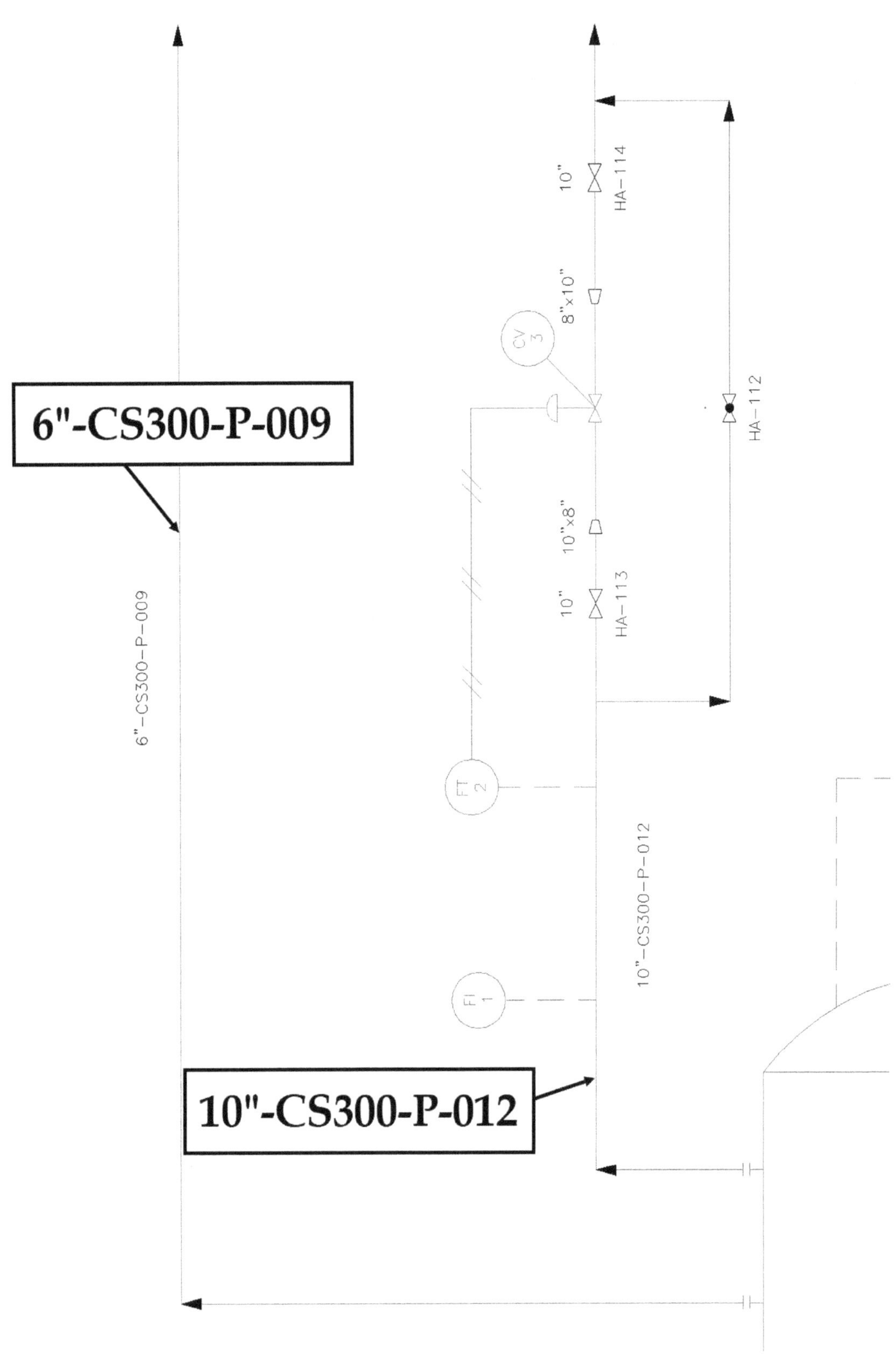
6"-CS300-P-009
6"-CS300-P-009
10"-CS300-P-012
10"-CS300-P-012
10"
HA-114
8"×10"
CV
3
HA-112
10"×8"
10"
HA-113
FT
2
FI
1

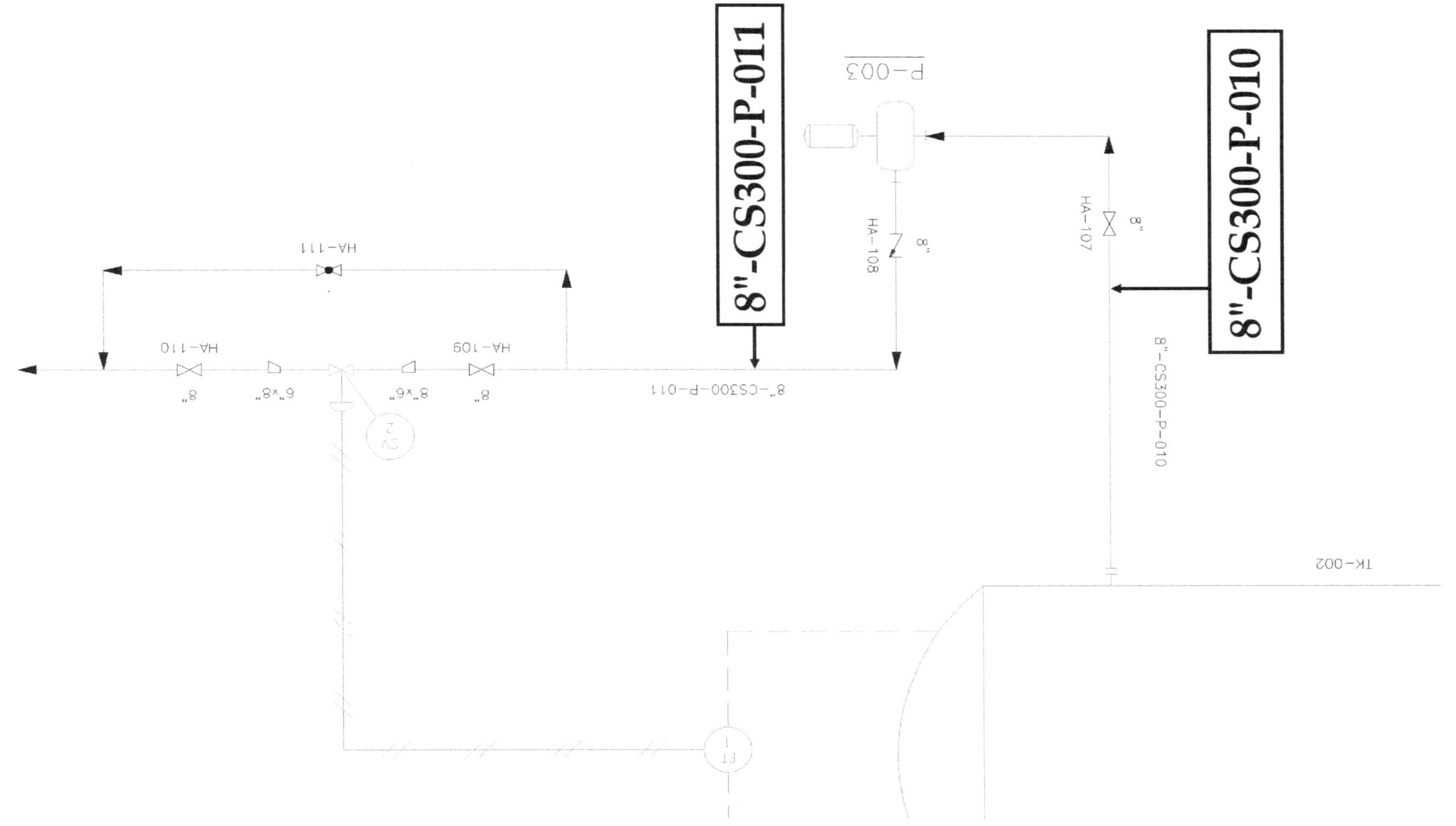
HA-111
HA-110
8"
6"x8"
8"x6"
HA-109
8"
CV 2
8"-CS300-P-011
8"-CS300-P-011
P-003
HA-108
8"
HA-107
8"
8"-CS300-P-010
8"-CS300-P-010
TK-002
FT

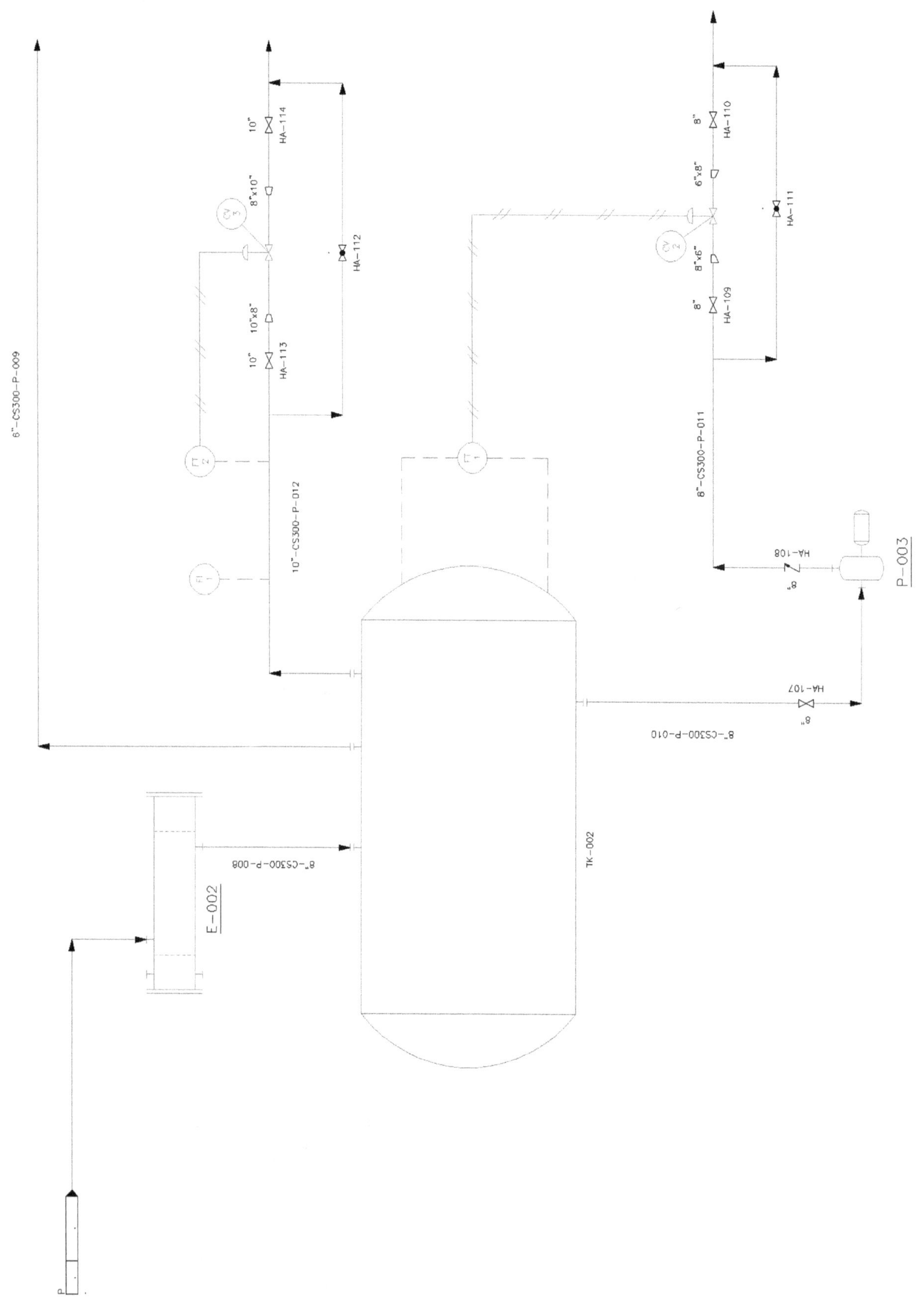
6"-CS300-P-009
10"
HA-114
8"x10"
HA-112
10"x8"
10"
HA-113
10"
10"-CS300-P-012
8"
HA-110
6"x8"
HA-111
8"x6"
8"
HA-109
8"-CS300-P-011
HA-108
P-003
8"
HA-107
8"
8"-CS300-P-010
TK-002
8"-CS300-P-008
E-002

Tutorial 3 (Editing the P&ID)

In this tutorial, you open the drawing created in **Tutorial 1** and modify it.

1. Right-click on **Tutorial1** in the **Project Manager** and select **Open** from the shortcut menu.

Applying Corners

1. To apply corners to a line, select the line connecting the bottom portion of the vessel.

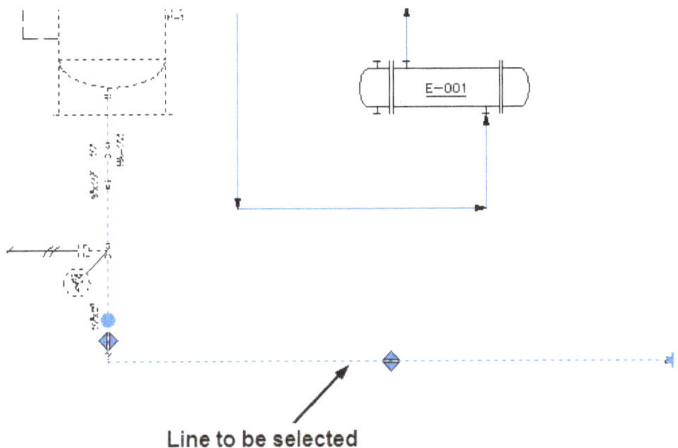

2. Right-click and select **Schematic Line Edit > Apply Corner**.

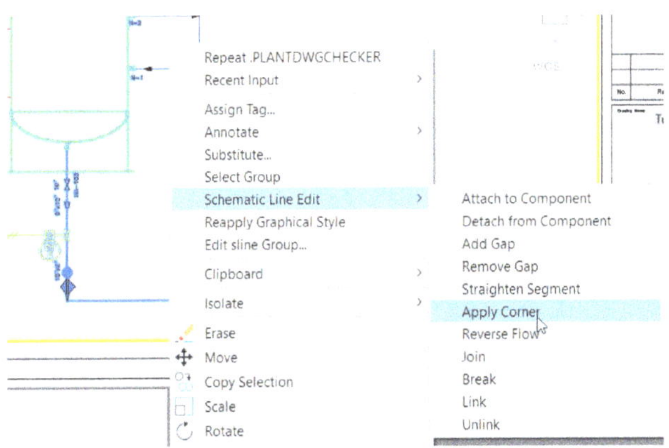

3. Select a point on the line to specify the corner point.

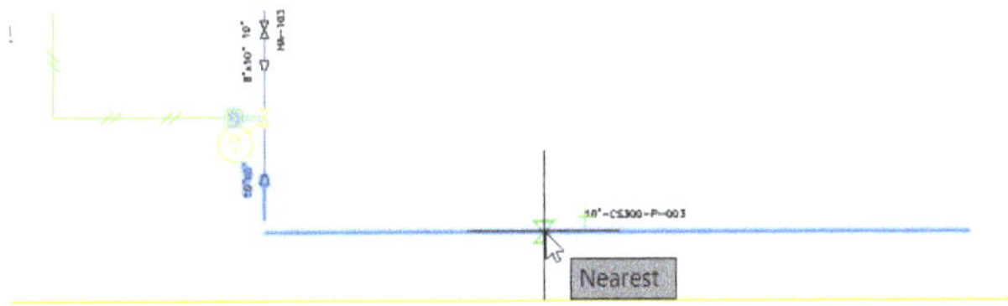

4. Move the pointer downward and click to specify the second point.

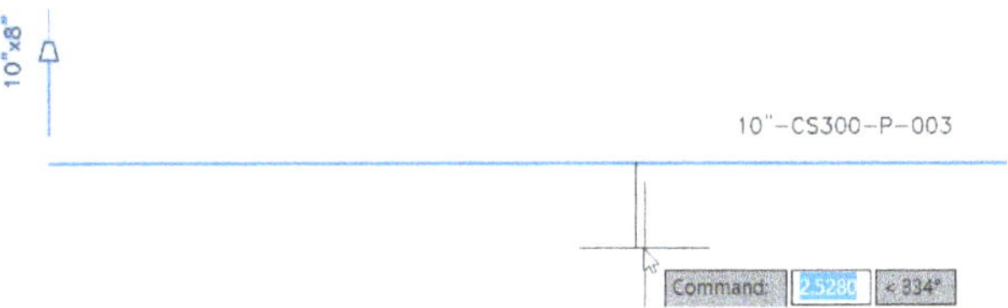

5. Select a point on the line to specify the side of the corner.

The corner is applied to the line.

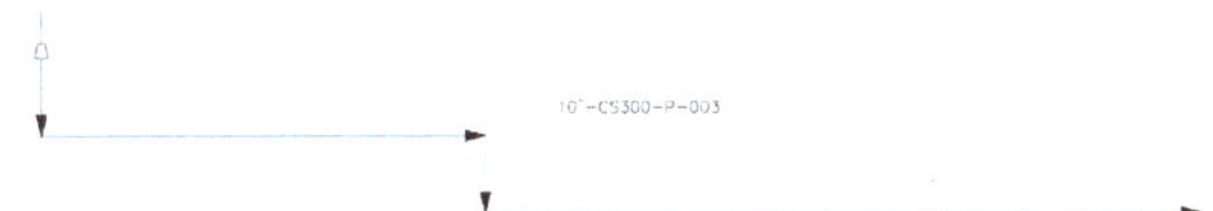

Adding Gaps to lines

In this section, you add gaps to lines. Before adding gaps, you need to create lines passing over equipment.

1. Create two lines passing through the heat exchanger, as shown.

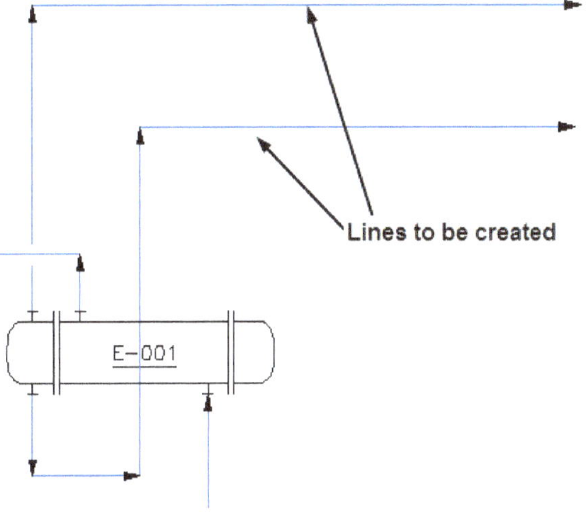

2. Click the **Edit** button on the **Schematic Lines** panel of the **Home** ribbon.

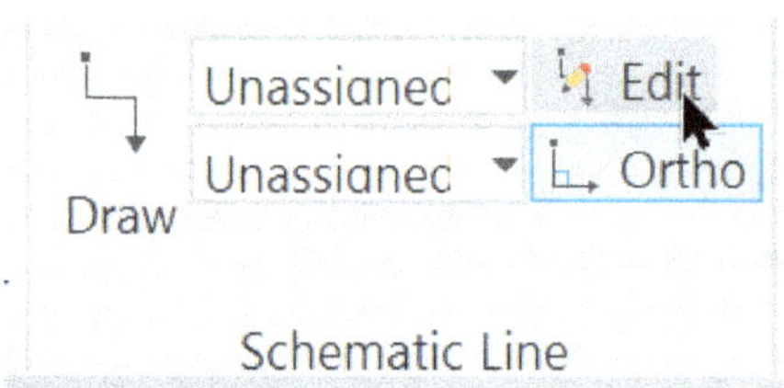

3. Select the line passing over the heat exchanger.

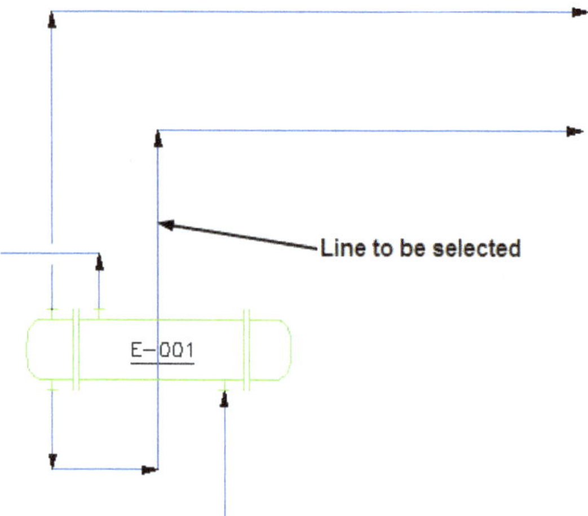

4. Select the **Gap** option.

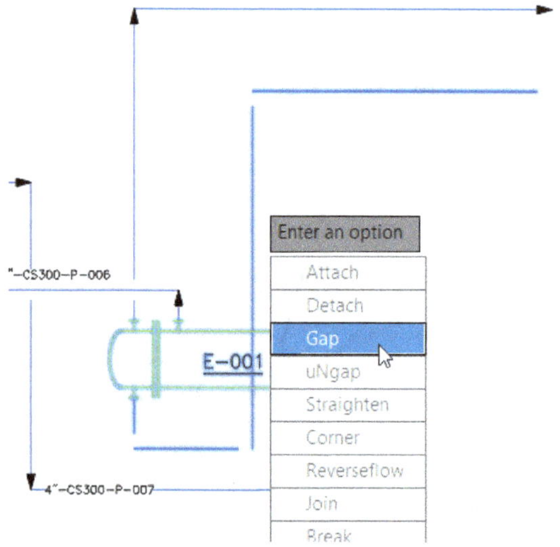

5. Select the first point of the gap.

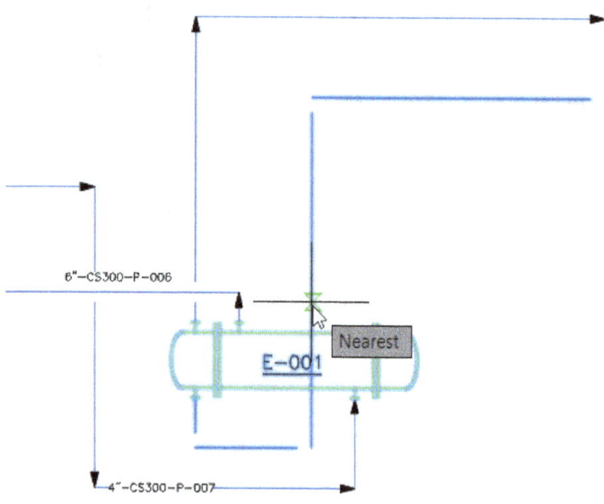

6. Select the second point of the gap.

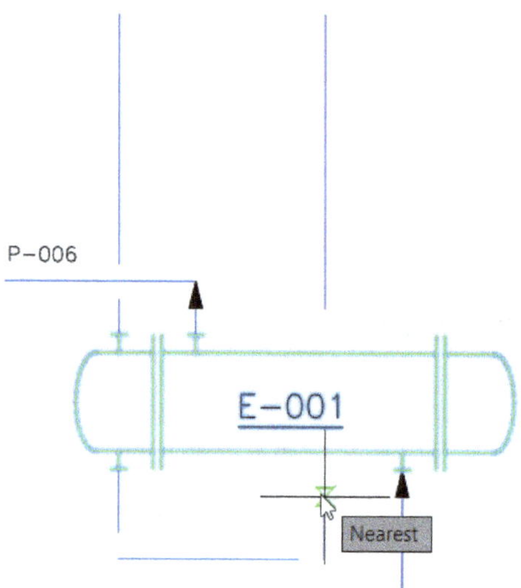

7. Press **Enter** key to create a gap.

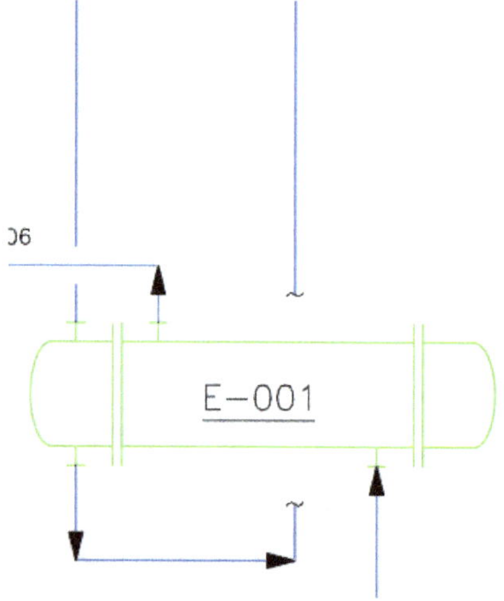

Reversing the Flow Direction

Sometimes you may create a line with the wrong flow direction. For example, the line connecting the heat exchanger is created in the opposite flow direction, see figure below. You need to reverse the flow direction.

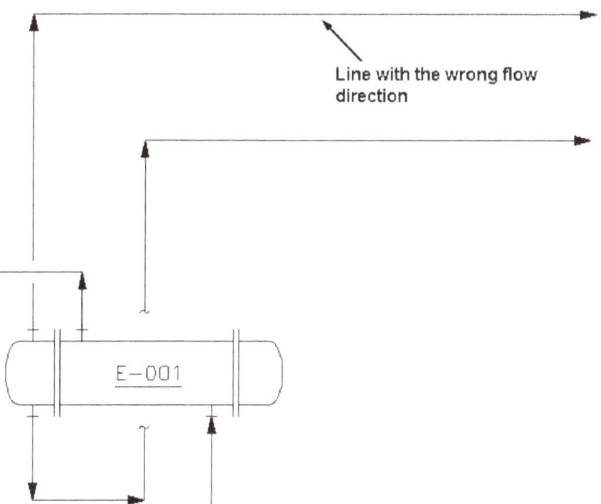

1. Right click on the line, and select **Schematic Line Edit > Reverse Flow**.

The flow direction of the line is reversed.

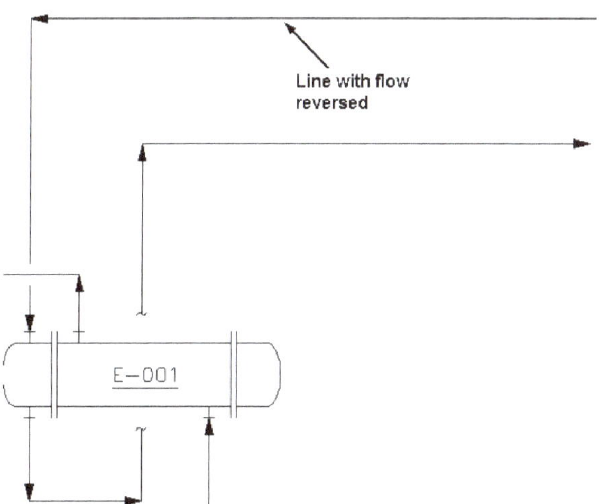

Modifying the lines using grips

In AutoCAD P&ID, you can modify a line using the grips displayed on it.

1. To modify a line using grips, first select it; the Move Schematic line grips appear at the midpoints of the line.

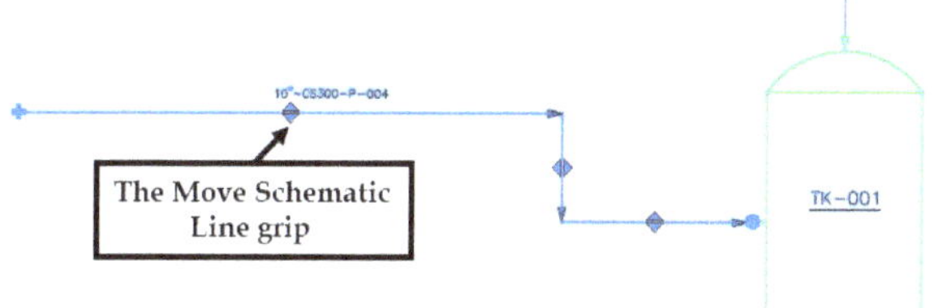

2. Select the **Move Schematic line** grip and move the line downwards.

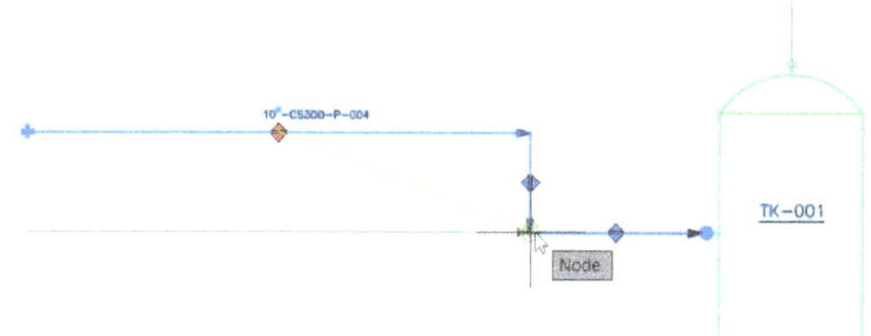

3. Select a point in line with the nozzle. The line is modified.

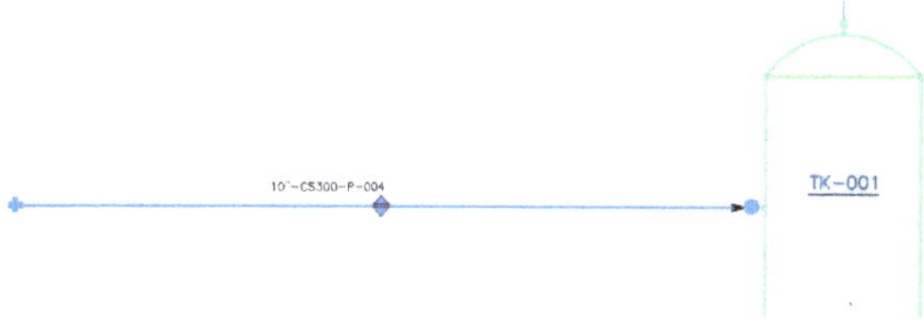

4. To disconnect the line from a P&ID component, select the Connection point grip displayed on the line and move the pointer away from the component. The line is detached from the component.

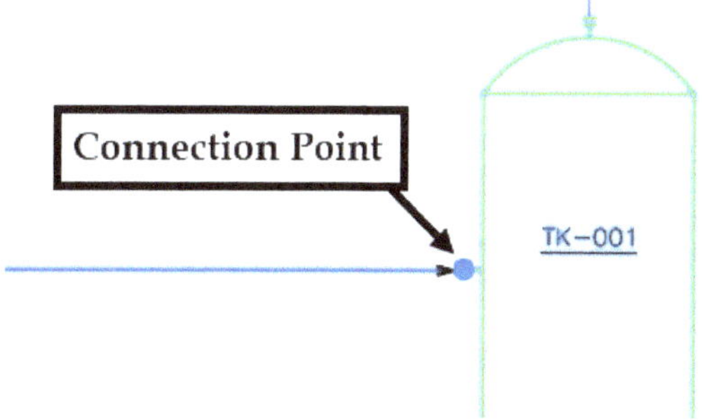

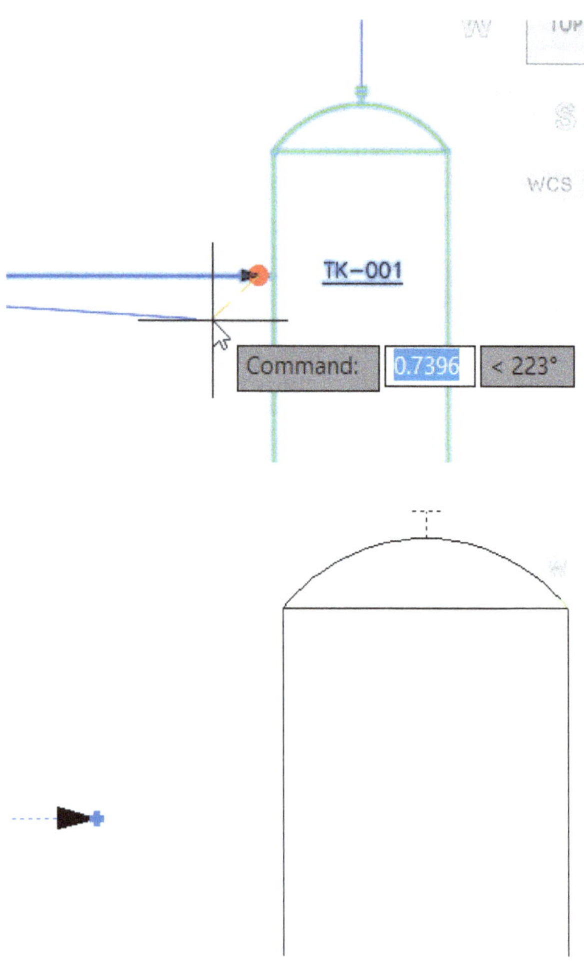

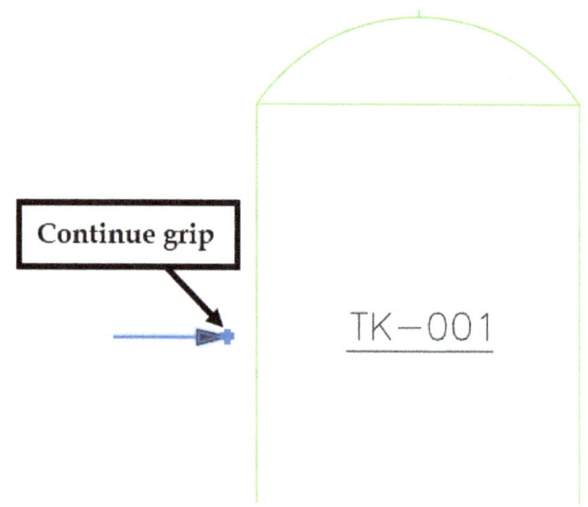

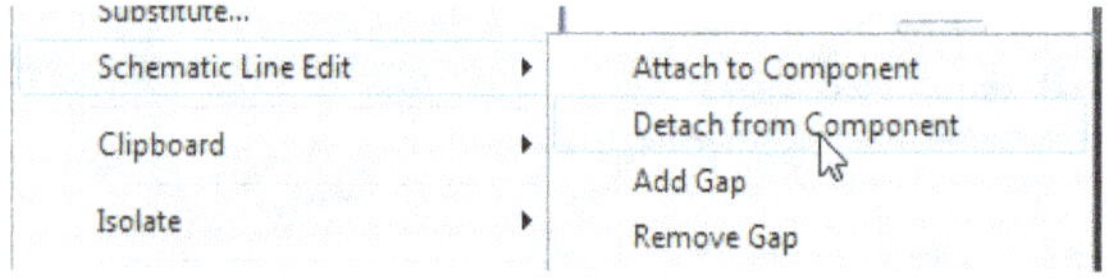

You can also detach a line from a component by using the **Detach** option. To do this, right-click on the line and select **Schematic Line Edit > Detach from component**. Next, specify the endpoint of the line.

Substitute...		
Schematic Line Edit ▸	Attach to Component	
	Detach from Component	
Clipboard ▸	Add Gap	
Isolate ▸	Remove Gap	

To reattach the line to the component, click on the **Continue grip** and connect it to the component.

Substituting the Symbols

In AutoCAD P&ID, you can replace symbols by substituting them with another symbol of the same group.

1. To substitute a valve symbol, select the **Check valve** placed on the line connected to the centrifugal pump. The Substitute grip appears on it.

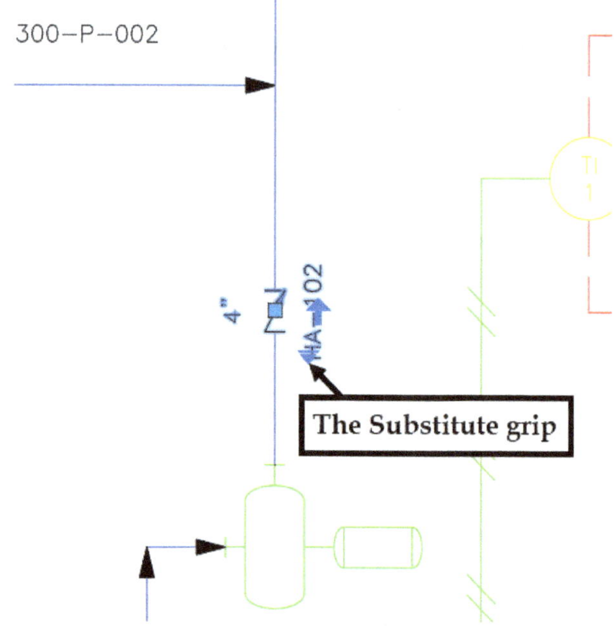

2. Click on the substitute grip to display various valve symbols.
3. Select the Globe Valve.

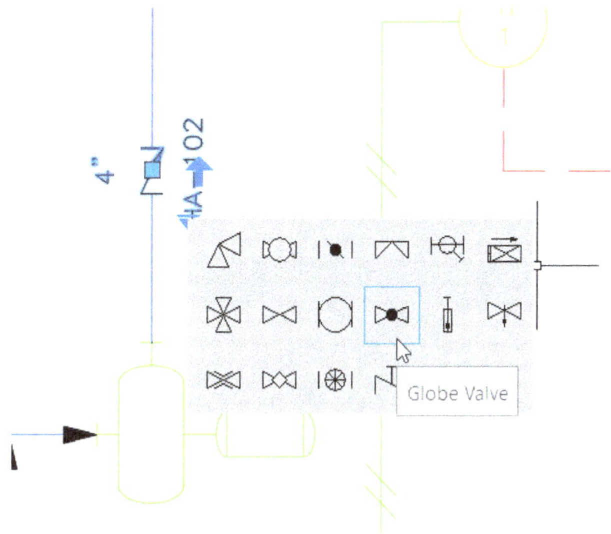

The Globe valve replaces the Check Valve.

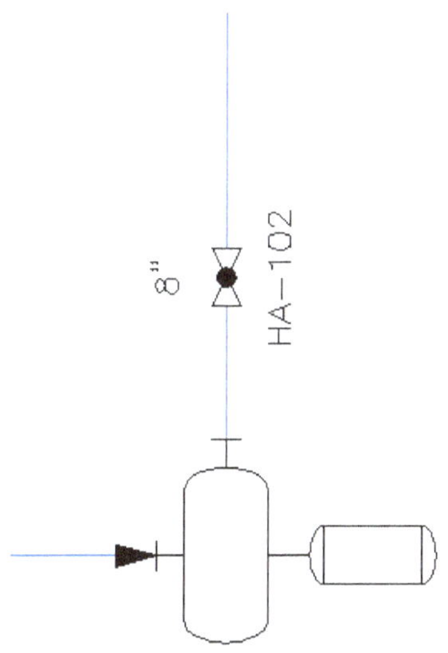

Substituting Instrument symbols

1. To substitute an instrument symbol, select the Temperature Indicator symbol connected to the vessel.
2. Click the Substitute grip.
3. Select **Primary Accessible DCS**.

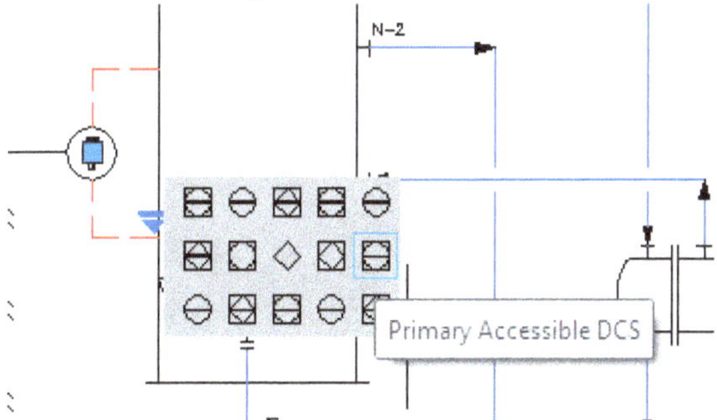

The instrument symbol is replaced.

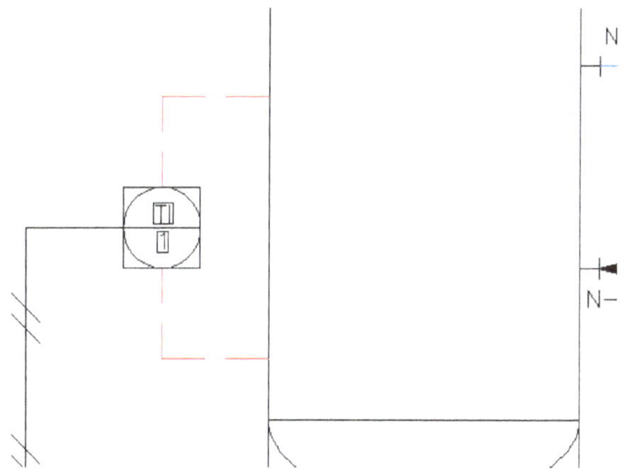

You can also substitute equipment symbols. However, you have to reconnect the pipelines after substituting. For example, on substituting a centrifugal pump with a vertical inline pump, the pipeline is disconnected. You need to connect the pipelines using the grips.

4. Save the P&ID drawing. Do not close it.

Tutorial 4 (Defining a new Class)

In this tutorial, you create a block of a symbol and add it to the category list of the project.

1. Start a new drawing by clicking the **New** button on the Quick Access toolbar.

2. Create the symbol, as shown.

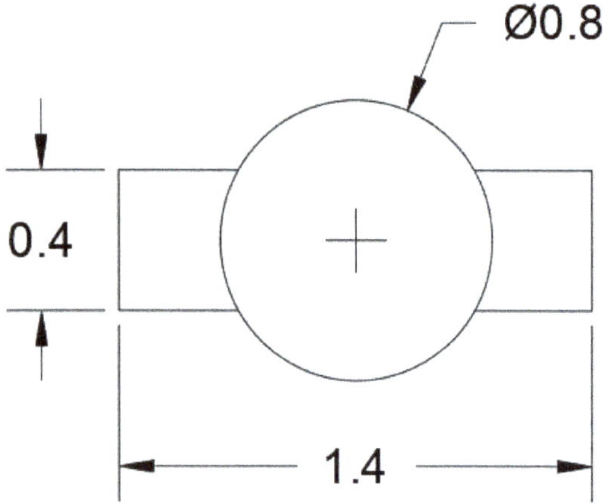

3. Select all the entities of the symbol.

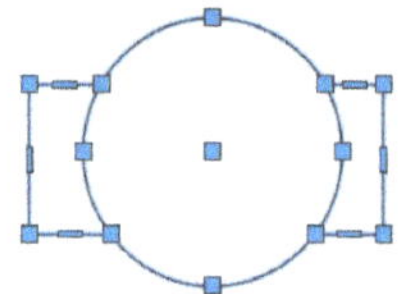

4. Click the **Create Block** button on the **Block Definition** panel of the **Insert** tab.

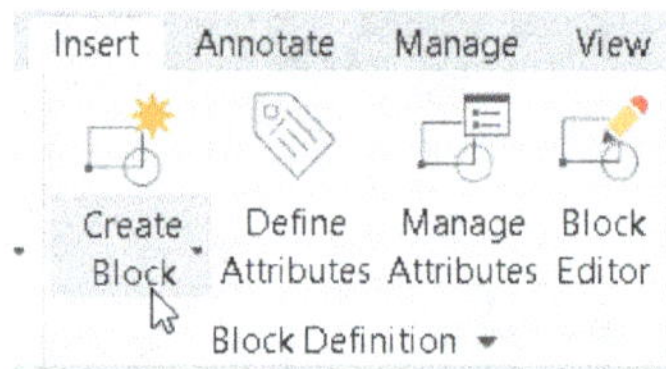

5. In the **Block Definition** dialog, enter **Vacuum Pump** in the **Name** edit box.
6. Click the **Pick Point** button on the **Block Definition** dialog.

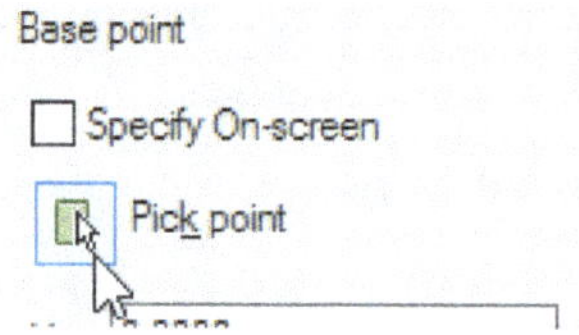

7. Select the center point of the circle as a base point.

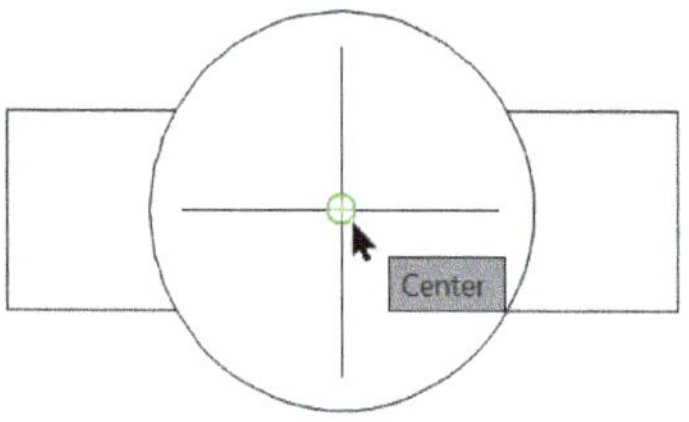

8. Click the **OK** button to create a block.
9. Save the file with the name *Vaccum_Pump.dwg* in the **TUTORIAL PROJECT** folder.

Next, you need to define a new class using the **Project Setup** dialog.

10. Open the **TUTORIAL PROJECT** project, if not already opened.

- To open a project, click the **Open** option on the drop-down in the **Project Manager**.

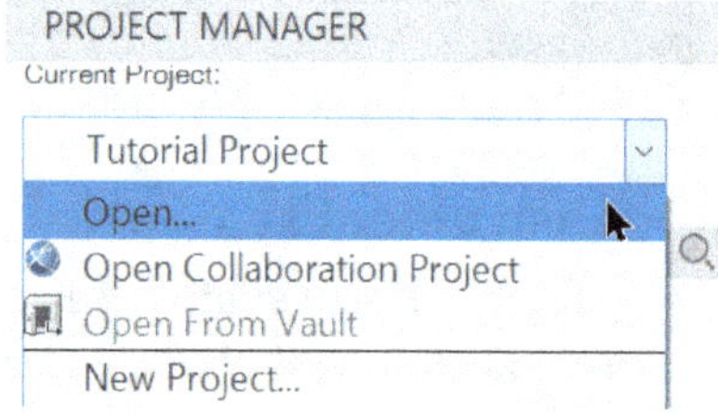

- Browse to the **TUTORIAL PROJECT** folder and double-click on the **Project.xml** file.

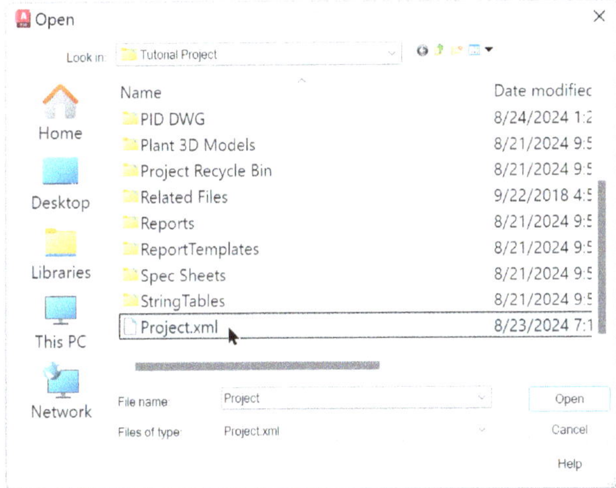

11. On the **Home** ribbon tab, click the **Project Setup** button from the **Project** drop-down in the **Project** panel.

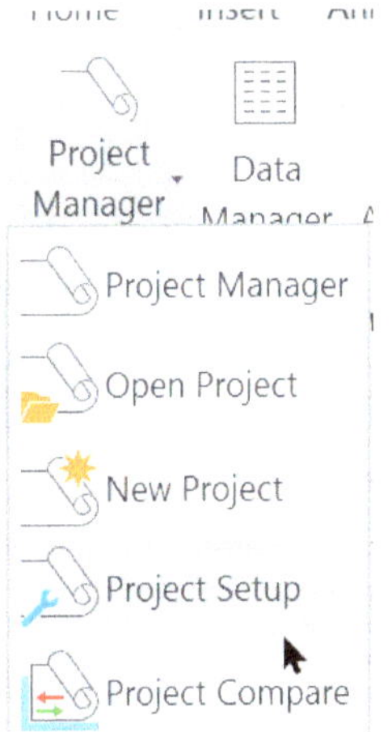

The **Project Setup** dialog appears.

12. Expand the **P&ID DWG Settings** node.

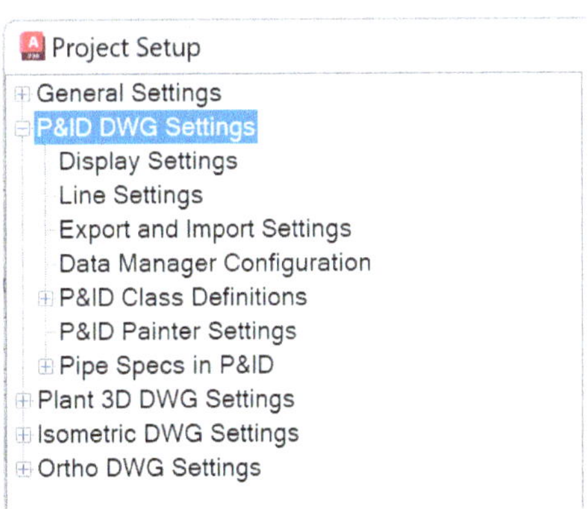

13. In the **P&ID DWG Settings**, expand **P&ID Class Definitions > Engineering Items > Equipment > Pumps**.

14. Right-click on **Pumps** and click **New**.

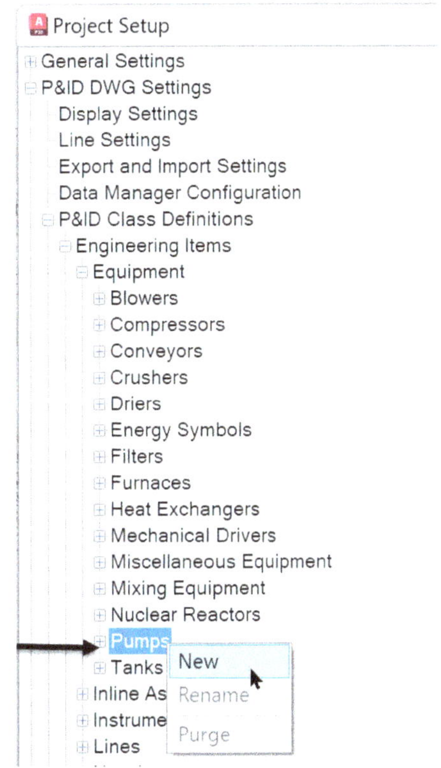

15. In the **Create Class** dialog, enter **Vacuum_Pump** in the **Class Name** field.

16. Type **Vacuum Pump** in the **Display Name of the Class** field.

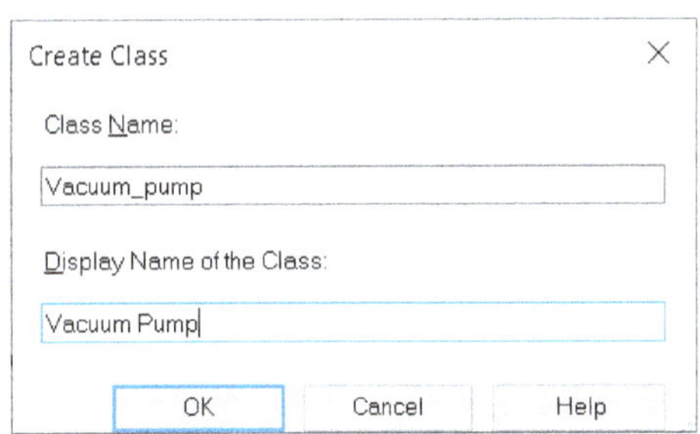

17. Click the **OK** button.

The new class is displayed under the **Pumps** list.

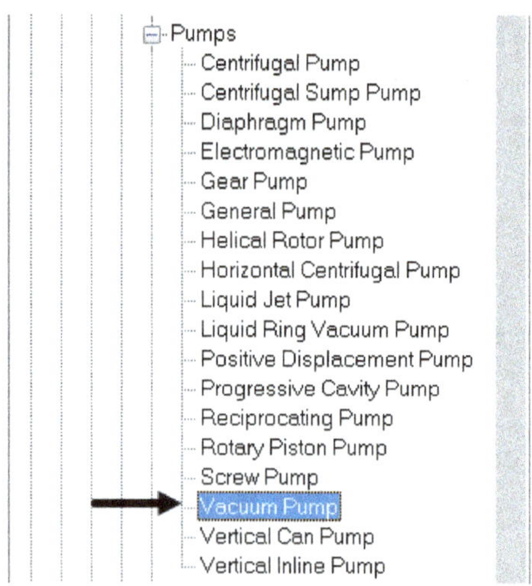

18. Select the **Vacuum Pump** class from the list and click the **Add Symbols** button under the **Symbol** section.

The **Add Symbols** dialog appears.

19. In this dialog, click the **Browse** button next to the **Selected Drawings** field.

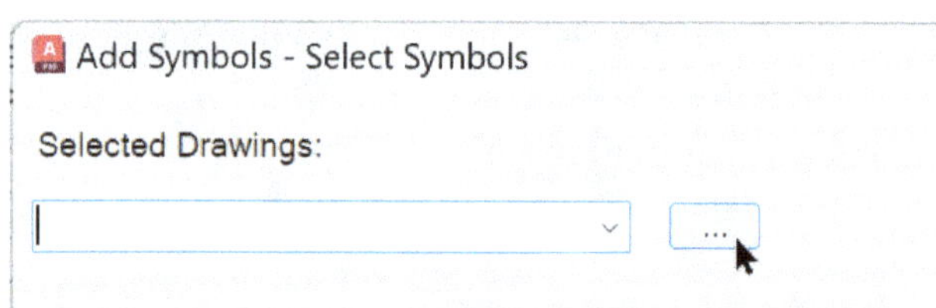

20. In the **Select Block Drawing** dialog, browse to the **TUTORIAL PROJECT** folder and double-click on the **Vacuum_Pump.dwg**.

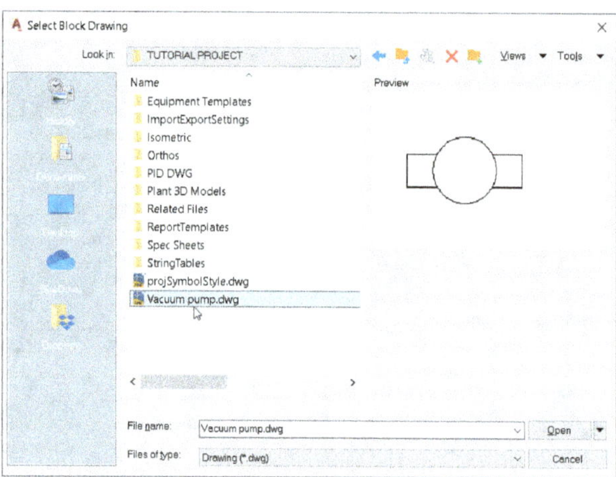

21. In the **Add Symbols** dialog, select **Vacuum_Pump** from the **Available Blocks** list and click the **Add** button.

22. Click the **Next** button.

The **Add Symbols-Edit Symbol Settings** dialog appears.

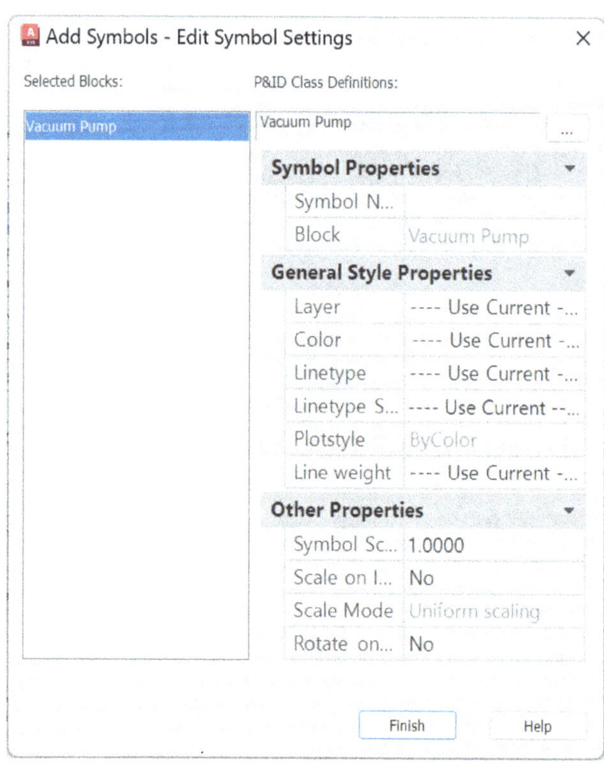

23. Type **Vacuum Pump** in the **Symbol Name** edit box.
24. Specify the other properties, as shown.

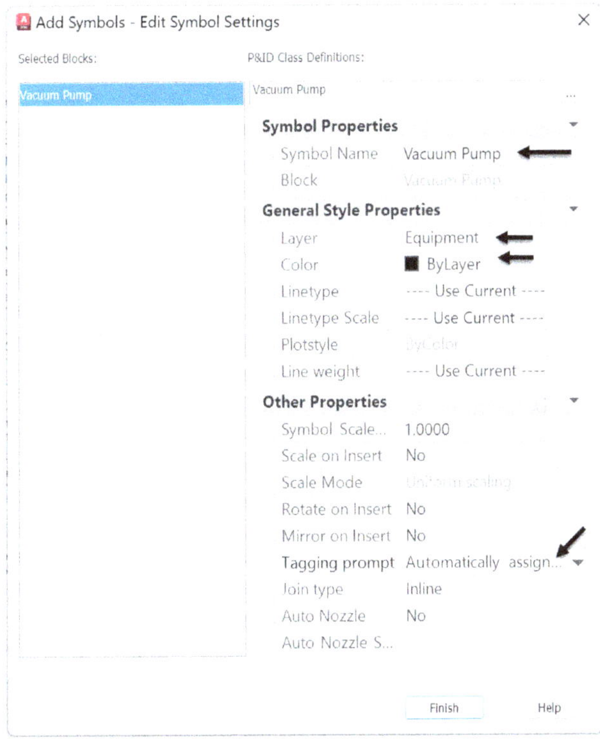

25. Click the **Finish** button to add the symbol to the list.
26. Click the **Edit Block** button under **Class settings: Vacuum Pump**.

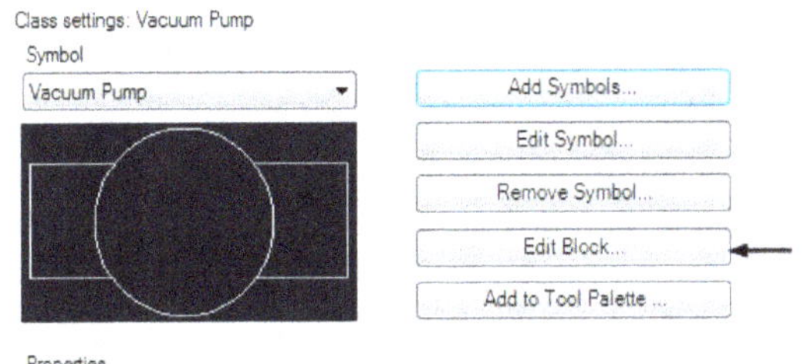

The block editor is opened.

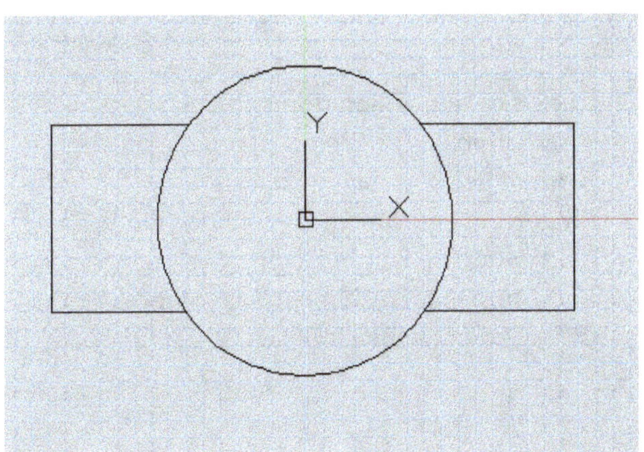

27. Select the **Parameters** tab from the **Block Authoring Palettes** tool palette.

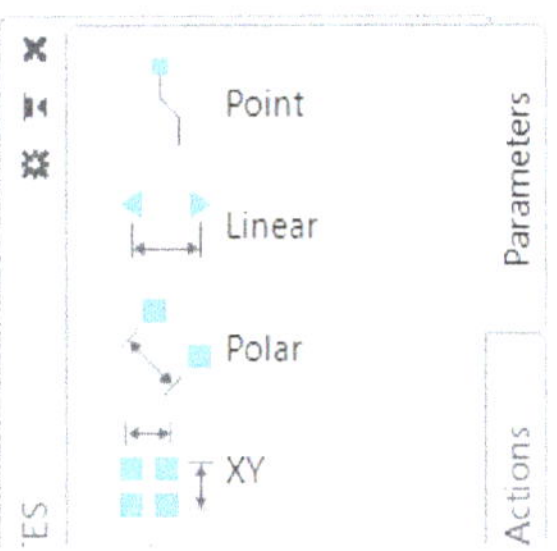

28. Select the **Point** button from the tool palette
29. Press and hold the **Shift** key and right-click to display the shortcut menu.
30. Click **Midpoint** on the shortcut menu.

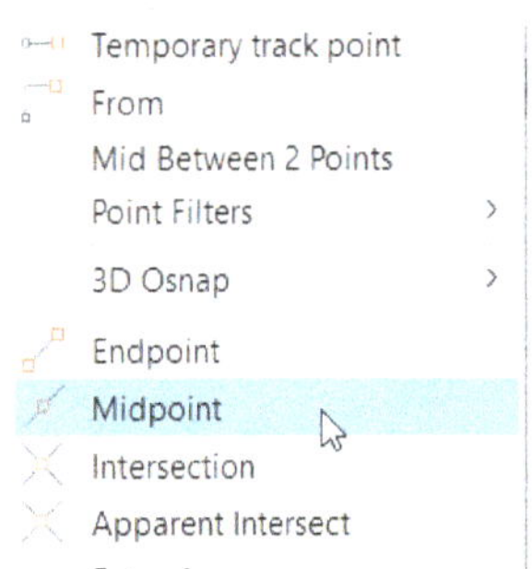

31. Select the midpoint of the left vertical line.

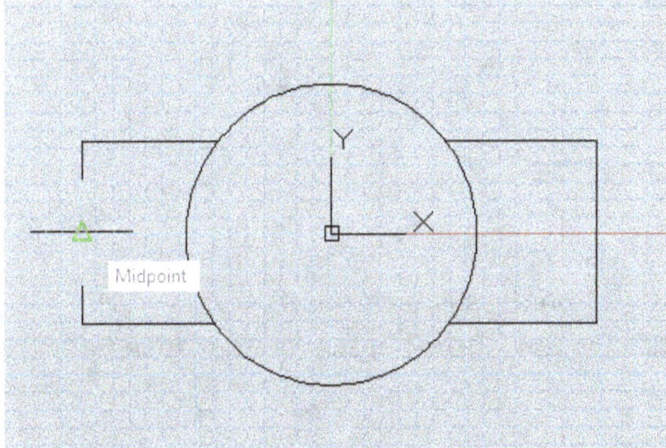

32. Move the pointer toward the left and click.

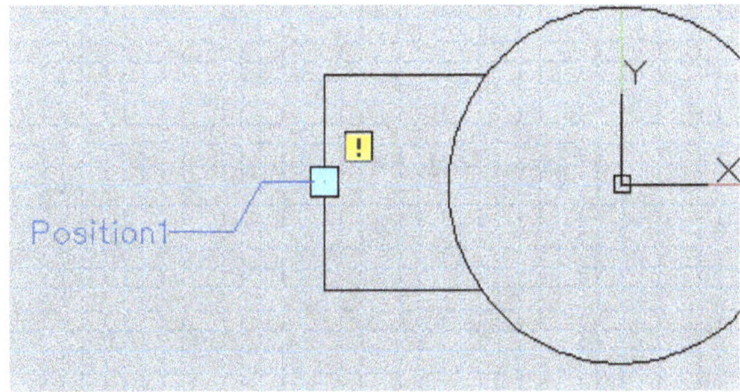

33. Likewise, add another point on the right vertical line.

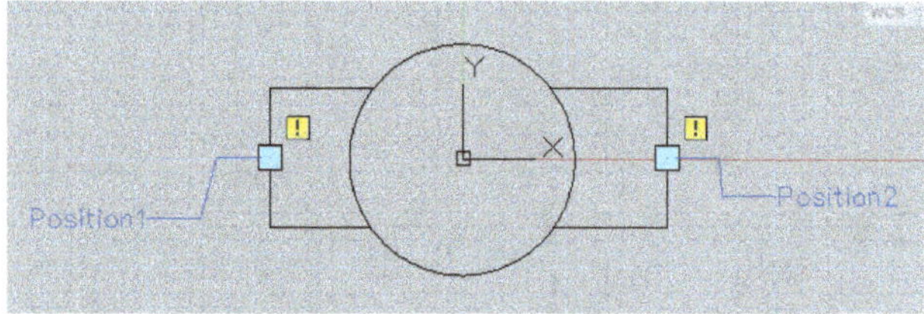

34. Click on the yellow grip displayed on the left point, right click, and select **Properties**; the **Properties** palette is opened.

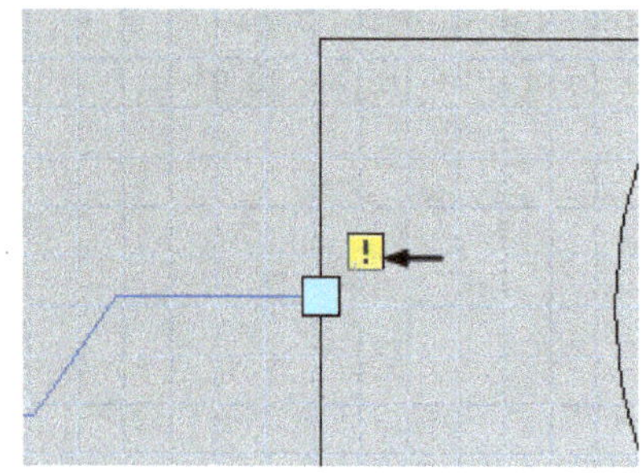

35. In the **Properties** palette, under the **Property Labels**, enter **AttachmentPoint1** in the **Position name** field.

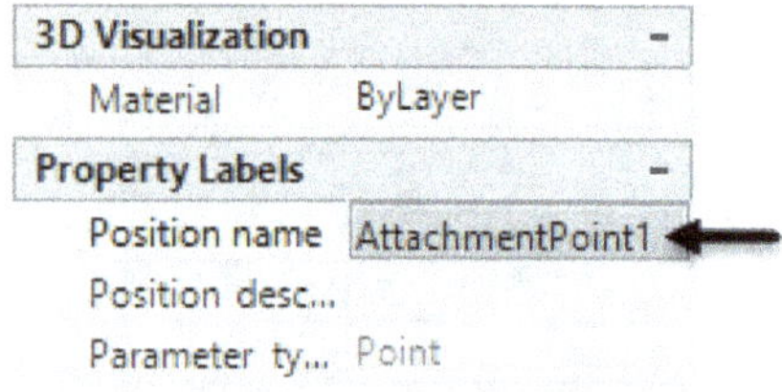

36. Likewise, specify the **Position name** of the second point as **AttachmentPoint2**.
37. Click the **Save Block** button on the **Open/Save** panel.

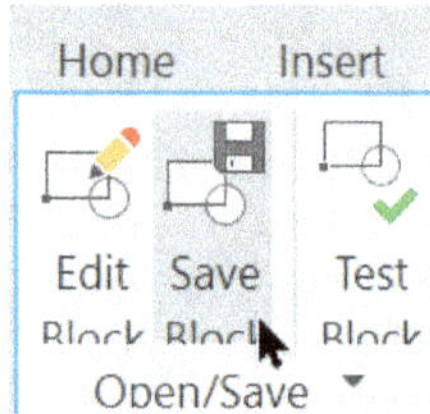

38. Click the **Close Block Editor** button.

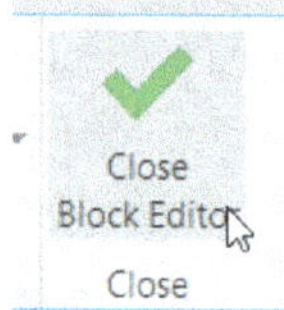

Next, you need to add this symbol to the tool palette.

39. Make sure that the **Equipment** tab is opened in the P&ID PIP tool palettes.
40. Click the **Add to Tool Palette** button under **Class Settings: Vacuum Pump** in the **Project Setup** dialog.

The **Vacuum Pump** is added to the tool palette.

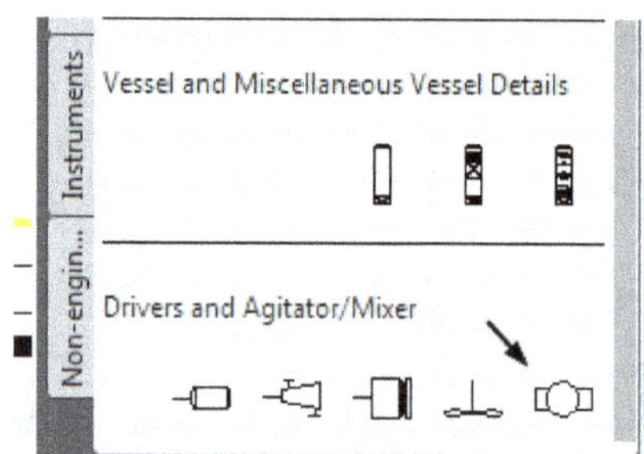

Adding Annotations to the Symbol

Now, you need to add annotations to the symbol.

1. To add annotations to the symbol, make sure that **Equipment tag** is selected in the drop-down available under **Annotation**.

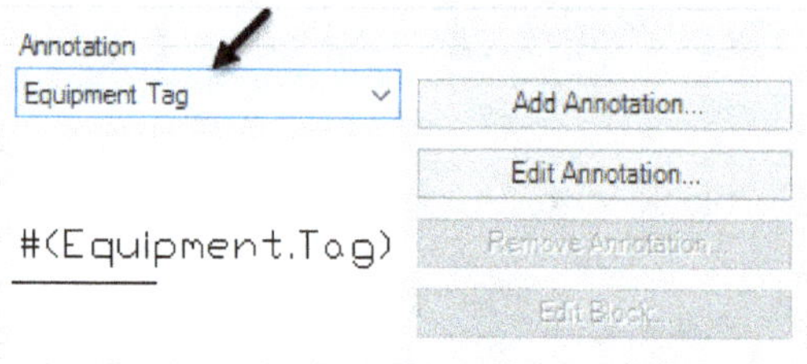

2. Click the **Add Annotation** button under **Annotation** on the **Project Setup** dialog; the **Symbol Settings** dialog appears.
3. Enter **New Equipment tag** in the **Symbol Name** field under the **Symbol Properties** group.
4. Make sure that **Equipment Tag_block** is displayed in the **Block** field.

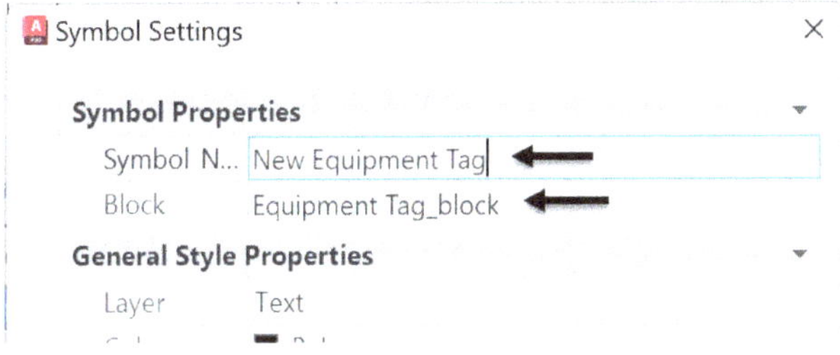

5. Click **OK**.

Now you need to assign a format to the annotation.

6. Click the **Edit Block** button under **Annotation** on the **Project Setup** dialog.

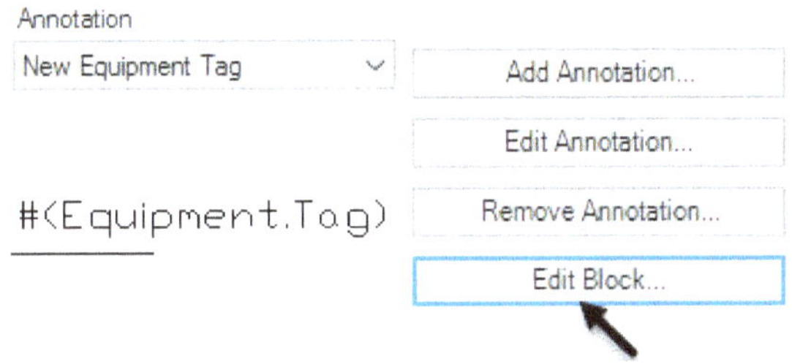

The **Block Editor** is opened.

7. Click the **Assign Format** button on the **Annotation** toolbar.

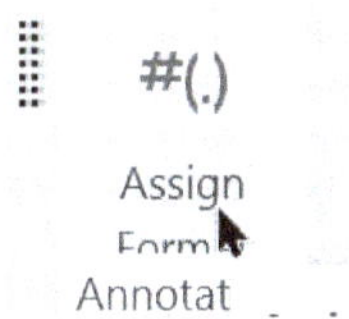

8. Select the **#(Equipment Tag)** attribute from the graphics window; the **Assign Annotation Format** dialog appears.
9. Click the **Select Class Properties** button on the **Assign Annotation Format** dialog.

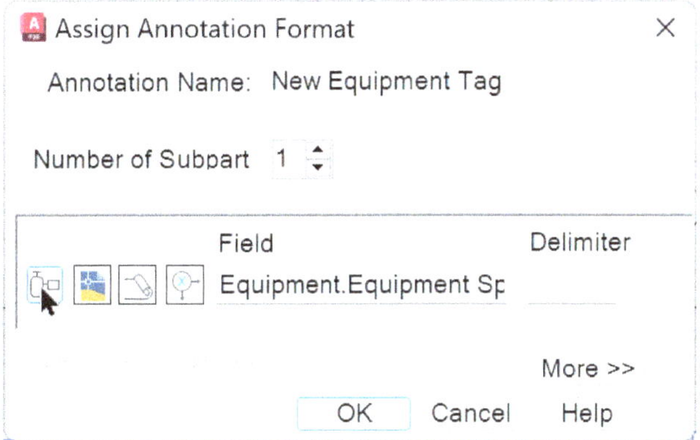

The **Select Class Property** dialog appears.

10. In the **Select Class Property** dialog, select **Engineering Items > Equipment**.
11. Select **Equipment Spec** from the **Property** list.

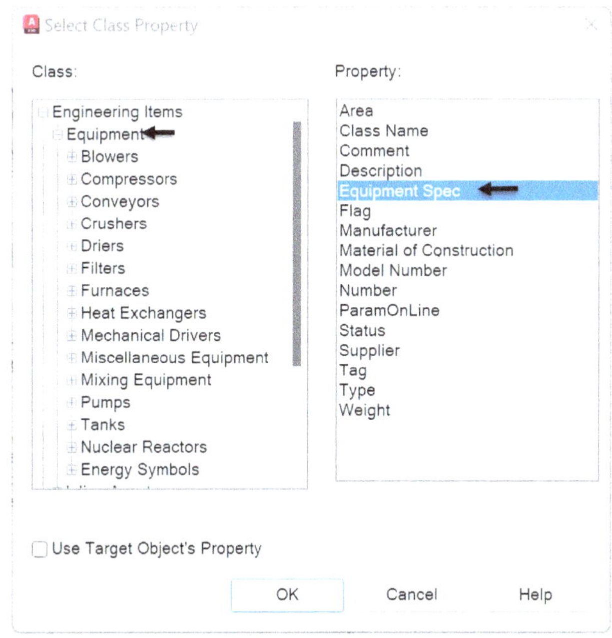

12. Click **OK** on the **Select Class Property** dialog.
13. Click **OK** on the **Assign Annotation Format** dialog.
14. Close the **Block Editor** and save the changes made.

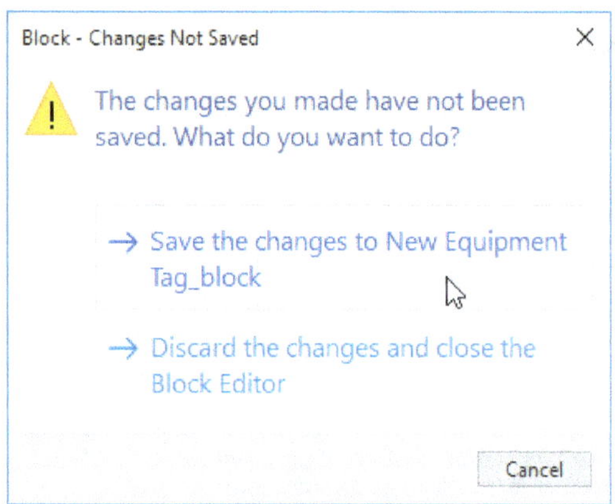

15. In the **Project Setup** dialog, make sure that **Vacuum Pump** is selected in the **Category** list.

16. Set **New Equipment Tag** as the **Default Value** for the **AnnotationStyleName**.

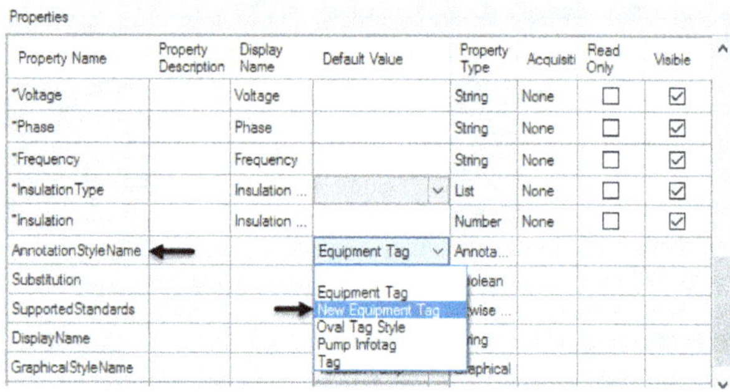

17. Click the **Apply** button.
18. Click the **OK** button.

Chapter 2: Data Manager

In this chapter, you will learn to use the Data Manager to view, export, and import project. Also, you will learn to create reports, customize reports, and customize the Data Manager views.

Tutorial 1 (Managing Data)

In this tutorial, you will learn to view, export, and import P&ID data. You need to use the Data Manager to view, export, or import data.

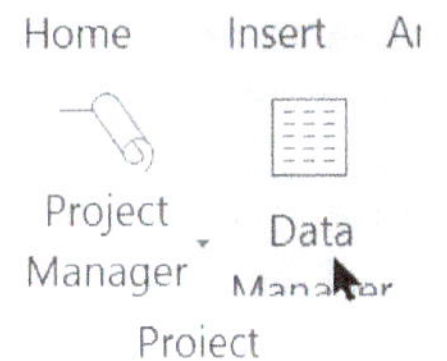

1. To open the Data Manager, click the **Data Manager** button on the **Project** panel of the **Home** ribbon.

The **Data Manager** appears as shown next. Various components of the **Data Manager** are shown in the figure.

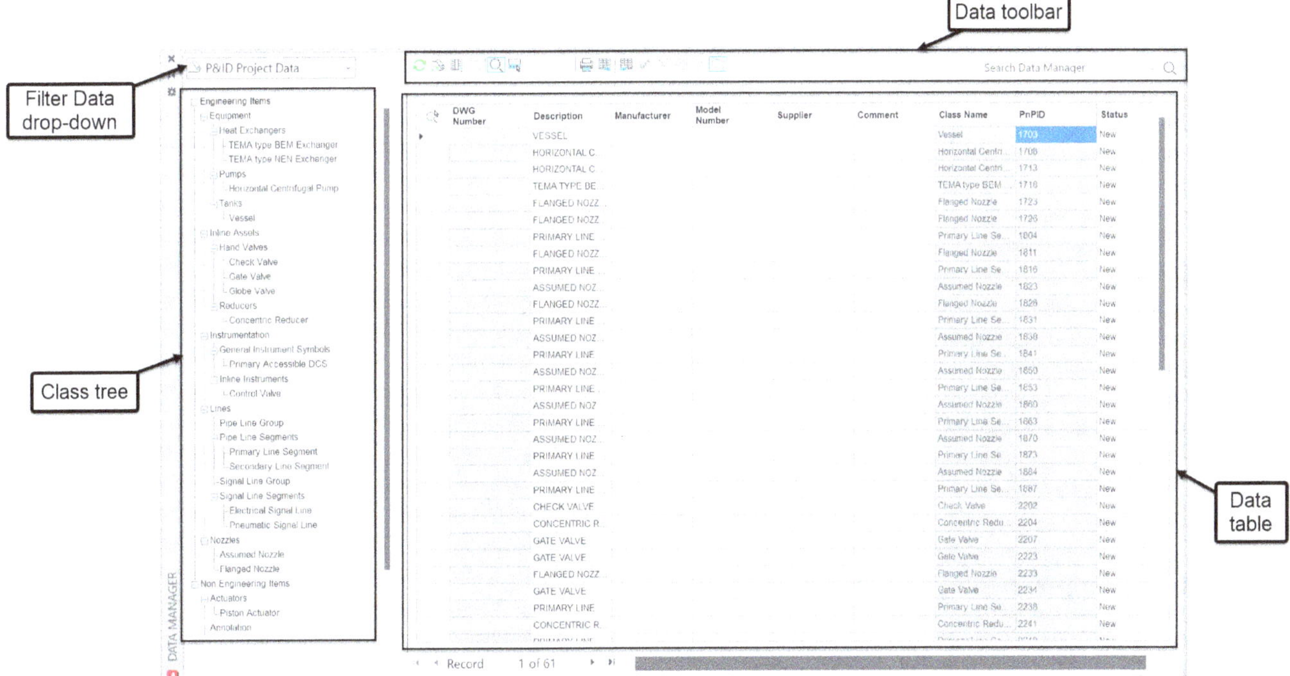

The **Filter Data** drop-down is used to select the type of data to be displayed in the **Data Manager**. You can select the **Current Drawing Data**, **P&ID Project Data,** or the **Project Reports.**

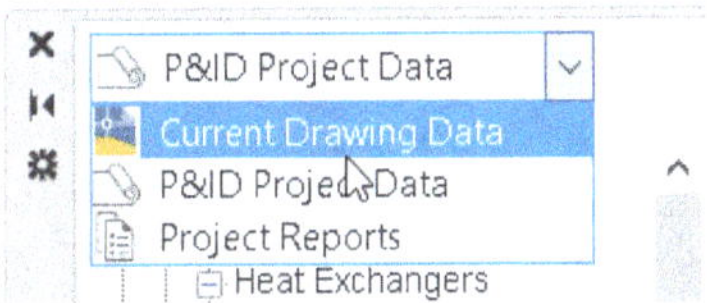

The **Class** tree is used to select the required P&ID class. The data related to the selected class is displayed.

The **Data Manager** toolbar is used to perform various operations such as import, export, view data, and so on.

The **Data** table is similar to a spreadsheet and displays data.

Filtering the Data

1. Open the **Tutorial1.dwg**, if not already opened.
2. Open the **Data Manager** by clicking the **Data Manager** button on the **Project** panel.

3. Click **Current Drawing Data** on00 the
    Filter data drop-down to view the data of
    the currently opened drawing file.
4. Click **Equipment** from the **Class** tree to
    view all the equipment in the drawing,

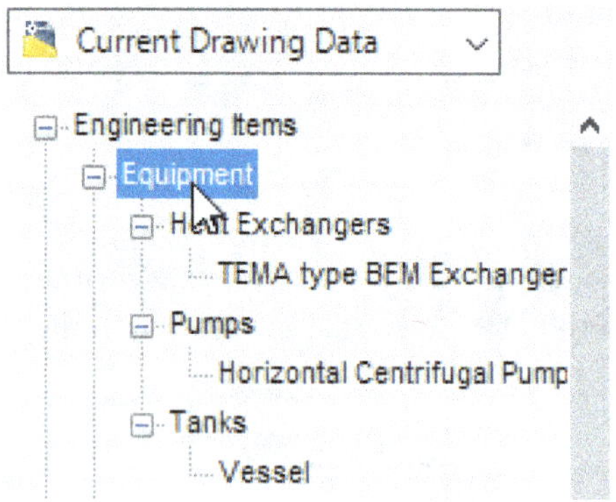

Tag	Size	Spec	Description	Mar
N-1	6"	CS300	FLANGED N...	
N-2	4"	CS300	FLANGED N...	
N-3	8	CS300	FLANGED N...	
N-1	4"	CS300	ASSUMED N...	
N-4	4"	CS300	FLANGED N...	
N-1	4"	CS300	ASSUMED N...	
N-2	6"	CS300	ASSUMED N...	
N-2	?	?	ASSUMED N...	
N-1	4"	CS300	ASSUMED N...	
N-2	6"	CS300	ASSUMED N...	
N-5	10"	CS300	FLANGED N...	
N-6	10"	CS300	FLANGED N...	

Tag	Type	Description	Manufacturer	Model Number
TK-001	TK	VESSEL		
P-001	P	HORIZONTA...		
P-002	P	HORIZONTA...		
E-001	E	TEMA TYPE...		

5. Click **Nozzles** in the **Class** tree to view the
    nozzle data

The nozzle data appear in the Data table.

6. To filter the data, right-click on the **4"** size in the
    Size column and select **Filter By Selection**.

Tag	Size	Spec	Description	Mar
N-1	6"	CS300	FLANGED N...	
N-2	4"	CS300	FLANGED N...	
N-3	8			
N-1	4"			
N-4	4"			

The nozzle data is filtered, and the Data table
displays only the 4" size nozzles.

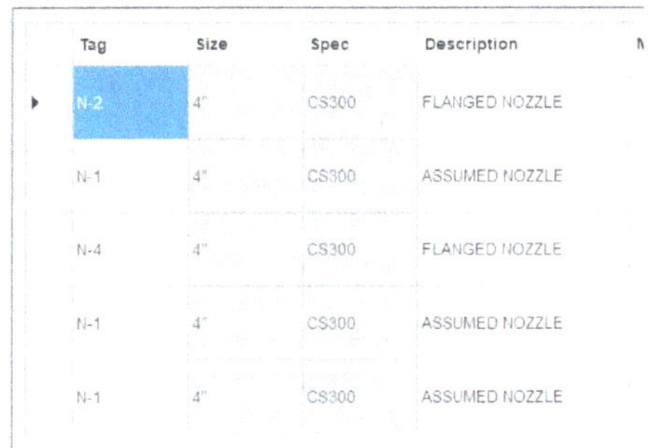

7. To remove the filter, right-click in the **Data** table and select **Remove Filter**.

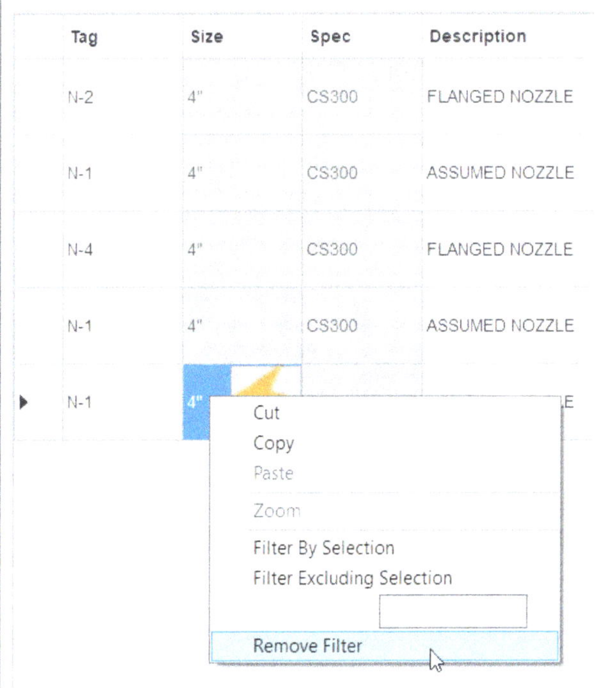

8. To filter by excluding the selection, right-click on the cell with '**?**' value and select **Filter Excluding Selection**.

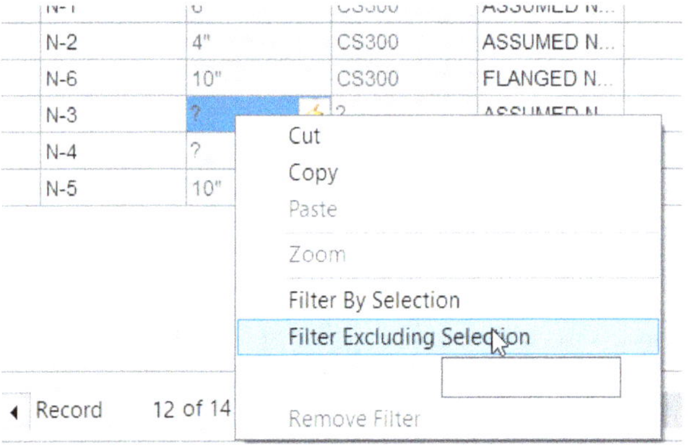

Now, you need to add some information to the Data table.

9. Add the manufacturer information in the **Manufacturer** column.

10. Hide the empty columns by clicking the **Hide Blank Columns** button on the **Data Manager** toolbar.

Exporting the Data

1. Export the data by clicking the **Export** button on the **Data Manager** toolbar.

The **Export Data** dialog appears.

2. Click the **Active node only** option under **Include child nodes**.

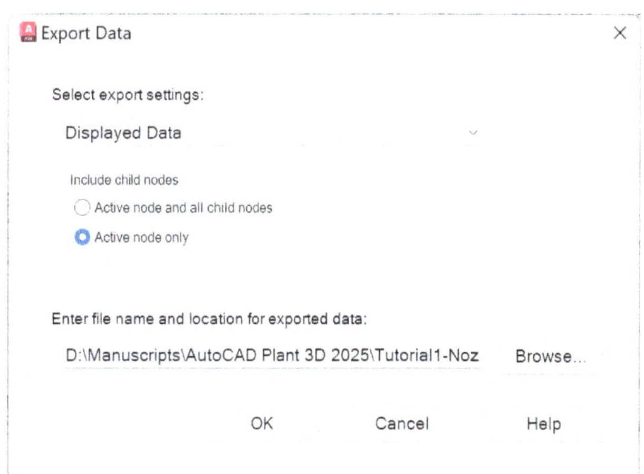

3. Click the **Browse** button and specify the location of the export file.
4. In the **Export To** dialog, specify the file type using the **File of type** drop-down.

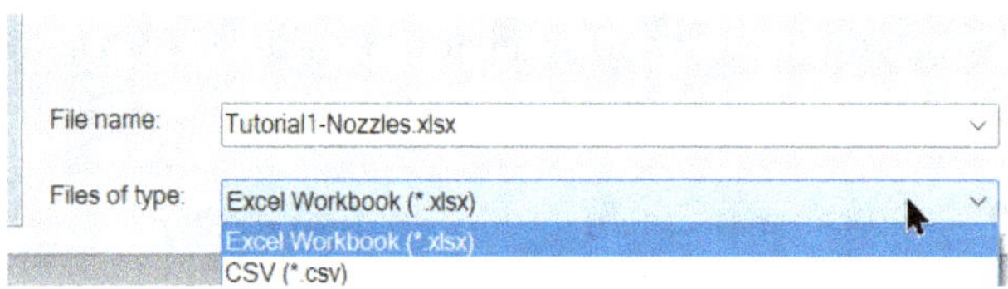

5. Click the **Save** button
6. Click **OK** to export the data.
7. Browse to the location of the exported file and open it.

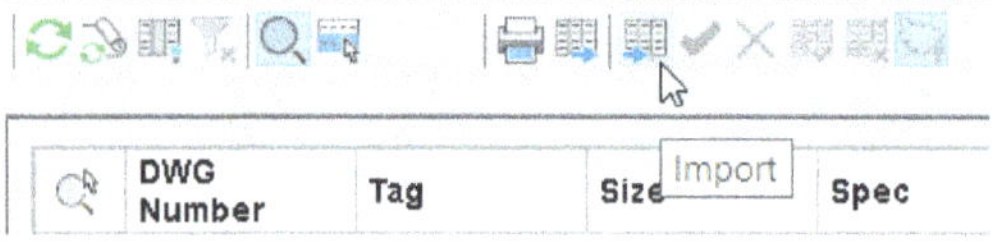

8. Enter the **Manufacturer** information.

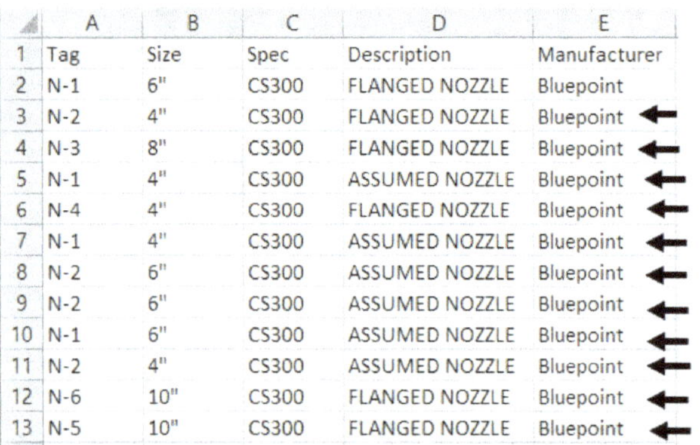

	A	B	C	D	E
1	Tag	Size	Spec	Description	Manufacturer
2	N-1	6"	CS300	FLANGED NOZZLE	Bluepoint
3	N-2	4"	CS300	FLANGED NOZZLE	Bluepoint
4	N-3	8"	CS300	FLANGED NOZZLE	Bluepoint
5	N-1	4"	CS300	ASSUMED NOZZLE	Bluepoint
6	N-4	4"	CS300	FLANGED NOZZLE	Bluepoint
7	N-1	4"	CS300	ASSUMED NOZZLE	Bluepoint
8	N-2	6"	CS300	ASSUMED NOZZLE	Bluepoint
9	N-2	6"	CS300	ASSUMED NOZZLE	Bluepoint
10	N-1	6"	CS300	ASSUMED NOZZLE	Bluepoint
11	N-2	4"	CS300	ASSUMED NOZZLE	Bluepoint
12	N-6	10"	CS300	FLANGED NOZZLE	Bluepoint
13	N-5	10"	CS300	FLANGED NOZZLE	Bluepoint

9. Save the spreadsheet.

Now, you need to import the spreadsheet.

10. Click the **Import** button on the **Data Manager** toolbar.

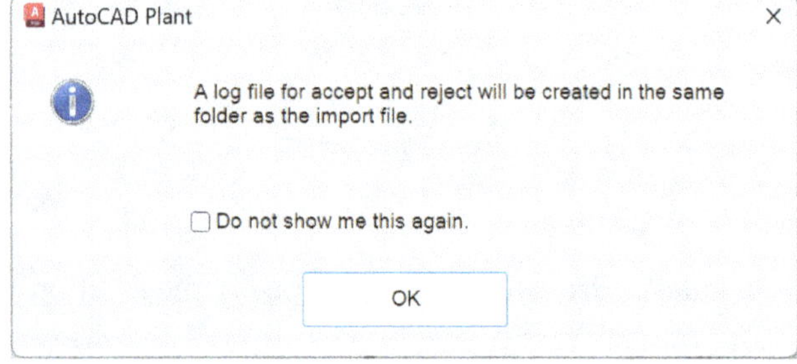

The **AutoCAD Plant** message box appears.

A log file for accept and reject will be created in the same folder as the import file.

☐ Do not show me this again.

OK

11. Click **OK**.

12. In the **Import From** dialog, browse to the location of the spreadsheet and double-click to open the file. The **Import Data** dialog appears.

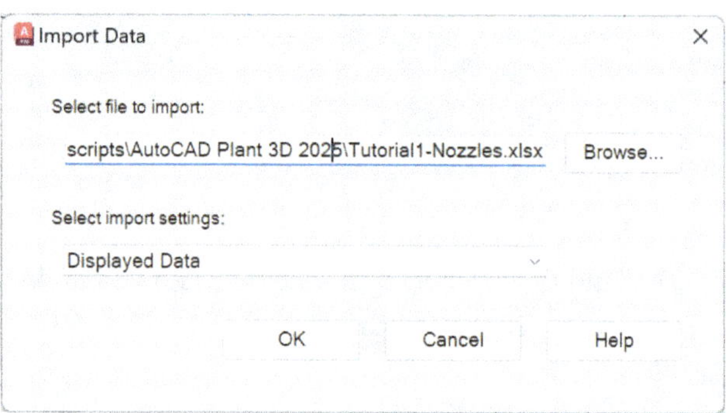

13. Click **OK** to import the data.

You notice that all the edited cells are highlighted in yellow color.

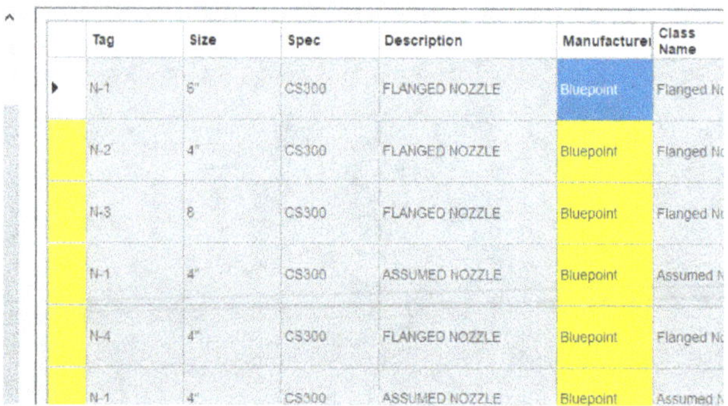

14. Click in the row of N-3 nozzle; the drawing is zoomed to the related nozzle.

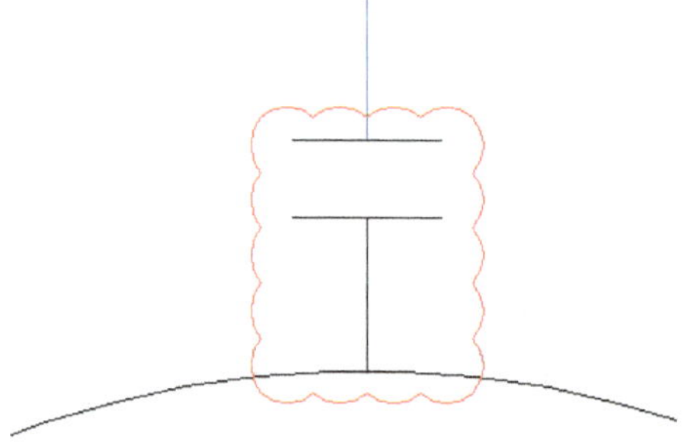

	Tag	Size	Spec
▶	N-1	6"	CS300
	N-2	4"	CS300
	N-3	8"	CS300
	N-1	4"	CS300
	N-4	4"	CS300

You notice that a revision cloud appears on the nozzle. Also, revision clouds appear on other modified nozzles.

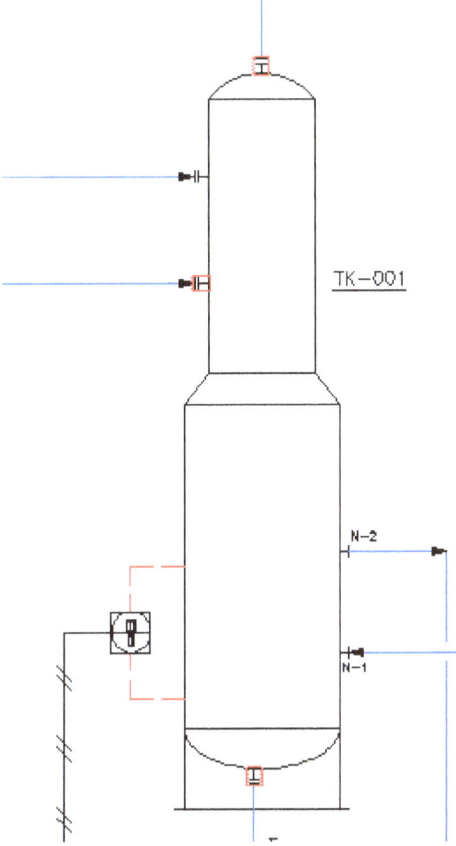

15. Click the **Accept** button on the **Data Manager** toolbar to accept the edited value; the revision cloud around the N-3 nozzle disappears.

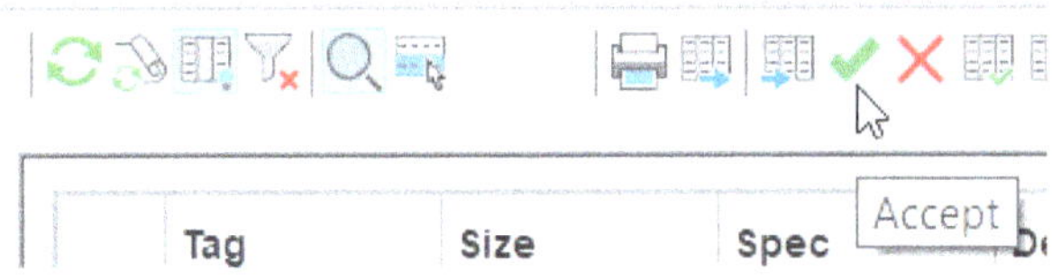

16. Click the **Accept All** button to accept all the edited values.

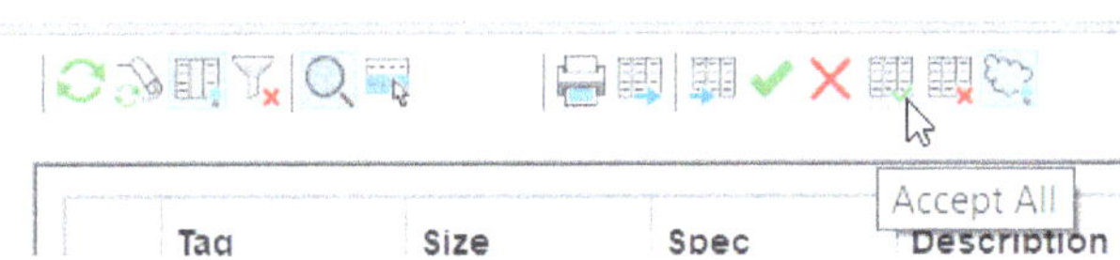

Assigning Tags using the Data Manager

You can use the Data Manager to assign tags to the P&ID components.

1. Make sure that the Tutorial 1 file is open.

2. On the Data Manager, click the **Engineering Items > Nozzles > Assumed Nozzle**. You notice that many nozzles have the same tag information. Now, you need to assign a unique tag to each nozzle.

3. Click **Engineering Items > Nozzles > Flanged Nozzle**. You notice that tag information for nozzle N-1 to N-6 is already defined.

4. Click **Nozzles > Assumed Nozzle**.

5. Double-click in the N-1 cell in the **Tag** column.

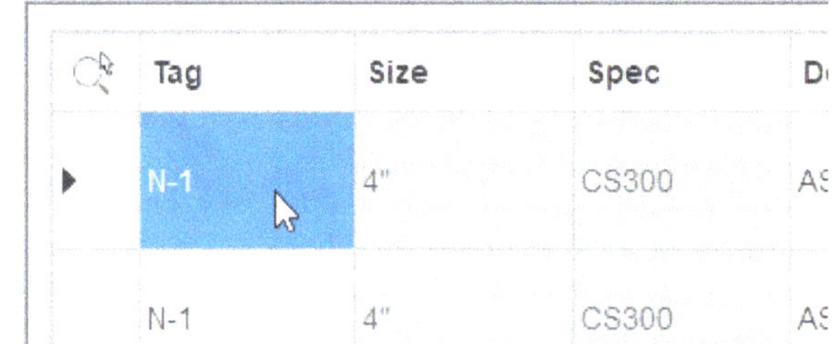

6. On the **Assign Tag** dialog, check the Parent Equipment. It shows P-001, which is the centrifugal pump.

7. Type-in **7** in the **Number** box and click **Assign**.

8. Place the tag next to the nozzle.

9. Likewise, assign tags to other nozzles, as shown.

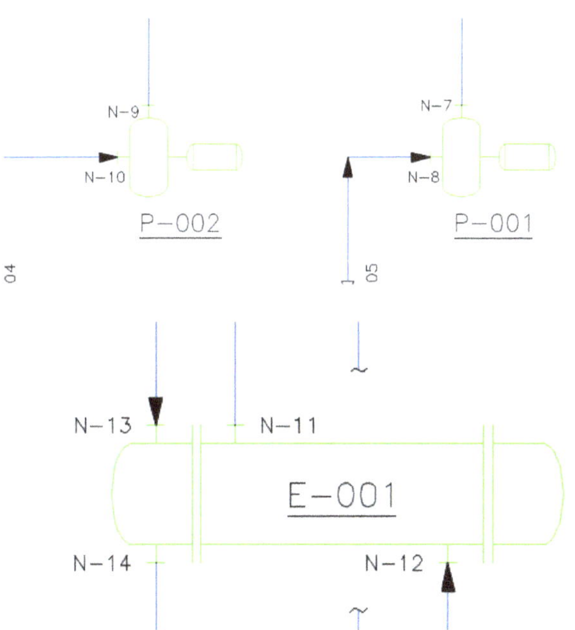

10. Save and close all the files.

Tutorial 2 (Creating Project Reports)

In this tutorial, you will learn to create project reports using the Data Manager.

1. Open the Tutorial 1 file.
2. On the ribbon, click **Home > Project > Data Manager**.
3. On the Data Manager, click **Select Data Manager Mode** drop-down > **Project Reports**.

The **Project Reports** tree displays the default project reports available in the Data Manager, such as Control Valve List, Equipment List, and so on.

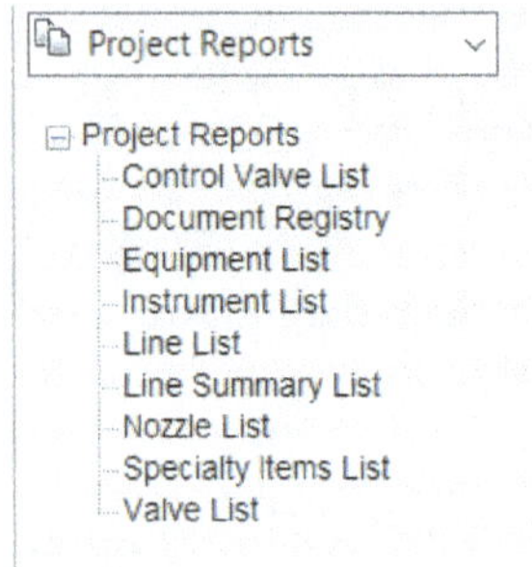

1. Click the **Equipment List** in the **Project Reports** tree.

Notice that there are many blank columns in the Equipment List Report.

2. Click the **Hide Blank Columns** icon to hide the blank columns.

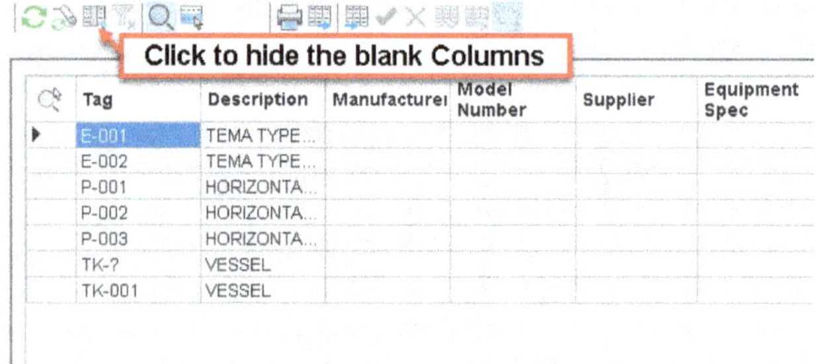

3. Click **Export** on the **Data Manager** toolbar.

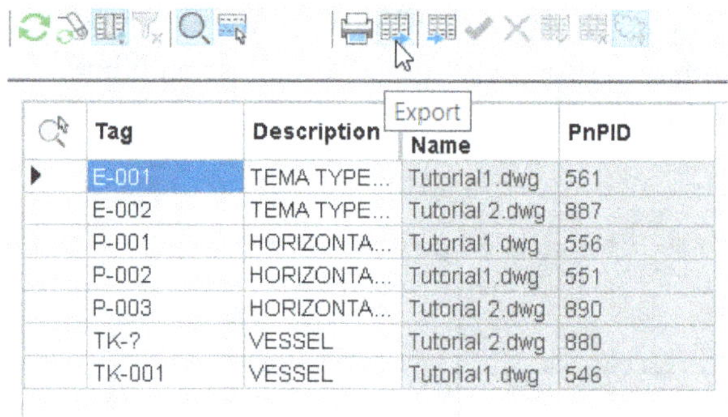

4. Browse to a location on your computer and click **Save**.
5. Open the exported file and notice that the hidden columns are also displayed in the exported file.

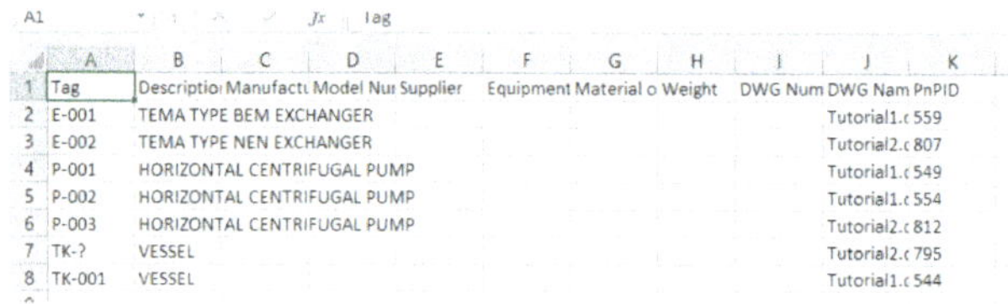

6. Close the exported file.

Modifying the Project Reports

You can modify the project reports by adding or removing columns from them.

1. On the ribbon, click **Home > Project > Project** drop-down > **Project Setup**.

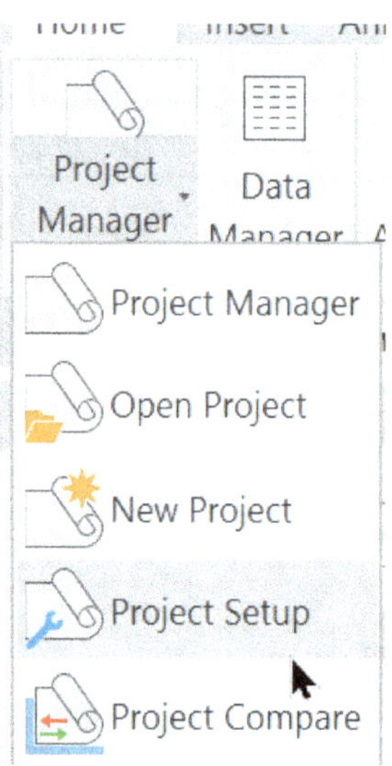

2. On the **Project Setup** dialog, click **General Settings > Reports**.

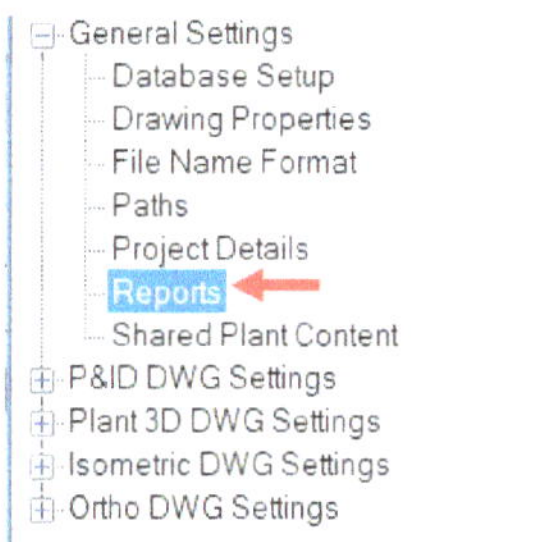

3. On the **Project Reports** page, select **Equipment List** from the **Defined Reports** section.
4. Click the **Modify** button.
5. On the **Modify Reports –Equipment List** dialog, expand the **P&ID Object Properties** node, and then expand the **Equipment** node under it.
6. Under the **Equipment** node, uncheck the properties, as shown.

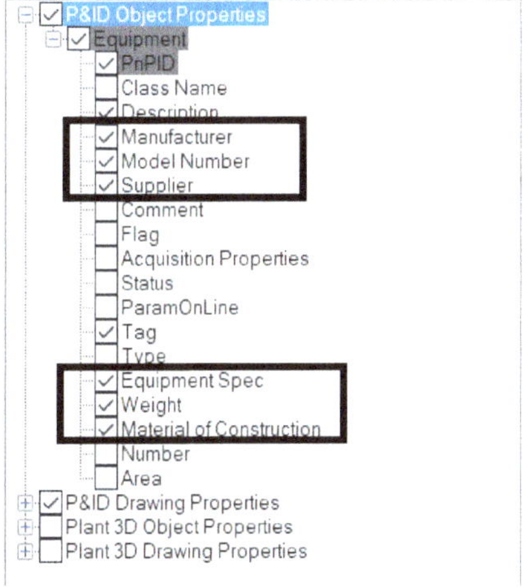

7. Expand the **P&ID Drawing Properties** node, and then uncheck the **DWG Number** property.

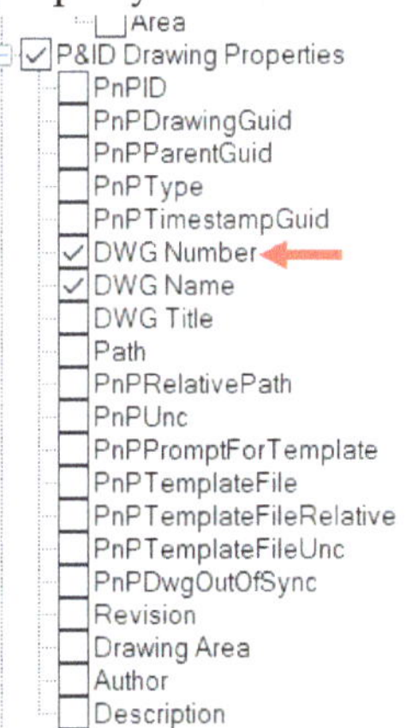

The **Property Order** section displays the properties that will be shown in the Equipment List report. You can also add properties to the report by simply checking them in the **Select properties to include** tree.

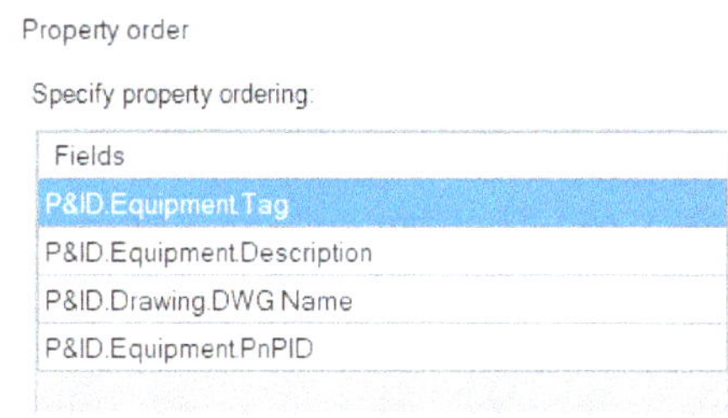

You can reorder the property using the **Up** ▲ and **Down** ▼ arrow button located in the **Property** order section.

8. Click **OK** on the **Modify Report** dialog; the report preview is displayed on the **Project Setup** dialog.

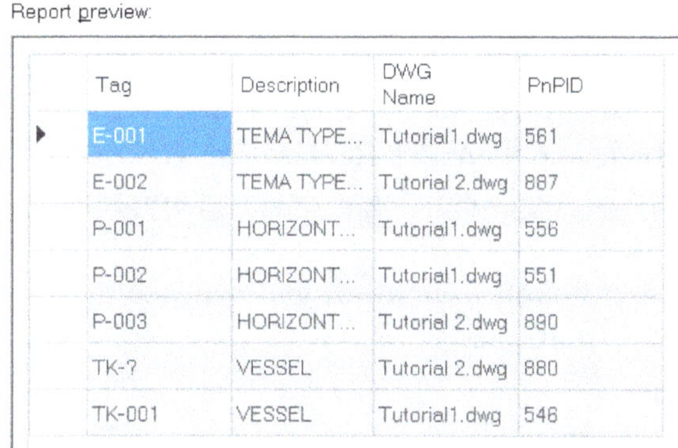

9. Click **Apply** and **OK** on the **Project Setup** dialog.
10. Export the **Equipment List** report and notice that only selected properties are displayed in it.

	A	B	C	D
1	Tag	Description	DWG Name	PnPID
2	E-001	TEMA TYPE BEM EXCHANGER	Tutorial1.dwg	559
3	E-002	TEMA TYPE NEN EXCHANGER	Tutorial2.dwg	807
4	P-001	HORIZONTAL CENTRIFUGAL PUMP	Tutorial1.dwg	549
5	P-002	HORIZONTAL CENTRIFUGAL PUMP	Tutorial1.dwg	554
6	P-003	HORIZONTAL CENTRIFUGAL PUMP	Tutorial2.dwg	812
7	TK-?	VESSEL	Tutorial2.dwg	795
8	TK-001	VESSEL	Tutorial1.dwg	544

Defining New Reports

In the earlier section, you have learned to modify an existing report. Now, you will learn to define a new report.

1. On the ribbon, click **Home > Project** > **Project** drop-down > **Project Setup**.
2. On the **Project Setup** dialog, click **General Settings > Reports**.
3. On the **Project Reports** page, select **Equipment List** from the **Defined reports** section.
4. Click the **New** button.
5. On the **New Report** dialog, type **Pump List** in the **New Report Name** box.

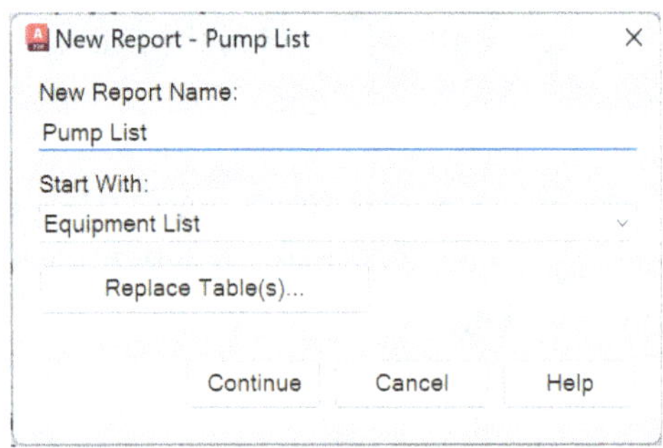

6. Select **Equipment List** from the **Start With** drop-down, and then click **Replace Table(s)**.
7. On the **Replace** dialog, check the **Equipment** option.
8. Select **Pumps** from the drop-down, and then click **Continue**.

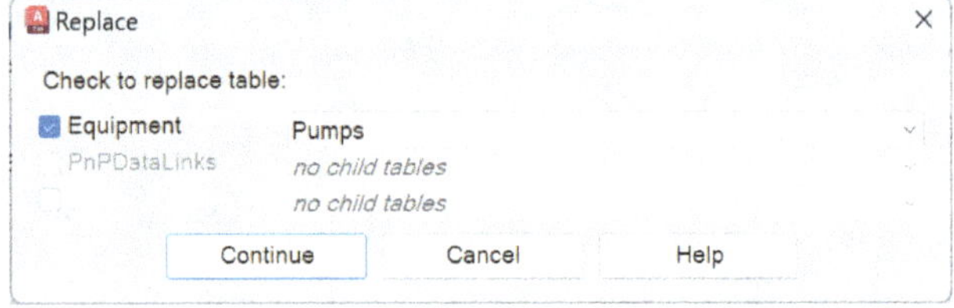

9. Click **Continue** on the **New Report** dialog.
10. On the **New Report** dialog, add or remove properties, if required.
11. Click **OK**.
12. Click **Apply** and **OK** on the **Project Setup** dialog ⊞ .
13. On the ribbon, click **Home > Project** > **Data Manager**.

14. On the **Data Manager**, select the **Pump List** option from the **Project Reports** tree; all the pumps in the project are displayed.

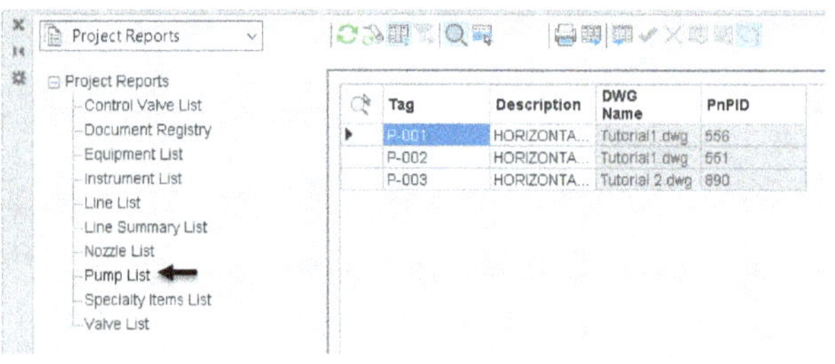

Data Manager Configuration

The Data Manager shows displays the data in a default format. Most of the time, it shows unwanted data. You can filter them using the options available on the Data Manager. However, it is very tedious to filter the data frequently. AutoCAD Plant 3D offers you customize the data manager so that you are not required to filter the data, frequently.

1. On the ribbon, click **Home > Project** > **Project** drop-down > **Project Setup**.
2. On the **Project Setup** dialog, select **P&ID DWG Settings > Data Manager Configuration**.

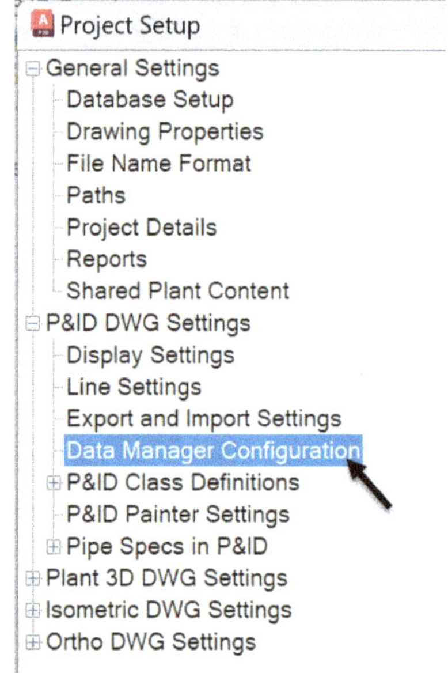

3. Click the **Create View** button.
4. Type **Line List** in the **Name** box.
5. Select **Scope > Project Data**.
6. Click the **New Level** button.

7. On the **Select Class Property** dialog, select
    **Engineering Items > Lines > Pipe Line
    Segments**.
8. Select **Description** from the **Properties** section.

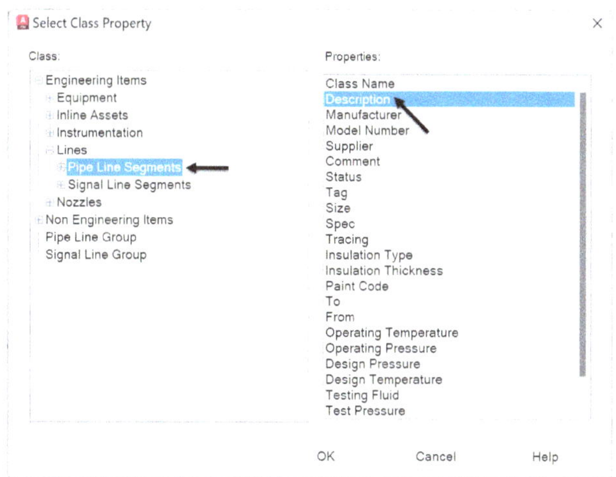

9. Click **OK**.
10. Likewise, define three more levels, as shown.

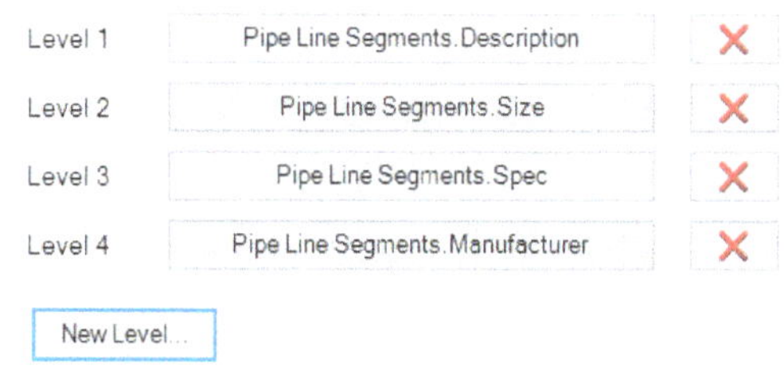

11. Click **Apply** and **OK** on the **Project Setup** dialog.
15. On the ribbon, click **Home > Project > Data
    Manager**.
12. On the Data Manager, click **Select Data Manager
    Mode drop-down > Project Custom Views**.

The Data Manager displays the Line list view. You
can filter the data by selecting the different nodes
under the **Line List** tree.

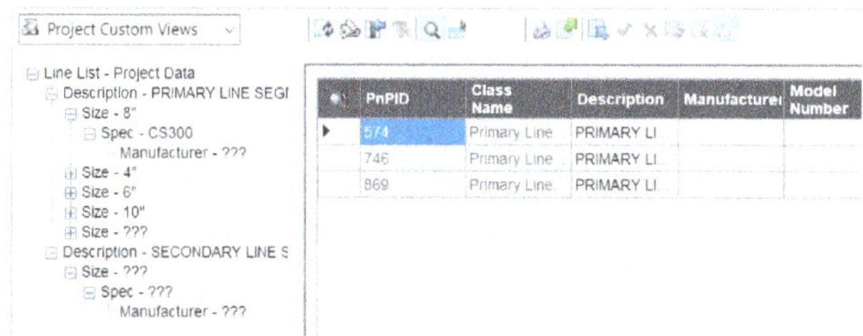

Chapter 3: Creating Reports

In this chapter, you will learn to create reports using the Report Creator.

Tutorial 1 (Generate Reports)

Earlier, you have learned to export data using the Data Manager. However, to generate data in a format that meets the client standards, you need to use the **Report Creator for AutoCAD Plant 3D 2025** application that comes with AutoCAD Plant 3D. In this tutorial, you generate reports using the Report Creator.

1. Type 'report' in the search bar located on the left side of the taskbar, if you are working in Windows 10 or more.
2. Select **Report Creator for AutoCAD Plant 2025 – English** from the search results.

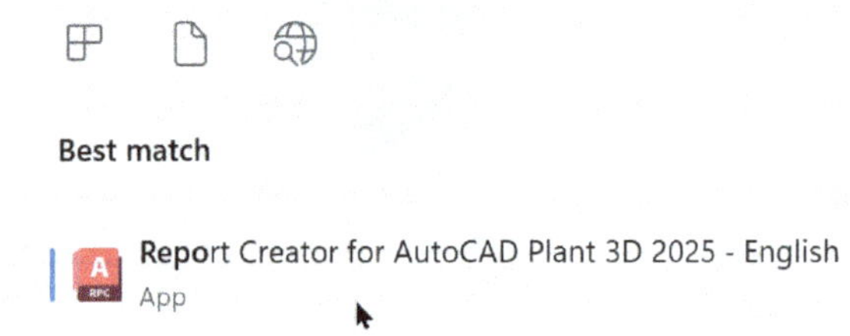

Best match

Report Creator for AutoCAD Plant 3D 2025 - English
App

The **Settings** dialog appears.

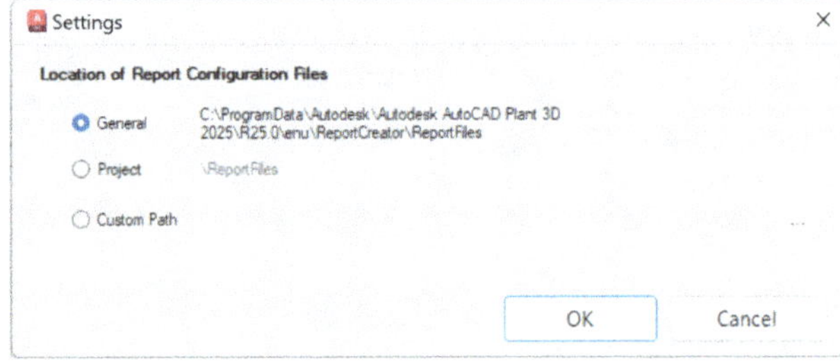

In this dialog, you can define the location of the report configuration files. The report configuration files define the type of report that you want to create. In simple words, a report configuration file is a query. There are many predefined queries such as line list, valve list, drawing list, equipment list, and so on. In addition to that, you can create your query. By default, these report configuration files (queries) are located inside the **Program Data** folder on your C drive.

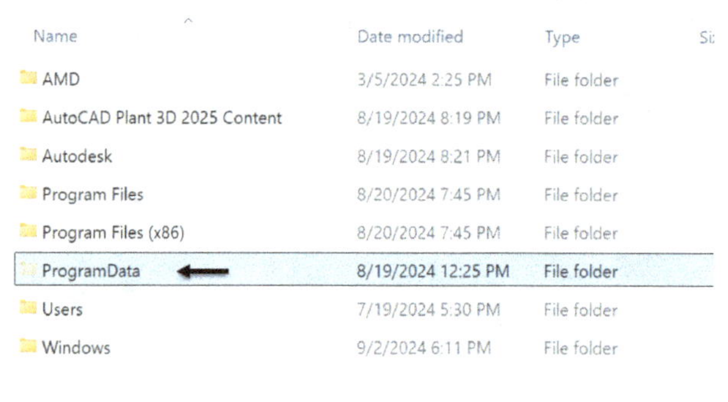

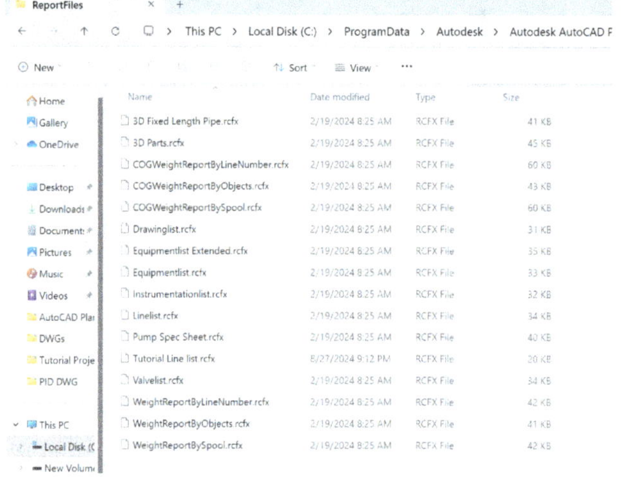

The **General** option allows you to create reports using the report configuration files located inside the **Program Data** folder.

The **Project** option is used to create reports using the report configuration files available in the **ReportFiles** folder under the current project directory. By default, there are no report files in this folder. You need to copy and paste the default report configuration files or save new ones in this folder.

The **Custom Path** option allows you to access the report configuration files saved at a location other than the **Program Data** folder and project directory. For example, you have created a custom report configuration file specific to a project. Now, you have to place this file on a network location so that all the team members can use it. The team members should use the **Custom Path** option to access the file and create reports.

3. Select the **General** option from the **Settings** dialog and click **OK**.
4. Click the **Open** option on the **Project** drop-down in the **Autodesk AutoCAD Plant Report Creator**.

5. Browse to location ….**TUTORIAL PROJECT\Project.xml**.
6. Click the **Open** button to set the project for generating the reports.
7. Select **Linelist** from the **Report Configuration** drop-down.

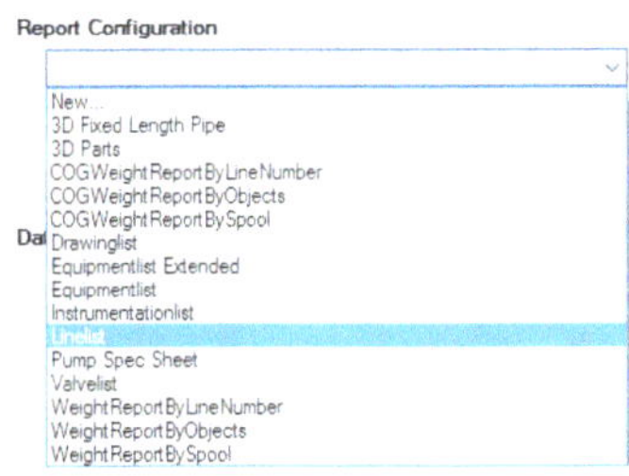

Next, you need to select an option from the **Data Source** section: **Project Data** or **Drawing Data**. The **Project Data** option, if selected, will show the data of the entire project. For example, if you select **Linelist** from the **Report Configuration**, the **Project Data** option generates the linelist data of the entire project.

The **Drawing Data** option generates the data of the selected drawing only.

8. Select the **Project Data** option as the **Data Source**.
9. Click the **Preview** button; the **Preview** window appears.

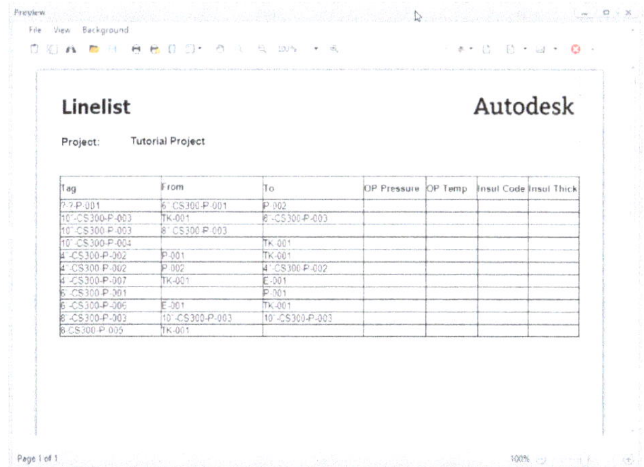

Using the options in this window, you can modify the display of the report by changing the background color, page setup, and so on. You can also specify the export format of the report.

You can also save the changes as a template. Click **Export Document > PDF File** on the Toolbar; the **PDF Export Options** dialog appears. Click the **OK** button; the **Save As** dialog appears. Specify the location of the template file.

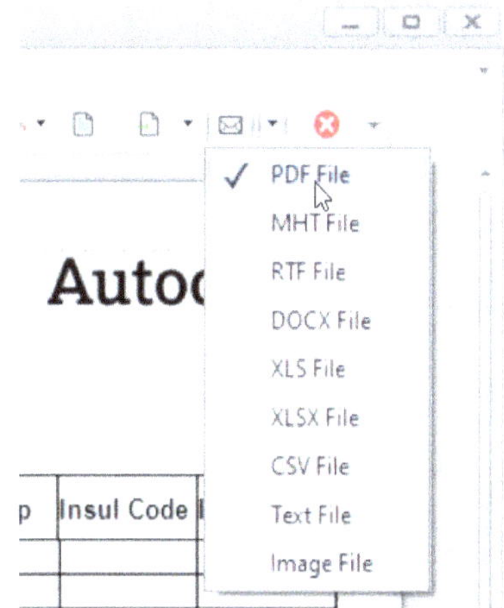

10. Close the **Preview** window.
11. Click **Print/Export**; the **PDF Export Options** dialog appears.

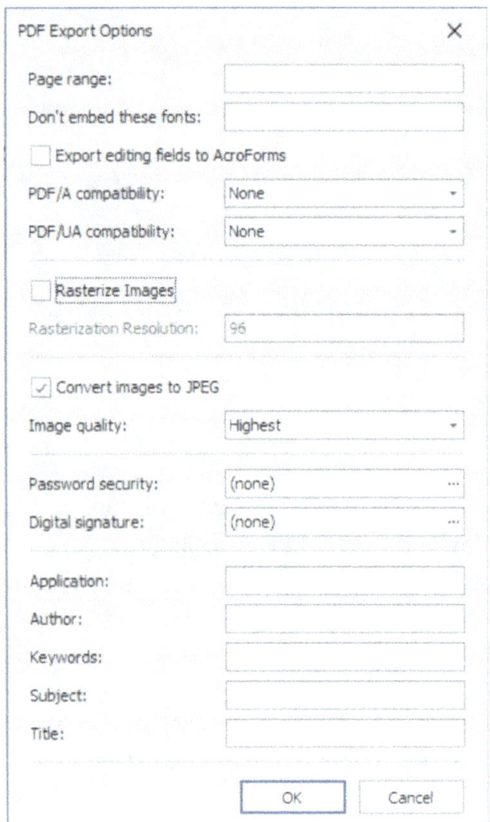

12. Click the **OK** button; the **Export Results** dialog appears.

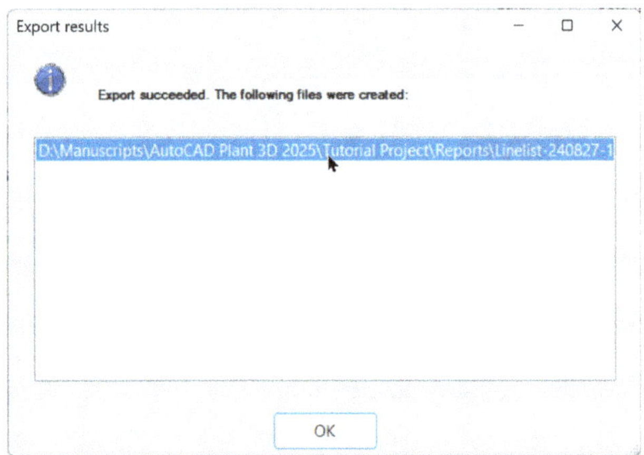

13. Double-click on the listed PDF file in the **Export results** dialog; the PDF file is opened.
14. View the report in a PDF file.

Linelist

Project: TUTORIAL PROJECT

Tag	From	To	OP Pressure	OP Temp	Insul Code	Insul Thick
?-?-?-?		E-001				
?-?-?-?	E-001					
?-?-?-?		E-001				
?-?-?-?	E-001					
?-?-?-?		TK-001				
?-?-P-001	10"-CS300-P-001	P-002				
?-?-P-009	8"-CS300-P-009	8"-CS300-P-009				
?-?-P-010	10"-CS300-P-010	10"-CS300-P-010				
10"-CS300-P-001		P-001				
10"-CS300-P-003	8"-CS300-P-003					
10"-CS300-P-003	TK-001	8"-CS300-P-003				
10"-CS300-P-010	8"-CS300-P-010					
10"-CS300-P-010	TK-002	8"-CS300-P-010				
6"-CS300-P-007	TK-002					
6"-CS300-P-009	8"-CS300-P-009	8"-CS300-P-009				
8"-CS300-P-002	P-002	8"-CS300-P-002				
8"-CS300-P-002	P-001	TK-001				
8"-CS300-P-003	10"-CS300-P-003	10"-CS300-P-003				
8"-CS300-P-005		E-002				
8"-CS300-P-005	TK-001					
8"-CS300-P-006	E-002	TK-002				
8"-CS300-P-008	TK-002	P-003				
8"-CS300-P-009	6"-CS300-P-009					
8"-CS300-P-009	P-003	8"-CS300-P-009				

11. Close the report file.

Tutorial 2 (Creating a New Report Configuration File)

In the last tutorial, you have created a report using the default report configuration file. In this tutorial, you will create a new report configuration file, and then generate a report using it.

1. Start **Report Creator for AutoCAD Plant 2025 – English**.
2. Click **Project** drop-down > **Open**.
3. Browse to location ….**TUTORIAL PROJECT\Project.xml**.
4. Click the **Open** button to set the project for generating the reports.
5. Select **New** from the **Report Configuration** drop-down.
6. On the **New Report Configuration** dialog, select **From existing report** and then select **Linelist** from the drop-down.
7. Click **OK**.
8. Type **Tutorial Line list** in the **Report Configuration** box.
9. Click the **Edit query** button; the **Query Configuration** dialog appears.

In this dialog, there are three query types: **P&ID Classes**, **Drawings**, and **Plant 3D Classes**.

10. Select the **P&ID Classes** option. This option allows you to query from the P&ID Classes database.

Notice that the **Included Classes** section displays the **Pipe Line Segment** in it. You can add more classes to the **Included Classes** list by selecting them from the **Available Classes** tree and clicking the Add (**>**) button. In addition to that, you can filter the data using the fields available in the section below the **Included Classes** section.

The **Report Creator** provides you with various examples of how to filter the data. Click the **Show Filter Examples** button located at the bottom left corner to view the examples.

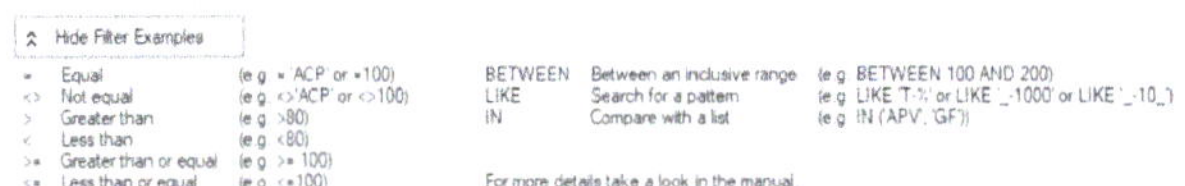

11. Click in the **Filter** box of the **Size** field and type = '**6"**'.

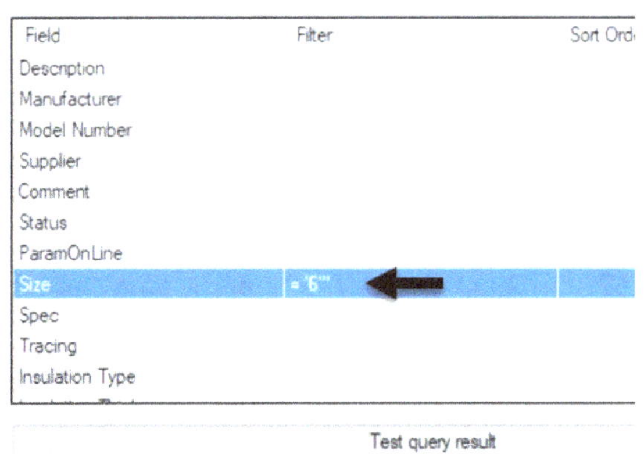

12. Click the **Test query result** button.
13. On the **Query result** dialog, scroll to the PipeLines_size field and notice that only the 6" pipes are displayed in the result.
14. Click **Close** on the **Query result** dialog.
15. Click **OK** on the **Query Configuration** dialog.
16. Select **PDF File** from the **Target** drop-down.
17. Click **OK**.
18. Click **Preview** on the **Report Creator**. It shows only the 6" line list.

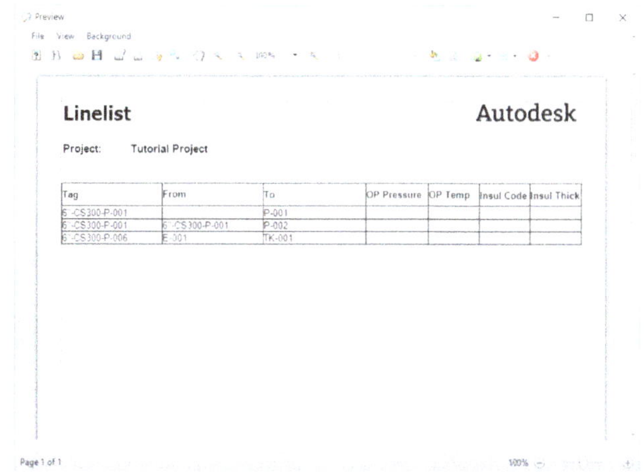

19. Click the **Print/Export** button to export the results.

Tutorial 3 (Editing the Report Layout)

In the previous tutorials, you have created reports using the default layouts available in Report Creator. However, your client may want reports to look like their company reports. You can customize the report layout by adding logos, changing font type and size, and so on.

1. Start **Report Creator for AutoCAD Plant 2025 – English**.
2. Click **Project** drop-down > **Open**.
3. Browse to location ….**TUTORIAL PROJECT\Project.xml**.
4. Select **Tutorial Line list** from the **Report Configuration** drop-down, and then click the **Edit** button.
5. On the **Report Configuration** dialog, click the **Edit report layout** button; the **Report Designer** window appears.
6. Double-click in the header and type **Tutorial Line list**.

7. On the **Properties** section located at the bottom right corner, scroll to the Font

property, and then click the three dots displayed next to it; the **Font** dialog appears.

8. On the **Font** dialog, change the **Font** to **Arial** and **Font Style** to **Bold**.
9. Click **OK**.
10. Click the drop-down next to the **Foreground Color** property, and then select **Maroon**.

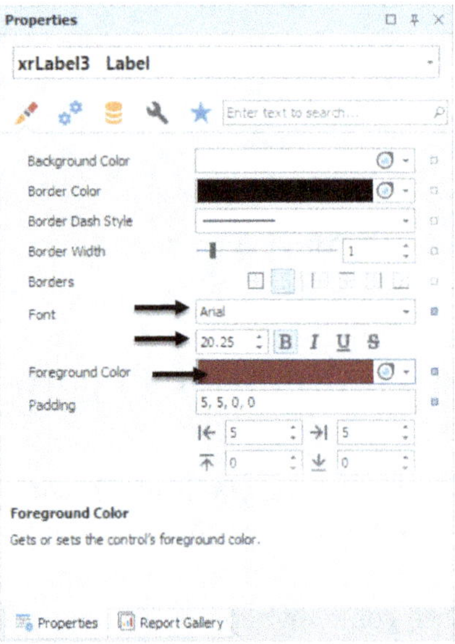

11. Likewise, change the **Foreground Color** of the text, as shown.

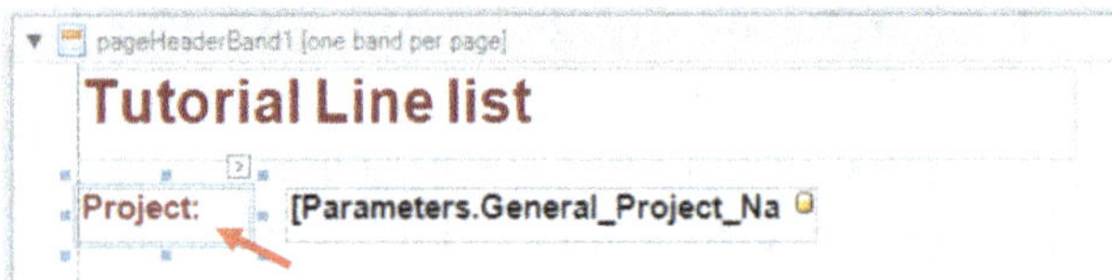

You can also change the values to be displayed in the table. For example, if you want the Paint Code to be displayed in the table instead of the Insulation Code, then you need to change the heading.

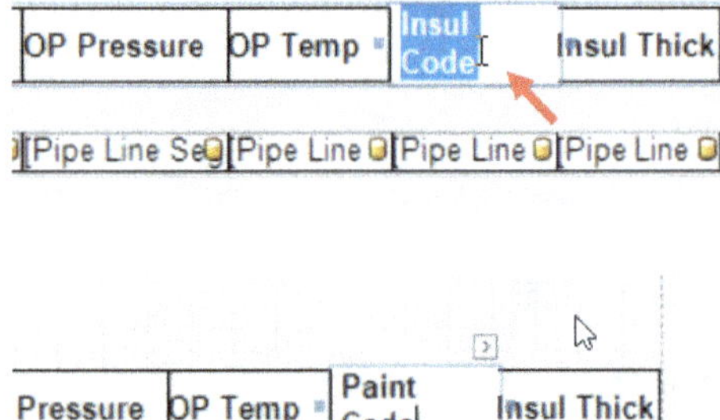

Next, click the **Field List** tab on the **Report Explorer** section; the field is displayed. Click and drag the **Pipe Line Segment _Paint Code** field, and then drop it under the **Paint Code** heading in the table.

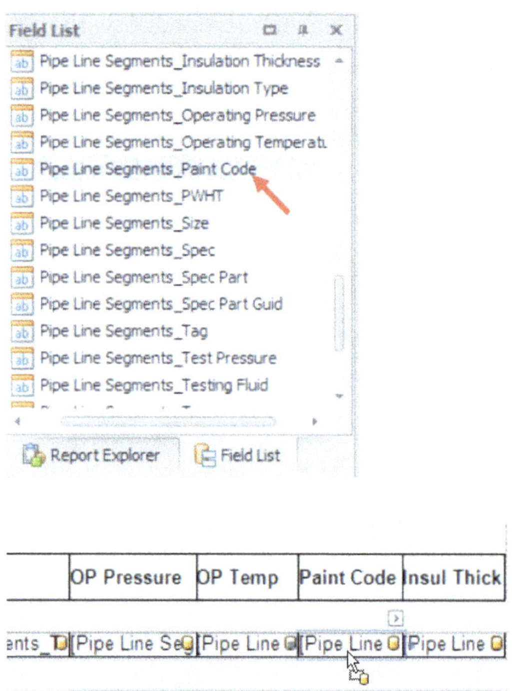

12. Click on the Autodesk logo image.
13. On the **Properties** section, click the **Behavior** tab.
14. Scroll down to the **Sizing** field, and then select **Zoom Image** from the drop-down located next to it.

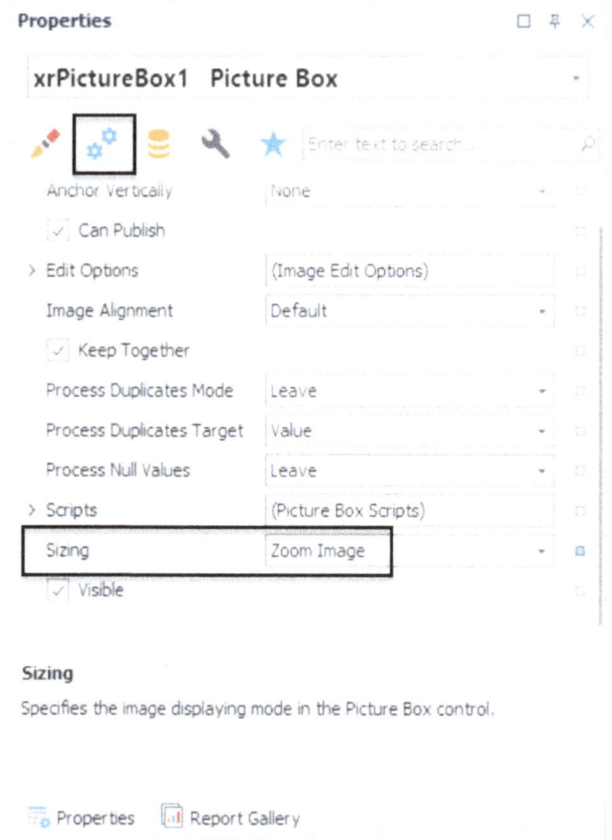

15. Click the **Appearance** tab.
16. Click in the **Size** field and type **370, 256**.

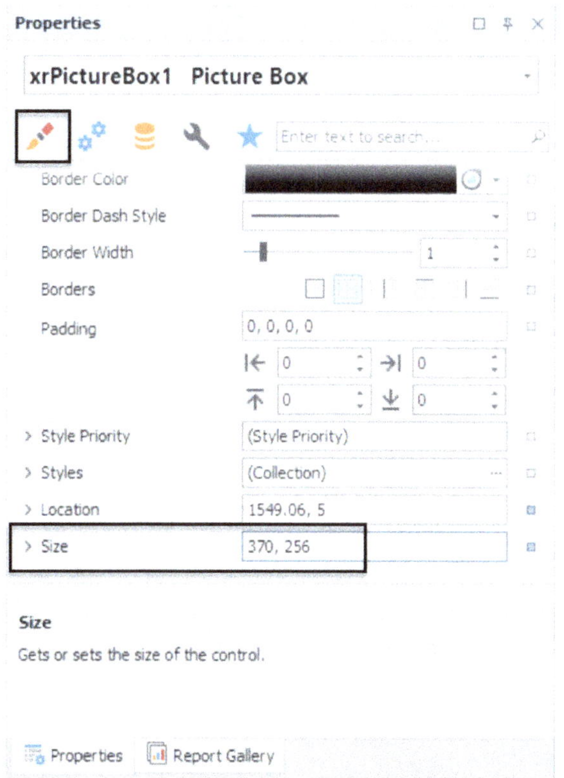

17. Click the **Data** tab.
18. Click in the **Image URL** field, and then click the three dots located next to it.

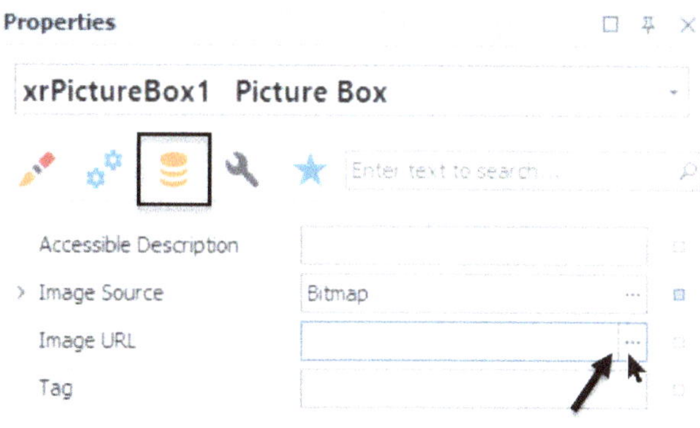

19. Browse to the location of the logo image, and then double click on it.
20. Click **Save** on the ribbon, and then close the Report Designer.
21. Click **OK** on the **Report Configuration** dialog.
22. Click **Preview** on the Report Creator and notice the changes in the layout.

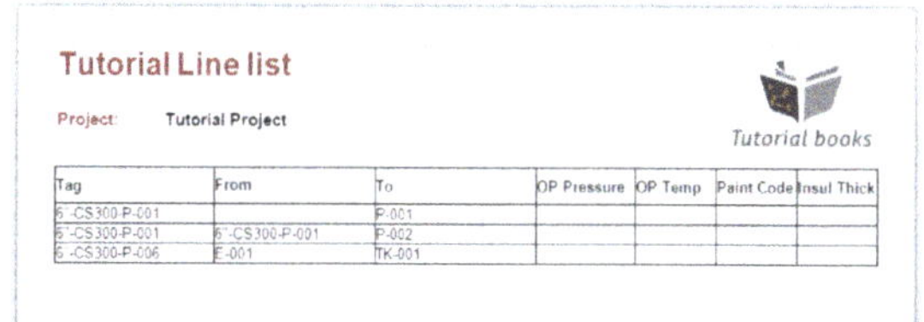

23. Close the Report Creator.

Chapter 4: Creating a Plant 3D Model

In AutoCAD Plant 3D, you can use the information from the P&ID to create the 3D model. The 3D model can be used to visualize a plant. In addition to that, you can create orthographic views, sections, elevations, and isometric drawings. These drawings are updated when you modify the 3D model.

In this book, you use the Tutorial 1 P&ID to create a 3D model. The steps to create a 3D model in plant 3D are given below:

- Create structural Model
- Create Equipment
- Create piping
- Create inline assets and pipe supports

Creating a Plant 3D Drawing

1. Activate the Tutorial Project using the **Current Project** drop-down located on the **Project Manager**.
2. Click the right mouse button on the **Plant 3D Drawings** folder and select **New Drawing**.

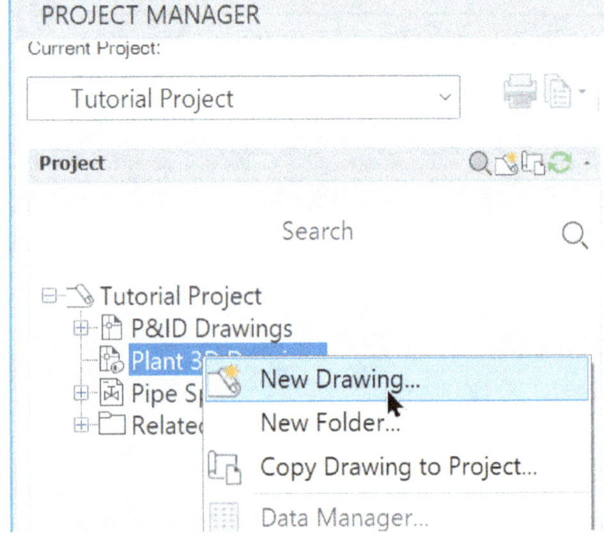

3. On the **New DWG** dialog, type-in **Master Model** in the **File name** box and click **OK**.
4. In the graphics windows, click on the **In-canvas tools** located at the top left corner and select **SW Isometric**.

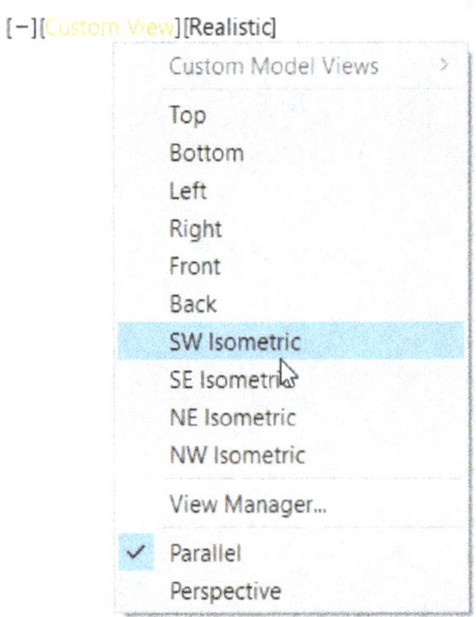

5. Change the workspace to **3D Piping**.

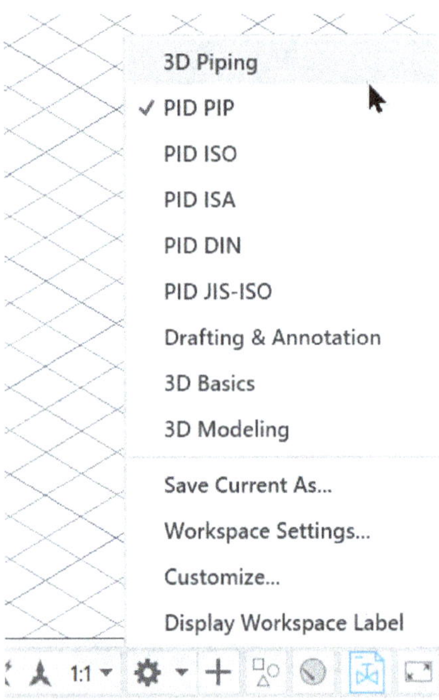

Tutorial 1 (Creating Structural Model)

AutoCAD Plant 3D provides a set of commands to create a structural model. These commands are available on the **Structure** tab of the ribbon. You can then use this structural model as a reference to design the plant model. If you want more complex structural models, you can create them in other applications such as Autodesk Revit and AutoCAD Architecture, and then import them.

Creating Layers

AutoCAD provides you with a feature called layers, which help you to arrange objects. You can learn about layers from the Help file. In this book, you will create layers and use them to arrange different objects of a plant 3D model.

1. On the ribbon, click **Structure > Layers > Layer Properties** .

2. Click the **New layer** button on the **Layer Properties Manager**. Enter **Grid** in the **Name** field.

3. Click the **Color** swatch of the grid layer; the **Select Color** dialog appears.

4. On the **Select Color** dialog, click the **Index Color** tab.

5. Select the Index color **250**, and then click **OK**.

6. Likewise, create other layers, and then assign colors to them, as shown.

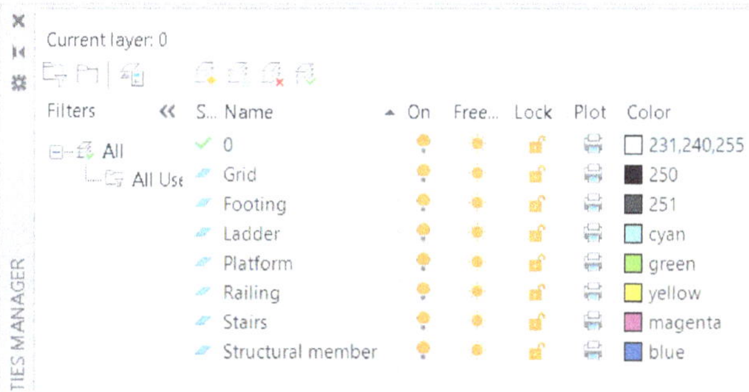

Creating the Grid

1. Change the view orientation to **SW Isometric**.

2. On the **Layer Properties Manager**, double click on the **Grid** layer to set it as current.

3. Close the **Layer Properties Manager** by clicking the **X** (Close) icon at the top left corner.

4. On the ribbon, click **Structure > Parts > Grid**.

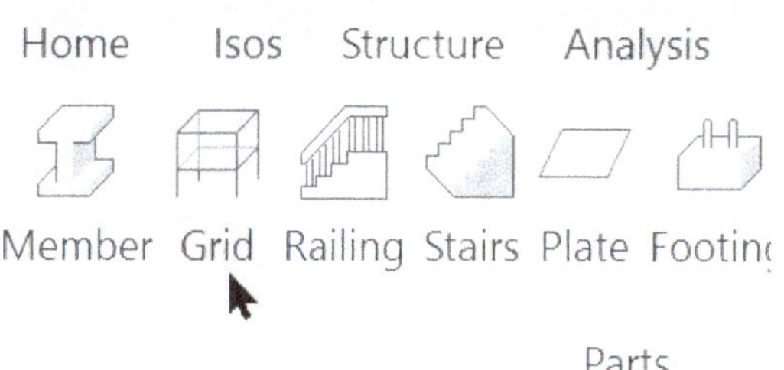

5. On the **Create Grid** dialog, type-in **Platform Grid** in the **Grid name** box. Next, you have to type-in values in the boxes available on the dialog.

6. Click the arrow button next to the **Axis name** box. You notice that the alphabets A, B, C are added. These alphabets represent the grid names along the X-axis.

7. Type-in 0, 150, 300, 450 in the **Axis value** box. The values in this box represent the grid spacing along the X-axis. You have to enter values separated by a comma.

8. Type-in 0, 150, 300 in the **Row value** box. These values define the grid spacing along the Y-axis.

9. Click the arrow next to the **Row name** box. The values in the **Row name** box represent the grid names along the Y-axis.

10. Type-in 0,24, 300 in the **Platform value** box. These values define the grid spacing along the Z-axis.

11. Click the arrow next to the **Platform name** box. The values in the **Platform name** box represent the grid names along the Z-axis.

On the dialog, you can type in a new value in the **Font size** box. The program changes the font size of the grid names.

12. Click **Create** to create a grid.
13. Type **Zoom** in the command line, and then press Enter.
14. Select **All** from the command line; the grid is fitted in the graphics window.

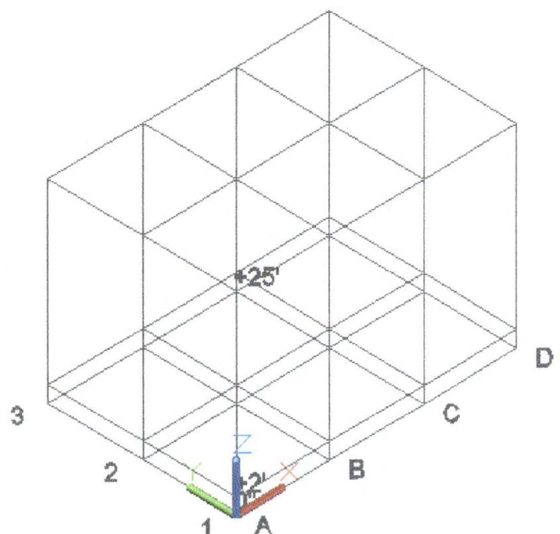

Structural Member Representation

In AutoCAD Plant 3D, you can represent structural members using four different options. You can select these options from the drop-down available on the **Parts** panel.

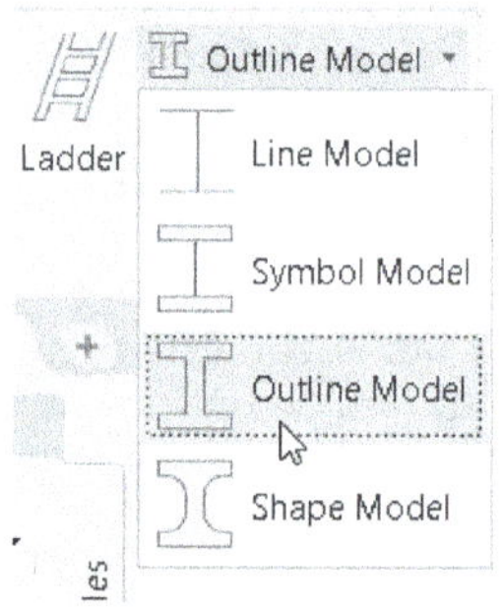

These options are explained in the following illustrations.

Line Model

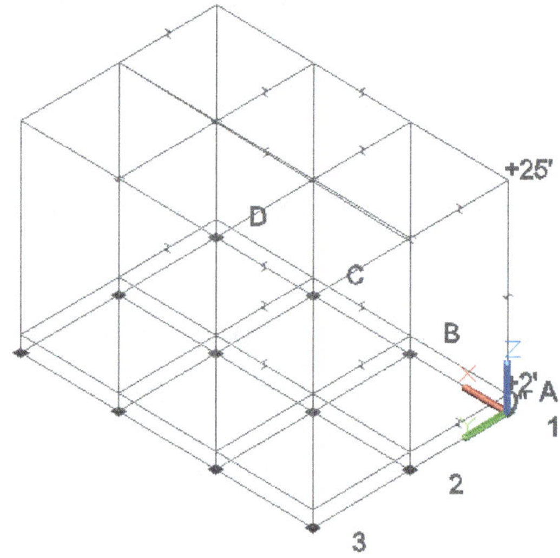

Symbol Model

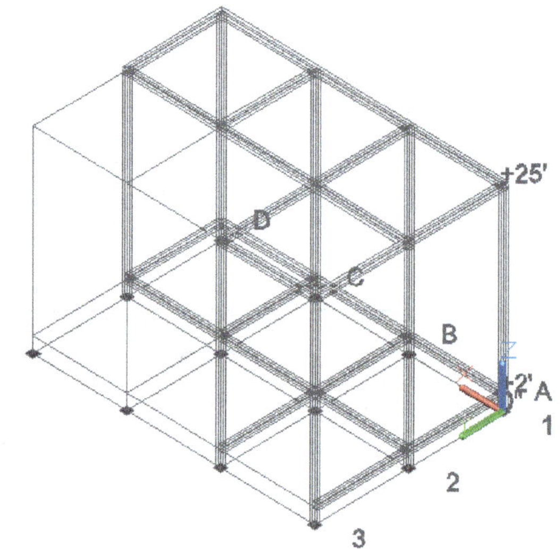

Outline Model

Shape Model

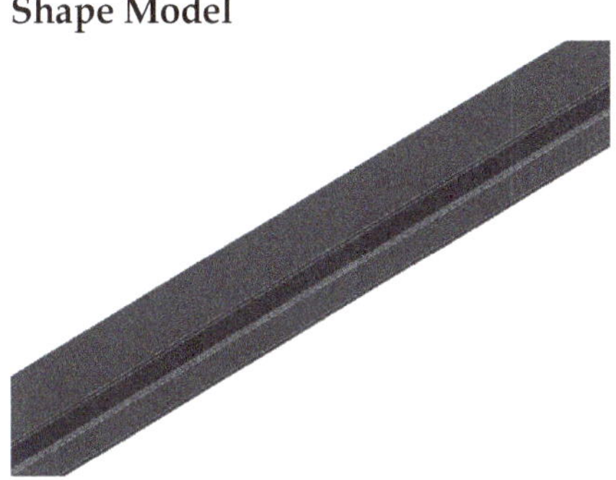

Creating Footings

1. On the ribbon, click **Structure > Parts > Structure Representation > Outline Model**.

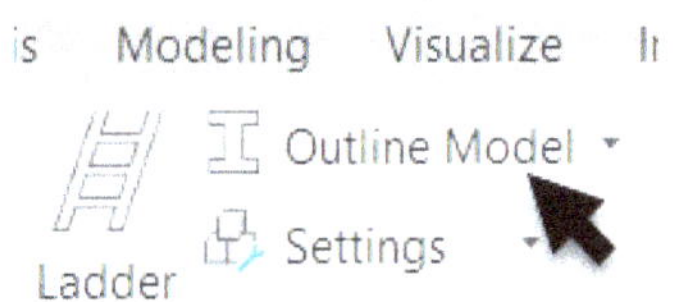

2. On the Status bar, click the down-arrow next to the **Object Snap** icon and select the **Endpoint**, **Node**, and **Intersection** options. Disable all the other options.

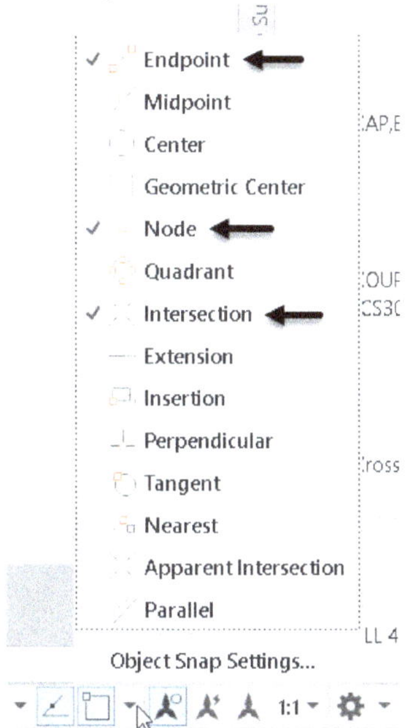

3. On the ribbon, click **Structure > Layers > Layer drop-down > Footing**.

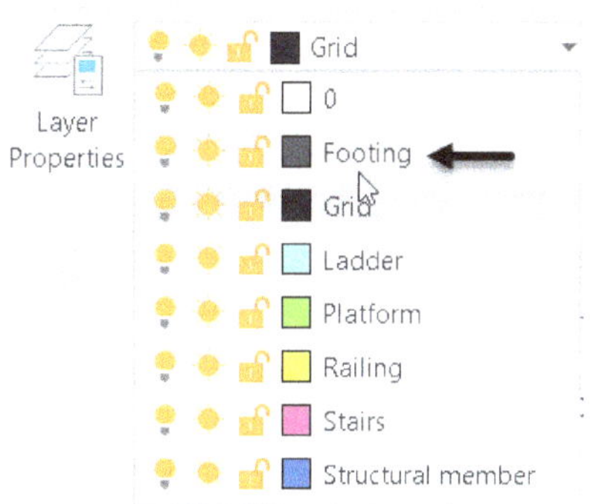

4. On the ribbon, click **Structure > Parts > Footing**.

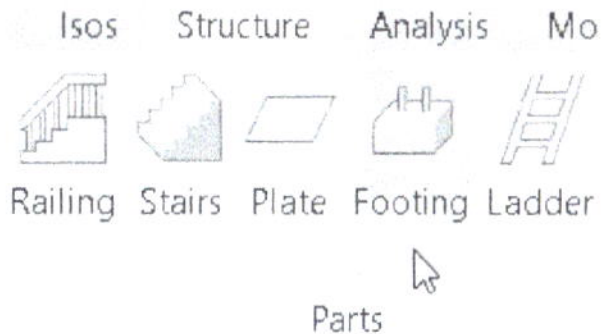

5. Click **Settings** in the command line.
6. On the **Footing Settings** dialog, set the **Standard** to **ASTM** and **Code** to **CONCRETE**.
7. Leave the default dimensions of the footing and click **OK**.

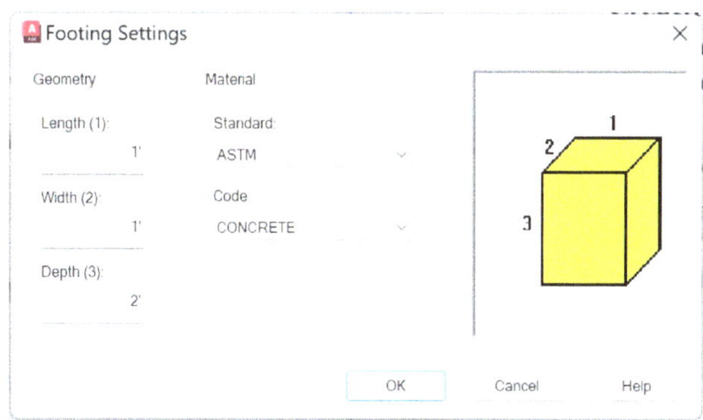

8. Click the lower intersection point of the grid in order to place the footing.

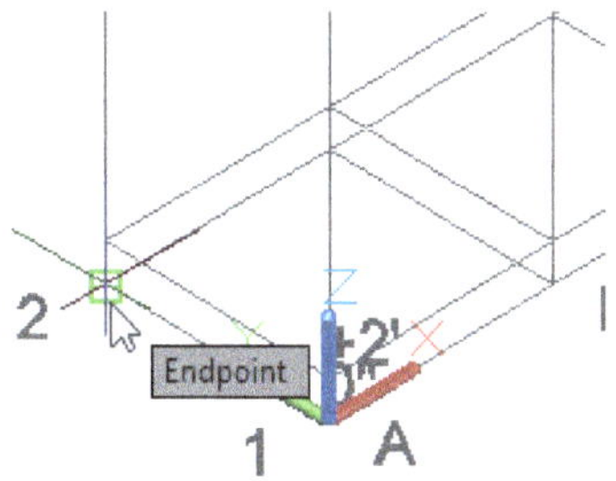

Likewise, place the other footings.

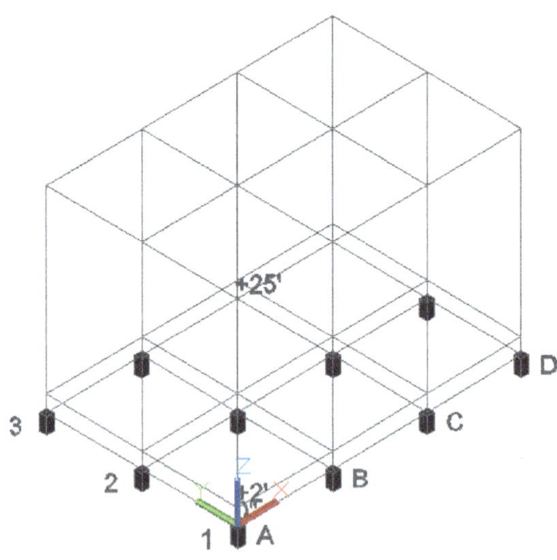

Creating Structural Members

1. On the ribbon, click **Structure > Layers > Layer drop-down > Structural Members**.

2. Activate the **Orthomode** on the Status bar. Alternatively, press **F8** to activate the orthomode.

3. Change the view orientation to **Left**.

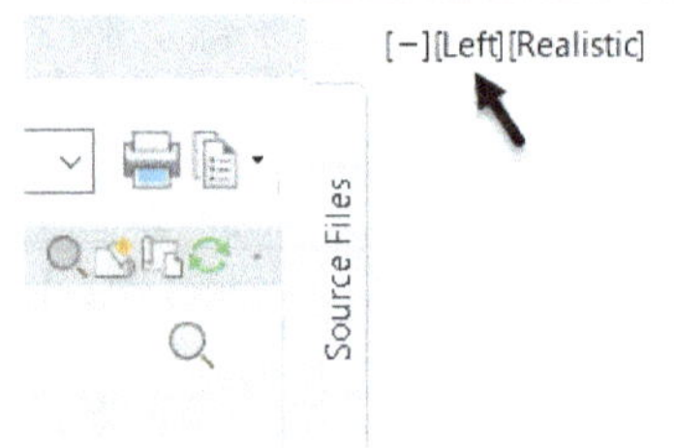

4. On the ribbon, click **Structure > Parts > Member**.

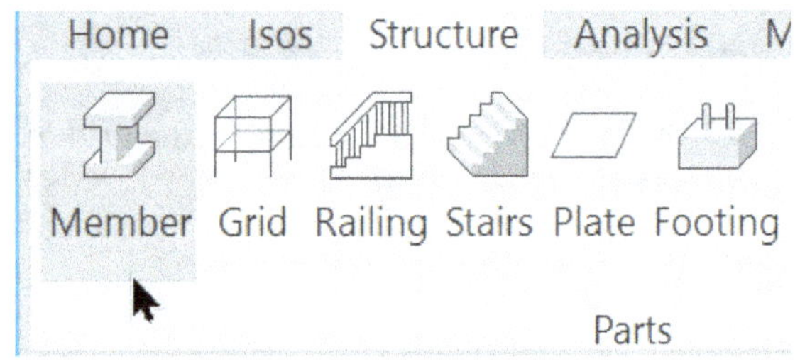

5. Click **Settings** in the command line.

On the **Member Settings** dialog, you can define the parameters of the structural member such as the shape standard, material standard, material code, and shape type and size. You can also set the orientation of the cross-section.

6. Set the **Shape type** to **W** and **Shape Size** to **W8X40**.

7. Leave the other default values and click **OK**.

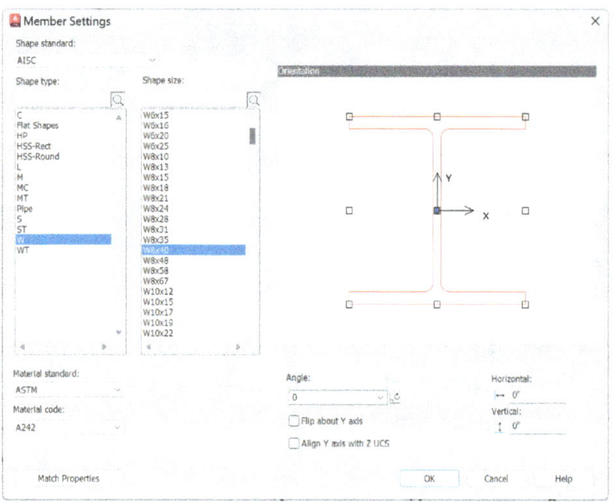

8. Click the lower right intersection point of the grid.

9. Move the pointer up and click the intersection point between the vertical and horizontal grid lines. The **Member** command creates a vertical structural member. You can select further points to create multiple members.

10. Move the pointer toward the right and click the intersection point between the horizontal and vertical grid lines. The command creates a horizontal structural member.

11. Move the pointer down and click the lower intersection point.

12. Press **Esc** to deactivate the command.

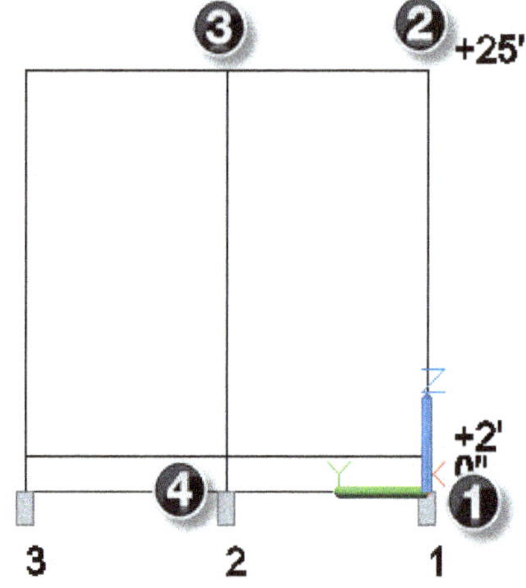

13. Change the view orientation to **SW Isometric**.

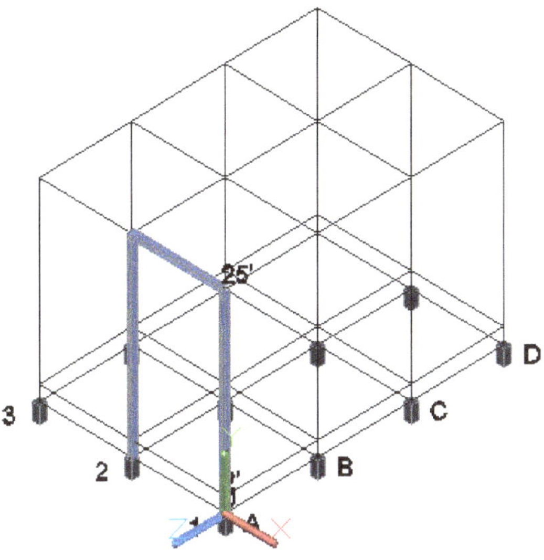

You can create other structure members or copy the existing ones.

14. Select the three structural members, and then click the right mouse button. Select **Copy Selection** from the menu.
15. Select the **+25'** grid point to define the base point of the copy.
16. Select the intersection points, as shown. The **Copy** command defines the destination points and places copies of the selected objects.
17. Press **Esc**.

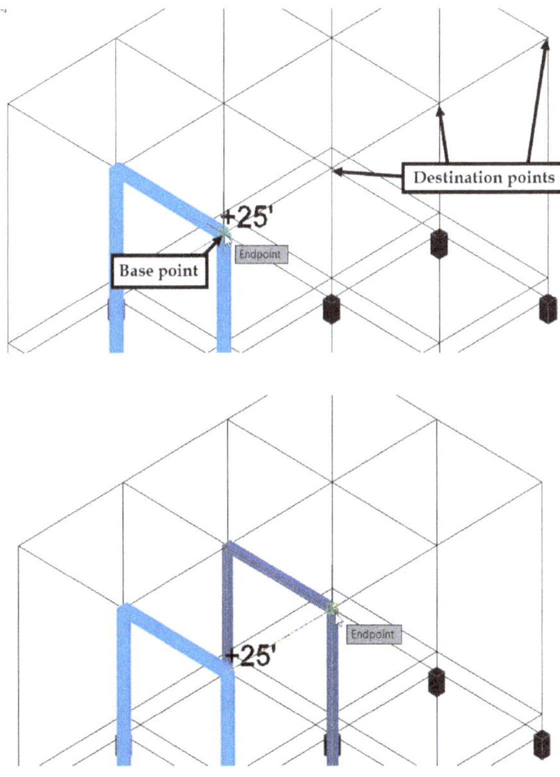

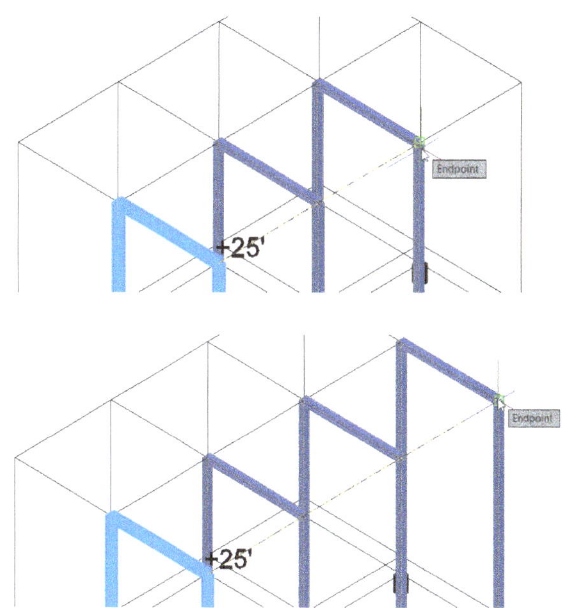

*Tip: You can make a selection easily in the **Line Model** representation.*

18. Create other vertical and horizontal structures. The sequence in which the points are to be selected is shown in the figure.

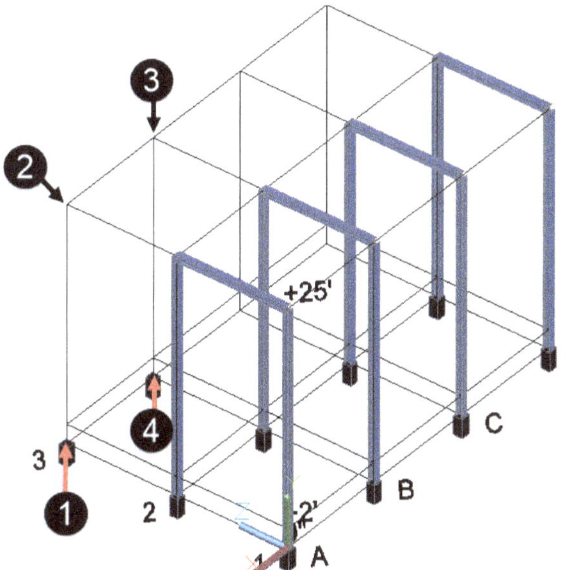

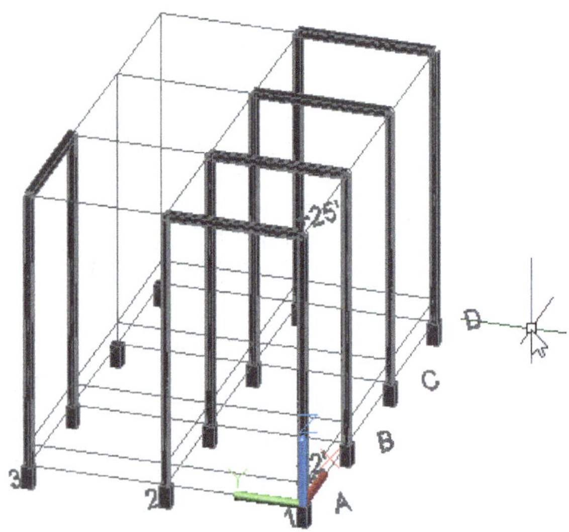

19. Create horizontal structures by selecting the intersections between the gridlines, as shown.

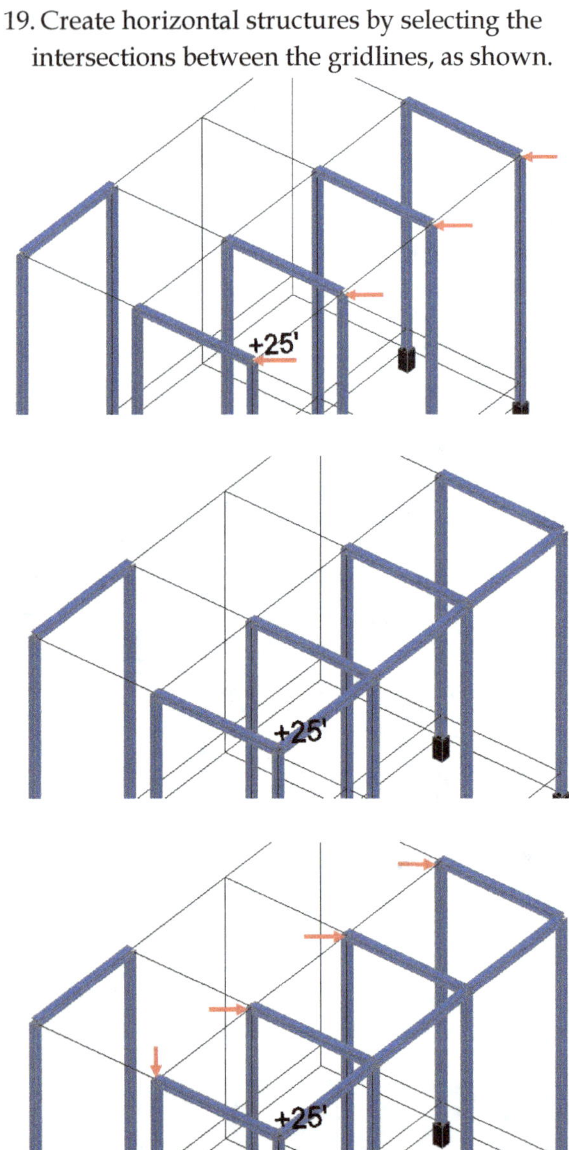

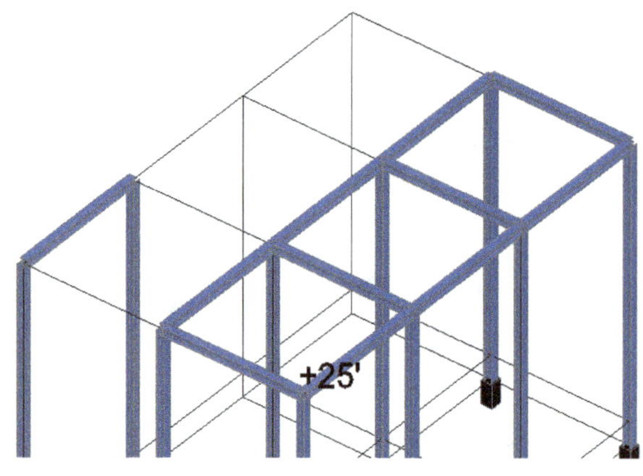

20. Create horizontal structural members by selecting the intersection points between the vertical gridlines and the second platform.

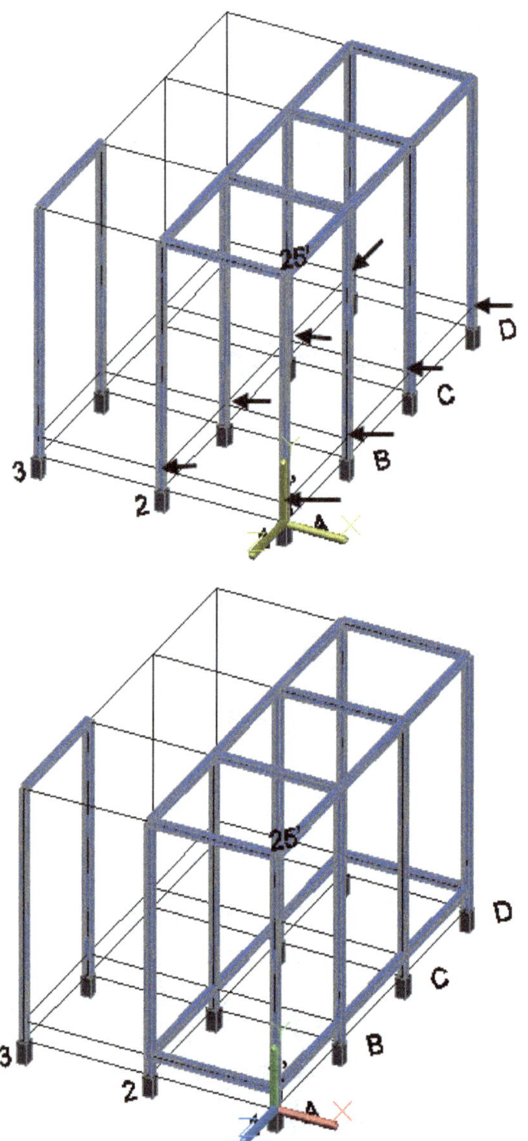

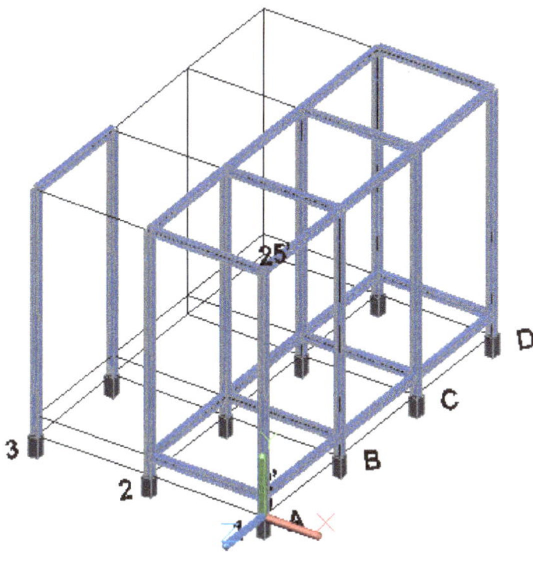

Increasing the length of the Structural Members

1. Click on the horizontal structural member located at the top, as shown.

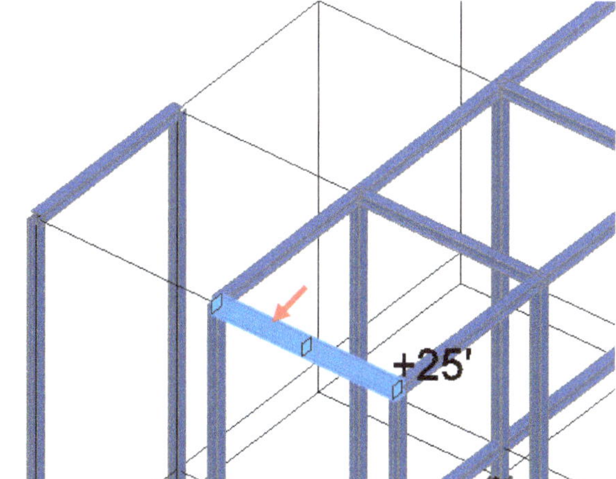

2. Click on the left end grip of the structural member.

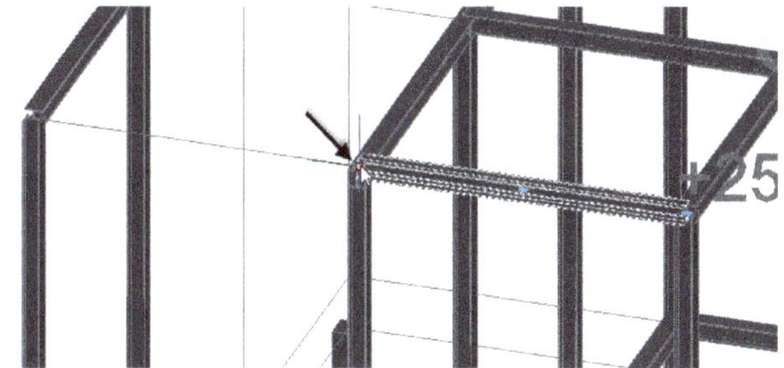

3. Move the pointer and click on the grid point, as shown.

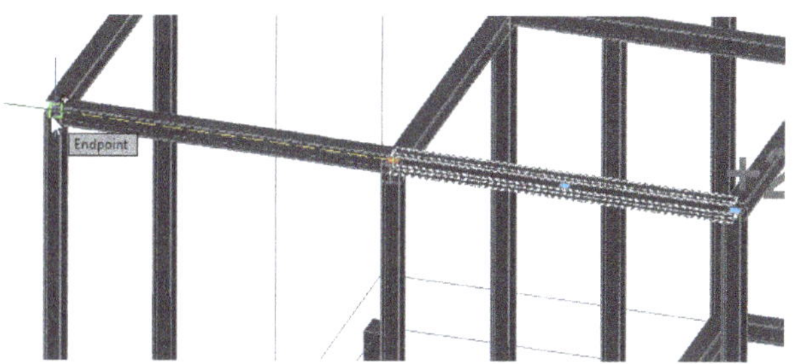

4. Click **Undo** on the **Quick Access toolbar** to restore the structural member to its original length.

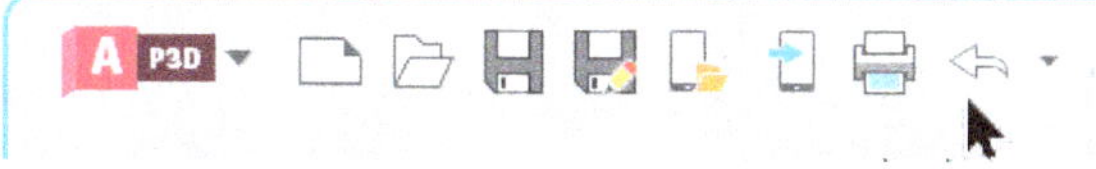

5. On the ribbon, click **Structure > Cutting > Lengthen Member**.

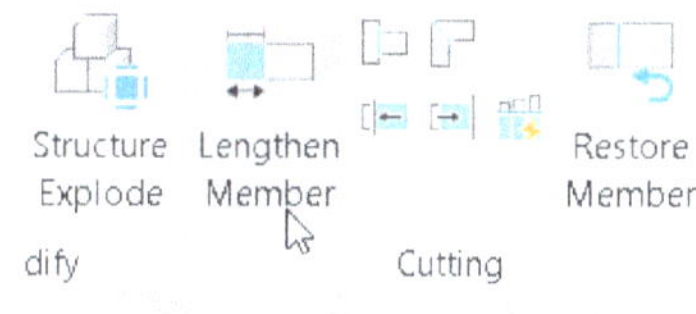

6. Click **Total** in the command line. This option sets a new length of the structural member. The **Delta** option specifies the increase in the length of the structural member.
7. Type **25′** in the command line and press Enter.
8. Select the horizontal structural member, as shown. The **Lengthen Member** command increases the total length of the member.

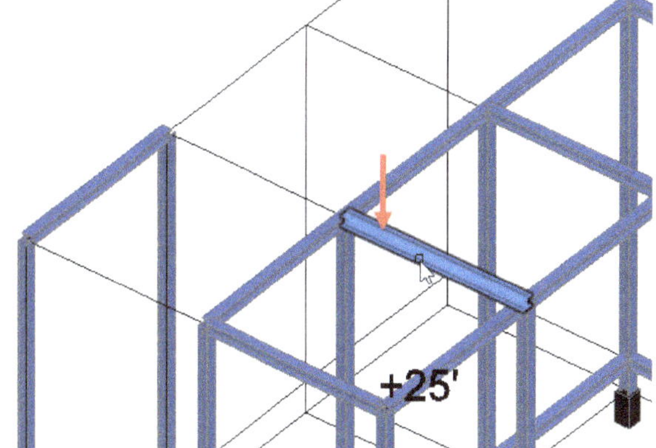

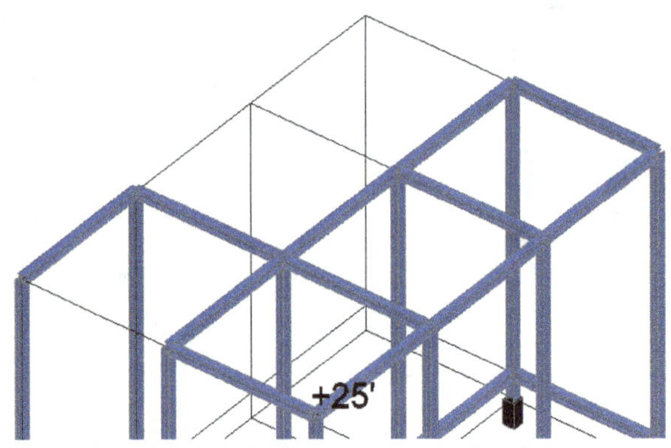

9. On the ribbon, click **Structure > Cutting > Restore Member** .

10. Select the lengthened structural member to restore it to the original length.

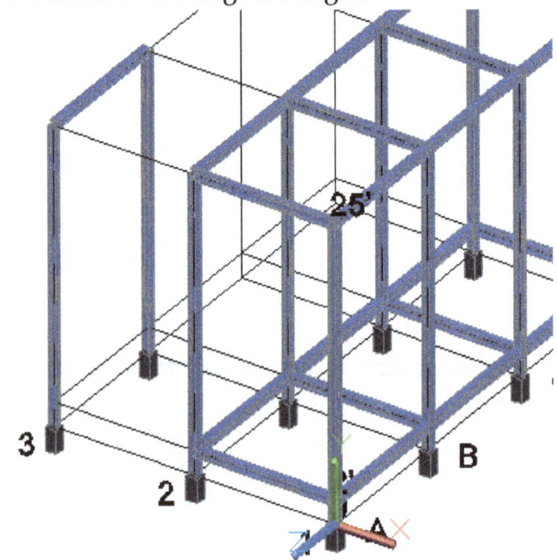

6. Create two horizontal structural members up to the left end.

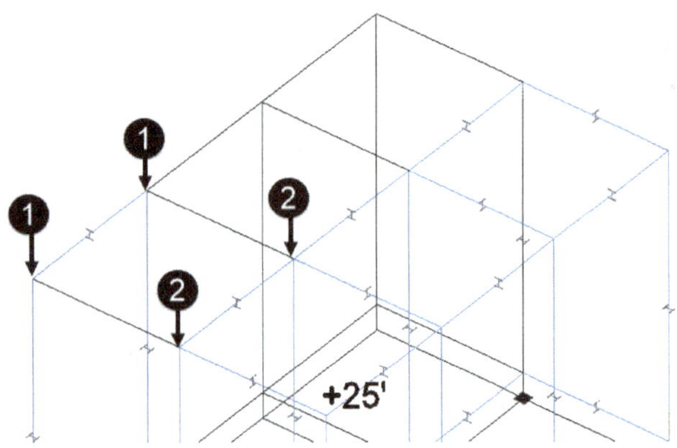

Extending the Structural Members

1. Change the view orientation to **NW Isometric**.
2. On the ribbon, click **Structure > Cutting > Extend Member**.

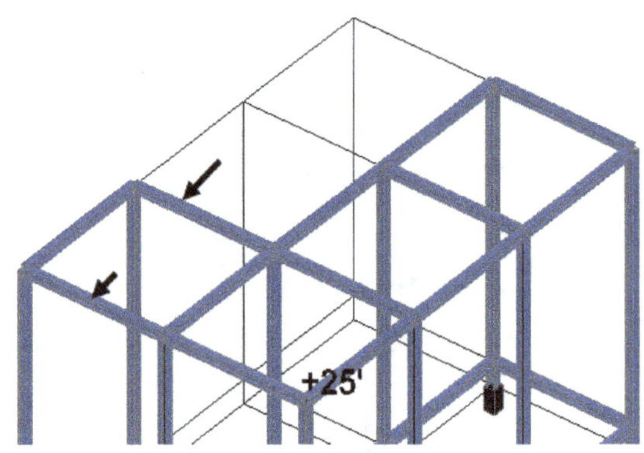

3. On the **Extend to Plane** dialog, select **3Points** and click **OK** to define the method to create a boundary plane.
4. Select the grid points, as shown in the figure. A boundary plane is set.
5. Select the lower horizontal structural member, as shown in the figure. The **Extend Member** command extends the structural members up to the boundary plane.

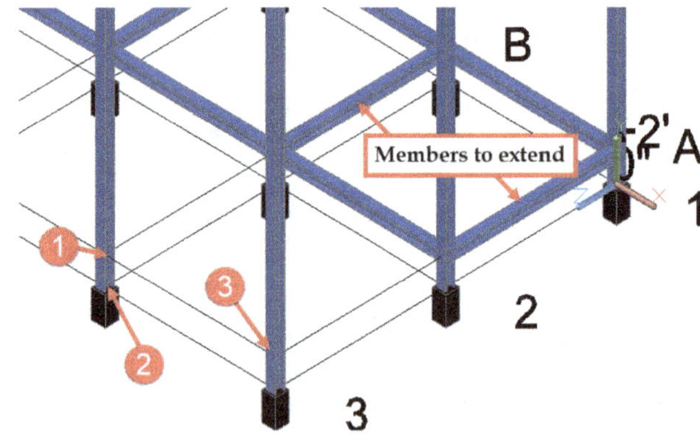

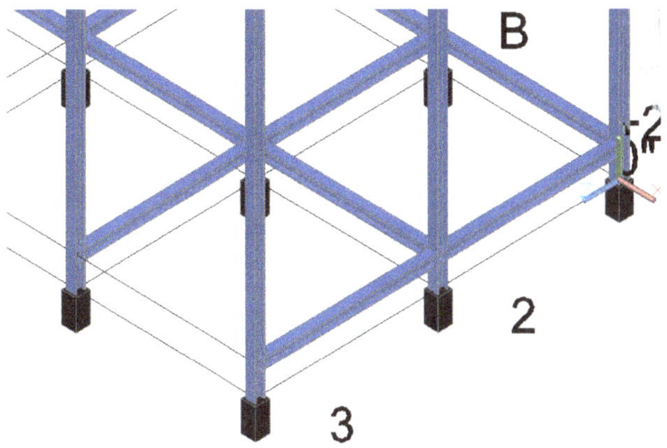

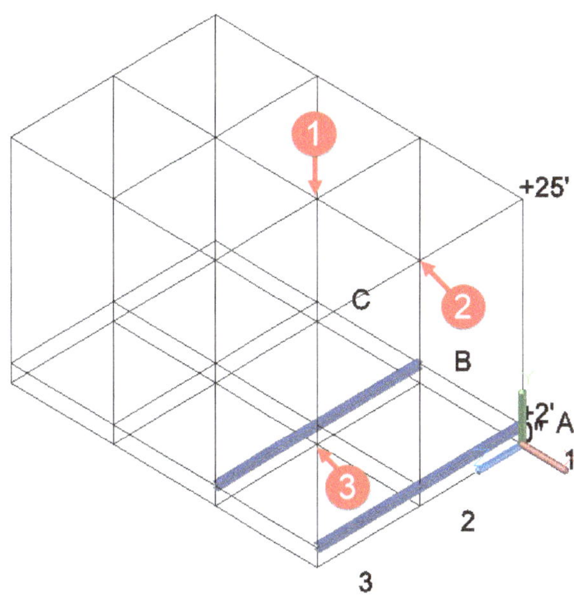

Trimming the Structural Members

1. On the ribbon, click **Structure > Visibility > Hide Others**.

2. Select the structural members and the grid, as shown.

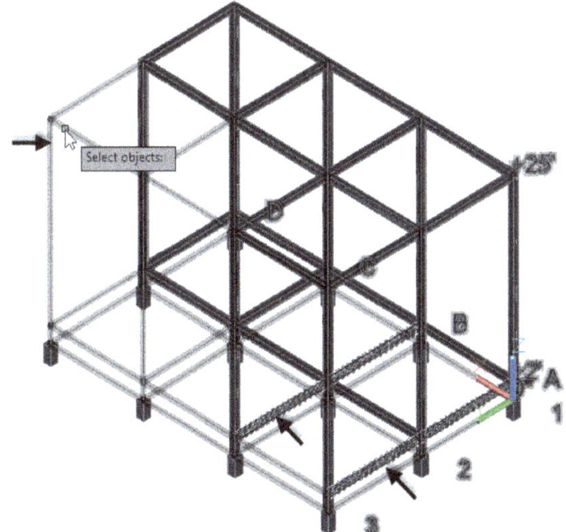

3. Press Enter. All the other objects except the selected ones are hidden.
4. On the ribbon, click **Structure > Cutting > Trim Member** .
5. On the **Trim to Plane** dialog, select **3 Points** option, and click **OK**.
6. Select the grid intersection points, as shown.

7. Select the portions to trim, as shown. The **Trim Member** command trims the structures by using the intersecting plane created by the three points.

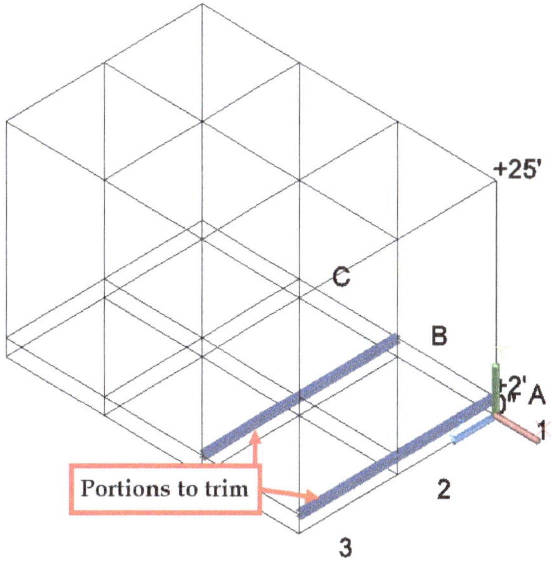

8. On the ribbon, click **Structure > Visibility > Show All** .

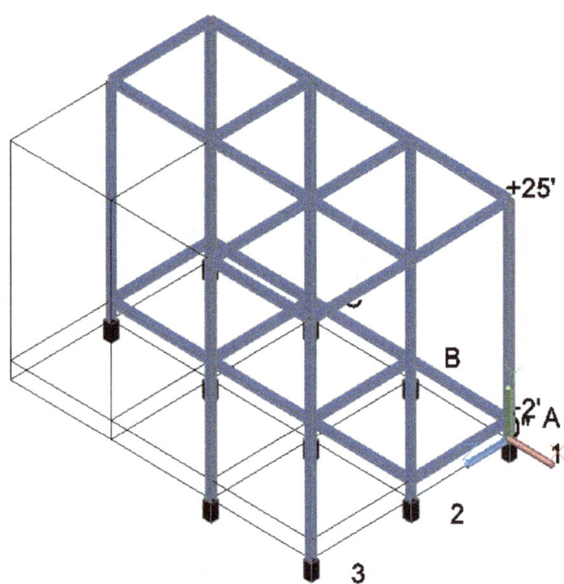

9. Change the view orientation to **SW Isometric**.

Using the Cut Back Member command

1. Zoom-In to the intersection between the members, as shown.

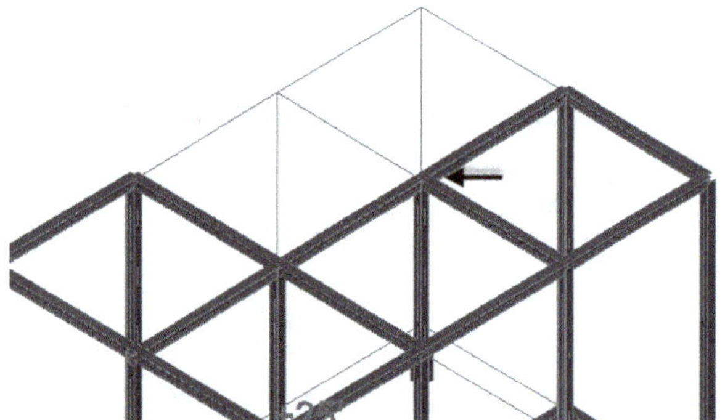

2. On the ribbon, click **Structure > Cutting > Cut Back Member**.

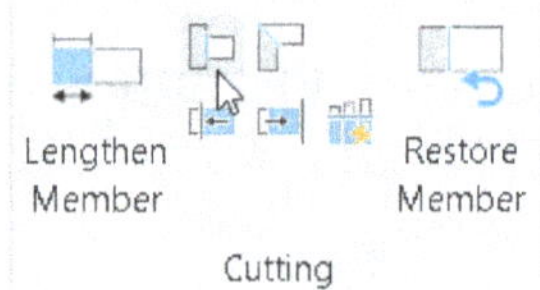

3. Select the limiting member and member to cut. The **Cut Back Member** command cuts the second selection.

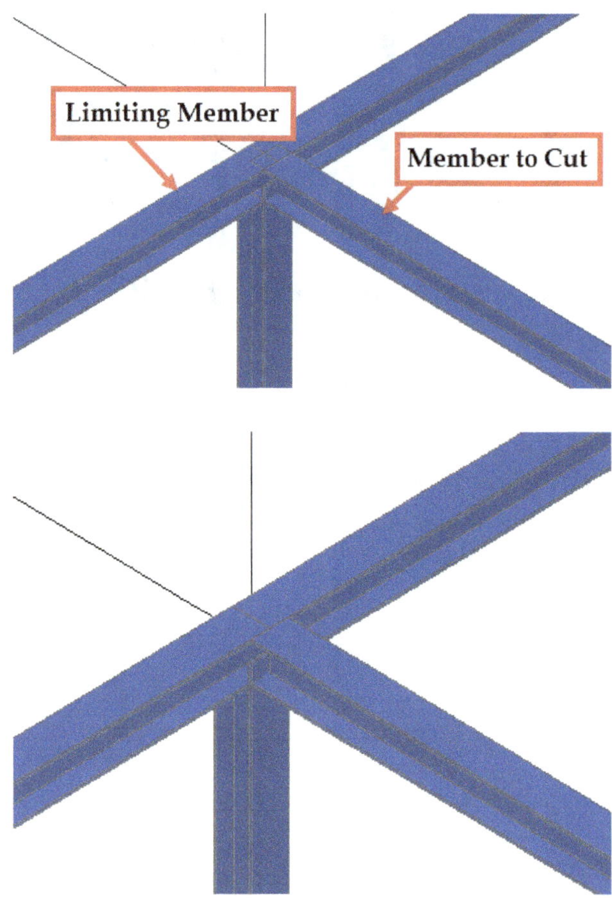

The **cut Both** option in the command line cuts both the members.

The **Gap** option adds a gap between the two members.

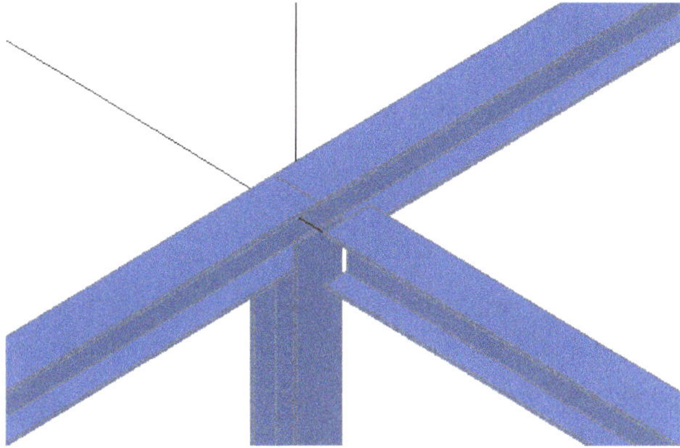

4. Likewise, cut the other members, as shown.

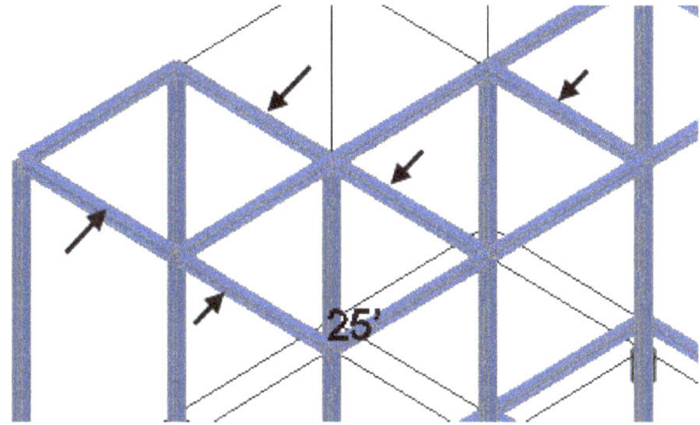

Using the Miter Cut Member command

The **Miter Cut Member** command creates a corner at the intersection point between two structural members.

1. On the ribbon, click **Structure > Cutting > Miter Cut Member**.

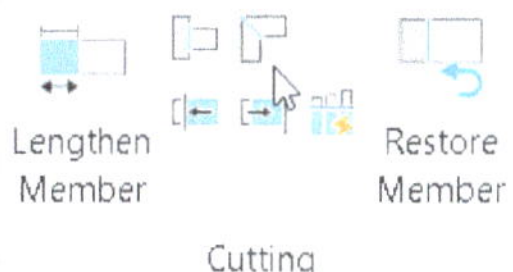

2. Select the two intersecting structural members. The **Miter Cut Member** cuts the structural members to form a corner.

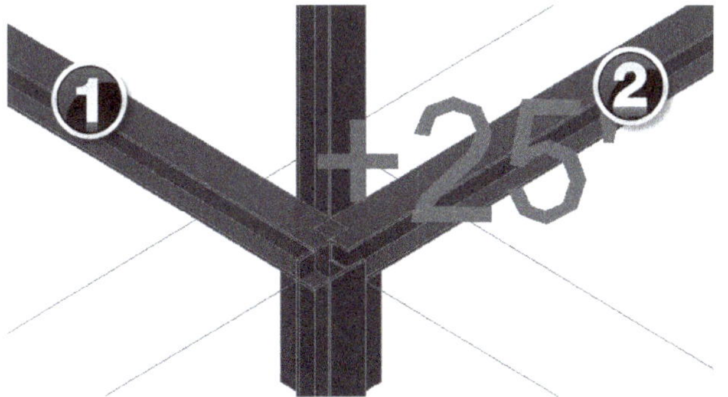

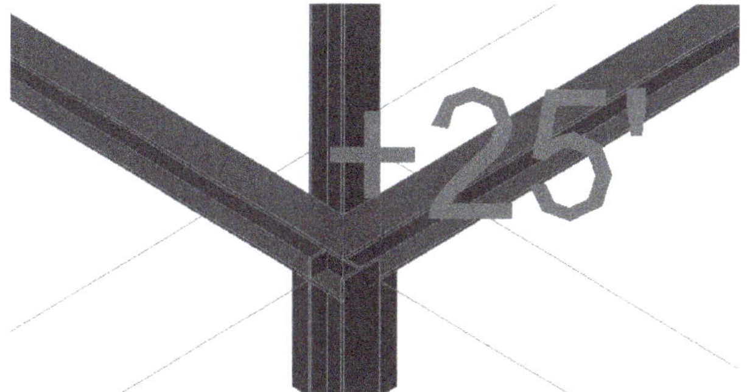

The **Gap** option adds a gap between the two members.

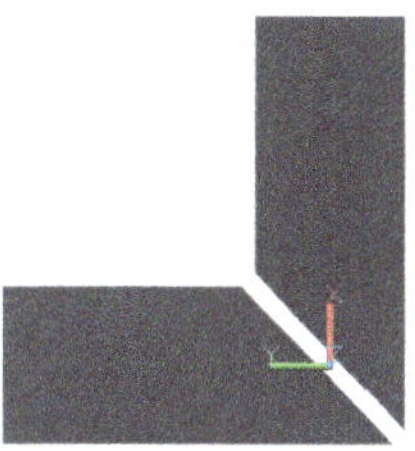

3. Miter the other corners.

Using the Structure Edit command

The **Structure Edit** command edits the structural members, stairs, ladders, grid, footings, and railings.

1. Select the top horizontal structural members one-by-one, as shown.

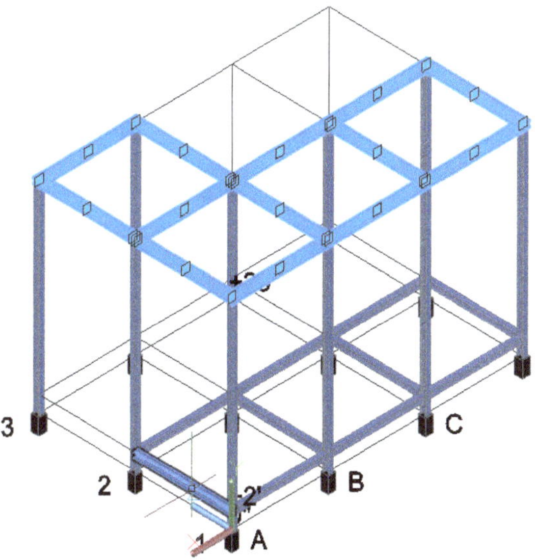

2. On the ribbon, click **Structure > Modify > Structure Edit**.

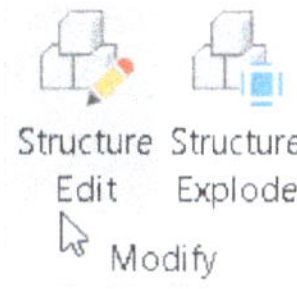

On the **Edit Member** dialog, you can modify the properties of the structural member. Likewise, if you select any other type of structural element, the dialog related to it would appear. You can modify the properties on the dialog and click **OK**.

3. On the **Edit Member** dialog, under the **Orientation** section, click the top center point of the cross-section. Click **OK**. The orientation of the structural members is changed to the top center.

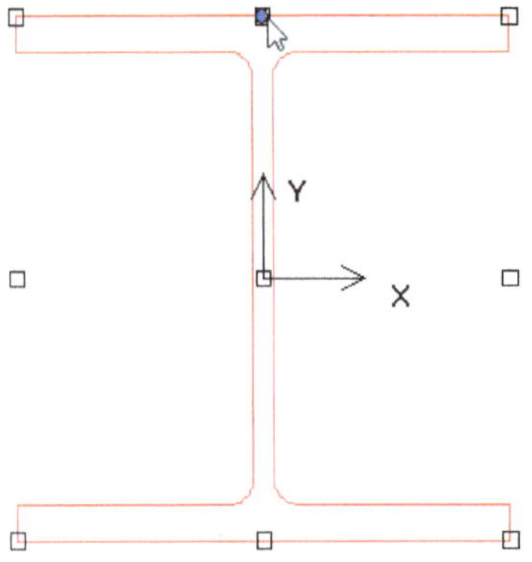

4. Likewise, change the orientation of the structural members on the bottom platform to the top center.

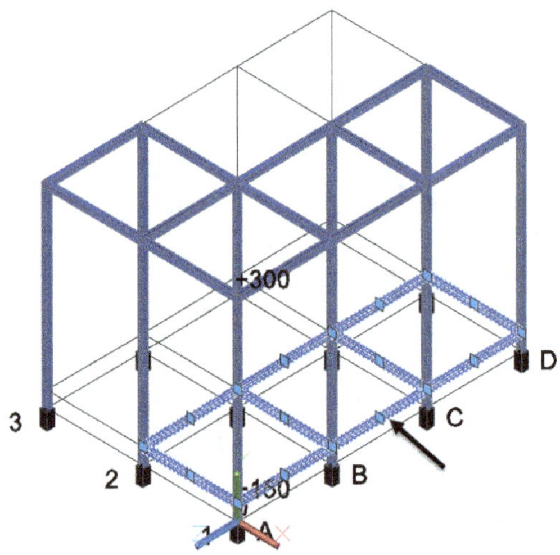

5. Use the **Cut Back Member** command to cut the intersecting portions of the structural members.

Adding Platforms

After creating the structural frame, you have to add platforms to accommodate equipment.

1. On the ribbon, click **Structure > Layers > Layer** drop-down **> Platform**.
2. Click the right mouse button, and select **Isolate > Isolate Objects**.
3. Select the grid and press Enter; all elements except the grid is hidden.
4. On the ribbon, click **Structure > Parts > Plate**.

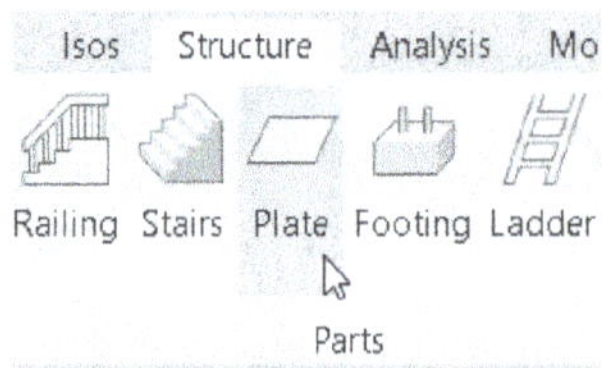

5. On the **Create Plate/Grate** dialog, select **Type > Plate**.
6. Select the **Material Standard** and **Material Code** based on the location of your project.
7. Set the **Thickness** value to **1"**.
8. Set the **Justification** to **Top**.
9. Set the **Shape** to **New rectangular**.
10. Click **Create** and select the grid points, as shown.

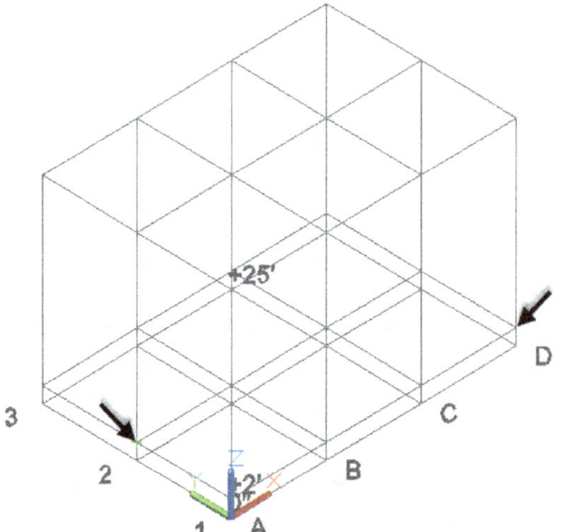

The plate is created.

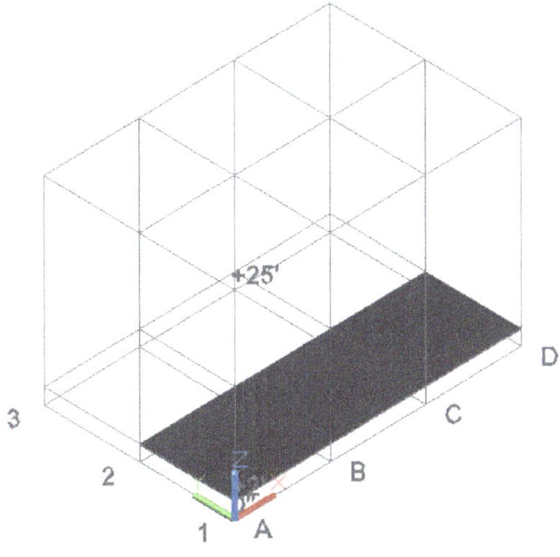

Now, you have to create the top platform.

11. On the ribbon, click **Structure > View > Restore View > Top**.

12. On the ribbon, click **Structure > Parts > Plate**.
13. On the **Create Plate/Grate** dialog, select **Type > Grating**.
14. Select the **Material Standard** and **Material Code** based on the location of your project.
15. Set the **Thickness** value to 1".
16. Set the **Justification** to **Top**.
17. Set the **Hatch Pattern** to **GRATE**.
18. Set the **Shape** to **New polyline**.
19. Click **Create** and select the grid points, as shown.

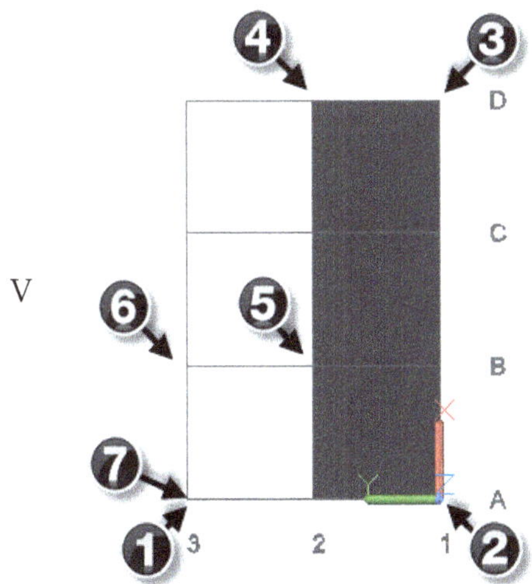

Change the orientation to **SW Isometric**. You notice that the platform is created at the bottom.

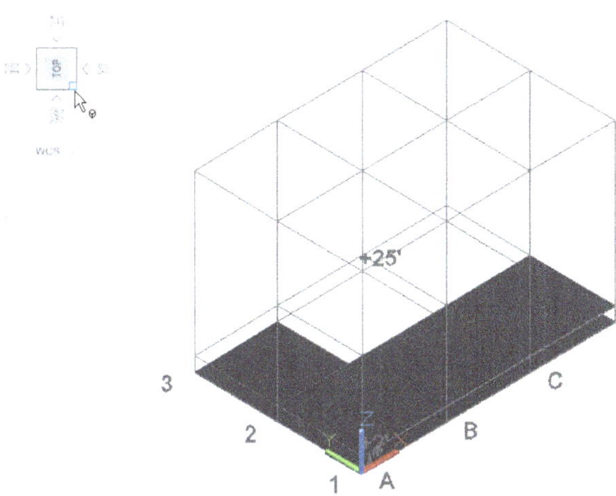

20. Click the right mouse button on the bottom plate and select **Properties**.
21. On the **Properties** palette, scroll down to the **Structural** section. You notice the structural properties of the plate. You can modify these properties.
22. Under the **Geometry** section of the **Properties** palette, click in the **Position Z** box, and then type-in **25'**. The bottom plate will be moved to the top.

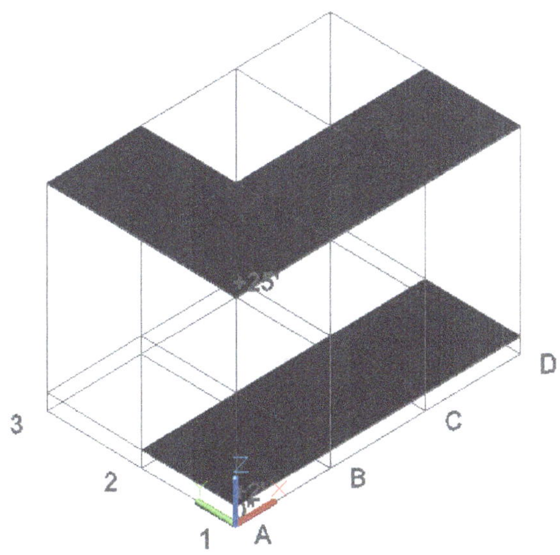

23. Right-click and select **Isolate > End Object Isolation**.

Adding Stairs

1. On the ribbon, click **Structure > Layers > Layer drop-down > Stairs**.
2. Change the view orientation to top.

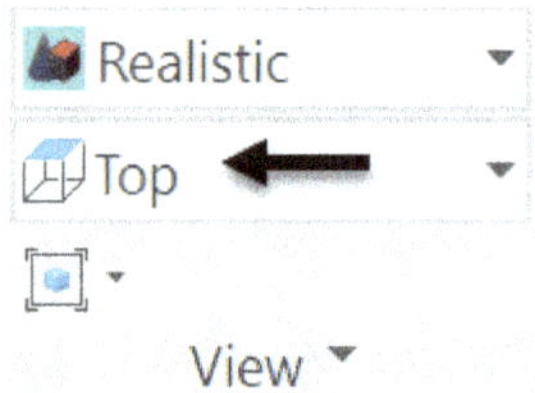

3. Turn on the **Orthomode** on the status bar.

4. Type-in **LINE** in the command line and press Enter.

5. Type-in **-3',0** in the command line, and then press Enter to define the starting point of the line.

6. Move the pointer up and type-in **150** in the command line. Press Enter to create the line.

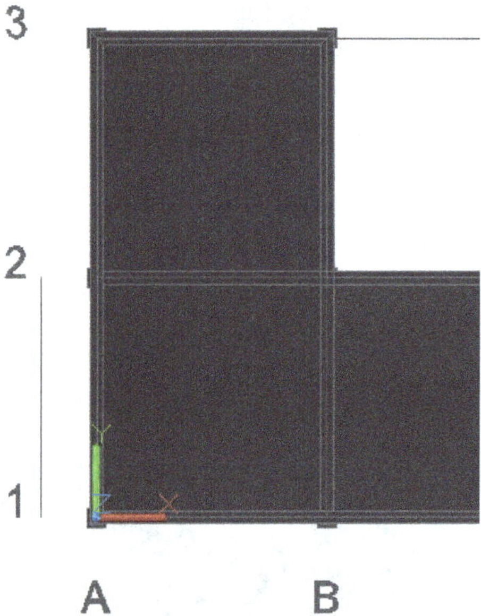

7. Press **Esc** to deactivate the **Line** command.

8. Change the view orientation to **SW Isometric**.

9. On the ribbon, click **Structure > Parts > Stairs** .

10. Click **Settings** in the command line.

On the **Stair Settings** dialog, the boxes in the **Geometry** section define the dimensions of the stair set. You can type-in the **Stair width** (inside distance between the stairs) and the **Maximum tread distance** (distance between the steps).

11. Leave the default settings in the **Geometry** section.

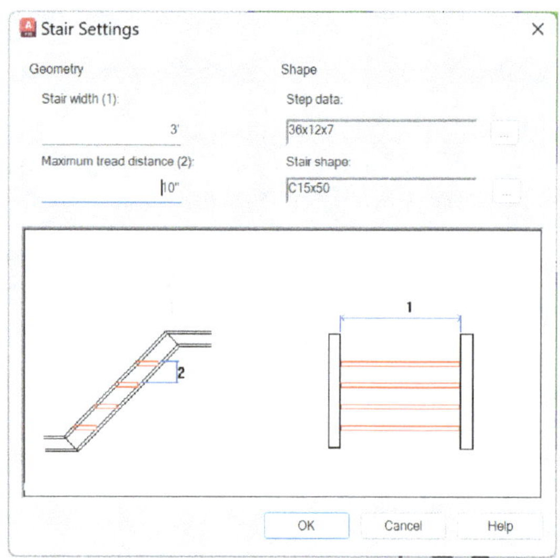

In the **Shape** section, you can define the shape and size of the steps and stairs.

12. To define the step geometry, click the button next to the **Step data** box.

On the **Select Step** dialog, select the **Tread standard** based on the location of the project. You can also select the **User defined** standard. Next, define the dimensions of the tread by selecting any one of the existing configurations from the **Tread shape** section. You can also add a new configuration to this section. To do this, type-in values in the **Dimensions** section, and then click the **Add** button.

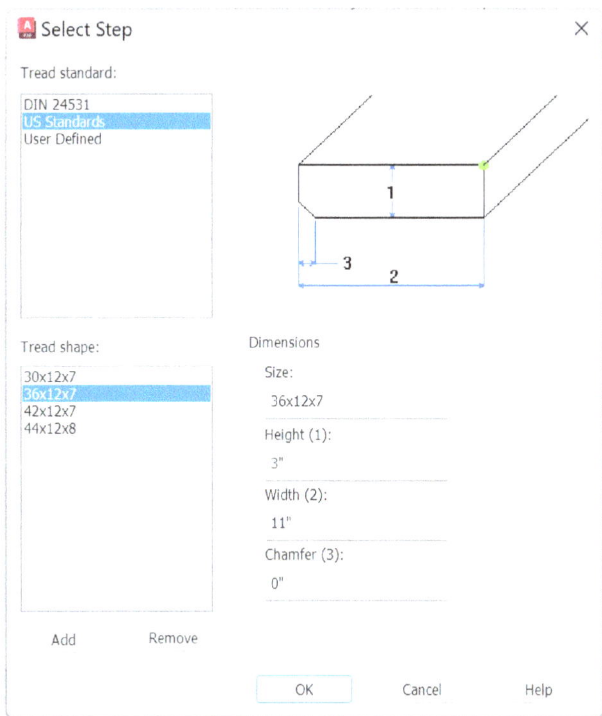

24. Click **OK** on the **Select Step** dialog.
25. Click the button next to the **Stair shape** box.

On the **Select Stair Shape** dialog, you can define the shape standard, shape, and size of the stair. Note that you cannot change the orientation and material of the stairs.

26. Leave the default settings on this dialog and click **Select**.
27. Click **OK** on the **Stair Settings** dialog.
28. On the Status bar, click the down-arrow next to the **Object Snap** icon and select **Midpoint**.

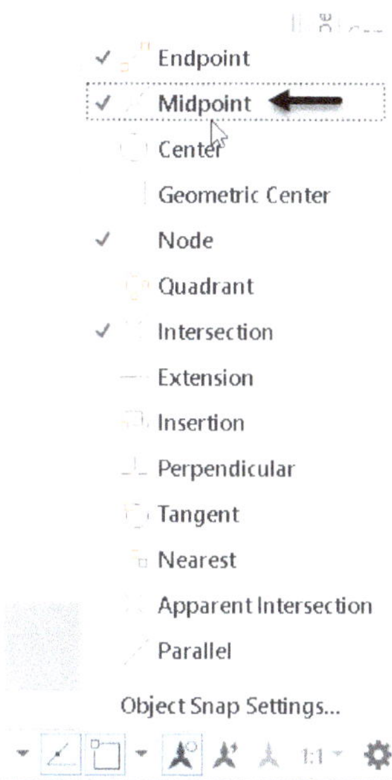

29. Select the midpoint of the line to define the starting point of the stairs.
30. Select the midpoint of the top edge of the platform to define the endpoint of the stair.

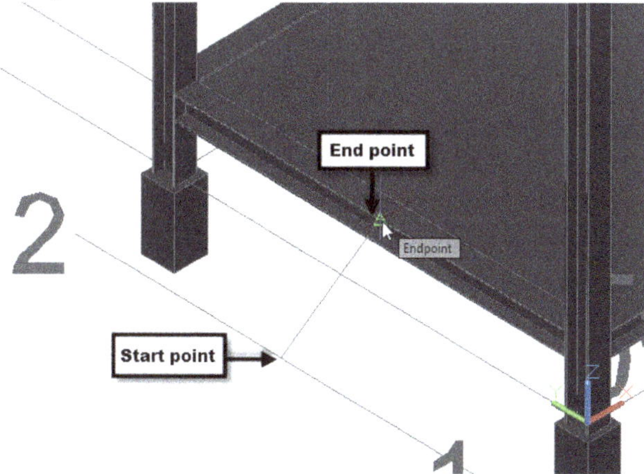

31. Press Enter to create the stairs.

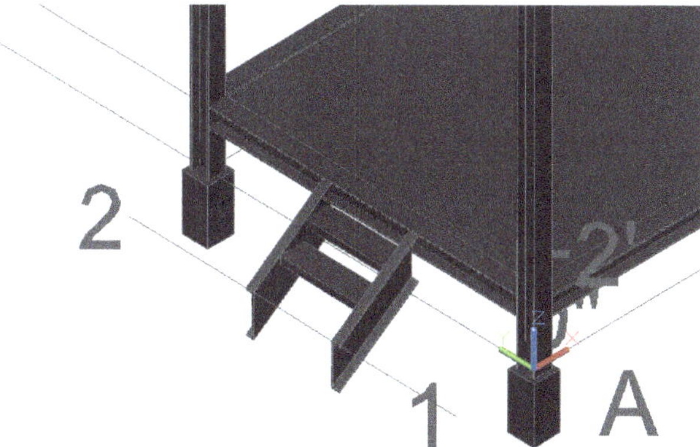

32. Select the stairs, and notice the grips on it. You can use these grips to modify the stairs.

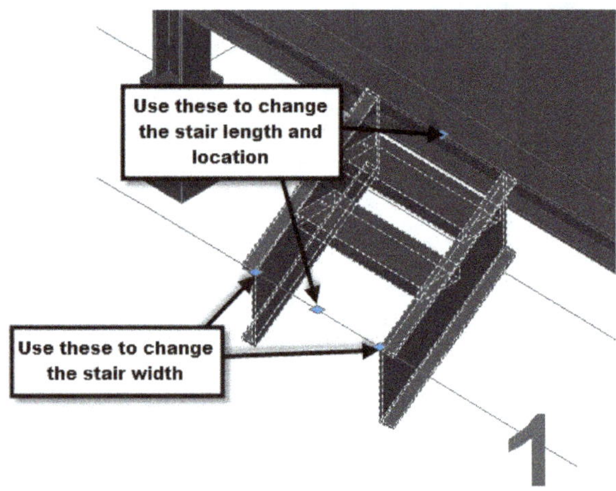

You can also use the **Structure Edit** command to modify the stairs.

Adding Railings

1. On the ribbon, click **Structure > Layers > Layer drop-down >Railing**.
2. On the ribbon, click **Structure > Parts > Railing** .
3. Click **Settings** in the command line.

On the **Railing Settings** dialog, the boxes in the **Geometry** section define the distances between the elements of the railing. On the dialog, you can view the image to get a better understanding of these parameters.

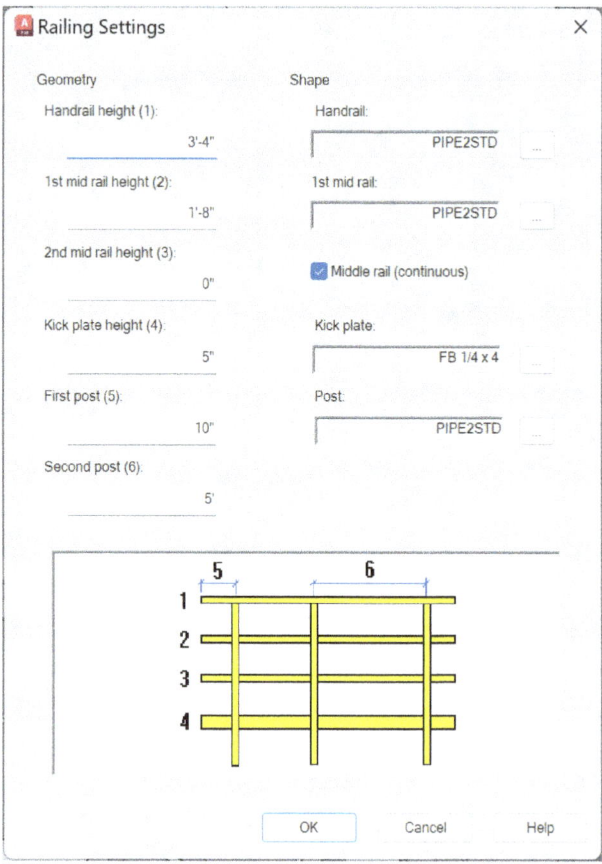

The options in the **Shape** section define the shapes and sizes of the railing elements. For example, to define the shape of the handrail, click the button next to the **Handrail** box. On the **Select Handrail Shape** dialog, select the shape standard, shape type, and size. Click **Select** to return to the **Railing Settings** dialog.

4. Leave the default settings on the **Railing Settings** dialog and click **OK**.
5. Click **Object** in the command line and select the stairs. The railing is added to the stairs. You can also add a railing by selecting two points. Click **2Point** in the command line and specify the start and endpoints of the railing.

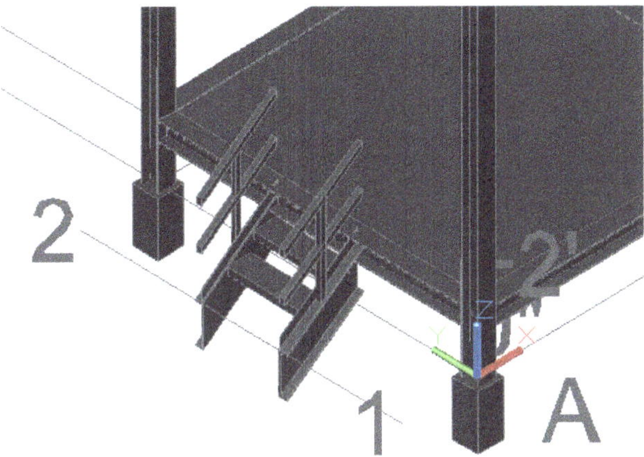

6. Likewise, create railings by selecting the structural members on the top platform.

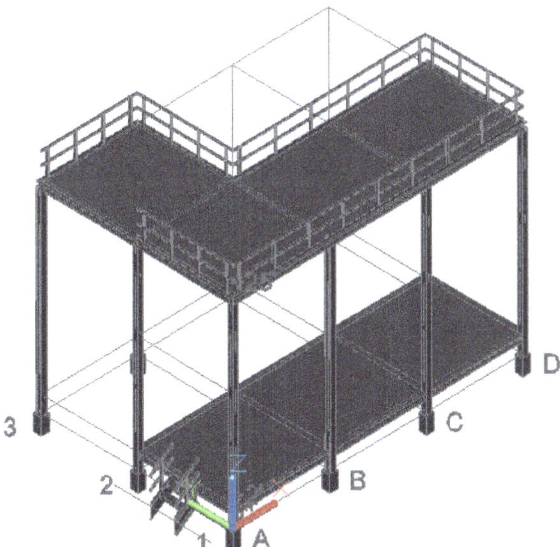

Using the Structure Explode command

This command explodes the grouped structure into individual elements so that they can be modified separately.

1. On the ribbon, click **Structure > Layers > Layer drop-down > Stairs**.
2. On the ribbon, click **Structure > Modify > Structure Explode**.

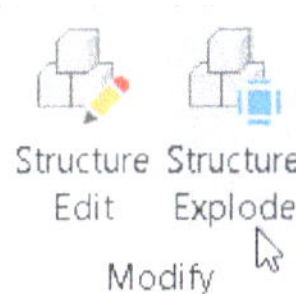

3. Select the stairs and press Enter. Now, you can select the individual elements of the stairs.
4. On the ribbon, click **Structure > Cutting > Trim Member**.

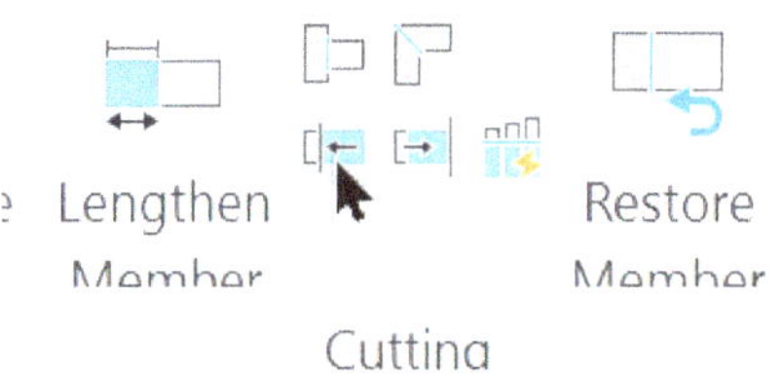

5. Select **XY WCS** and click **OK** on the **Trim to Plane** dialog.
6. Click on the upper portions of the structural members of the two stairs.

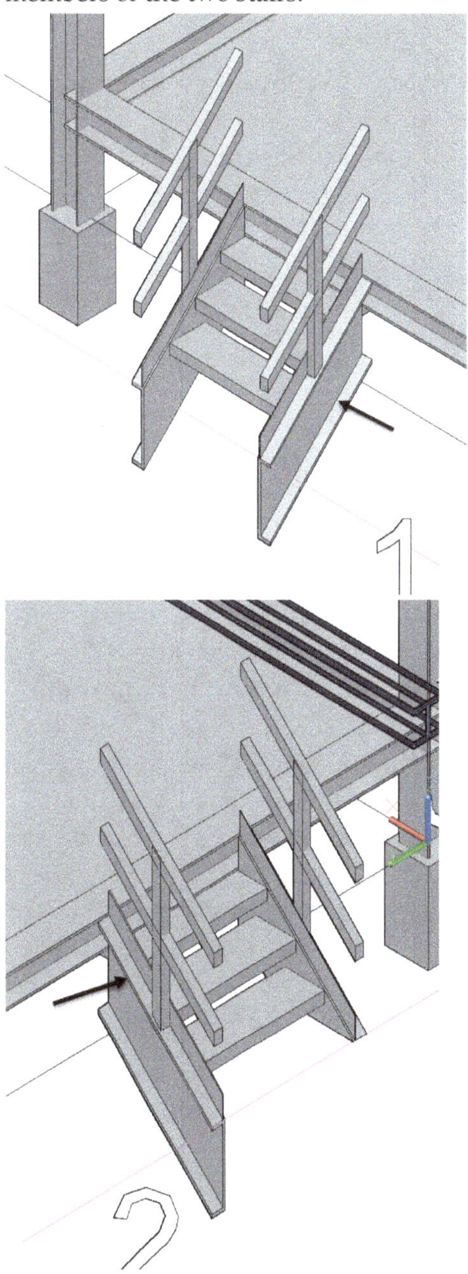

The **Trim member** command trims them using the XY plane of the world coordinate system.

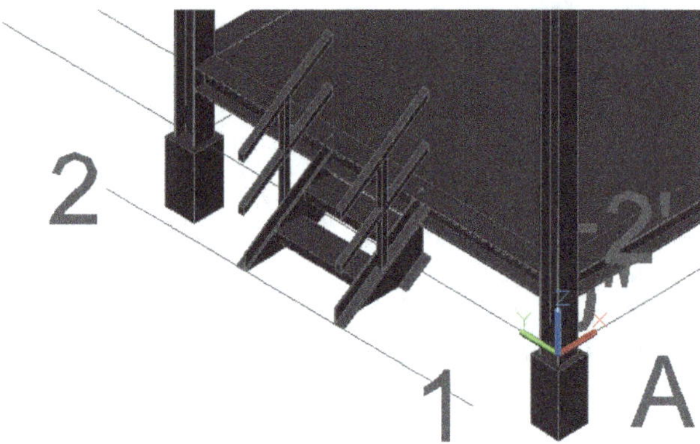

Adding Ladders

1. On the ribbon, click **Structure > Layers > Layer drop-down > Ladder**.
2. On the ribbon, click **Structure > Parts > Line Model**. The model representation changes to the line.

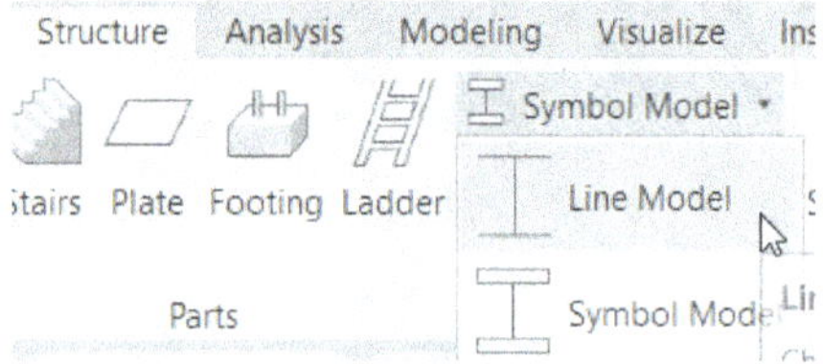

3. On the ribbon, click **Structure > Parts > Ladder** .
4. Click **Settings** in the command line.

On the **Ladder Settings** dialog, the boxes in the **Geometry** section define the dimensions between the ladder elements. The **Width** and **Exit width** boxes define the starting and exit width of the ladder. The **Projection** box determines the extension of the ladder beyond the top point. The **Rung distance** determines the distance between the rungs.

The **Shape** section defines the shapes and sizes of the ladder and rungs. For example, click the button next to the **Ladder Shape** box to change the shape of the ladder. On the **Select Ladder Shape** dialog, define the shape standard, shape type and size of the ladder, and then click **Select**.

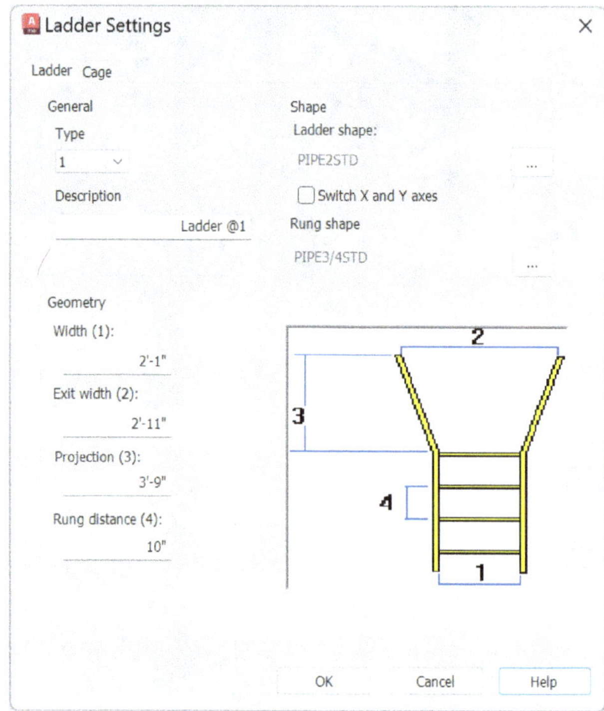

5. Click the **Cage** tab on the **Ladder Settings** dialog.

On the **Cage** tab, check the **Draw Cage** option to create the ladder with a cage. This option avoids the worker from falling.

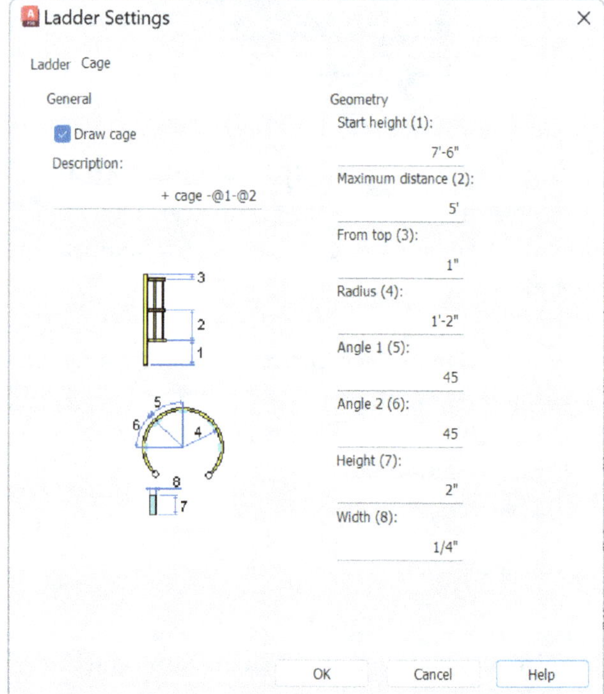

The boxes in the **Geometry** section define the spacing between the cage elements. The **Start height** box defines the starting point of the cage from the bottom. The **Maximum distance** box determines the distance between the bands. The **From top** box determines the distance between the top ends of the ladder and cage. The **Radius**, **Angle 1**, **Angle 2** boxes define the cage radius, angular locations of the frames on the cage. The **Height** and **Width** boxes define the size of the frames. View the image available on the dialog to understand the parameters.

6. Leave the default options and click **OK**.
7. Activate the **Orthomode** on the status bar.
8. Select the midpoint of the horizontal grid line between 2 and 3.
9. Move the pointer up and select the midpoint of the top platform.

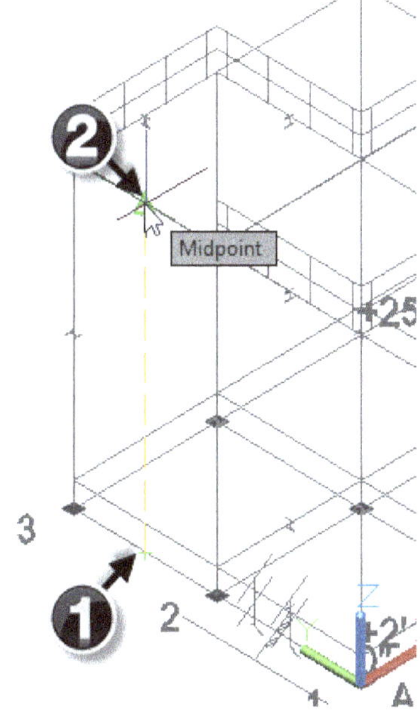

10. Move the pointer downward.
11. Move the pointer horizontally away from the grid up to a small range, and then click. The **Ladder** command creates the ladder at the specified distance from the platform.

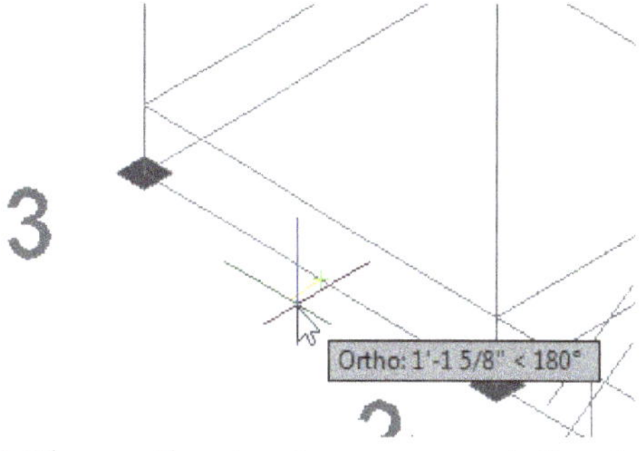

12. Change the structure representation to **Outline Model**.

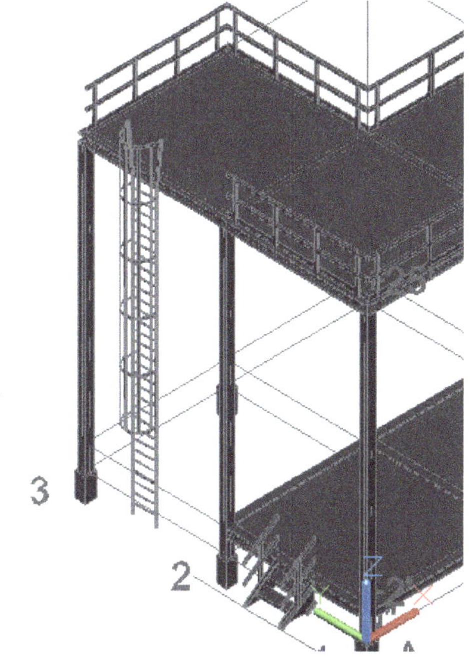

Tutorial 2 (Adding Equipment)

After creating the structural model, you can add process equipment. The equipment you add in a 3D model is always linked with its corresponding symbol in the P&ID. To understand this better, you need to open the **Project Setup** dialog and view which P&ID symbol is mapped to Plant 3D equipment.

1. On the ribbon, click **Home > Project > Project Manager > Project Setup**.

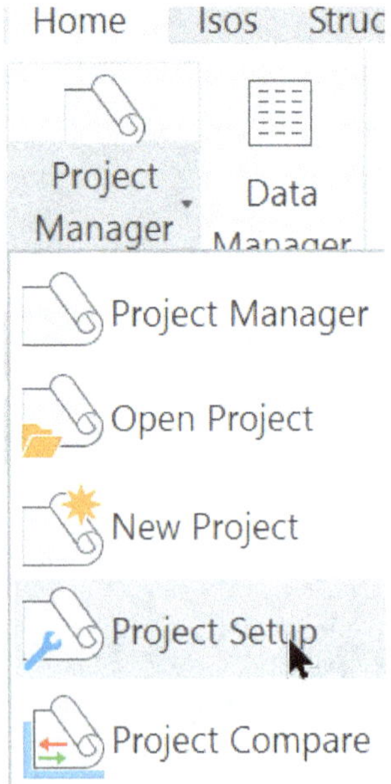

2. On the **Project Setup** dialog, select **Plant 3D DWG Settings > P&ID Object Mapping**.

3. Under the **P&ID Classes** section, click **Engineering Items >Equipment > Pumps > Centrifugal Pump**. The **Plant 3D Classes** section shows the 3D equipment mapped to the selected symbol.

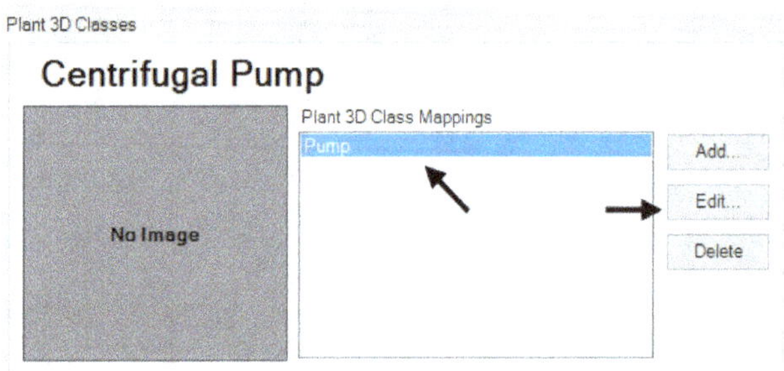

Notice the properties of the pump. Usually, most of the pump properties available in the **Property Mapping** section are linked to the properties of the pump symbols in the P&ID. For example, the **Manufacturer** property of the plant object is the same as that in the P&ID.

4. On the **Project Setup** dialog, select **Plant 3D DWG Settings > P&ID Object Mapping**.

5. Under the **P&ID Classes** section, select **Engineering Items > Equipment > Pumps > Centrifugal Pump**.

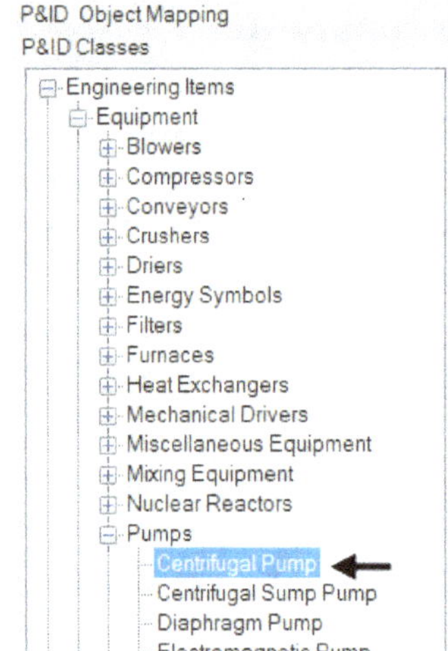

6. Select **Pump** from the **Plant 3D Class Mappings** section and click **Edit** to change the 3D model that is mapped to it. The **Select Plant 3D Class Mapping** dialog appears. In this dialog, you can control the symbols to which the 3D equipment is mapped.

7. Click **Cancel** on the **Select Plant 3D Class Mapping** dialog.

8. Close the **Project Setup** dialog.

Now, you need to place the pumps on the lower platform. Since the platform is at the 2' elevation, you need to create new UCS at this elevation.

9. Select the UCS (User Coordinate System) and click on its origin point.

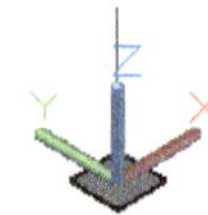

10. Move the pointer upward and type-in 2'. Press Enter to create a new User Coordinate System.

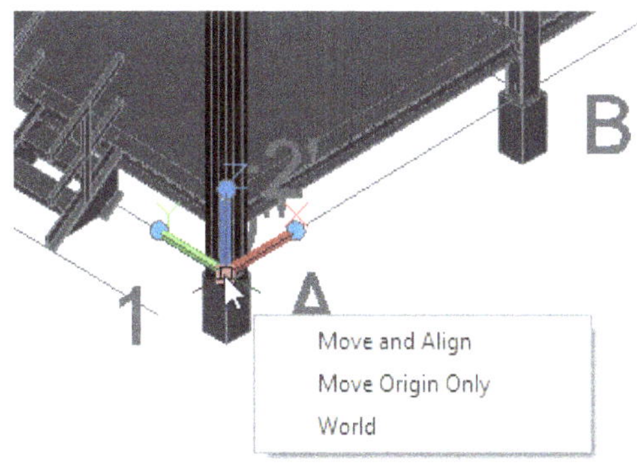

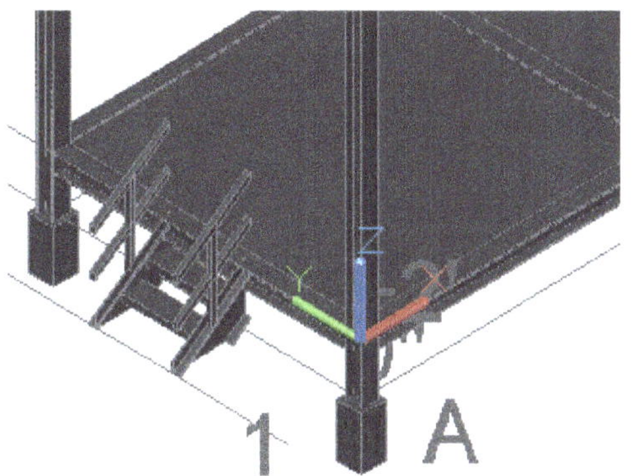

11. Select **Symbol Model** from the **Structural Representation** drop-down on the **Parts** panel of the **Structure** ribbon tab.
12. Change the view orientation to top.

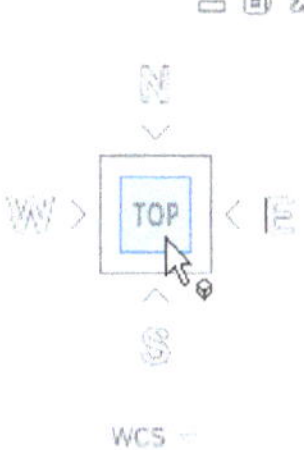

13. On the ribbon, click **Home > Layers > Layers Properties**.
14. On the **Layer Properties Manager**, create a new layer with the name **Equipment** and change its color to Index color **30**.

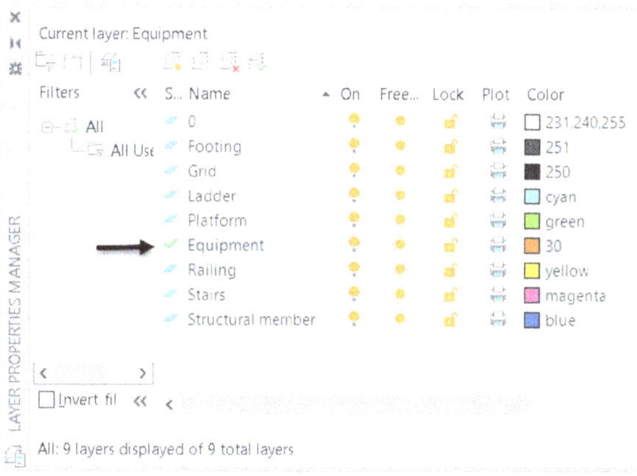

15. Set the **Equipment** layer as current, and then close the Layer Properties Manager.
16. On the ribbon, click **Home > Equipment > Create**.

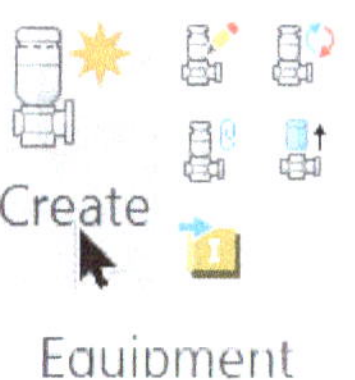

17. On the **Create Equipment** dialog, select **Pump > Centrifugal Pump** from the drop-down.

The **Equipment** tab on the dialog has the general information and dimensions of the pump.

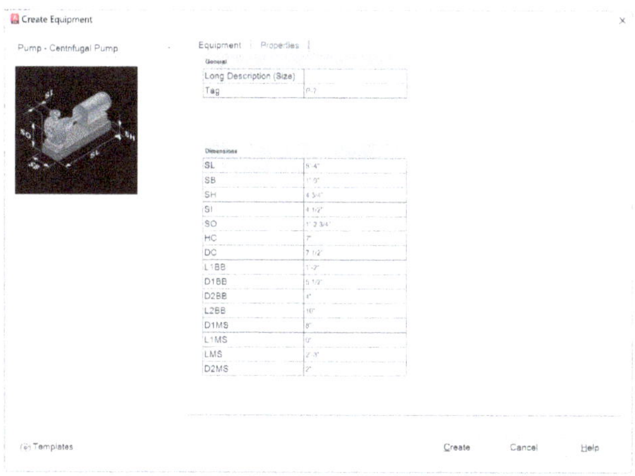

18. Click in the **Tag** box, and the **Assign Tag** dialog appears.
19. On the **Assign Tag** dialog, click in the **Number** box and select the button next to it. The number **001** is entered in the box.

20. Click **Assign**. AutoCAD Plant 3D creates a link between this pump and the Centrifugal Pump symbol in the P&ID with the P-001 tag.
21. Leave the default dimensions and click the **Properties** tab. The properties of the associated P&ID symbols are populated in this tab. You can also enter new data to link it to the P&ID symbol.

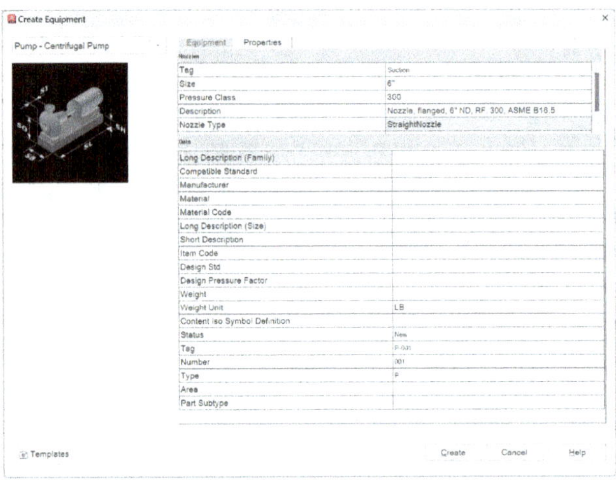

22. Click **Create** on the dialog.
23. Click between A and B, and rotate the pump by 90 degrees, as shown.

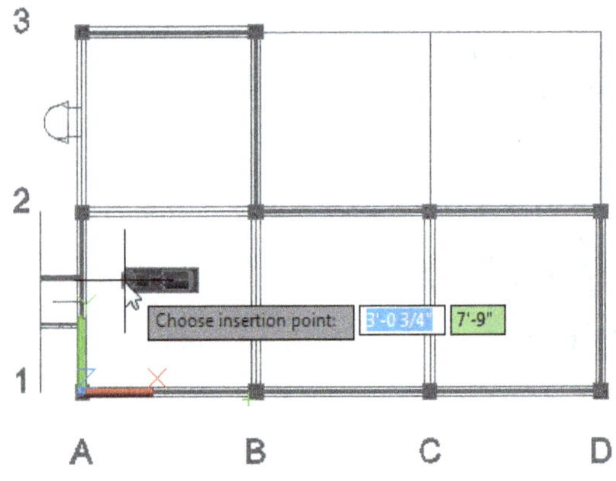

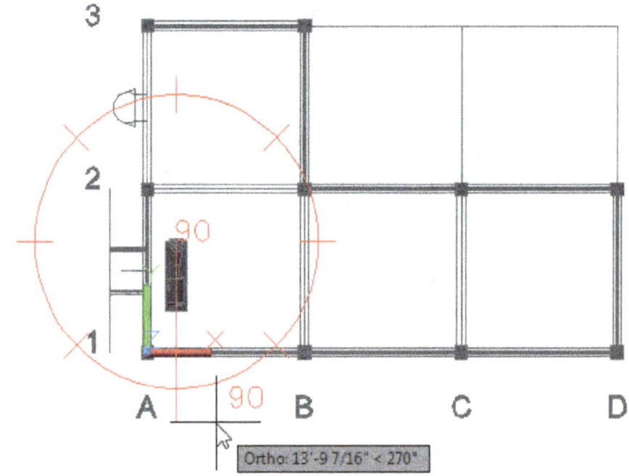

24. Select the pump.
25. On the ribbon, click **Modeling > Modify > Mirror**.

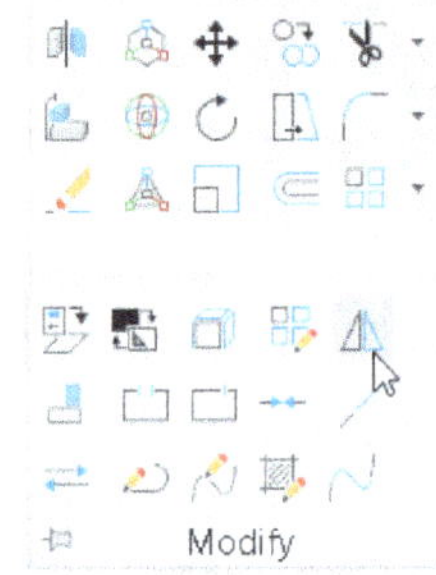

26. Click on the midpoint of the horizontal structural member.
27. Move the pointer downward and click to create the mirror line.

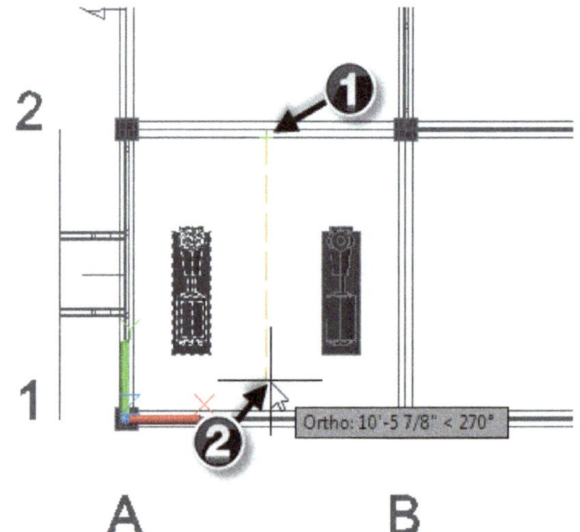

28. Click **No** in the command line.

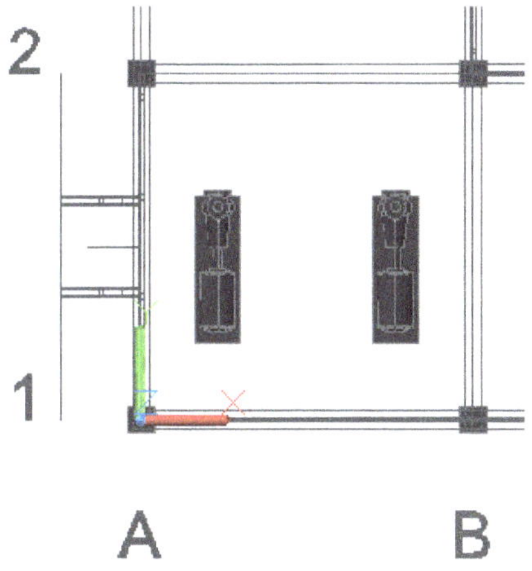

29. On the ribbon, click **Home > Part Insertion > Assign Tag**.

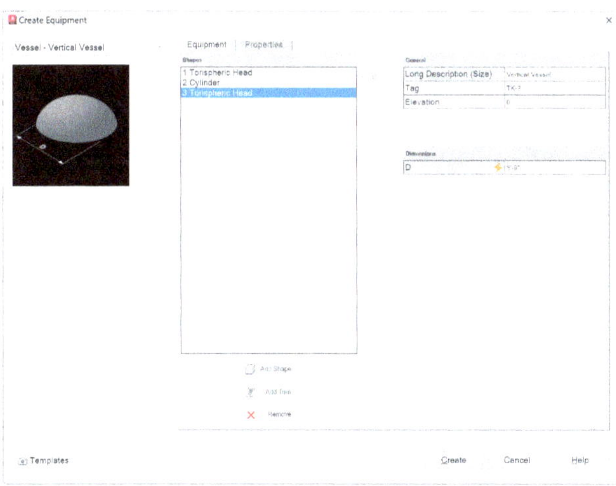

30. Select the mirrored pump to open the **Assign Tag** dialog.
31. On the **Assign Tag** dialog, click in the Number box, and then click the button next to it. The number **002** is entered into it. Click **Assign** to assign a tag. The program associates the mirrored pump with the P&ID symbol with the **P-002** tag.
32. Activate the **Create Equipment** command.
33. On the **Create Equipment** dialog, select **Vessel > Vertical Vessel** from the drop-down.

The **Add Trim** button at the bottom of the **Shapes** helps you to add a saddle, skirt, stiffening ring, lug, platform, leg, flange, and body flange to the vessel.

For example, if you want to add a platform to the vessel, you need to select the shape (from the **Shapes** list) to which you want to add the platform. Next, click the **Add Trim** button and select **Platform** from the menu. Next, specify the dimensions in the **Dimensions** section of the dialog. You can view the image available on the dialog to get a good idea about the dimensions.

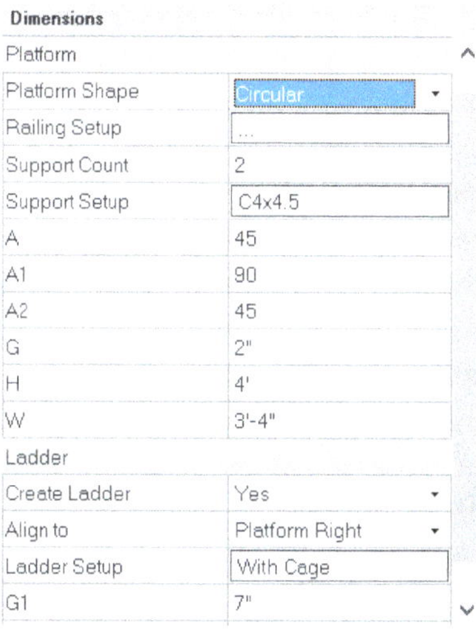

34. Click the **Equipment** tab and select **Torispheric Head** under the **Shapes** section.
35. Under **Dimensions**, type-in 7′6″ in the **D** box. The **D** box defines the diameter of the Torispheric head.
36. Under **Shapes**, click the **Cylinder** and type-in 7′6″ and 25′ in the D and H boxes, respectively.
37. Likewise, change the diameter of the bottom **Torispheric Head** to 7′6″.
38. Select the **Torispheric Head** at the bottom of the **Shapes** section, and then click the **Add Trim** button.
39. Select **Skirt** from the **Add Trim** menu.
40. Under the **Dimensions** section, select **Skirt Type > With Base Ring**.
41. Click in the **A1** dimension field and notice the image located on the top left corner of the dialog. It explains the **A1** and **W** dimensions.

42. Likewise, refer the image located on the top left corner of the dialog for the remaining dimensions in the **Dimensions** section.
43. Click in the **H** field in the **Dimensions** section and type 6'.
44. Leave the default values in the **Dimensions** section.
45. Click in the **Tag** box under the **General** section.
46. On the **Assign Tag** dialog, click in the **Number** box, and then click the button next to it. Click **Assign**. The program assigns the tag TK-001 to the vessel.
47. Under **General**, type-in 4' in the **Elevation** box to define the base point of the equipment at an elevation.
48. Click **Create** on the dialog.
49. Click in the space between 3 and 2 grid points.
50. Rotate the vessel by 180 degrees and click.

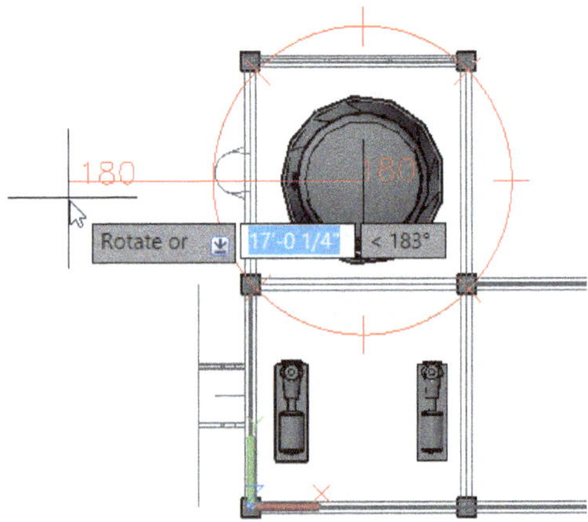

Creating an Equipment using Pre-Defined Shapes

AutoCAD Plant 3D offers you several equipment types. However, sometimes you may want to create equipment, which is not available in the library. In that case, you can use pre-defined shapes such as a rectangle, cylinder, elliptical head, and pyramid, and so on to create a new equipment type.

1. Change the view to **SW Isometric**.
2. Select the UCS located on the other platform.
3. Click on the origin of the UCS and move the pointer up.
4. Type-in 23' and press Enter. The UCS is moved to the top platform.

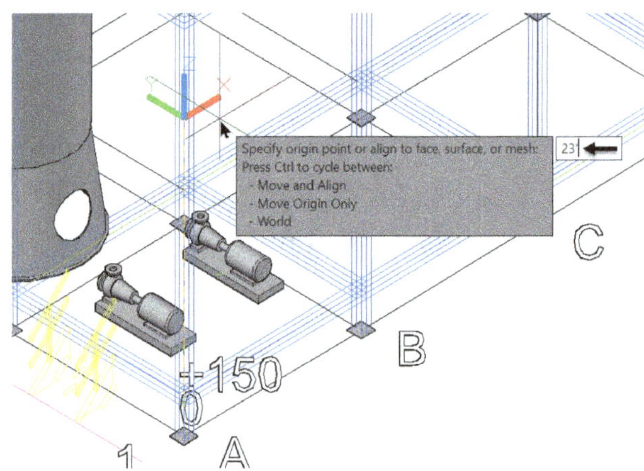

5. Change the view orientation to Top.
6. On the ribbon, click **Home > Equipment > Create**.
7. On the **Create Equipment** dialog, select **Heat Exchanger > New Horizontal Heat Exchanger** from the drop-down. The **Shapes** list appears empty. If not, select the existing shapes and click the **Remove** button.
8. Click the **Add Shape** button and select **2:1 Torispherical Head**.
9. Likewise, add other shapes using the **Add Shape** button.

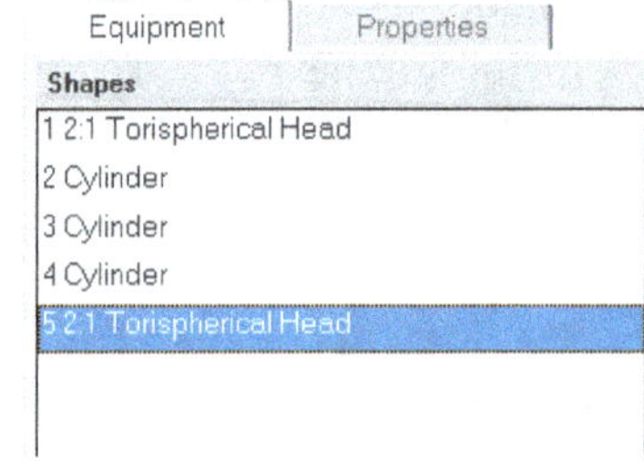

10. Under **Shapes**, click **Torispherical Head** located at the top.
11. Under **Dimensions**, type-in 1'8" in the **D** box. It defines the diameter of the Torispheric head.
12. Under **Shapes**, click the **Cylinder** located at the number 2 position.
13. Under **Dimensions**, type-in 1'8" in the **D** and **H** boxes, respectively.
14. Likewise, change the dimensions of other shapes. The dimensions of all the shapes are given below.

Shapes	D	H
Torispheric Head	1'8"	
Cylinder	1'8"	1'8"
Cylinder	1'8"	14'2"

Cylinder	1′8″	1′8″
Torispheric Head	1′8″	

15. Select the first **Cylinder** from the **Shapes** list.
16. Click the **Add Trim** button and select **Body Flange** from the menu.

17. In the **Dimensions** table, set the **Orientation** to **Mating Flange Set**, and then change the H value to 0.

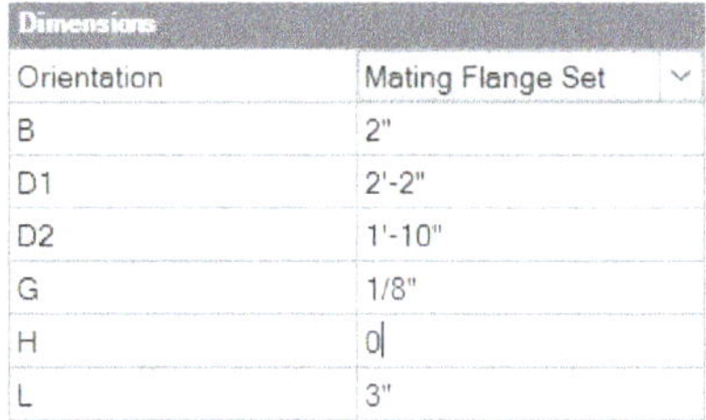

Dimensions	
Orientation	Mating Flange Set
B	2"
D1	2'-2"
D2	1'-10"
G	1/8"
H	0
L	3"

18. Select the **Cylinder** located at the number 4 position in the **Shapes** list.
19. Click the **Add Trim** button and select **Body Flange** from the menu.
20. In the **Dimensions** table, set the **Orientation** to **Mating Flange Set**, and then change the **H** value to 1′8″.
21. Select the **Cylinder** located at the number 3 position in the **Shapes** list.
22. Click the **Add Trim** button and select **Saddle**.
23. In the **Dimensions** table, set the **Orientation** to **Pair**.
24. Change the **L** and **L3** values to 0′8″ and 12′6″, respectively.
25. Click in the **Tag** box under the **General** section.
26. On the **Assign Tag** dialog, click in the **Number** box, and then click the button next to it. Click **Assign**. The program assigns the tag E-001 to the heat exchanger.

27. Under **General**, type-in 3′4″ in the **Elevation** box to define the base point of the equipment at an elevation.
28. Click **Create** on the dialog and position the heat exchanger at the location, as shown.

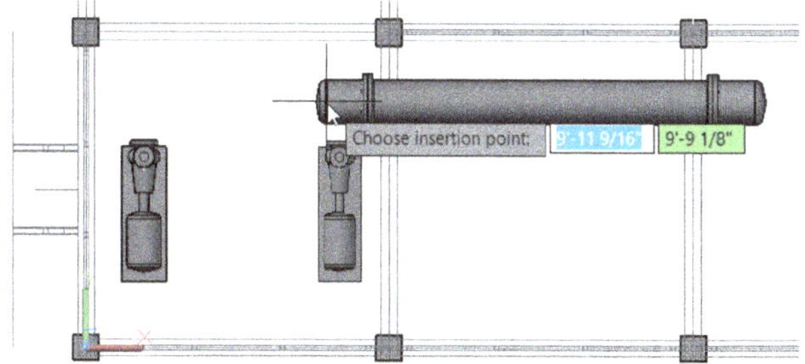

29. Type-in 0 as the rotation angle and press Enter.
30. Change the view orientation to **SW Isometric** and **View Style** to **Realistic**.

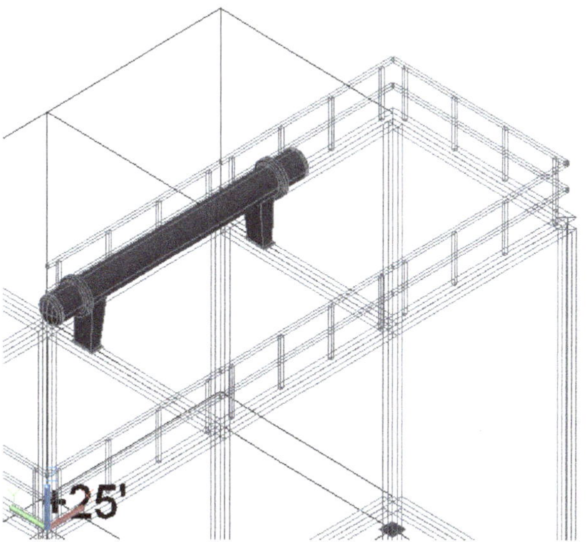

Adding Nozzles

Most of the equipment available in the AutoCAD Plant 3D library has nozzles. Nozzles are used to create pipe connections. However, when you create new equipment using predefined shapes, the nozzles are not added to them. You need to add nozzles manually to the equipment.

1. Click on the heat exchanger, and the nozzle symbol appears. It is called the **Add Nozzle** tool.
2. Click on the **Add Nozzle** tool. The **Add Nozzle** dialog appears.

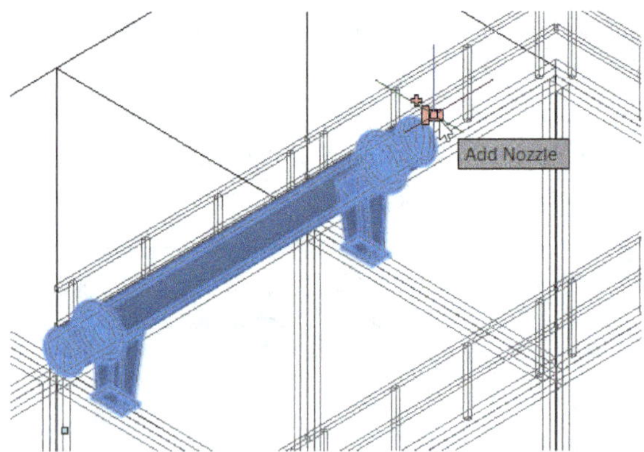

3. On the **Add Nozzle** dialog, click the **Change Type** tab.

On the **Change Type** tab, the top section is used to add a nozzle tag. You can enter the type and number values. The entered data is stored in the project database.

There are four nozzle types available on this dialog: **Straight Nozzle**, **Bent Nozzle**, **Vent Nozzle**, and **Manway**.

4. Type-in **13** in the **Number** box and click **Close**.

5. Select the **Straight Nozzle** type.
6. Set the **Size**, **End Type**, **Unit**, and **Pressure Class** to **4″**, **FL**, **in**, and **300**, respectively.
7. Select the RF nozzle from the list.

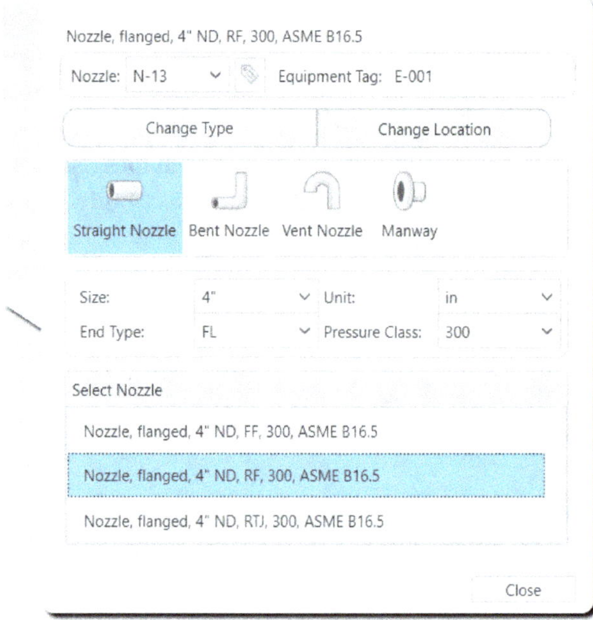

8. Click the **Change Location** tab and select **Nozzle Location > Radial**.
9. Type-in **8″**, **90** and **6″** in the **H**, **A,** and **L** boxes, respectively.
10. Click **Close,** and you notice that the nozzle is added to the Heat exchanger.
11. Likewise, add other nozzles to the heat exchanger. The nozzle tags should match the nozzles in the P&ID.

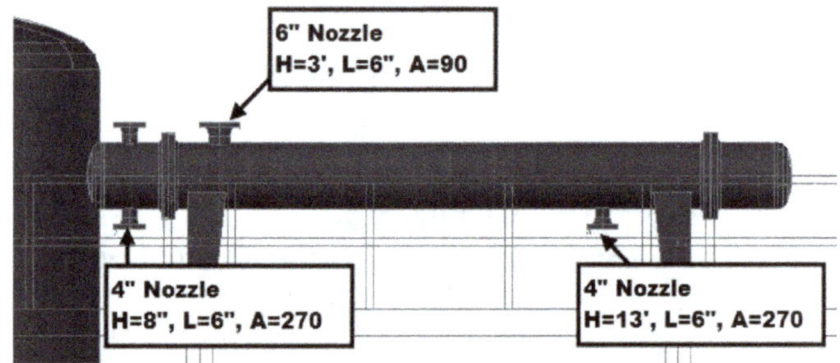

12. On the ribbon, click **Home > Equipment > Modify Equipment** and then select the heat exchanger.
13. On the dialog, click the **Templates** button and select **Save current settings as template**. The **Save Template To** dialog appears, and you will be taken to the **Equipment Templates** folder.
14. Type-in *Custom Heat Exchanger* in the **File name** box, and then click **Save**.
15. Click **OK** to close the **Create Equipment** dialog.

Using the Convert Equipment command

In addition to creating equipment using predefined shapes, you can create 3D models using the AutoCAD commands and convert them into equipment.

1. Create a 3D model using the AutoCAD commands. For example, create a cooler model, as shown.

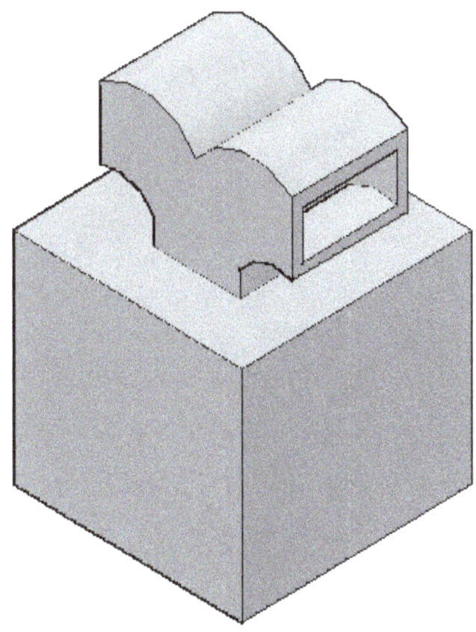

2. On the ribbon, click **Home > Equipment > Convert Equipment** .
3. Select the 3D model and press Enter.
4. On the **Convert to Equipment** dialog, select the equipment type. For this example, just select the **Misc equipment** type.
5. Click **Select**, and then select a point on the 3D model to define the insertion point.
6. On the **Modify Equipment** dialog, enter values in the **Equipment** and **Properties** tabs. You can use the **Templates** button if you want to save this equipment for further use. Click **OK** to close the dialog.

To add nozzles to the equipment, click on it and select the **Add Nozzle** tool displayed on it. Select a point on the equipment to define the center of the nozzle. Move the pointer and click to define the direction of the nozzle. On the **Add Nozzle** dialog, select the nozzle type and size. Click **Close**.

Modifying Nozzles

The nozzles that are added to the equipment may not be of the required size. You can modify the nozzles to change the size and location.

1. Zoom to the lower portion of the vessel.
2. Ctrl+click the nozzle located on the vessel.
3. Click the **Edit Nozzle** tool (pencil symbol).

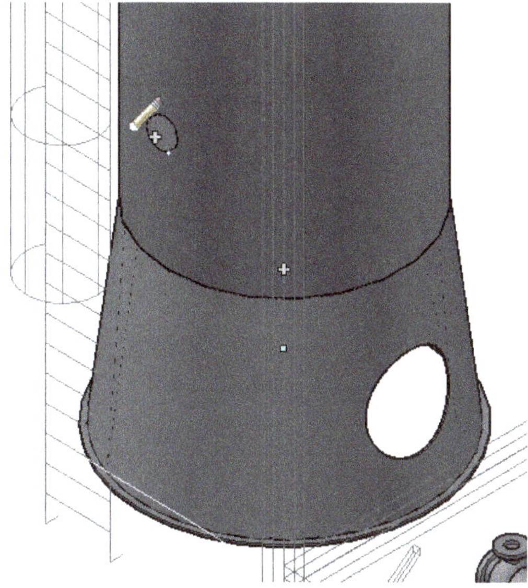

4. On the **Modify Nozzle** dialog, click the **Tag** button to expand the top section.
5. Type-in **4** in the **Number** box. Click **Close** to hide the top portion.
6. Click the **Change Location** tab and type-in 6″ in the **L** box.
7. Type-in 3′9″ in the **H** box.
8. Type-in 90 in the **A** box.
9. Click **Close** on the dialog.

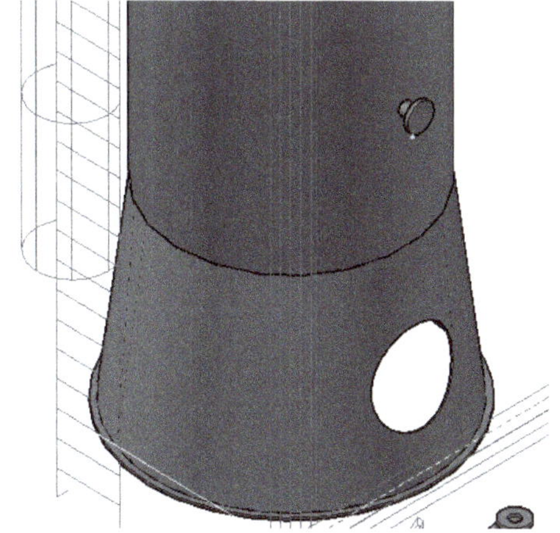

10. Likewise, add the 6″ and 4″ nozzles at 8′4″ and 5′ heights, respectively. The radial angle (A) is 180 degrees. The nozzle tags should be N-1 and N-2.

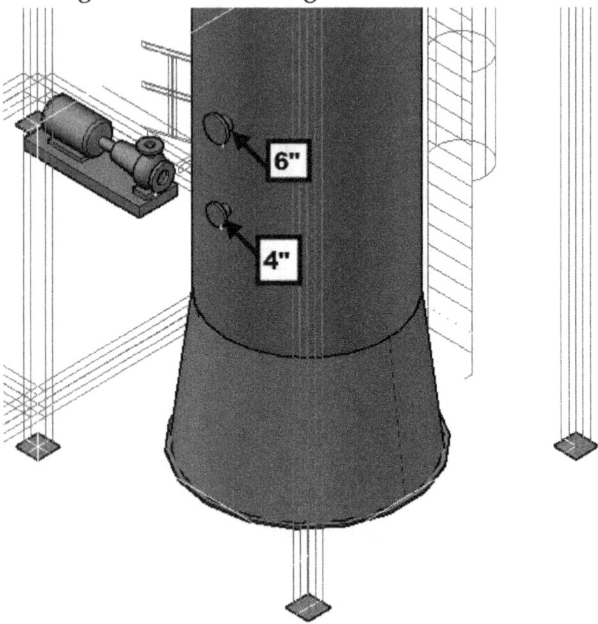

11. Change the nozzle tags of the pumps using the **Modify Nozzle** dialog.

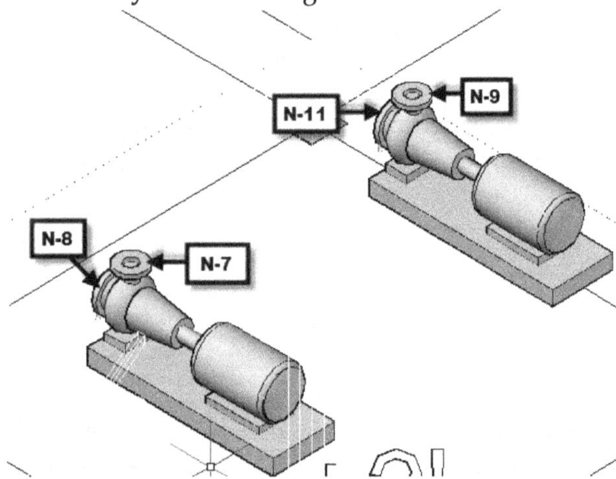

Chapter 5: Creating Pipes

AutoCAD Plant 3D provides various tools and techniques to create piping. In this tutorial, you will learn to create piping using these tools and techniques.

Using the Spec Viewer

To create piping in AutoCAD Plant 3D, you need to have a basic understanding of the piping materials. AutoCAD Plant 3D comes with a database of piping components. The information related to the piping components is stored in the specifications file. You can access different specifications by using the **Spec Viewer** (on the ribbon, click **Home > Part Insertion > Spec Viewer**).

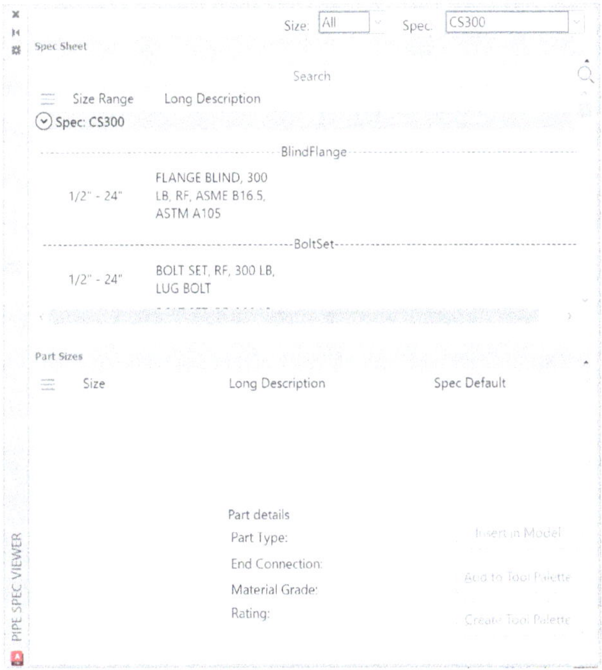

1. On the **Spec Viewer** palette, select the desired spec from the **Spec** drop-down.

You can view the piping components available in the selected spec under the **Spec Sheet** section. There are different categories of components, such

as blind flange, bolt set, cap, tees, and valves, and so on. Each category has different types of components. For example, scroll down to the **Valve** category to notice that there are different valve types (Ball Valve, Butterfly Valve, Check Valve, Gate Valve, Globe Valve, and Plug Valve) available. These valve types are available in different size ranges.

2. Select the butt weld Ball Valve (**Ball Valve, Long Pattern, 300 LB, BW, ASME B16.10, ASTM A216 Gr WPB, Hand Lever**).

The **Part Sizes** section lists the available sizes. These part sizes are based on industry standards. You can select a part size and insert it into the model.

There are three buttons available on the Spec Viewer. The **Insert in Model** button inserts the selected part size into the currently opened AutoCAD Plant 3D file. The **Add to Tool Palette** button adds the selected part size to the Dynamic Tool Palette. The **Create Tool Palette** button creates a new Tool Palette from the selected Spec.

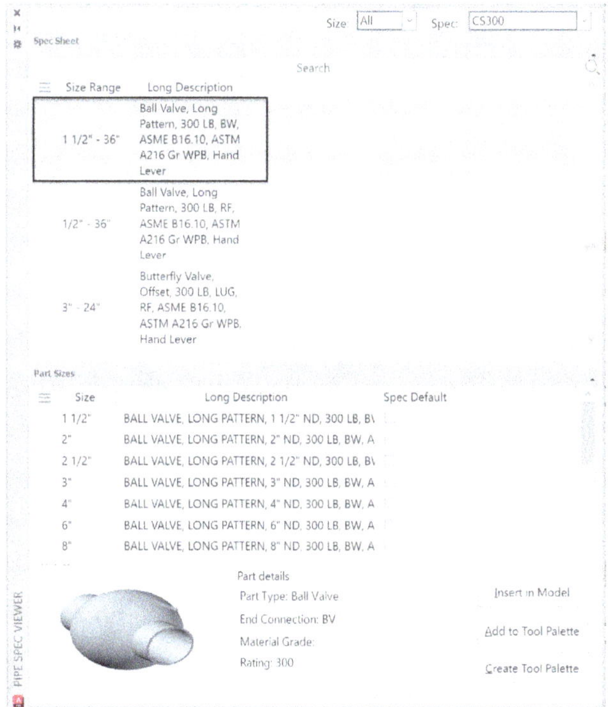

Editing Specs

Piping Specification, typically known as Spec, is one of the most important documents in a Plant 3D project. A piping spec is a list of all the pipe sizes, piping components, and material grades developed as per the fluid to be conveyed through the pipes. Each spec has a list of items based on the temperature and pressure ratings of the fluid. For example, the CS300 pipe spec contains only the component that fits with the Carbon steel 300 rating pipe.

A Catalog is a list of available parts. You can select the parts from the catalog, and then add them to the spec. The final spec is developed after adding necessary parts from the catalog to the spec. AutoCAD Plant 3D provides you with the separate **Spec Editor** application to work with specs and catalogs. You can create, open, and edit specs using this application. Click **Start** > **All apps** > **AutoCAD Plant 3D 2025** > **Spec Editor for AutoCAD Plant 3D 2025** icon to start this application. Next, close the dialog that pops up on the screen.

The **Spec Editor** user interface is divided into two portions: Spec Browser and Catalog Browser. The upper portion is the Spec Browser, whereas the lower portion is the Catalog Browser. The Spec Browser has parts filtered based on their sizes. They are also grouped based on their type. The Catalog Browser has many options to filter the parts available in a catalog.

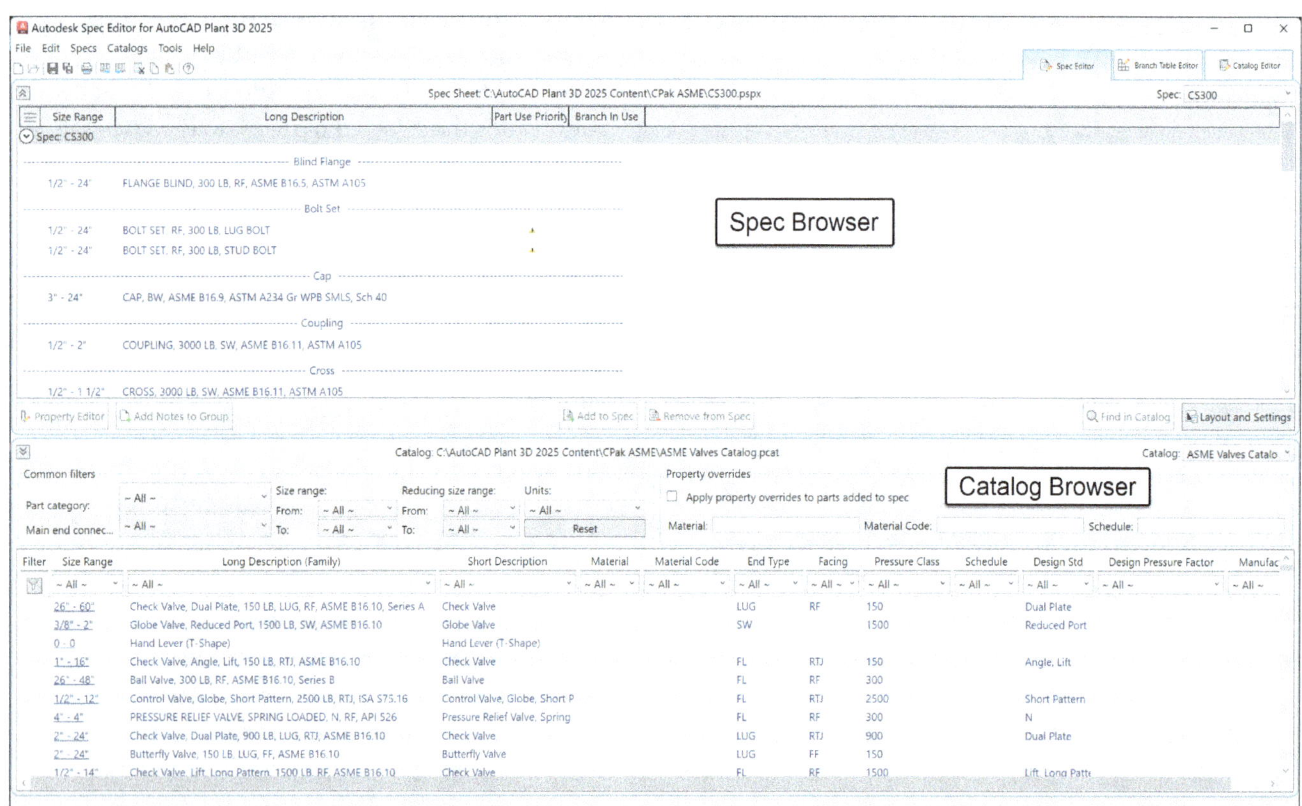

The menu bar located on the top left corner has the **File**, **Edit**, **Specs**, **Catalogs**, **Tools**, and **Help** menus.

The **File** menu has the option to create new specs, open an existing spec or catalog, save, export, and close files. You can also import the specification files from other software's such as AutoPLANT and CADWorx, and then convert it into AutoCAD Plant 3D format. To do this, click **File > Convert** and select an option from the menu.

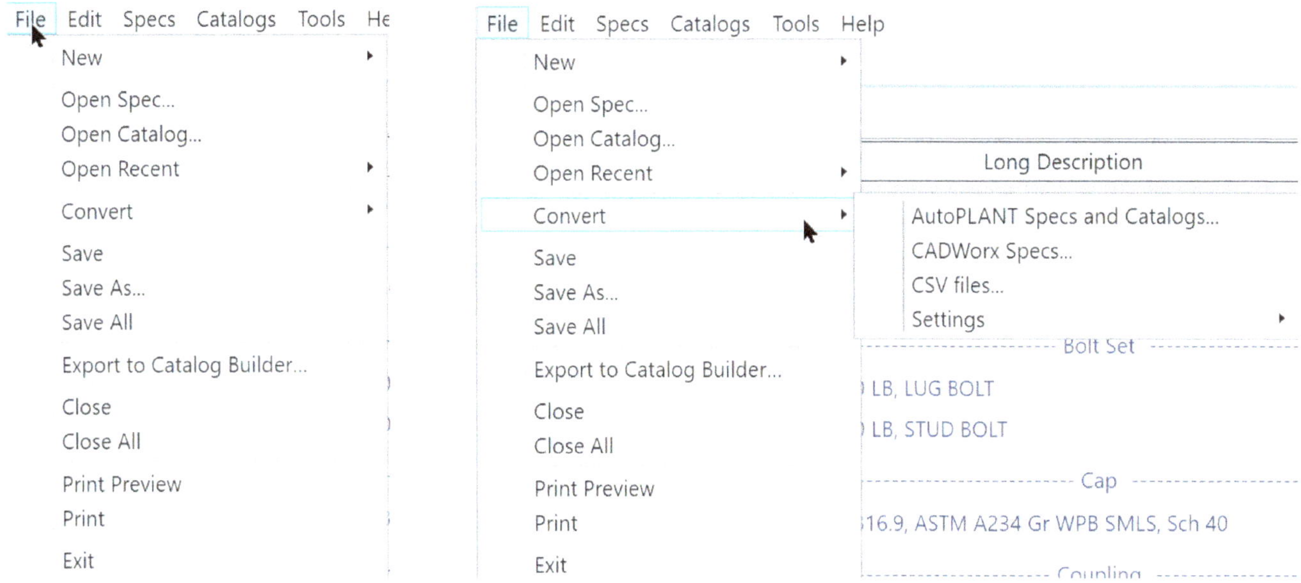

The **Edit** menu can be used to perform tasks such as **Cut**, **Copy**, **Paste**, **Undo**, and **Redo**.

The **Specs** menu has options to perform some important tasks related to specs.

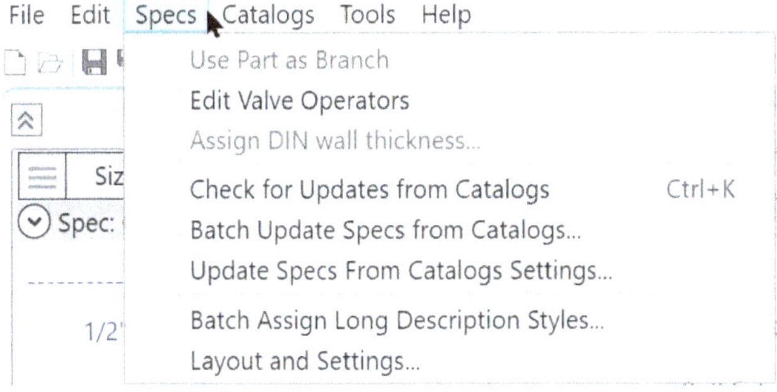

The **Catalogs** menu can be used to modify catalog properties, duplicate components, edit catalog in different units, and so on.

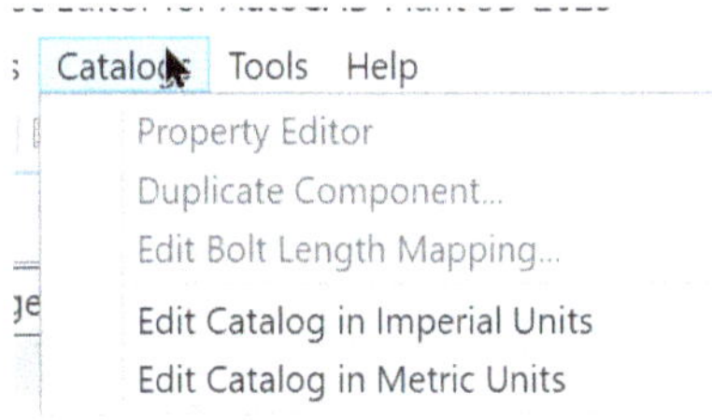

The **Tools** menu has options to launch the catalog builder, migrate specs and catalogs to other applications, and modify the shared content folder.

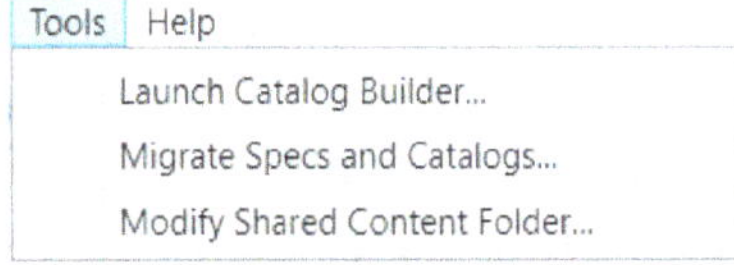

Opening Specs

To open a spec, click File > Open Spec on the Menu bar; the Open dialog pops up and takes you to the location: *C:\AutoCAD Plant 3D 2025 Content\CPak ASME*. Select the required spec (CS300 in this case) and click **Open**. If you have a custom spec located on your computer or network, then browse to the location and open it.

Creating a New Spec

AutoCAD Plant 3D Spec Editor allows you to create a spec using any one of the two options: **Create Spec** and **Create a Spec from Existing**. On the menu bar, click **File > New > Create Spec** to create a completely new spec. On the **Create Spec** dialog, type in the name and description in the **New Spec name** and **Spec Description** boxes, respectively. Next, click on the **Load Catalog** drop-down and select **ASME Pipe and Fittings Catalog** (or) select the **Browse** button, and then select your own catalog. Click the **Create** button to create the new spec. Notice the spec details at the top left of the Spec Browser. You can edit the description by right-clicking on it and selecting **Edit Spec Description**. Note that you cannot rename the spec. You can only save it with a different name (click **File > Save As** on the Menu bar).

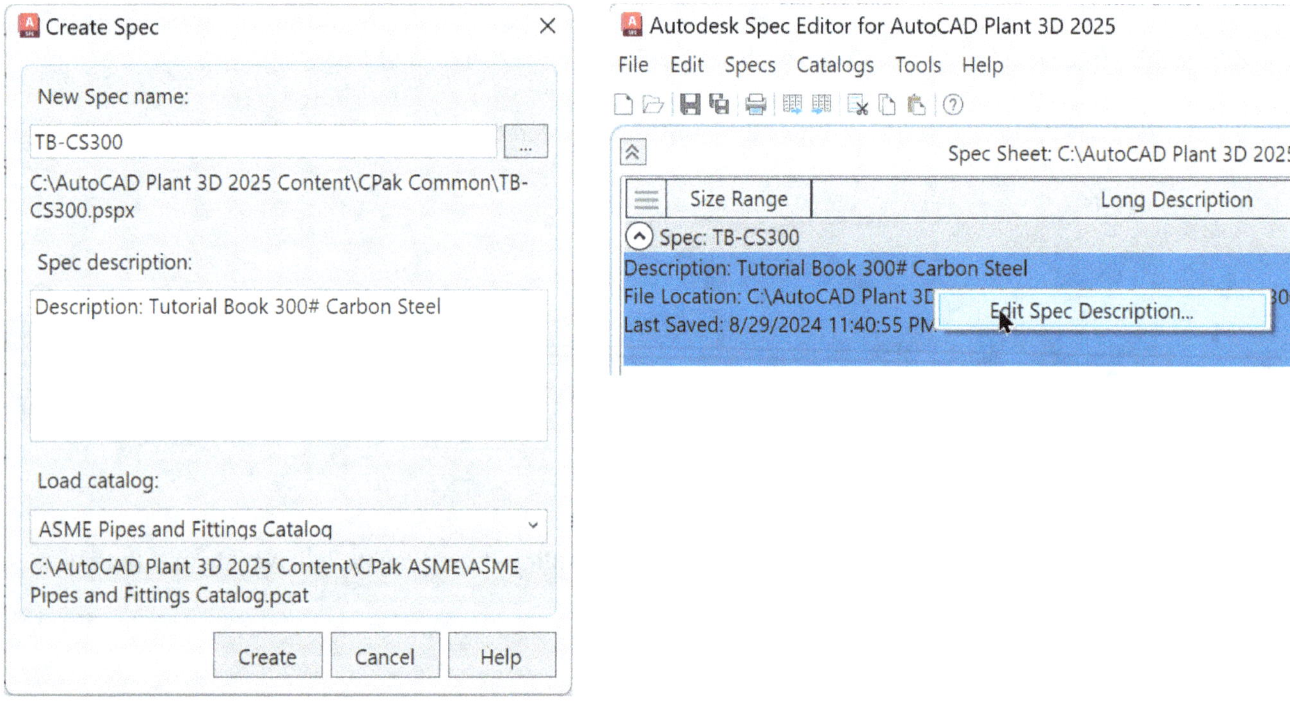

Using the Common Filters in Catalog Browser

The Catalog Browser located at the bottom has a large number of part data displayed in it. It makes it difficult to select the required part from the catalog browser, and then add it to the spec. However, the Catalog Browser has many filters available in the **Common Filters** area. You can start filtering the part data by starting with the Part Category. For example, select the **ASME Pipes and Fittings** option from the **Catalog** drop-down located at the top right corner of the Catalog Browser. Next, select **Fittings** from the **Part Category** drop-down; only fittings are displayed in the Catalog Browser.

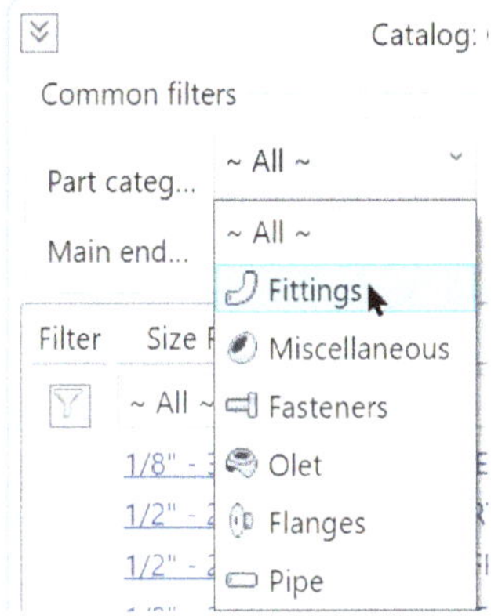

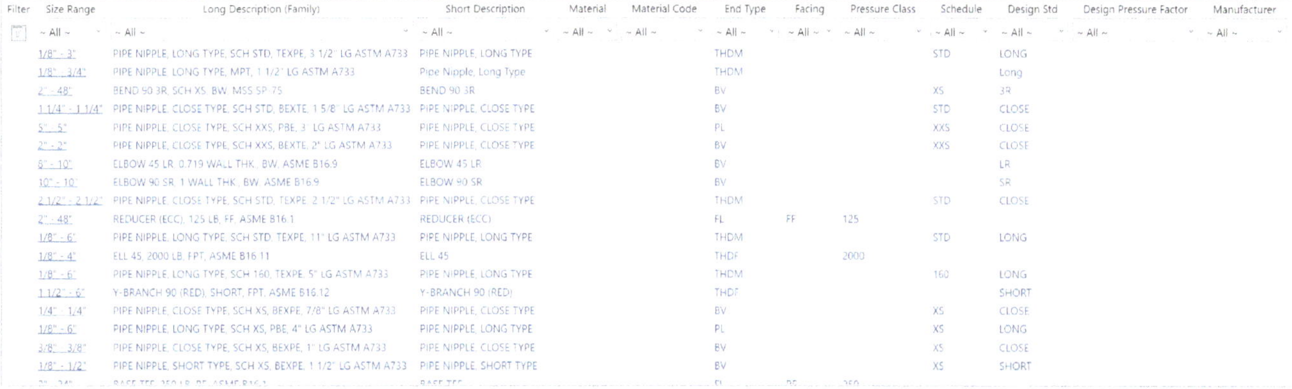

Filter	Size Range	Long Description (Family)	Short Description	Material	Material Code	End Type	Facing	Pressure Class	Schedule	Design Std	Design Pressure Factor	Manufacturer
~ All ~	~ All ~	~ All ~	~ All ~	~ All ~	~ All ~	~ All ~	~ All ~	~ All ~	~ All ~	~ All ~	~ All ~	~ All ~
	1/8" - 3"	PIPE NIPPLE, LONG TYPE, SCH STD, TEXPE, 3 1/2" LG ASTM A733	PIPE NIPPLE, LONG TYPE			THDM			STD	LONG		
	1/8" - 3/4"	PIPE NIPPLE, LONG TYPE, MPT, 1 1/2" LG ASTM A733	Pipe Nipple, Long Type			THDM				Long		
	2" - 48"	BEND 90 3R, SCH XS, BW, MSS SP-75	BEND 90 3R			BV			XS	3R		
	1 1/4" - 1 1/4"	PIPE NIPPLE, CLOSE TYPE, SCH STD, BEXTE, 1 5/8" LG ASTM A733	PIPE NIPPLE, CLOSE TYPE			BV			STD	CLOSE		
	5" - 5"	PIPE NIPPLE, CLOSE TYPE, SCH XXS, PBE, 3" LG ASTM A733	PIPE NIPPLE, CLOSE TYPE			PL			XXS	CLOSE		
	2" - 2"	PIPE NIPPLE, CLOSE TYPE, SCH XXS, BEXTE, 2" LG ASTM A733	PIPE NIPPLE, CLOSE TYPE			BV			XXS	CLOSE		
	6" - 10"	ELBOW 45 LR, 0.719 WALL THK, BW, ASME B16.9	ELBOW 45 LR			BV				LR		
	10" - 10"	ELBOW 90 SR, 1 WALL THK, BW, ASME B16.9	ELBOW 90 SR			BV				SR		
	2 1/2" - 2 1/2"	PIPE NIPPLE, CLOSE TYPE, SCH STD, TEXPE, 2 1/2" LG ASTM A733	PIPE NIPPLE, CLOSE TYPE			THDM			STD	CLOSE		
	2" - 48"	REDUCER (ECC), 125 LB, FF, ASME B16.1	REDUCER (ECC)			FL	FF	125				
	1/8" - 6"	PIPE NIPPLE, LONG TYPE, SCH STD, TEXPE, 11" LG ASTM A733	PIPE NIPPLE, LONG TYPE			THDM			STD	LONG		
	1/8" - 4"	ELL 45, 2000 LB, FPT, ASME B16.11	ELL 45			THDF		2000				
	1/8" - 6"	PIPE NIPPLE, LONG TYPE, SCH 160, TEXPE, 5" LG ASTM A733	PIPE NIPPLE, LONG TYPE			THDM			160	LONG		
	1 1/2" - 6"	Y-BRANCH 90 (RED), SHORT, FPT, ASME B16.12	Y-BRANCH 90 (RED)			THDF				SHORT		
	1/4" - 1/4"	PIPE NIPPLE, CLOSE TYPE, SCH XS, BEXPE, 7/8" LG ASTM A733	PIPE NIPPLE, CLOSE TYPE			BV			XS	CLOSE		
	1/8" - 6"	PIPE NIPPLE, LONG TYPE, SCH XS, PBE, 4" LG ASTM A733	PIPE NIPPLE, LONG TYPE			PL			XS	LONG		
	3/8" - 3/8"	PIPE NIPPLE, CLOSE TYPE, SCH XS, BEXPE, 1" LG ASTM A733	PIPE NIPPLE, CLOSE TYPE			BV			XS	CLOSE		
	1/8" - 1/2"	PIPE NIPPLE, SHORT TYPE, SCH XS, BEXPE, 1 1/2" LG ASTM A733	PIPE NIPPLE, SHORT TYPE			BV			XS	SHORT		

Next, you can filter the data by selecting an end connection from the **Main end connection** drop-down. For example, select **BV**(Beveled) from the **Main end connection** drop-down; all the fittings with beveled end connection type are displayed.

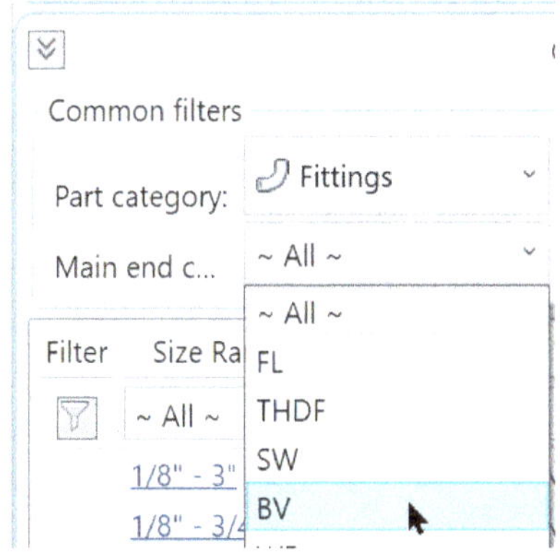

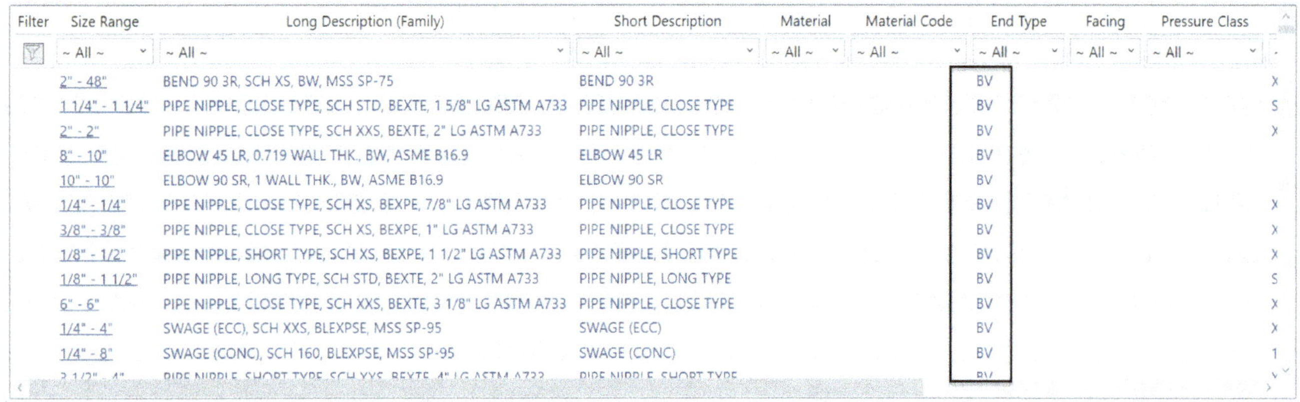

Filter the **Size range** by selecting the sizes from the **From** and **To** drop-downs located under **Size range**. For example, select 1 and 12 from the **From** and **To** drop-down, respectively; the parts within the size range of 1 and 12 are displayed.

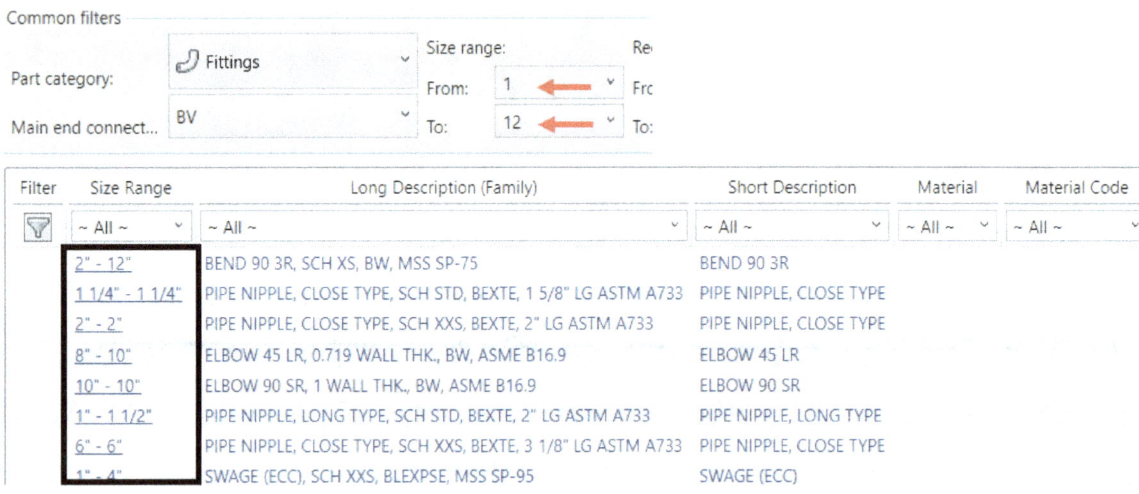

Notice that there are more filters available within the Catalog Browser. For example, you can filter the parts based on their **Short Description**. Select TEE or type 'tee' in the **Short Description** filter; only tees are displayed in the Catalog Browser.

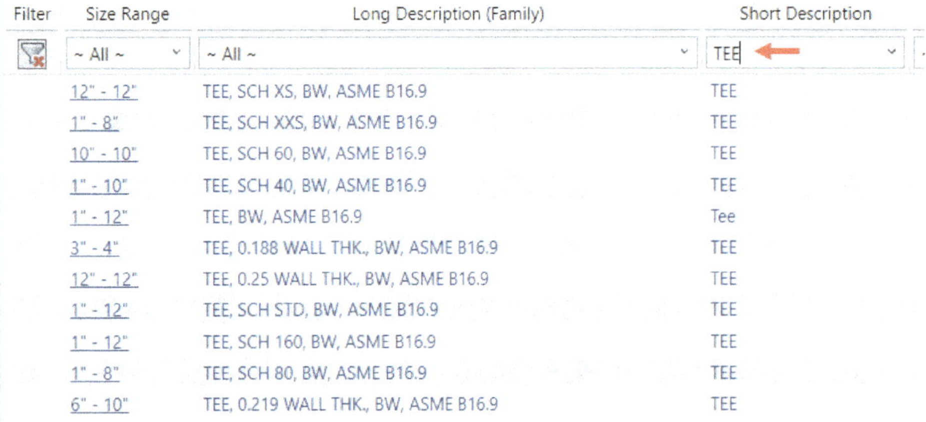

Adding Parts to the Spec

After filtering parts in the Catalog Browser, select a part and click the **Add to Spec** button located above the catalog browser. Use the **Remove from Spec** button, if you want to remove a part from the spec.

Editing Parts

The **Property Editor** button available at the bottom left corner of the spec editor allows you to edit the parts available in a spec. For example, select PIPE, SEAMLESS, PE,ASME B36.10,ASTM A106 Gr WPB from the Pipe section. Next, click the **Property Editor** button; the **Spec Property Editor** dialog pops up on the screen.

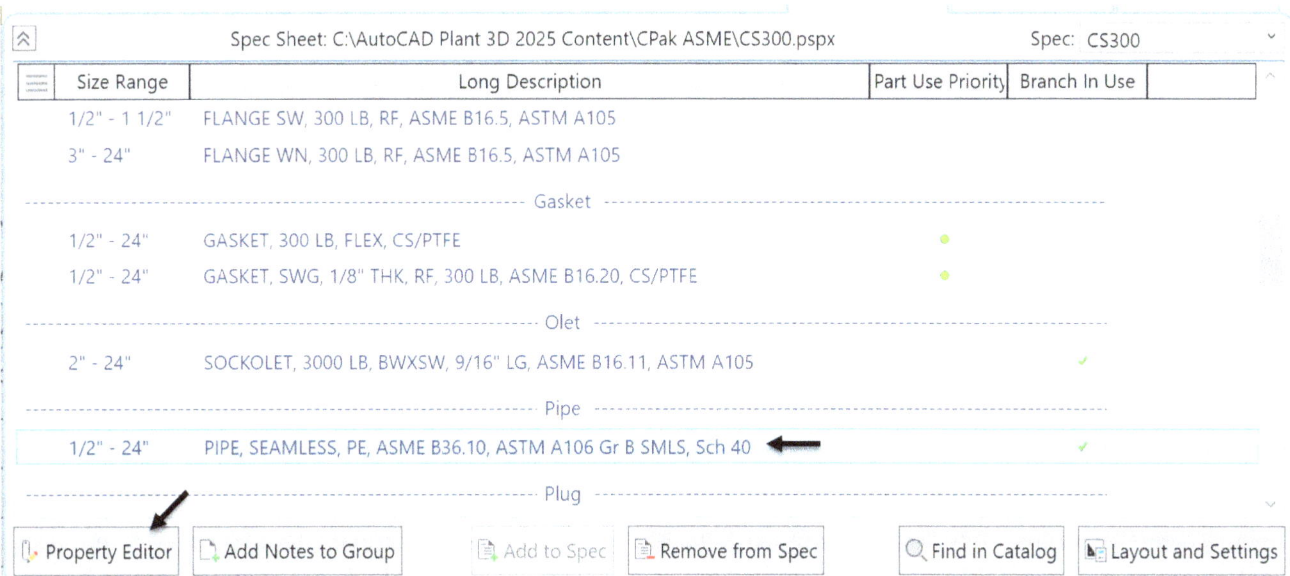

On the **Property Editor** dialog, you can remove the part sizes from the spec by checking the **Remove From Spec** options available next to them. Next, click **Apply** to remove the parts. On the dialog, select **Display** drop-down > **Hide parts marked 'Remove From Spec'** option to hide the removed parts from the parts list.

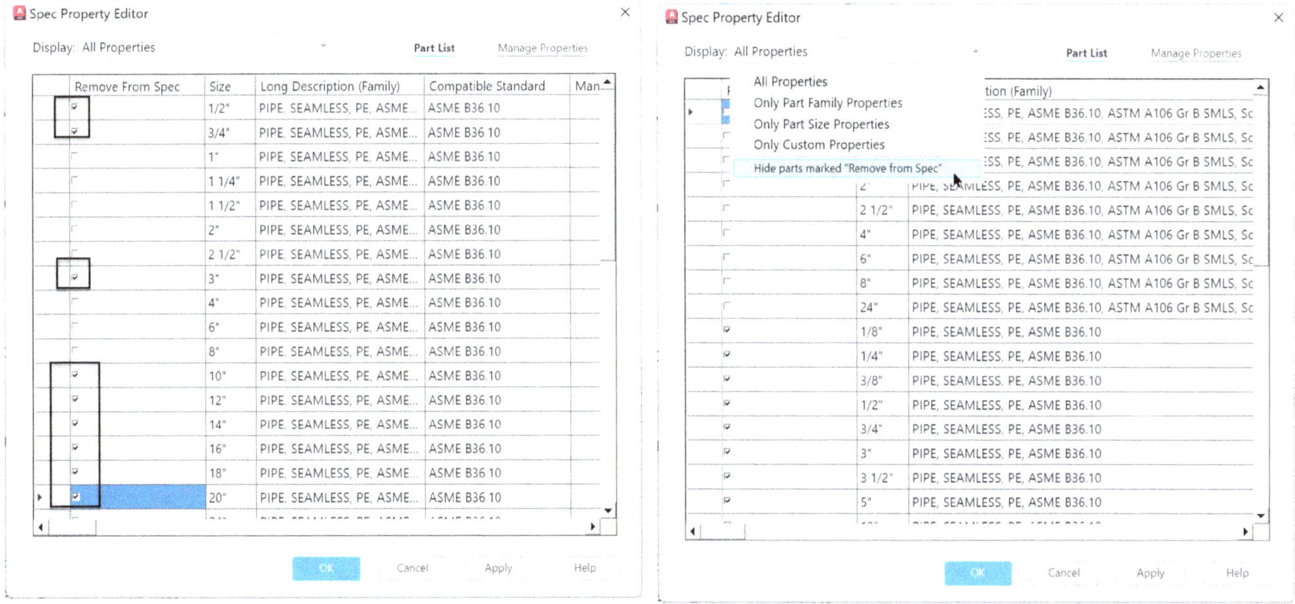

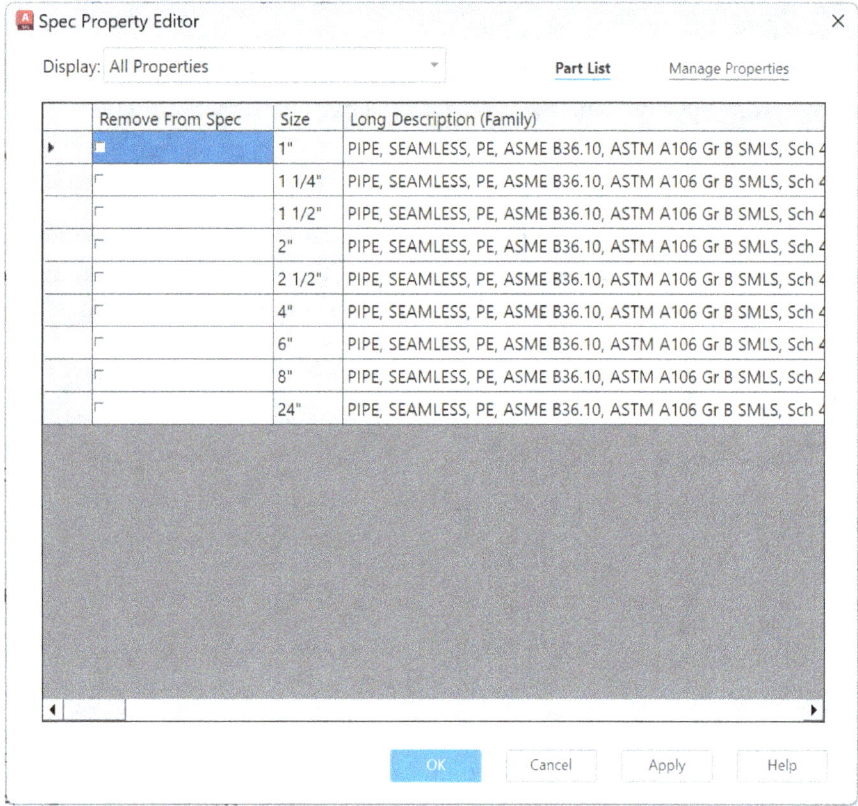

You can also add data in the **Manufacturer**, **Material**, **Material Code** columns, and so on. In addition to that, you can also create a custom property. To do this, click the **Manage Properties** tab on the **Spec Property Editor** dialog. Next, type-in a value in the **Display name** box and select **Field type**. Specify the **Field Size** value and click the **Add** button. Click **Apply** to add the property. Next, click the **Part List** tab and notice that the property is added to the table. Now, you can enter data in the newly added property column and click **OK**.

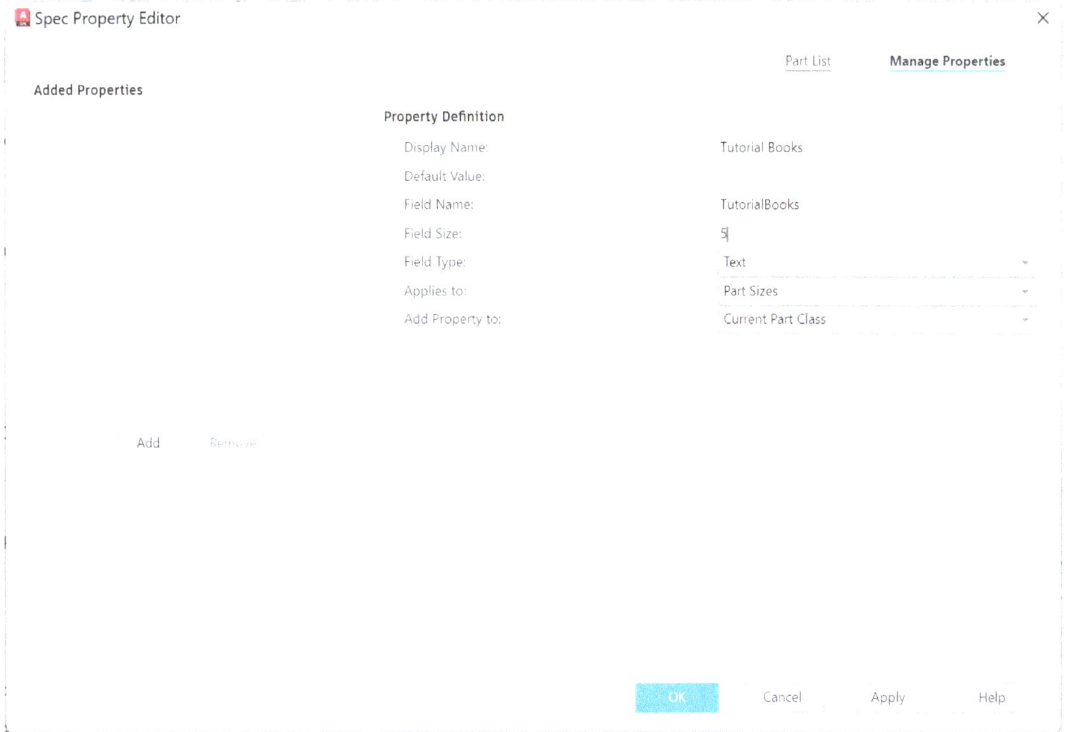

Likewise, you can edit various parts available in the spec.

Property overrides

The **Property overrides** section in the Catalog Browser allows you to add Material, Material Code, and Schedule to the parts at a time. It can be done while adding parts to the spec editor from the Catalog Browser. For example, filter the Catalog Browser and select the PIPE, SEAMLESS, 10, PE, ASTM A106 part.

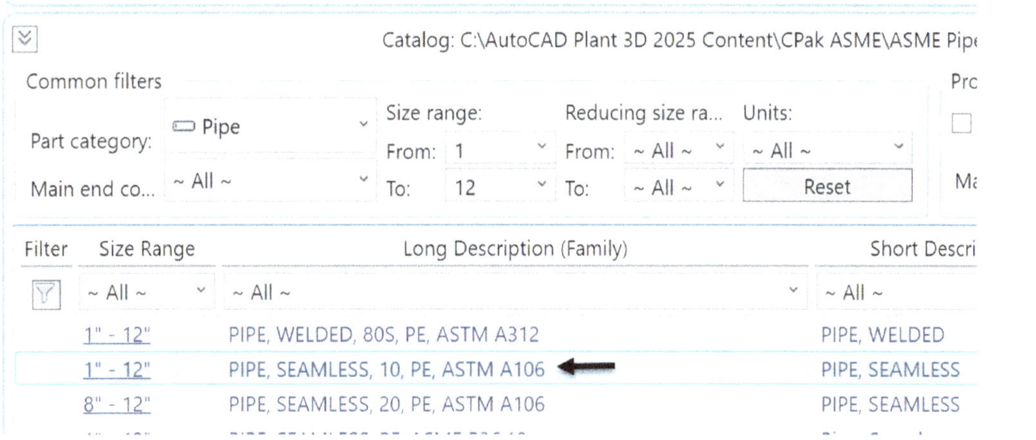

Check the **Apply overrides to parts added to spec** option in the **Property Overrides** section. Next, enter the data in the Material, Material Code, and Schedule boxes, and then click the **Add to Spec** button; the part is added to the spec.

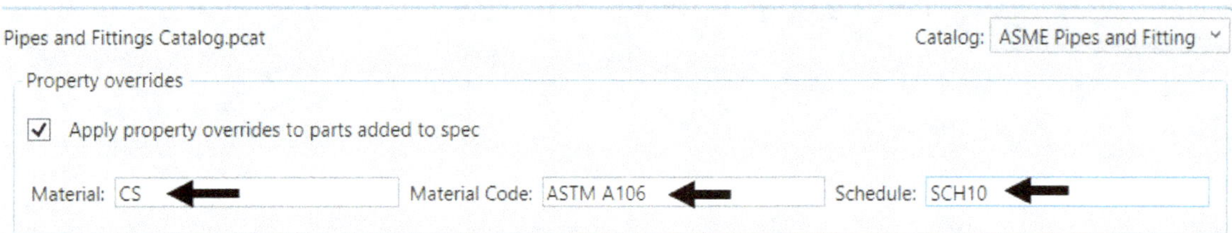

Select the newly added part from the spec editor and click the **Property Editor** button. On the **Spec Property Editor** dialog, notice that the properties in the **Property overrides** section is added to the parts.

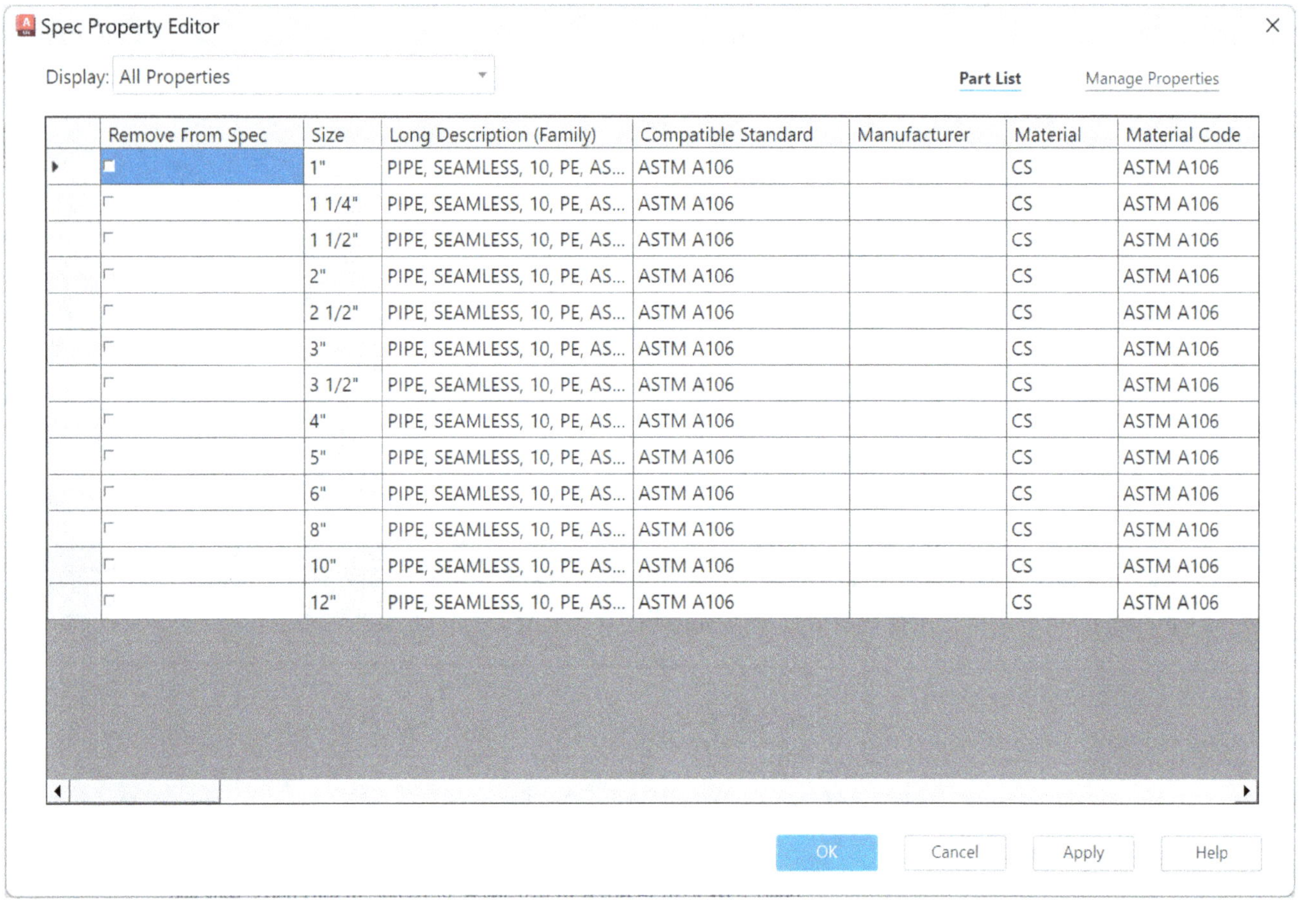

Remove From Spec	Size	Long Description (Family)	Compatible Standard	Manufacturer	Material	Material Code
	1"	PIPE, SEAMLESS, 10, PE, AS...	ASTM A106		CS	ASTM A106
	1 1/4"	PIPE, SEAMLESS, 10, PE, AS...	ASTM A106		CS	ASTM A106
	1 1/2"	PIPE, SEAMLESS, 10, PE, AS...	ASTM A106		CS	ASTM A106
	2"	PIPE, SEAMLESS, 10, PE, AS...	ASTM A106		CS	ASTM A106
	2 1/2"	PIPE, SEAMLESS, 10, PE, AS...	ASTM A106		CS	ASTM A106
	3"	PIPE, SEAMLESS, 10, PE, AS...	ASTM A106		CS	ASTM A106
	3 1/2"	PIPE, SEAMLESS, 10, PE, AS...	ASTM A106		CS	ASTM A106
	4"	PIPE, SEAMLESS, 10, PE, AS...	ASTM A106		CS	ASTM A106
	5"	PIPE, SEAMLESS, 10, PE, AS...	ASTM A106		CS	ASTM A106
	6"	PIPE, SEAMLESS, 10, PE, AS...	ASTM A106		CS	ASTM A106
	8"	PIPE, SEAMLESS, 10, PE, AS...	ASTM A106		CS	ASTM A106
	10"	PIPE, SEAMLESS, 10, PE, AS...	ASTM A106		CS	ASTM A106
	12"	PIPE, SEAMLESS, 10, PE, AS...	ASTM A106		CS	ASTM A106

Part Use Priority

In the Spec file, there are many piping components available of the same type and sizes. For example, there are two types of Bolt sets under the Bolt Set category. In this case, the program shows an error asking you to specify the part to be used first. You need to define the **Part Use Priority** to solve this error. For example, scroll down to the **Valve** category and click on the error ⚠ symbol in the **Part Use Priority** section of the Check Valve.

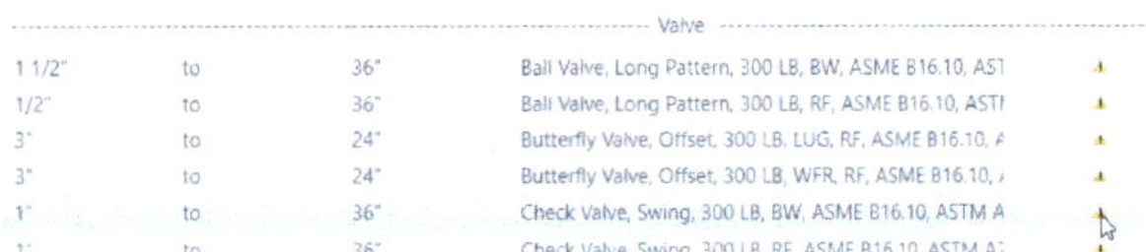

On the **Part Use Priority** dialog, click 4" from the **Size Conflicts** section. Under the **Spec Part Use Priority** Section, click Gate Valve, Solid Wedge, 300 LB. Next, keep clicking the **Up arrow** button to move the gate valve to top.

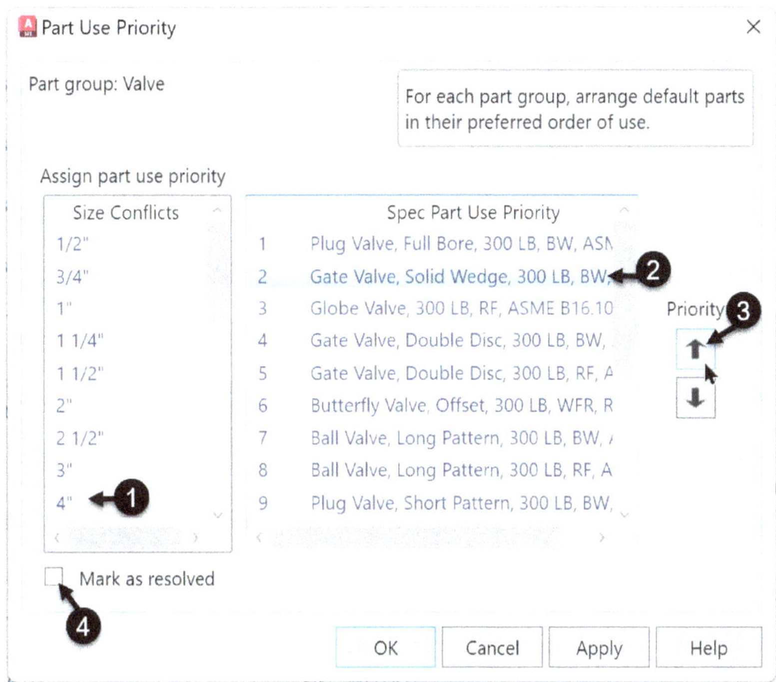

Likewise, set the **Part Use Priority** of the 6″ valve to Gate Valve, Solid Wedge. Check the **Mark as resolved** option and click **OK**. The error symbols still appear even after you have resolved the part use priority for 4″ and 6″ only.

Editing Specs in a Spreadsheet

AutoCAD Plant 3D Spec Editor allows you to edit the spec file in a spreadsheet. To do this, click the **Export to Excel** icon located below the menu bar. On the **Export Data** dialog, select an option from the **Select export settings** drop-down (**Spec sheet and branch display** or **Full spec data export**). The **Spec sheet and branch display** option exports the spec sheet and branch table only. In contrast, the **Full spec data export** option exports the complete spec file, including the part families. Next, click the **Browse** button and specify the location of the excel file. Type in a value in the **File name** box and click the **Save** button. Click **OK** to export the spec file.

Open the exported spreadsheet and add data in the columns. Note that you cannot add or remove columns and rows to the spreadsheet. Next, save and close the spreadsheet.

Click the **Import Excel file** icon located below the menu bar and select the spreadsheet file, and click **Open**; the **Resolve Excel Import Changes** dialog appears. On this dialog, expand the Spec Parts node in the tree located on the left side; the part families that are modified in the spreadsheet are highlighted in yellow color. Expand the part families and notice that the columns in which the new information is added are highlighted in yellow. Click the **Accept All** icon to accept all the changes, and then click **OK** to close the dialog.

Tutorial 1 (Using P&ID Line Lists to create Piping)

AutoCAD Plant 3D allows you to add pipes to a 3D model using different methods. You can just add pipes to a model or use the P&ID Line list. The pipes created using P&ID Line Lists are linked to the P&ID automatically. The P&ID Line list shows all the schematic lines that are created in the project P&ID. Follow the steps given below to create pipes using the P&ID Line List.

1. On the status bar, click the down arrow next to the **Object Snap** icon and make sure that only the **Node** option is selected.

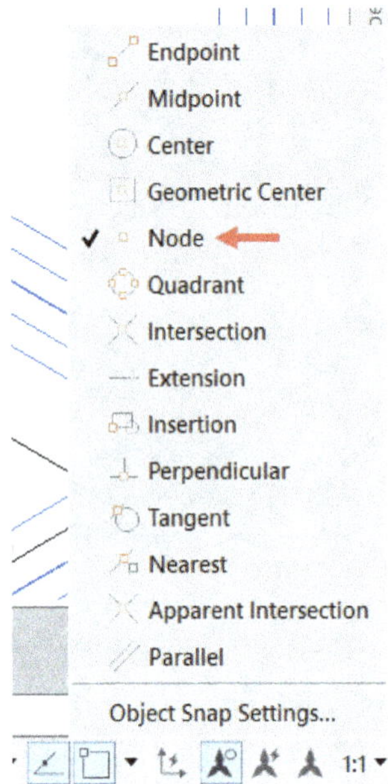

2. On the ribbon, click **Home > Part Insertion > P&ID Line List**.

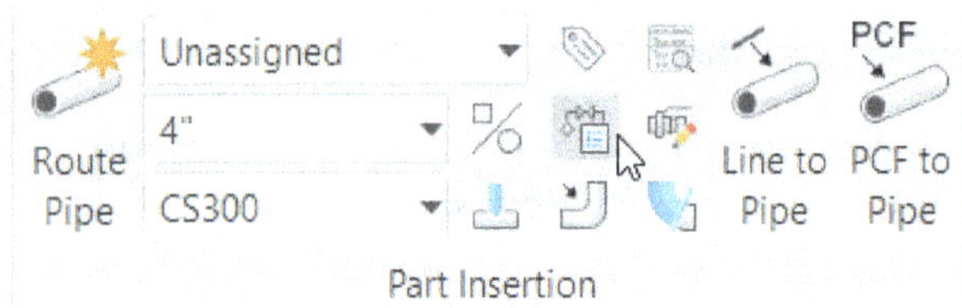

The **P&ID LINE LIST** palette appears showing the different line groups.

3. On the **P&ID LINE LIST** palette, select **Tutorial 1** from the drop-down located at the top.
4. Expand 002 line and select **4"-CS300-P-002**.

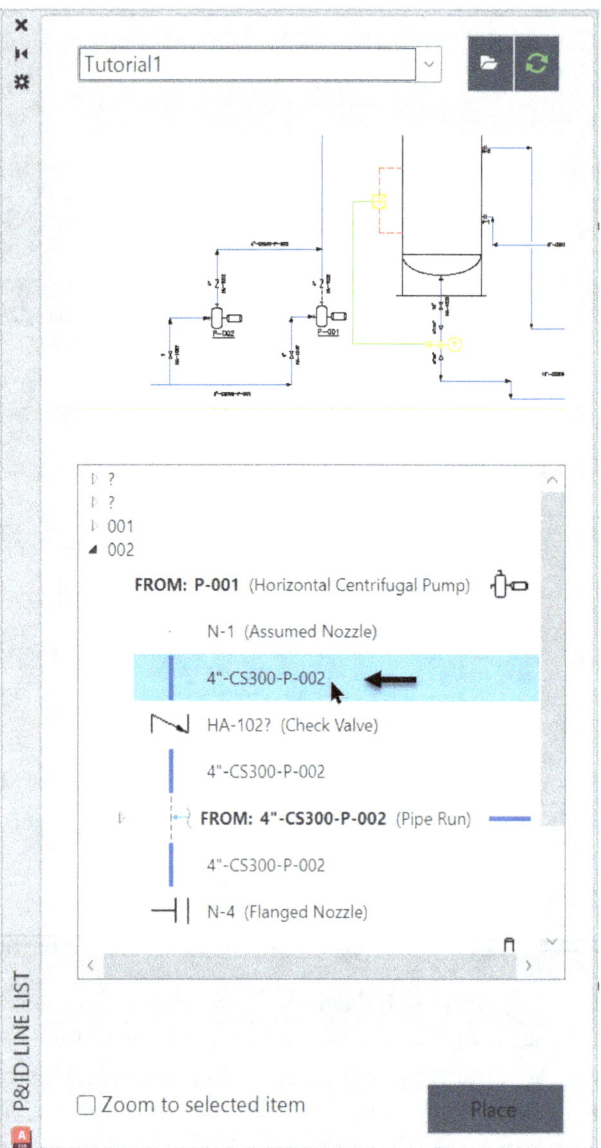

5. Click the **Place** button.
6. Place the pointer on the discharge nozzle of the left pump.
7. Click when the when a green circle is displayed on the nozzle and the pump is highlighted.

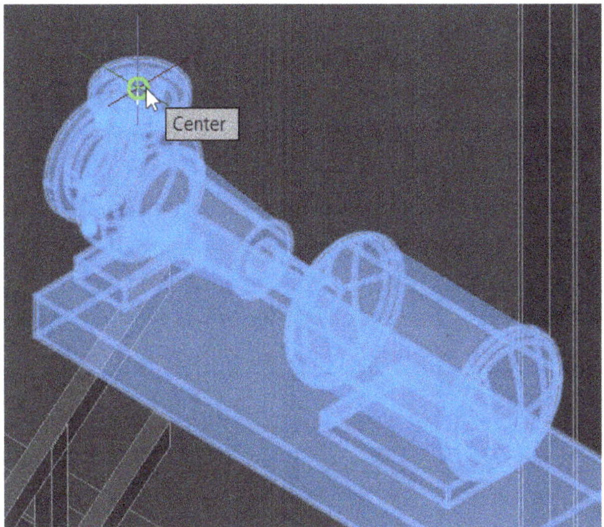

8. Move the pointer up.
9. Place the pointer on the nozzle attached to the vessel.
10. Select the node of the nozzle attached to the vessel.

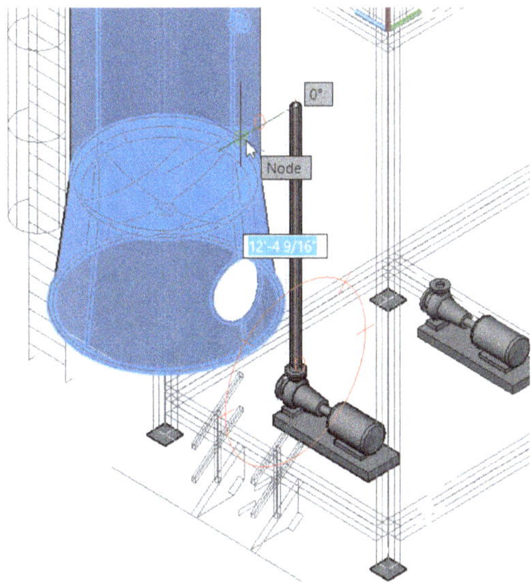

11. Click **Next** in the command line until the solution shown in the figure is displayed.

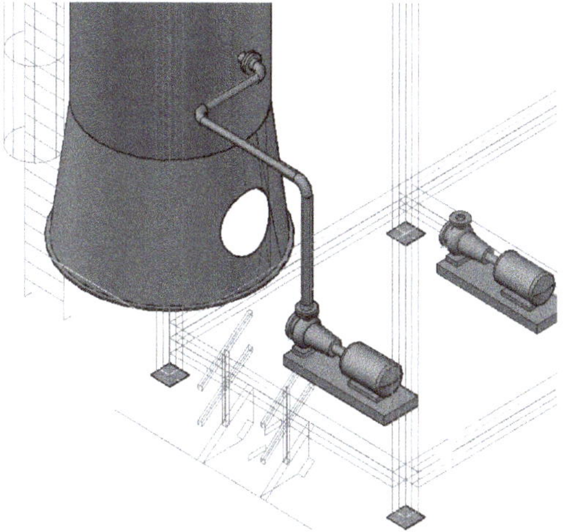

12. Click **Accept** in the command line to accept the solution.
13. Place the pointer on the pipe to view the tag information of the pipe. Now, you cannot assign a tag to the pipe as it is linked to the P&ID schematic line. Any change in the P&ID tag information is reflected in the pipe automatically.

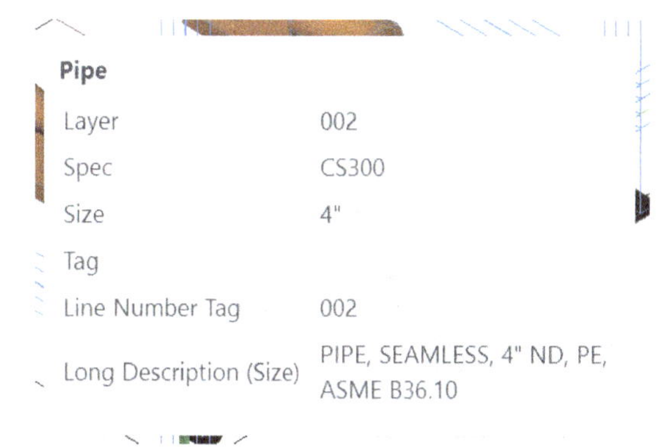

14. On the Status bar, click the down arrow next to the **Object Snap** icon and select the **Nearest** option.
15. On the **P&ID Line List** palette, expand the **4"-CS300-P-002** and select **Check Valve HA-101**.
16. Click **Place** and move the pointer on the horizontal pipe. The check valve is aligned to the pipe.

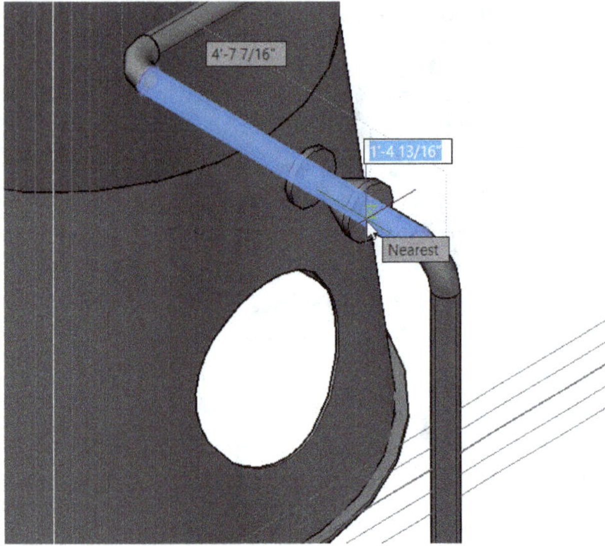

17. Select the endpoint of the pipe to place a check valve.

18. Press **Enter** to use the default rotation angle.

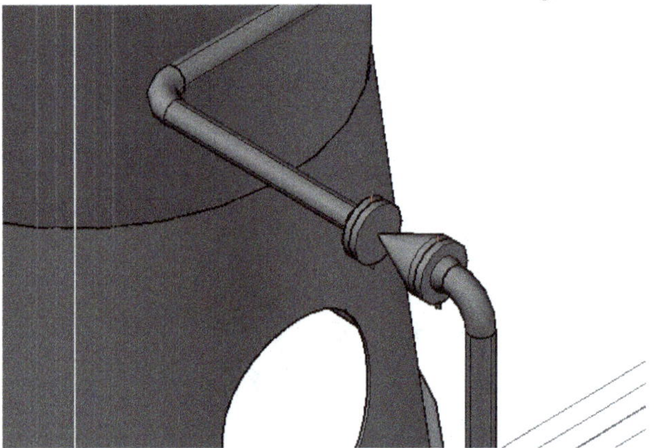

Tutorial 2 (Using the Routing tools to create Pipes)

On the **Part Insertion** panel, there are some routing tools (**Route Pipe**, **Route New Line**, **Line to Pipe**, and PCF to Pipe) to create pipes.

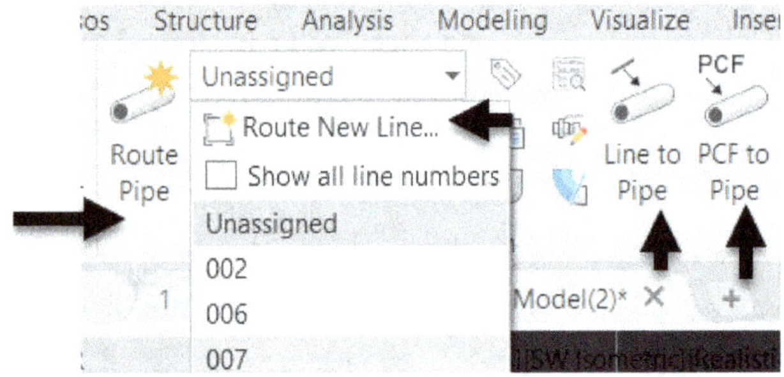

The **Route New Line** tool helps you to create a pipe by adding a new line number to it. This tool can be

useful to create a 3D piping model before creating the P&ID. This tool is available in the **Line Number Selector** drop-down. On this drop-down, the **Show all line numbers** option displays all the available line numbers in the project.

The **Route Pipe** tool creates a new pipe without assigning any tag to it. If you want to create a pipe using a P&ID line number, then select the line from the **Line Number Selector** drop-down and route the pipe.

The **Line to Pipe** tool converts a line or polyline into a pipe.

The **PCF to Pipe** tool creates piping using the **Piping Component File**.

Now, you create pipes using a P&ID Line number.

1. Change the view to NE Isometric.

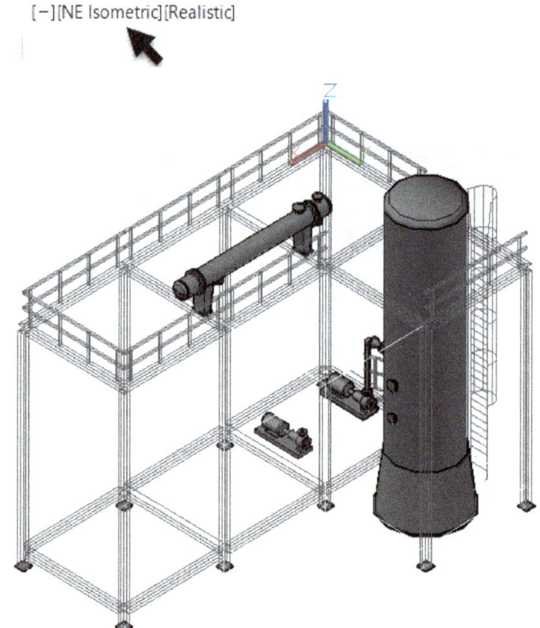

2. On the **Part Insertion** panel, click **Line Number Selector > Show all line numbers**.

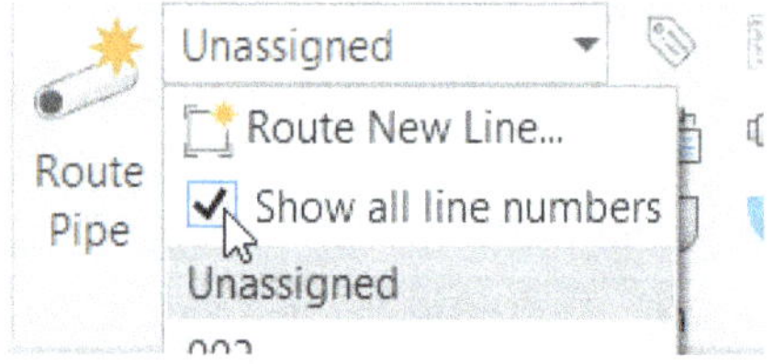

3. Select **006** from the **Line Number Selector** drop-down.
4. Select **6″** from the **Pipe Size Selector** drop-down.
5. Select **CS300** from the **Spec Selector** drop-down to define the pipe spec.

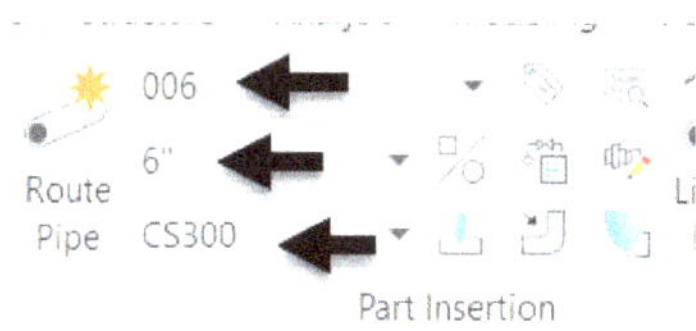

6. Click the **Route Pipe** icon on the **Part Insertion** panel.
7. Place pointer on the **6″** nozzle attached to the heat exchanger.
8. Click when the node of the nozzle and the heat exchanger are highlighted.

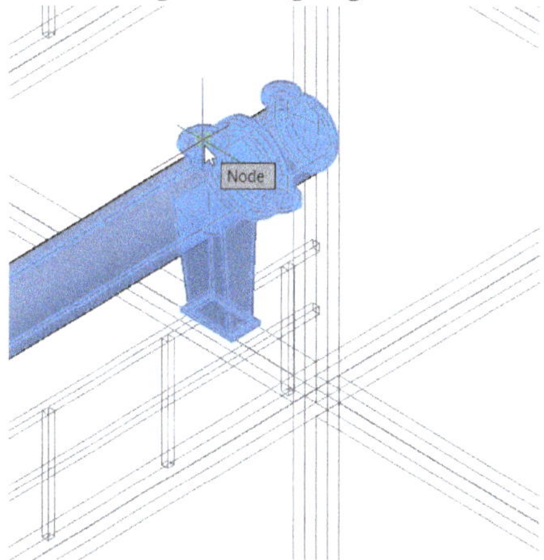

9. Move the pointer along the X-axis and type-in 2′. Press Enter.

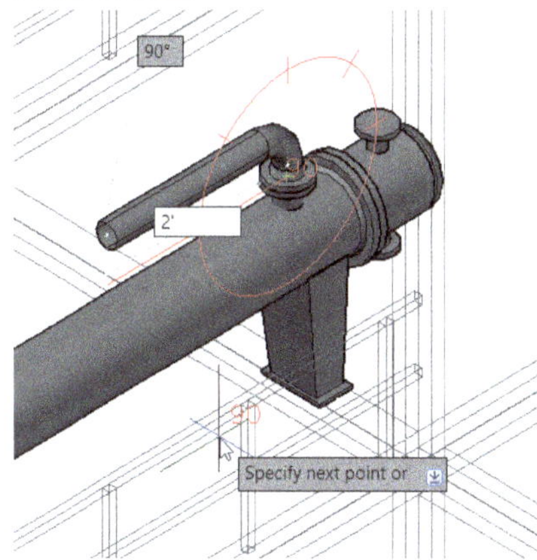

10. Click **Plane** in the command line until the pipe is oriented along the Y-axis.

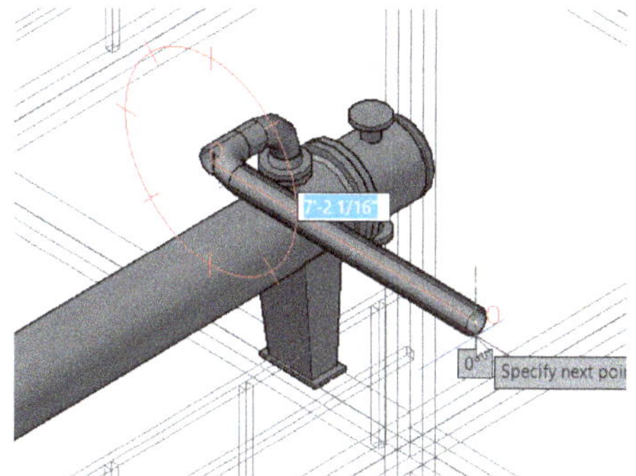

11. Type 4′ and press Enter.
12. Zoom to the vertical vessel and place the pointer on the 6″ nozzle attached to it.
13. Click when the node of the nozzle and the vertical vessel are highlighted.

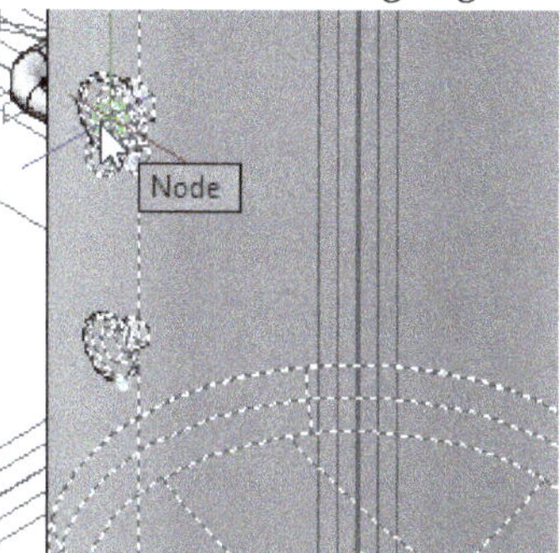

14. Click **Next** in the command line until the solution appears, as shown.

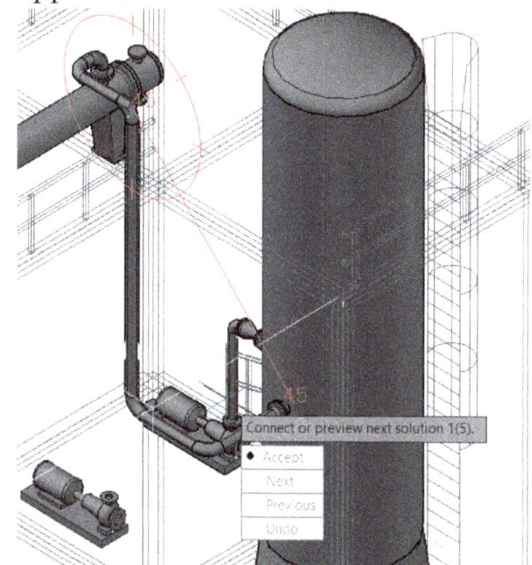

15. Click **Accept** to create the pipes.

A pipe connection is created between the selected nozzles. Place the pointer on the pipe connection, and you notice that the tag information of the 006 P&ID schematic line is assigned to it.

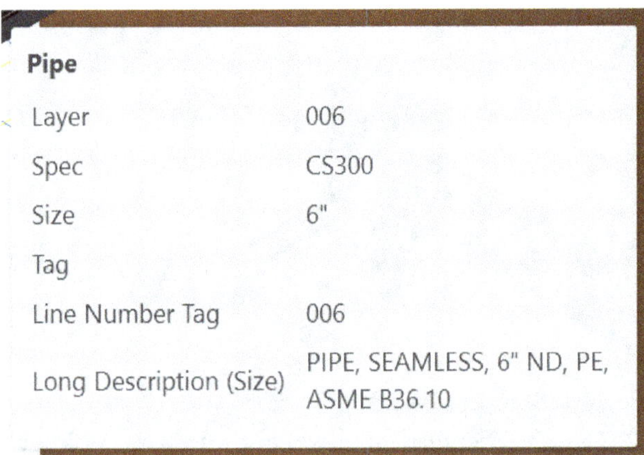

16. On the **Part Insertion** panel, click **Line Number selector > Unassigned**.
17. Change the view orientation to **SW Isometric**.

18. Click on the left pump to highlight it.
19. Zoom to the pump and select the + mark of the 6" nozzle, as shown.

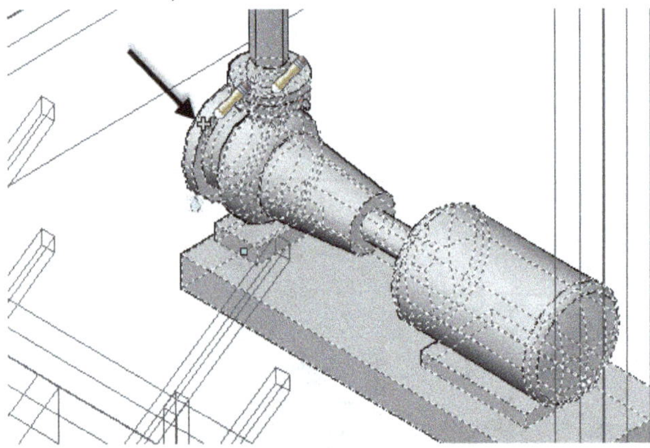

20. Move the pointer rightward and place the pointer on the 6" nozzle of the right pump. Select the **Plane** option from the command line if the Compass is oriented vertically.
21. Click when the node of the nozzle and the pump are highlighted.

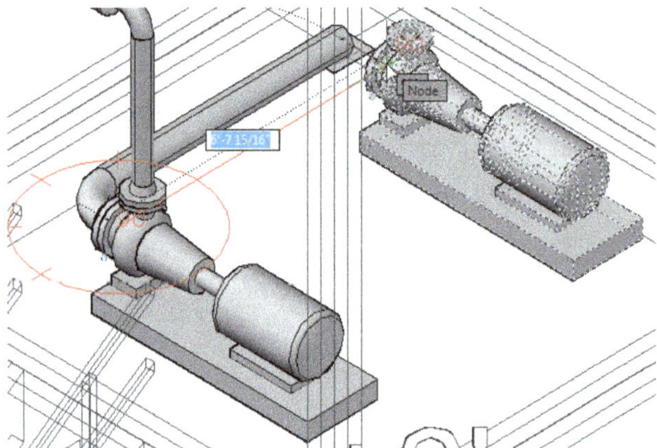

22. Click **Accept** in the command line.
23. Place the pointer on the pipe connection between the two pumps. You notice that the tag information is not assigned to the pipe.

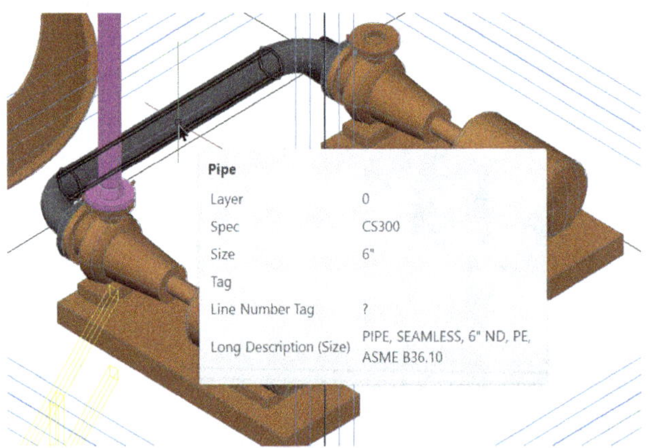

24. Click on the pipe, right click, and then select **Add to selection > Entire Line number**.

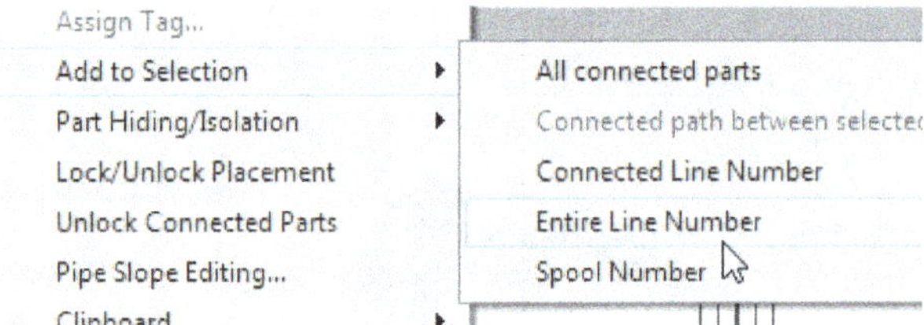

25. Right click and select **Properties**.
26. On the **Properties** palette, scroll down to the **Tag** section.
27. Under the **Tag** section, click **Line Number Tag > Show All line numbers**.

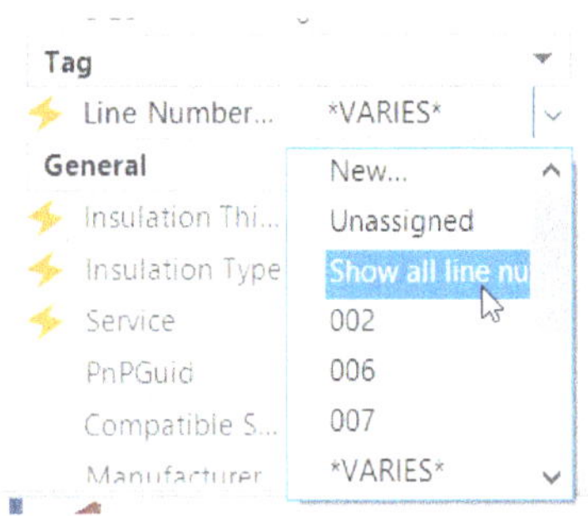

28. Select **Line Number > 007**. The line tag of the 007 P&ID schematic line is assigned to the pipe.

Tutorial 3 (Using the Line to Pipe command to create Pipes)

1. On the status bar, activate the **Ortho Mode** icon.
2. On the ribbon, click **Modeling > Draw > 3D Polyline**.

3. Zoom to the heat exchanger and select the node point of the 4" nozzle.

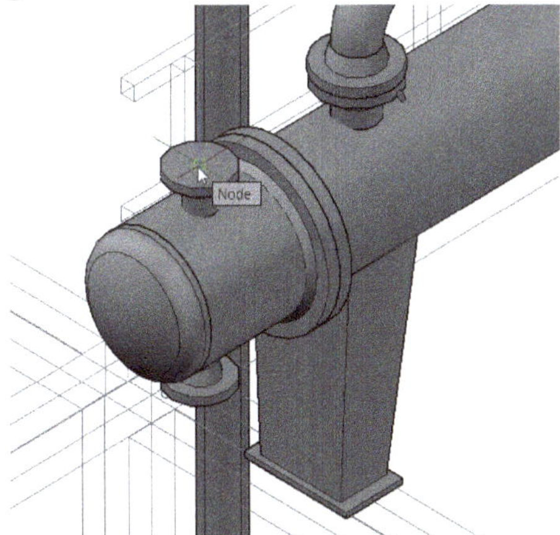

4. Move the pointer up and click to create a vertical line.
5. Likewise, create horizontal and vertical lines, as shown.
6. Right click and select **Enter**.

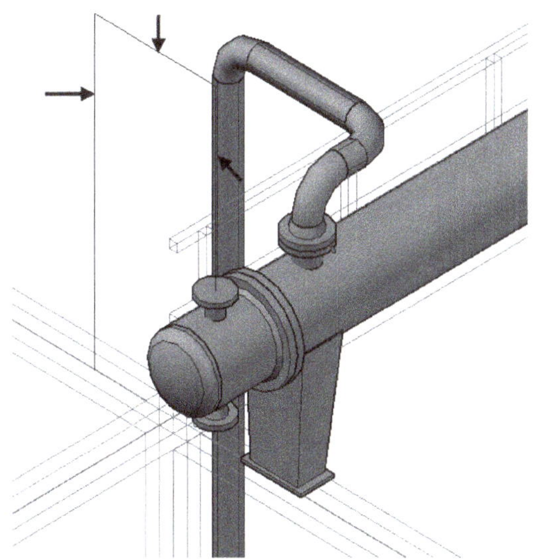

7. On the **Part Insertion** panel of the **Home** tab, select 4" from the **Pipe Size Selector** drop-down.

8. On the **Part Insertion** panel, click the **Line to Pipe** icon.
9. Click on the 3D polyline and press Enter. The line is converted to a pipe.

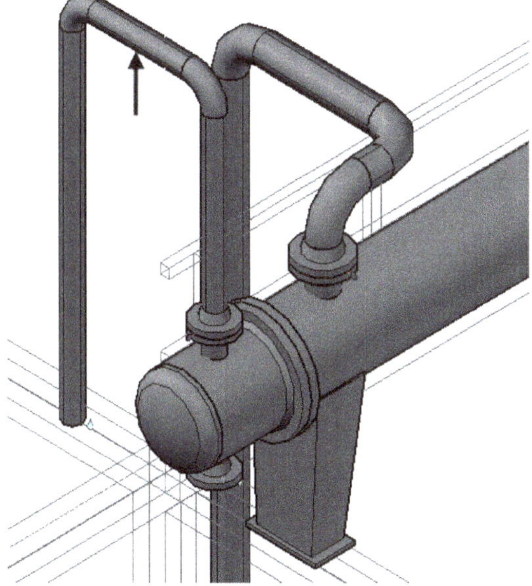

Knowing about the Compass

You may have noticed a red circle with tick marks while routing a pipe. It is called Compass, and it can be used to rotate the pipes. The settings related to Compass are available on the **Compass** panel of the ribbon.

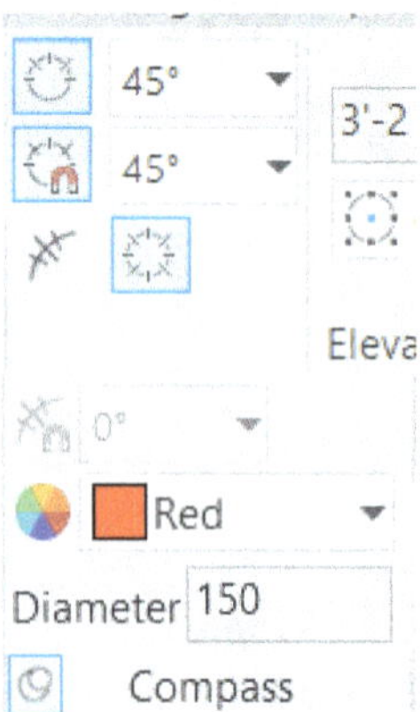

The **Toggle Tick Marks** icon hides/shows tick marks on the compass. You can type-in a value in the **Tick Mark Increments** box to define the angle between the tick marks.

The **Toggle Snaps** icon forces the pipe to rotate at the angular increments defined in the **Snap Increments** box.

The **Toggle Tolerance** icon enables the pipe to deflect slightly from the elbow angle. Activate this button and type-in a tolerance angle in the **Tolerance Snap Increment** box. The pipe is allowed to deflect within the specified tolerance angle.

The **Toggle Compass** icon shows/hides the Compass while routing a pipe.

On the expanded **Compass** panel, there are options to change compass color and diameter.

Tutorial 4 (Editing Pipes)

The process of editing pipes is similar to that of editing AutoCAD objects. AutoCAD Plant 3D offers various grips that appear when you select a pipe.

1. Zoom to the heat exchanger and select the horizontal portion of the pipe created by converting the 3D polyline.
2. Click on the Move Part grip located at the middle of the horizontal pipe.
3. Move the pipe downward and click to change the height.

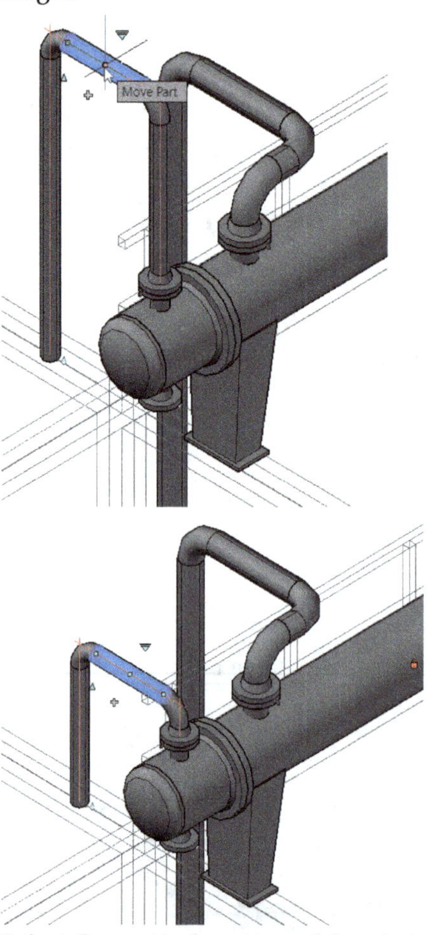

4. Select the vertical portion of the pipe connection, and then click on the Move part grip located at its end.
5. Move the pointer upward and click to reduce the length of the pipe. You can also type-in value to define the change in length.

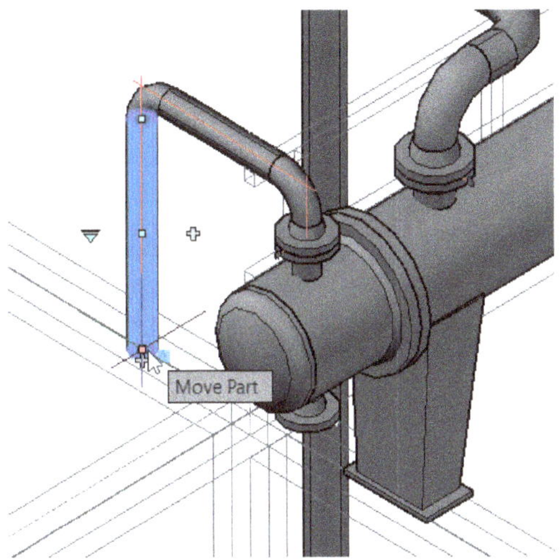

6. Change the view orientation to **Back**.

   [−][Back][Realistic]

7. Again, select the vertical portion of the pipe connection.
8. Click on the + mark to activate the PLANTPIPEADD command.

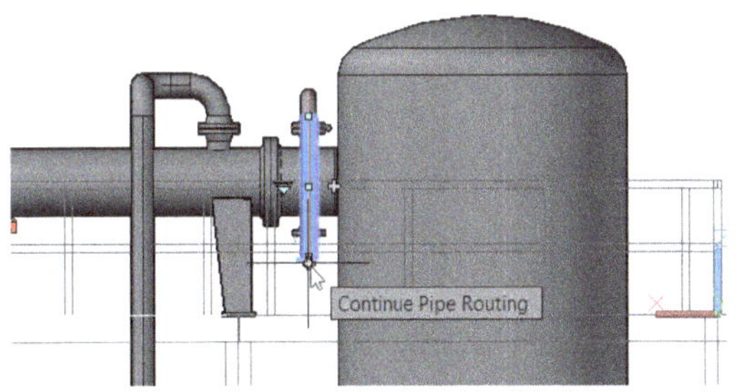

9. Now, continue routing the pipe, as shown.

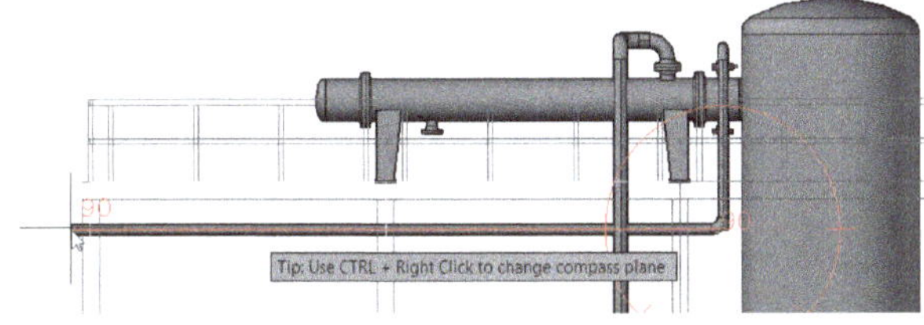

10. Press Esc to deactivate the command.
11. Change the view orientation to SW Isometric.
12. On the Status bar, click the down arrow next to **Object Snap** icon, and then select **Midpoint** from the menu.
13. Again, select the vertical portion of the pipe and click the Move Part grip located at the middle.
14. Move the pointer and select the midpoint of the horizontal pipe. The length of the horizontal pipe is changed.

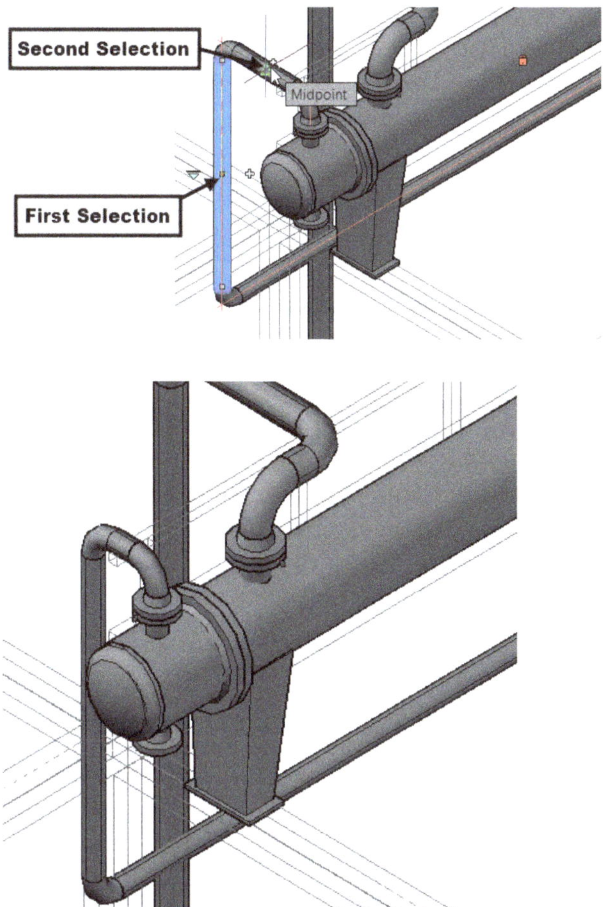

Tutorial 5 (Creating Stub-in and Tee joints)

A Stub-in joint creates a T-joint without using a fitting. This type of joint is useful if there are no fittings available for the selected pipe size.

1. Change the view orientation to Top.
2. On the ribbon, click **Home > Part Insertion > Route Pipe**.
3. Click **STub-in** in the command line.
4. Zoom to the area of the pump and click on the midpoint of the pipe connecting the 6" nozzles.

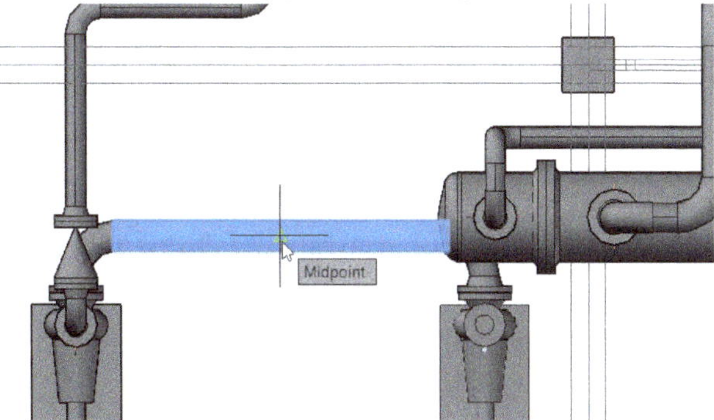

5. Move the pointer upward and click to create a stub-in joint.

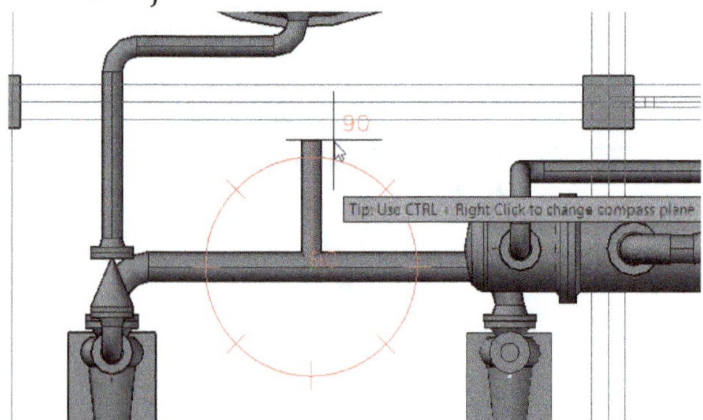

6. Press Esc to deactivate the active command.
7. Select the stub-in pipe and press Delete. The program deletes the stub-in joint.
8. Click on the pipe connecting the 6" nozzles. You notice a + mark in the middle.
9. Click on the + mark and move the pointer. A T-joint is created at the center.

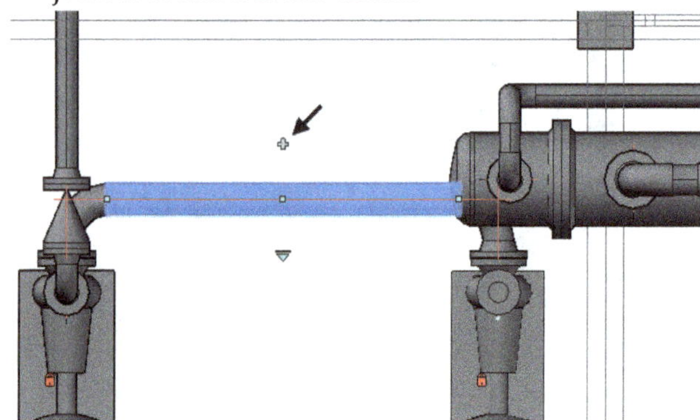

10. Move the pointer upward and click.

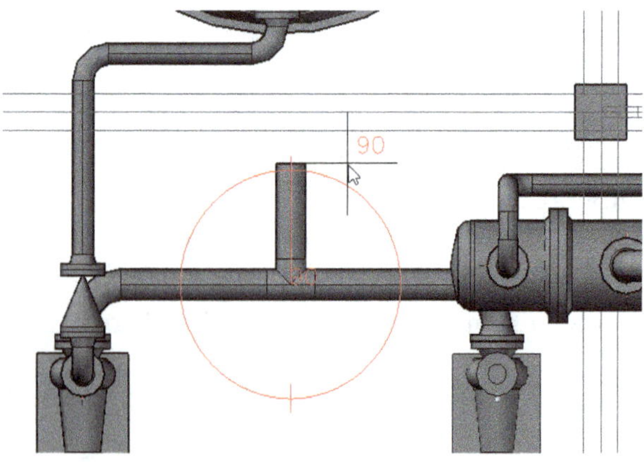

Creating Elbows and Pipe Bends

1. On the status bar, deactivate the **Ortho Mode** icon.
2. Rotate the pointer, and you notice the pipe rotates only at angle intervals (45 and 90).

3. On the **Part Insertion** panel, click the **Toggle Cutback Elbows** icon. The program activates the cutback elbow mode. The cutback elbow mode is used to create elbows at non-standard angles.

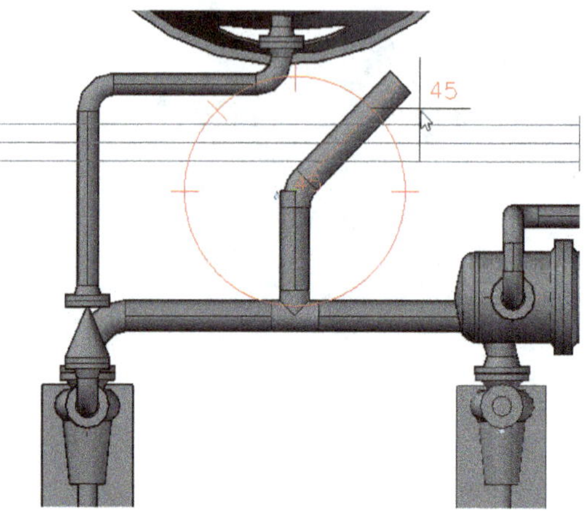

4. Rotate the pointer, and you notice that the pipe is rotated freely.

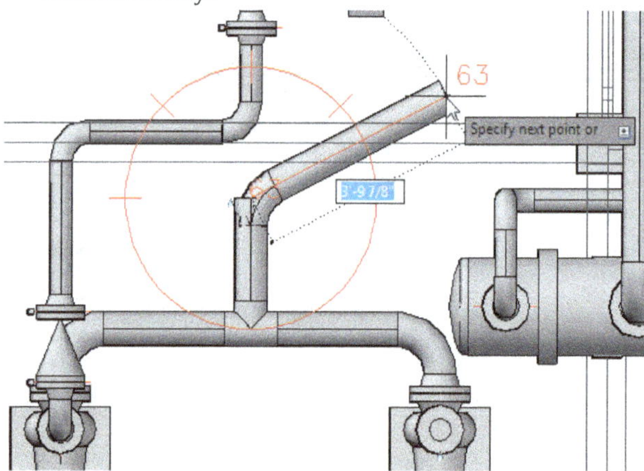

5. Turn on the Dynamic Input icon on the Status bar.

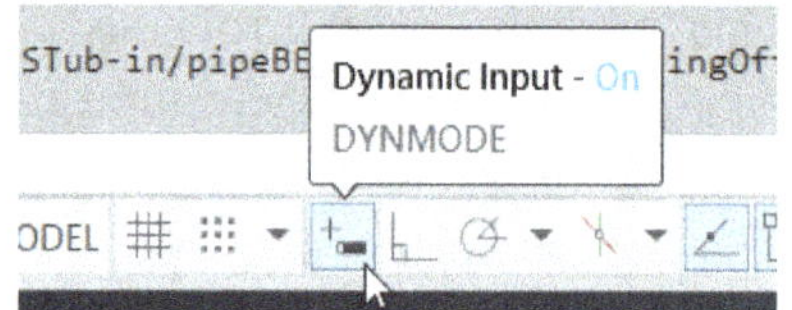

6. Press Tab key and type-in 68 in the angle box attached to the pipe.
7. Press Enter to create an elbow.

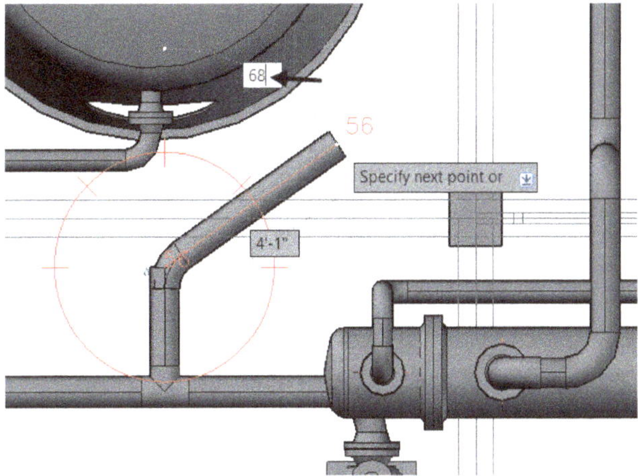

8. On the **Part Insertion** panel, click the **Toggle Pipe Bends** icon to activate the pipe bends mode. Notice that the cutback elbows mode is deactivated.

9. Rotate the pipe up to a 45-degree angle and click to create a bend.

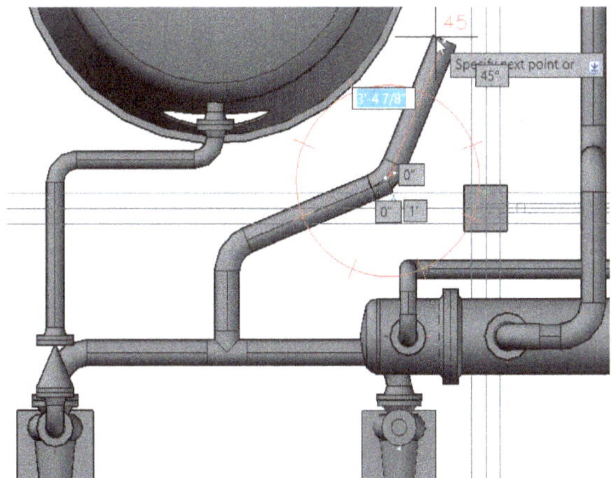

10. Press Esc to deactivate the active command.
11. Select the 45-degree bend; the two pipes connected to it are also selected.
12. Right click and select **Convert to Pipes and Bends** from the shortcut menu; the pulled pipe is converted into pipes and bends.

Tutorial 6 (Creating Sloped Pipes)

AutoCAD Plant 3D allows you to create sloped pipes.

1. Deactivate the **Toggle Pipe Bends**  icon on the Part Insertion panel.
2. On the **Slope** panel, type-in **1"** and **10"** in the **Slope Rise** and **Slope Run** boxes, respectively.
3. Click the **Toggle Slope** icon.

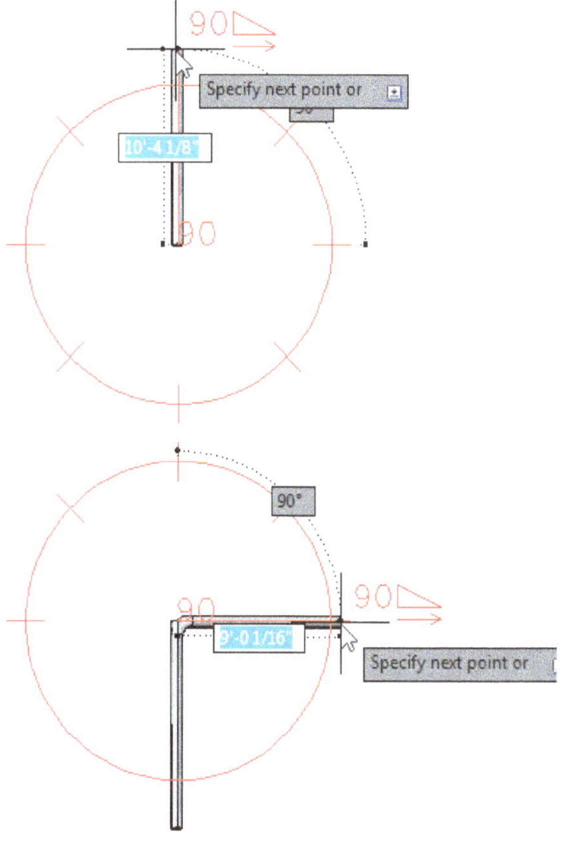

4. Create piping, as shown.

5. Change the view orientation to Front. You notice the sloped pipe.

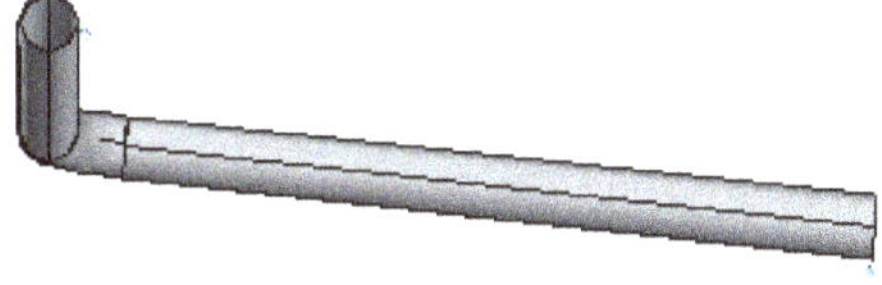

You can also change the slope, but it may result in disconnected pipes.

6. Click on the sloped pipe, right-click, and then select **Pipe Slope Editing**.

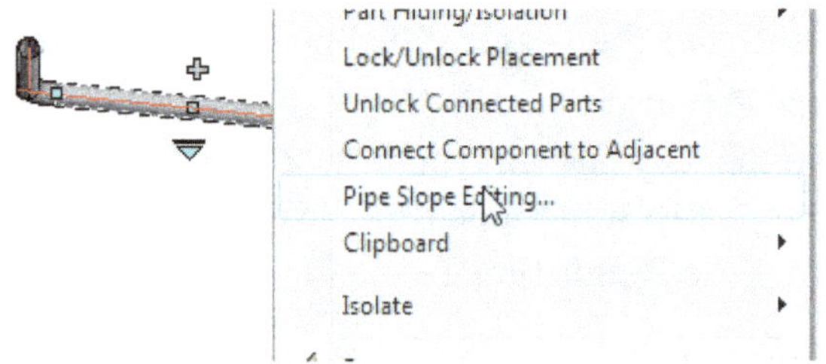

On the **Edit Slope** dialog, you can redefine the slope of the pipe by calculating the **Start Elevation, End Elevation,** or **Slope angle**.

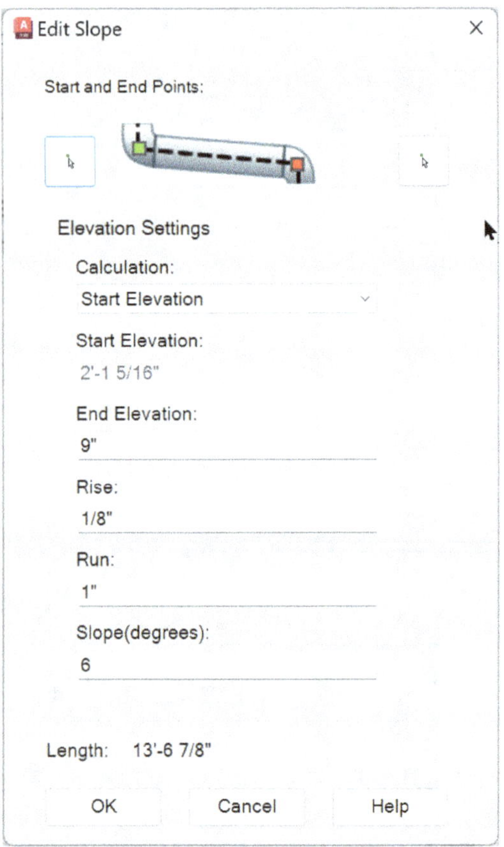

7. On the **Edit Slope** dialog, select **Calculation > End Elevation**.
8. Type-in 20 in the **Slope(degrees)** box and click **OK**. The **Slope Angle Exceeded** message box appears.
9. Click **Yes** to change the slope angle. It results in a broken connection.

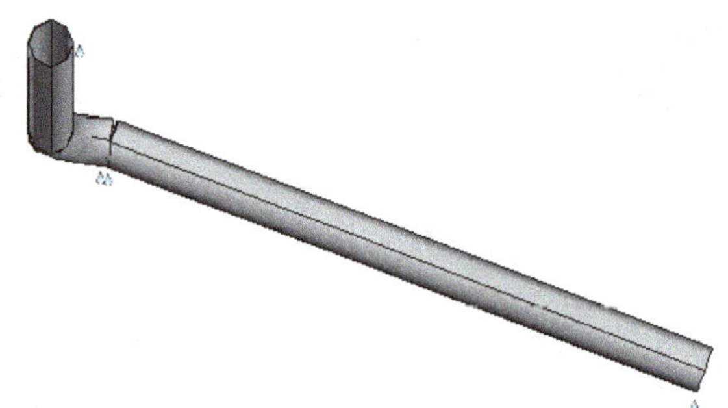

Tutorial 7 (Creating offset piping)

AutoCAD Plant 3D allows you to create pipes offset to a reference line.

1. Change the view orientation to Front.
2. Deactivate the **Toggle Slope** icon on the **Slope** panel.

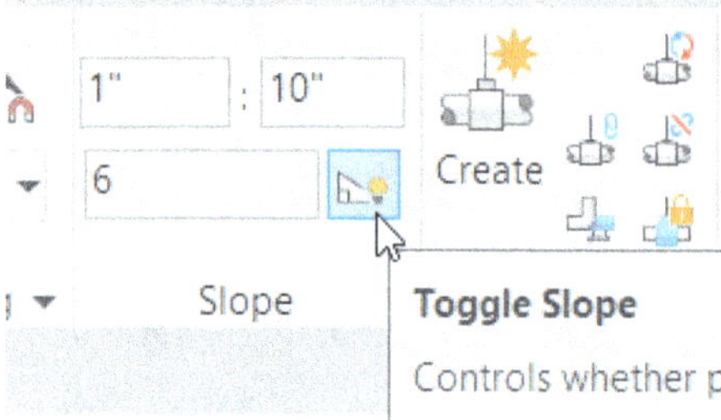

3. On the ribbon, click **Home > Part Insertion > Route Pipe**.
4. Click **routingOffset** in the command line.
5. Click **offsetDistance** in the command line.
6. Type 2' as the Horizontal distance and press Enter.
7. Type 2' as the Vertical distance and press Enter.
8. Select the grid points, as shown. Notice that the pipe is created at the specified offset distance from the select points.

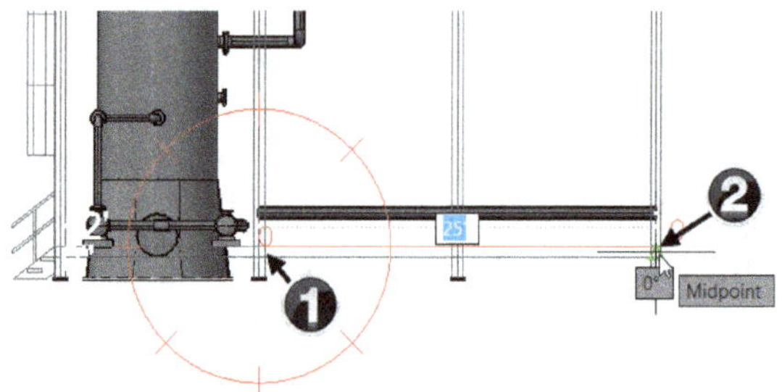

9. Move the pointer up and click.

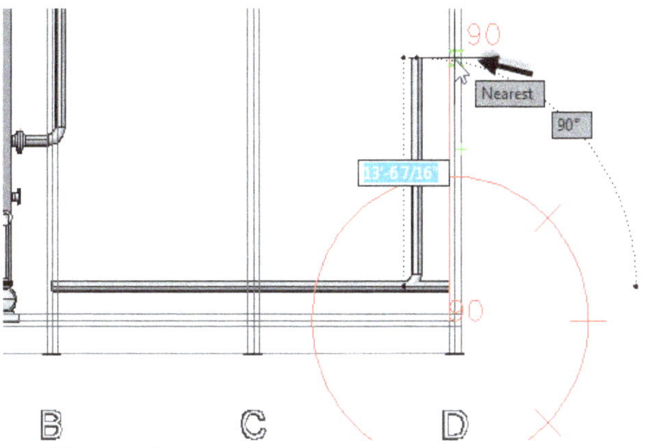

10. Change the view orientation to Top. You notice that the pipe is created at a horizontal offset as well.

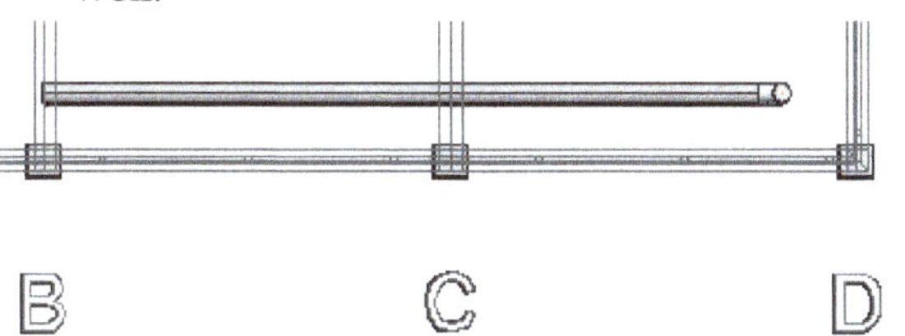

11. Press Esc to deactivate the active command.
12. To deactivate the offset routing, expand the **Elevation & Routing** panel and type-in 0 in the **Horizontal Offset** and **Vertical Offset** boxes.

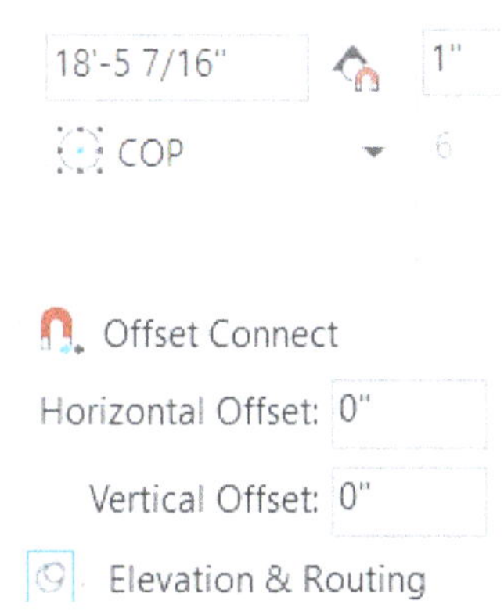

13. Zoom to a pipes' open end to notice the drop symbol, which indicates that the pipe is open. You can turn ON/OFF this symbol using the **Toggle Disconnect Markers** icon.

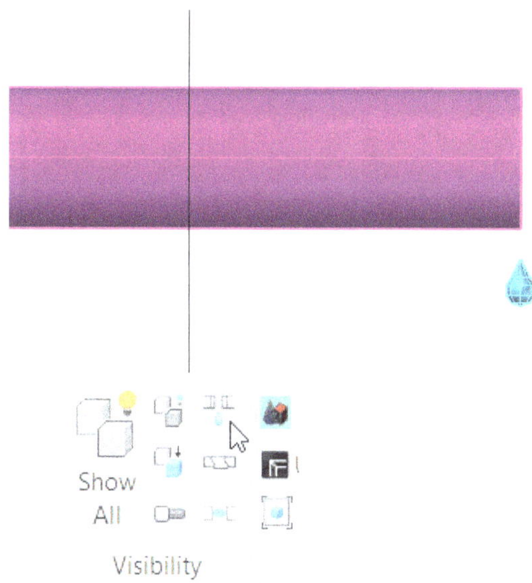

Tutorial 8 (Adding Insulation and Welds to Pipes)

1. Set the View orientation to Top.
2. Click on the pipe connected to the heat exchanger, right-click, and then select **Properties**.

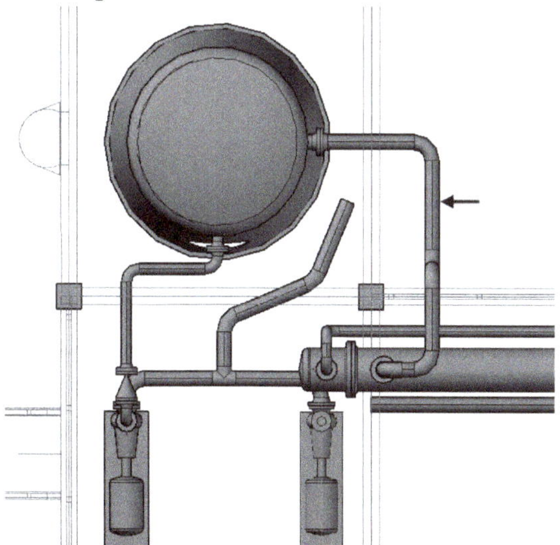

3. On the **Properties** palette, scroll down to the **Process Line** section, and set the **Service**, **Insulation Thickness** and **Insulation Type**.

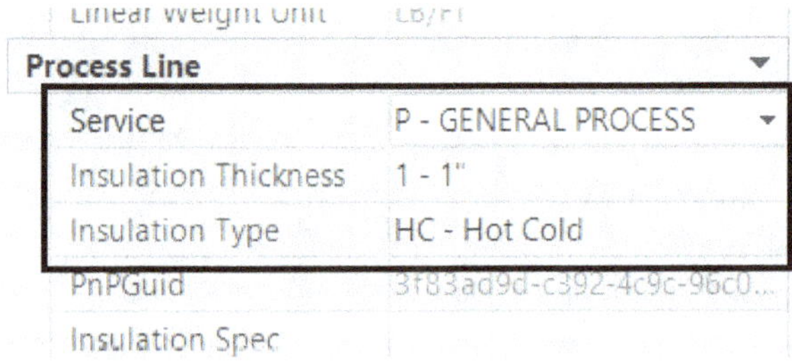

4. On the ribbon, click **Home > Visibility > Toggle Insulation Display** to display the insulation by increasing the thickness of the pipe.

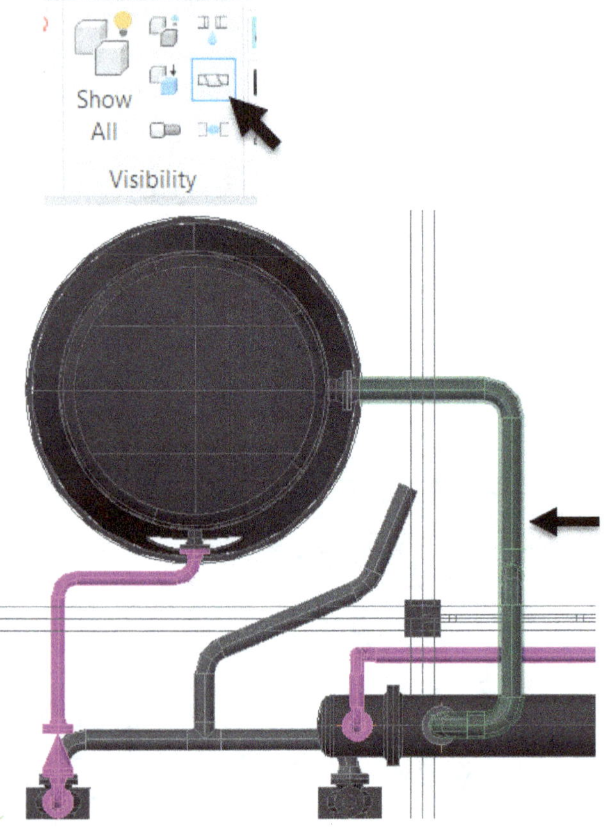

Welds are added by default when two pipe components are created continuously. However, you can add a weld when you want to break the pipe. To add welds, follow the steps given next.

5. Click on the pipe connecting the heat exchanger and vessel, right-click, and then select **Add Weld to Pipe**.
6. Move the pointer and click to define the location of the weld (or) type-in the distance value to locate the weld.

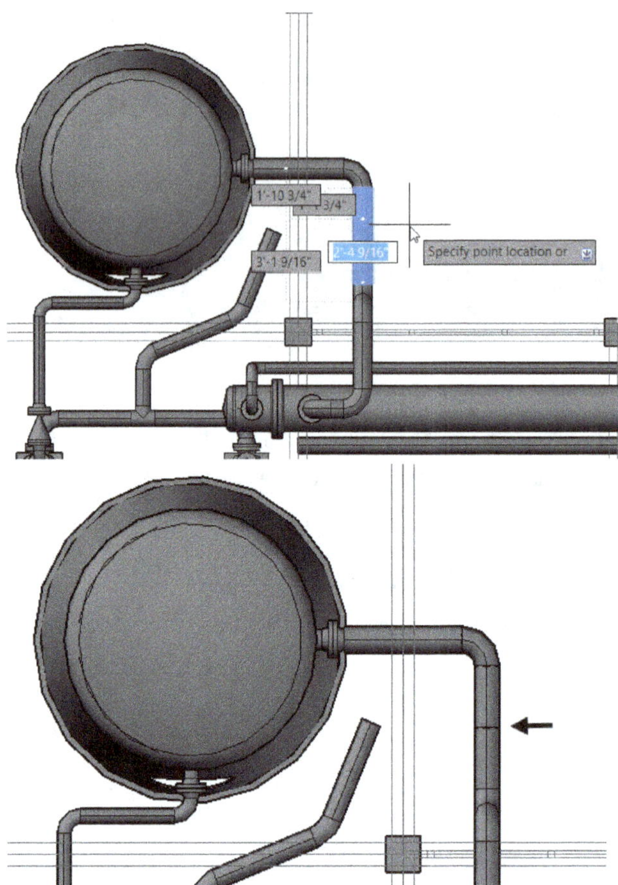

7. Click **eXit** in the command line.

Tutorial 9 (Adding Inline assets)

Before adding inline assets, create a pipe connection between the right pump and vessel.

1. Change the view orientation to **SW Isometric**.
2. On the **Part Insertion** panel, select **002** from the **Line Number Selector** drop-down.
3. Click on the right pump to highlight it.
4. Click on the + mark on the 4" nozzle.

116

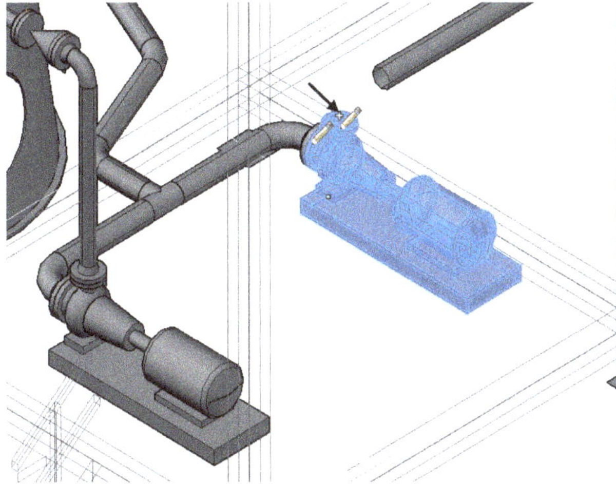

5. Move the pointer and select the midpoint of the elbow originating from the vessel.

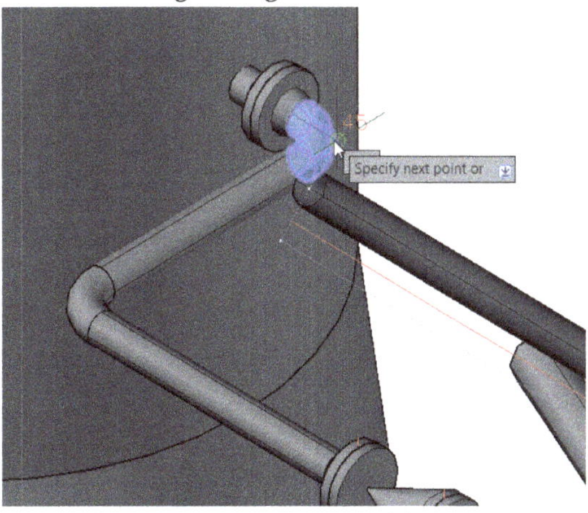

6. Click **Next** in the command line until the following solution is displayed.

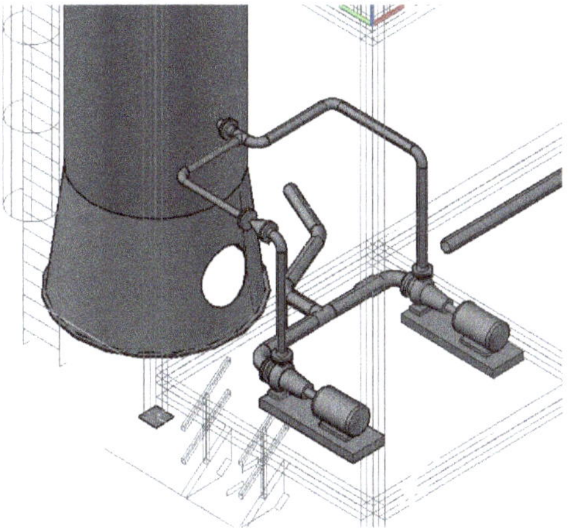

7. Click **Accept** to create the pipe connection.

After creating piping, you can add inline assets such as valves and fittings. There are three methods to add inline assets to the piping. Earlier, you have learned to add inline assets using the P&ID Line List palette. It is the best method to add pipe components to the 3D model as it links them to the corresponding P&ID symbols automatically. However, you can add inline assets using the Spec Viewer and Dynamic Tool Palette.

8. Make sure that the CS300 spec is loaded on the Dynamic Tool Palette.

9. On the Dynamic Tool Palette, scroll down to the **Valve** section and select **Globe Valve, FL, RF, 300, (CS300)**.

10. Move the pointer on the horizontal pipe connected to the right pump. You notice that the valve moves along the pipe.

11. Select the endpoint of the pipe. The valve is positioned at the selected point, and the compass appears. The valve rotates as you rotate the pointer.

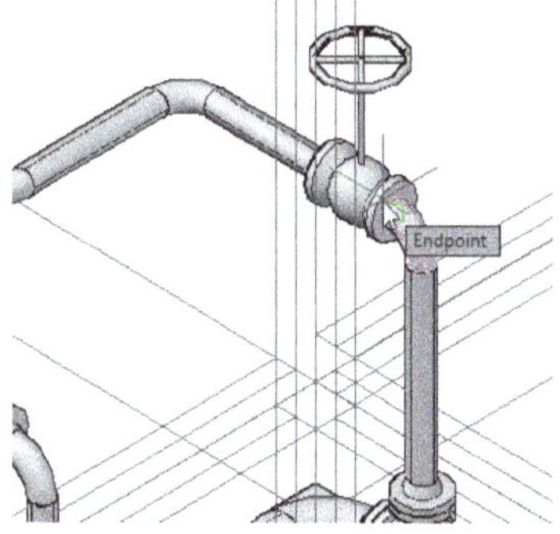

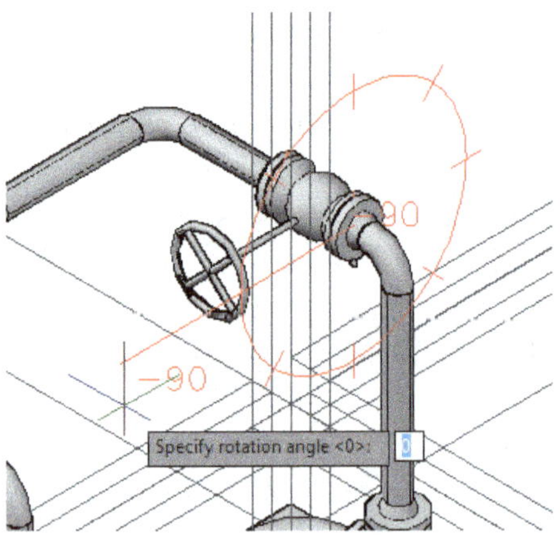

12. Press Enter to position the valve at the default angle.

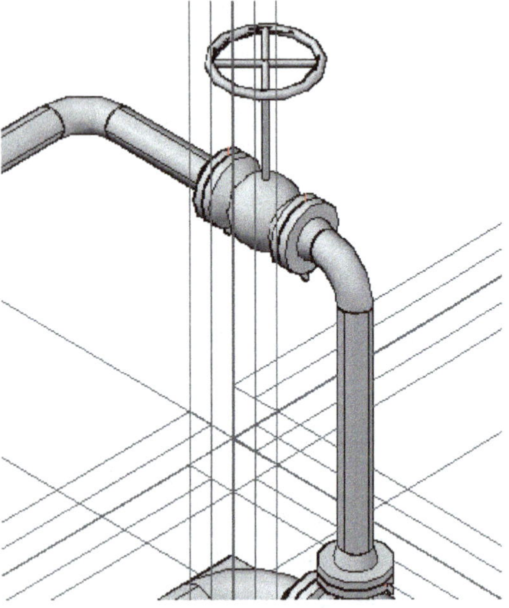

13. Press Esc.
14. Select the globe valve, click the right mouse button, and select **Properties**.
15. On the **Properties** palette, scroll down to the **Tag** section and click in the **Tag** box.
16. Click the icon next to the **Tag** box.

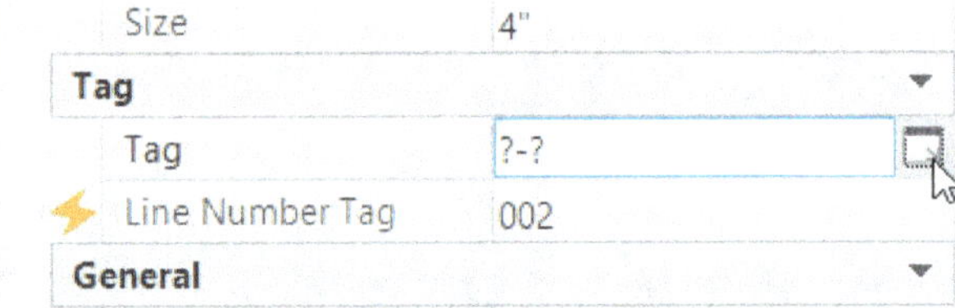

17. On the **Assign Tag** dialog, type-in HA and 102 in the **Code** box and **Number** boxes, respectively. Click **Assign**.

Editing Inline assets

1. Click the globe valve to highlight it. You notice many grips displayed on the valve.
2. Click on the circular grip and rotate the valve.
3. Type-in a new rotation value and press Enter.

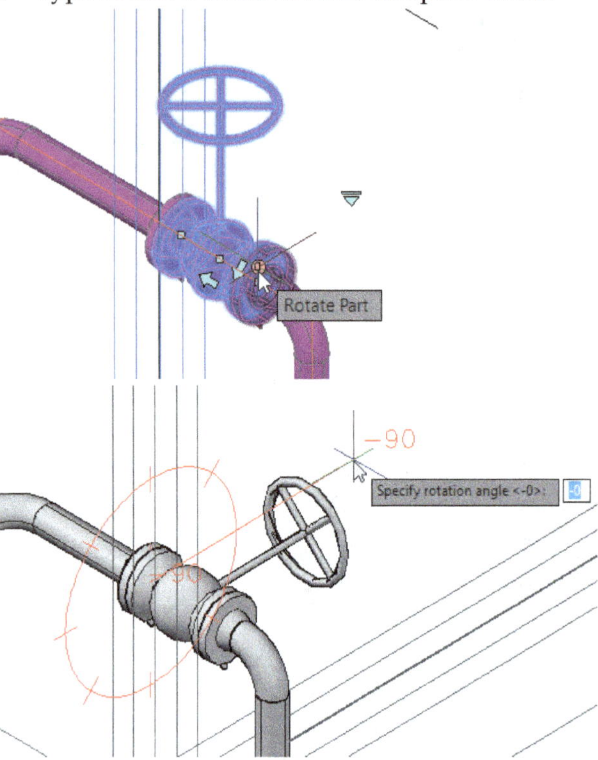

4. Again, select the globe valve and click on the vertical arrow grip. The grip flips the side of the valve.

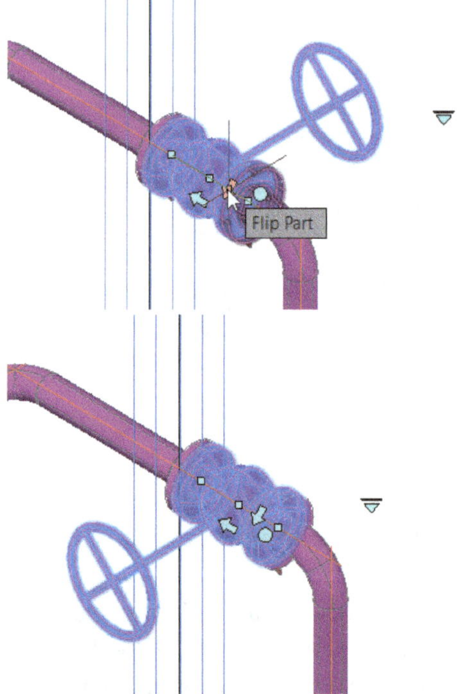

You can notice the three square grips displayed on the highlighted valve.

5. Click on the square grip of the valve, and then move the pointer. The valve moves along the pipe.

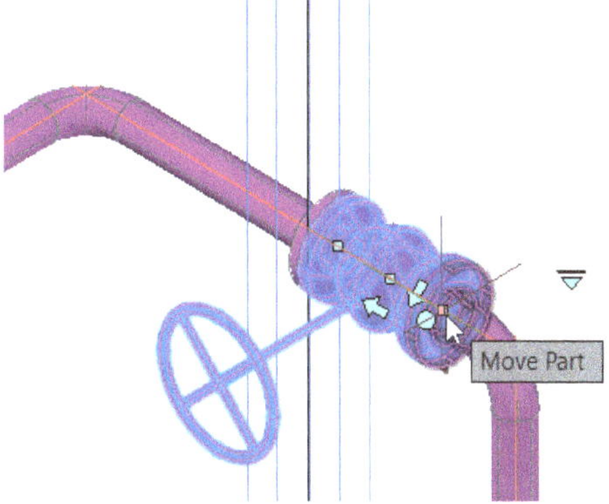

6. Click to define the new position of the valve or type-in the distance value to define the location.

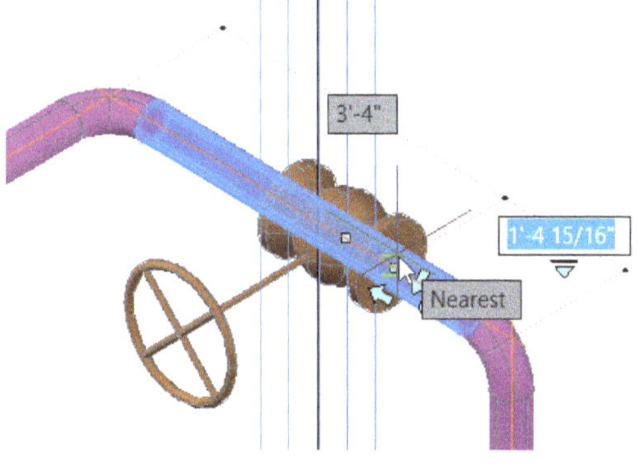

You can also place the valve on another pipe using the square grip.

7. Click on the check valve to highlight it.
8. Click on the horizontal arrow grip to flip the direction of the valve.

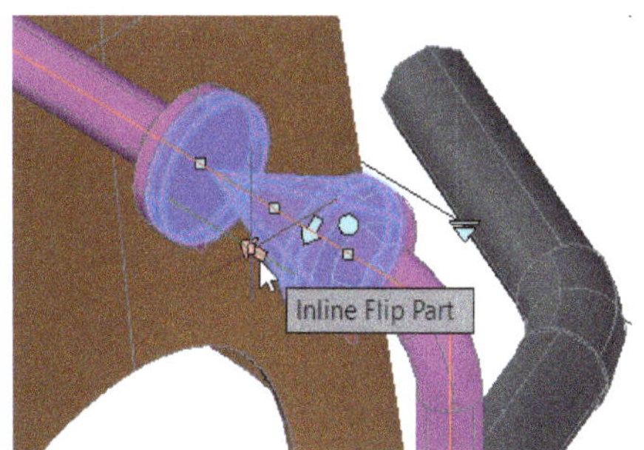

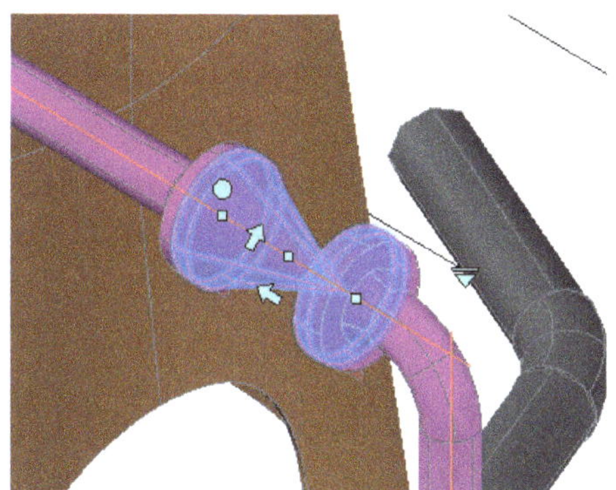

9. Click on the **Substitute Part** grip to open a menu. You can select the replacement part from this menu.

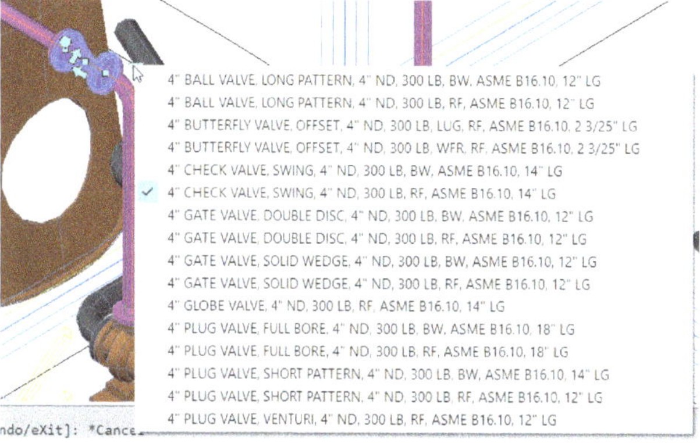

You can also change the valve operator.

10. Select the globe valve, click the right mouse button, and select **Properties**.
11. On the **Properties** palette, scroll down to the **Valve Operator** section and click in the **Operator** box.
12. Click the icon next to the **Operator** box.

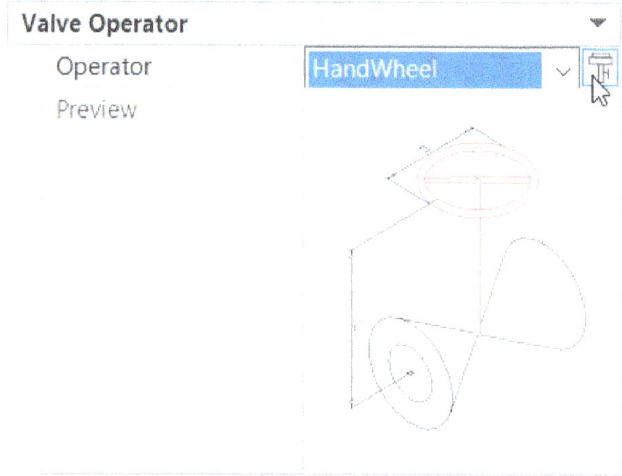

13. On the **Override Valve Operator** dialog, scroll right to see different operators.
14. Select the T-Crank operator, and you notice the preview image along with dimensions. Click **OK**; the operator of the globe valve is changed.

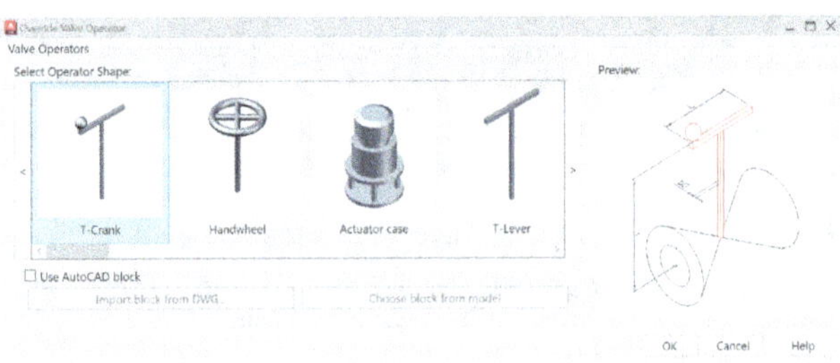

15. On the **Properties** palette, under the Valve Operator section, type-in values in the **Dimensions** sub-section.

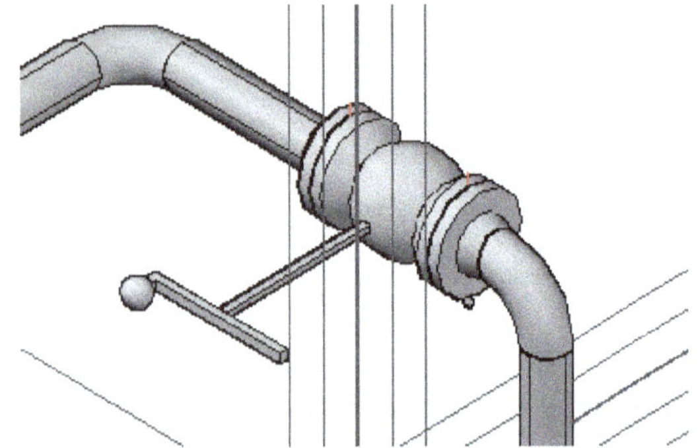

Adding Inline Assets at Pipe ends

1. Change the view orientation to NE Isometric.
2. Click on the vessel to highlight it.
3. Click the + mark on the 4" nozzle and start routing.

4. Click **pipeFitting** in the command line. The **Pipe Fittings** dialog appears. In this dialog, you can select the type of fitting.
5. On the dialog, click the **Flanges** button.
6. Select **Class Types > FLANGE BLIND**. A blind flange of 4" size is available. If you want a flange of different and size, then click **Change** at the top of the dialog. The additional options appear to change the size, spec, and end type.

7. Select the blind flange from the **Available Piping Components** section and click **Place**. The blind flange is attached to the pipe end.
8. Move the pointer and click to create a pipe with a blind flange.

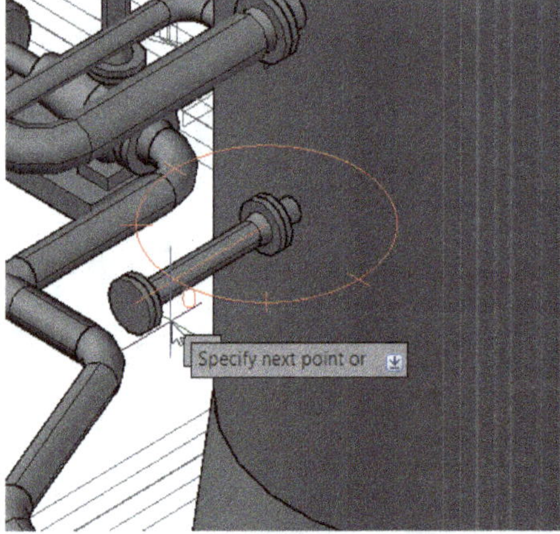

9. Press Enter to rotate the flange at the default angle.

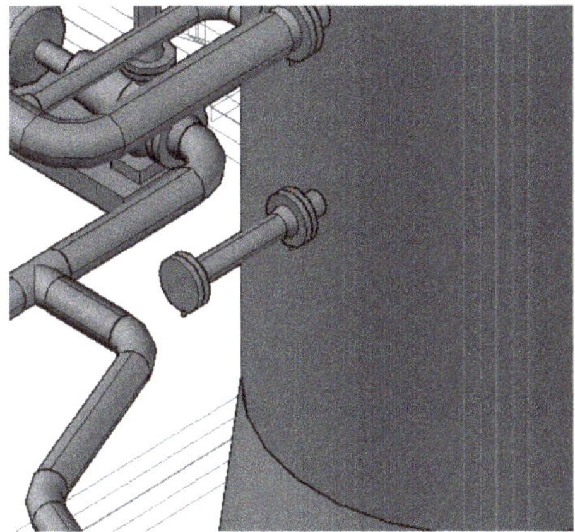

10. Select the pipe and blind flange, and then press **Delete**.

Adding Custom Parts

AutoCAD Plant 3D allows you to add custom parts to the 3D Model, which are not available in the selected spec file. You can also create your 3D blocks and add them to the Plant 3D model.

1. Change the view orientation to SW Isometric.
2. On the ribbon, click **Home > Part Insertion > Custom Part**.

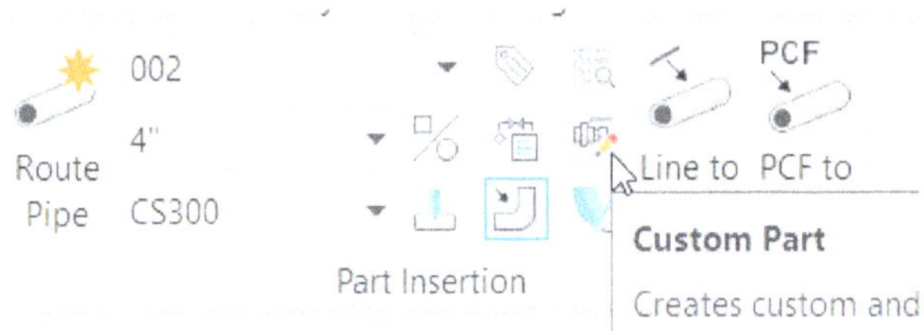

3. On the **CUSTOM PARTS BUILDER** palette, select **Part Type > Valve**.
4. Click the **Plant 3D Shape** tab under the **Graphics** section.
5. Click the **Shape Browser** button to open the **Plant 3D Shape Browser** dialog.
6. Click **Advanced shape options** to view the additional options on the left side of the dialog.
7. In the additional options, click **Pipe Run Component > Valve**. Only the valves appear in the browser.
8. Click the **Inline Shapes** button. The inline valve shapes are displayed on the dialog.

9. Click the down arrow in the search bar and select **Beveled (BV)**. The dialog filters the shapes based on the selected end type.
10. Select **Inline Valve, Cone Style (FLG/BW/PE)** from the browser, and then click **OK**.

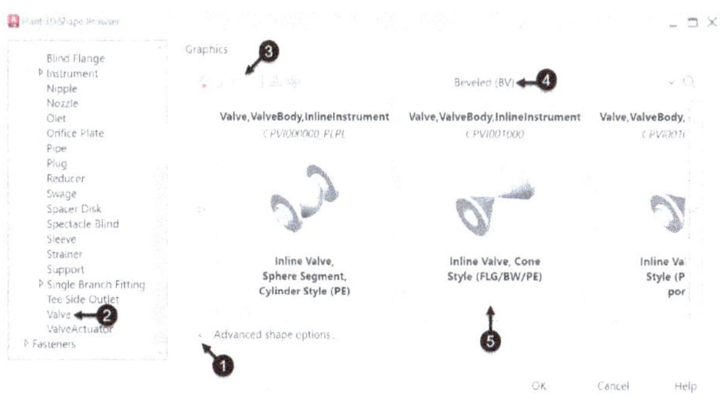

11. Under the **Part Properties** section, set **Tag** to **Do not prompt on Insert**.

12. Leave the default settings on the **CUSTOM PARTS BUILDER** palette and click **Insert in Model**.
13. Add the valve to the pipe connected to the heat exchanger.

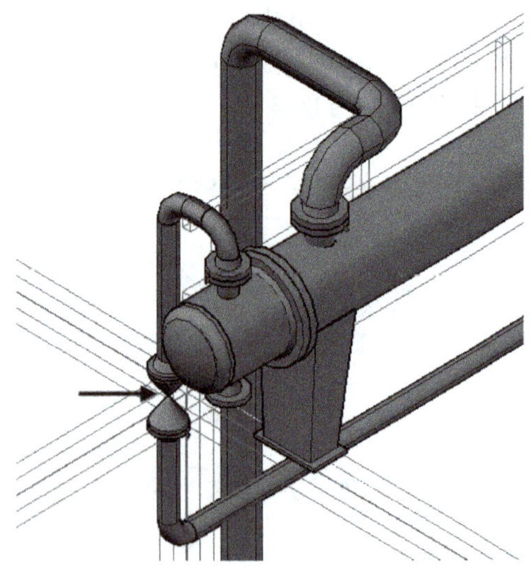

14. Press Esc twice.
15. Select the placeholder valve, click the right mouse button, and select **Properties**. The features of the valve appear in the **Properties** palette. You can change the dimensions of the valve, tag information, and other features.

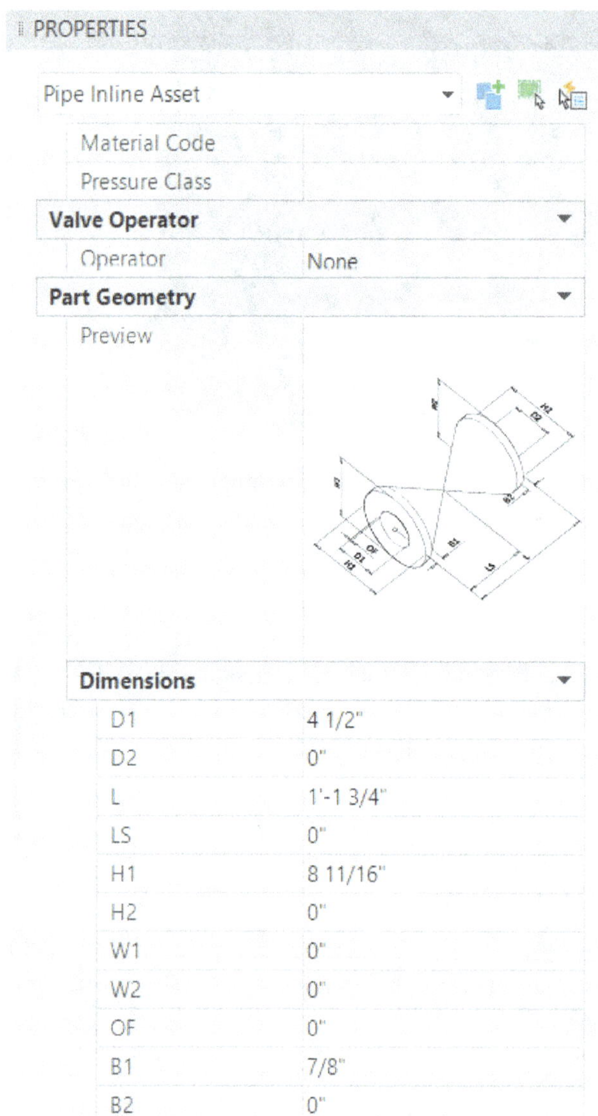

16. Select the custom valve and press **Delete**.

Tutorial 10 (Adding Pipe Supports)

After creating pipes, you can add pipe supports to them. The pipe supports are displayed in the isometric drawing.

1. On the ribbon, click **Home > Pipe Supports > Create**.

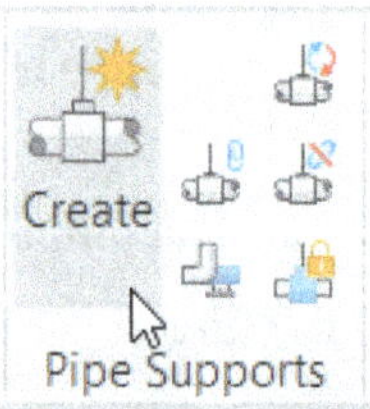

2. On the **Add Pipe Support** dialog, click the **Base Supports** icon.
3. Click the down arrow in the search bar and select **Clamped Supports**.
4. Select **Clamped Stanchion** and click **OK**.

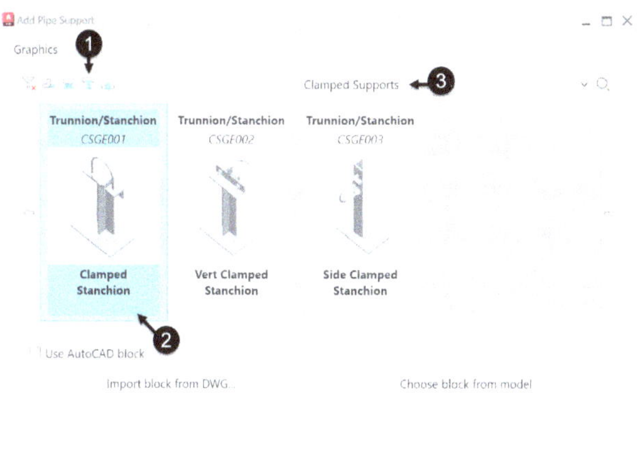

5. Move the pointer on the pipe, as shown. The pipe support aligns with the pipe.
6. Type-in a value (or) click at a point to define the location of the support.
7. Press Esc.

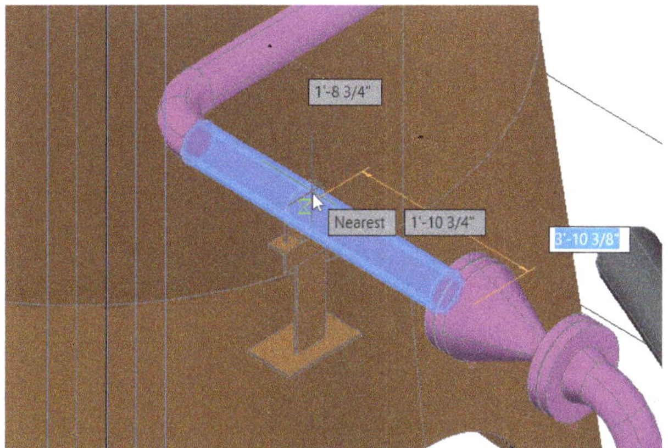

8. Change the view orientation to Left.
9. Click on the pipe support to highlight it.
10. Click on the down arrow grip located at the bottom of the pipe support.
11. Move the pointer down and click on the structural member located at the bottom. The program changes the height of the pipe support.

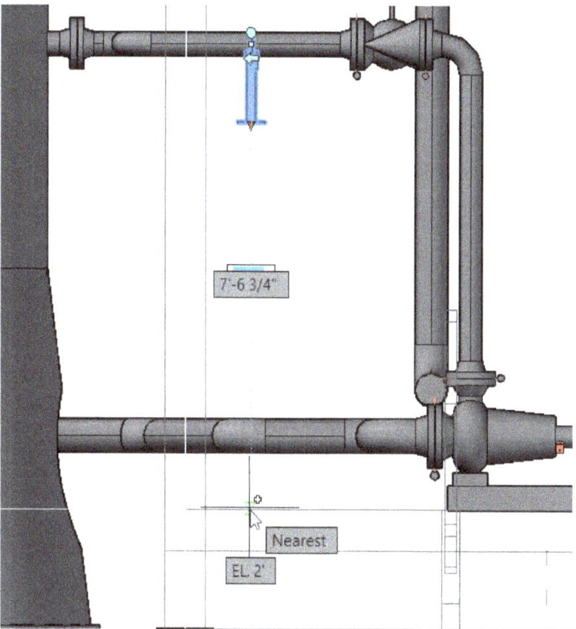

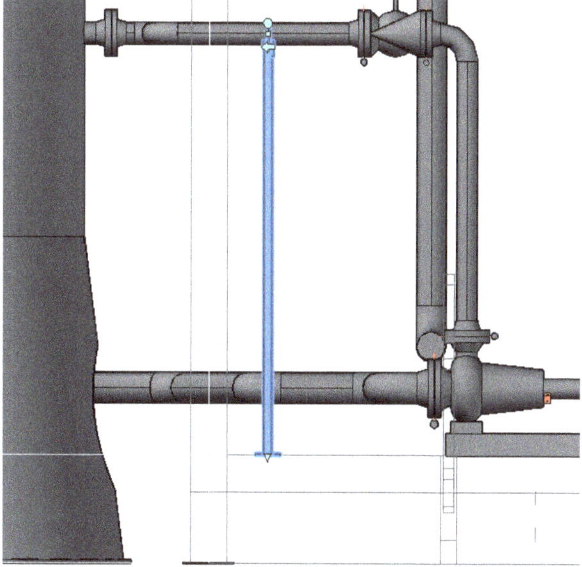

12. Save the file.

Tutorial 11 (Validating Project Drawings)

You need to validate a P&ID to check for errors. You can validate single or multiple drawings in a project. Before validating a drawing, you need to set the type of errors to be check during validation. These errors include non-terminating lines, orphaned annotations, spec mismatches, and more.

1. Switch to the **P&ID PIP** workspace.

2. Click the **Validate Config** button on the **Validate** panel of the **Home** ribbon; the **P&ID Validation Settings** dialog appears.

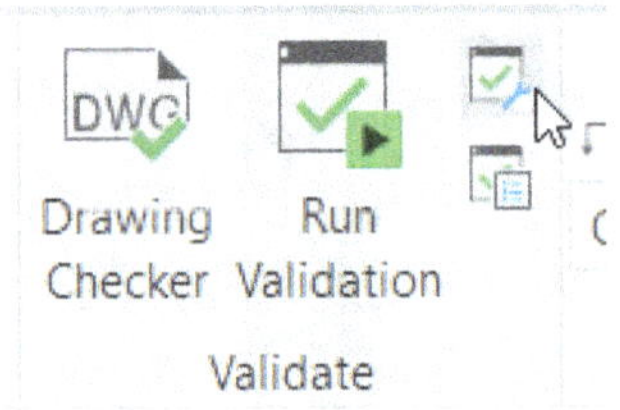

The **P&ID Validation Settings** dialog has four types of conditions to check for: P&ID objects, 3D Piping, Base AutoCAD objects, and 3D Model to P&ID checks.

You can select the type of errors to be checked by expanding the **P&ID objects** list. The P&ID is checked for errors such as size mismatches, spec mismatches, non-terminating lines, and so on.

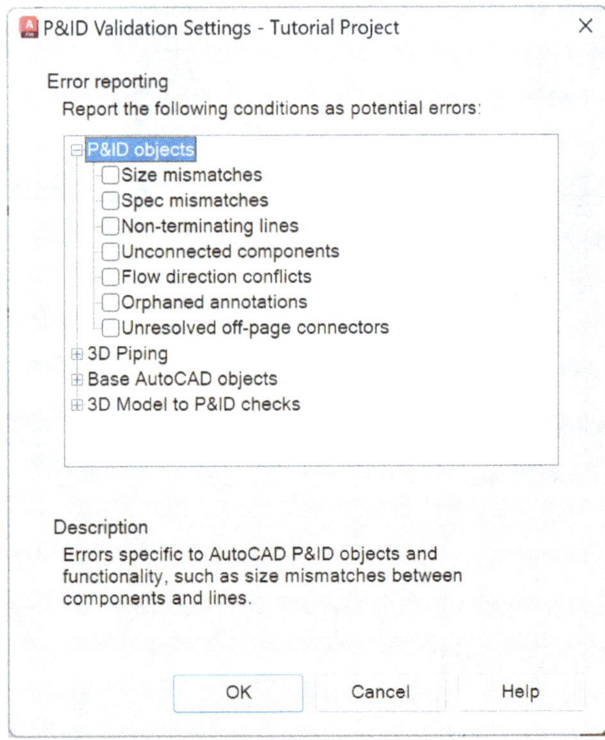

The **Size mismatches** option checks for schematic lines, which are connected but are of different sizes.

The **Spec mismatches** option checks for schematic lines that are connected but are of different spec.

The **Non-terminating lines** option checks for schematic lines that are not properly connected to the equipment or any component.

The **Unconnected components** option checks for equipment or components, which are not connected to any schematic lines. You need to make sure that there is at least one connection To/From the component.

The **Flow direction conflicts** option checks for any two schematic lines which have opposite flow directions.

The **Orphaned annotations** option checks for tags that are placed far away from the components. You can specify the distance up to which the annotations can be placed. To do so, select the **Orphaned annotations** option and type-in a value in the **Orphaned Annotation Distance** box.

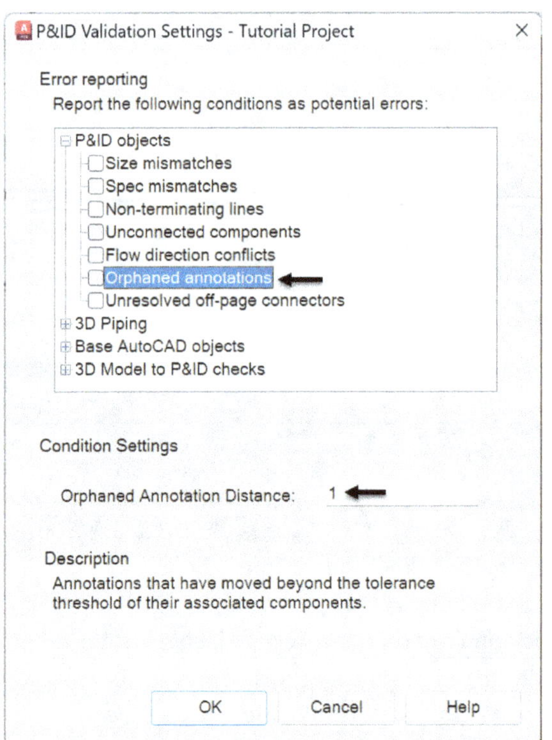

The **Unresolved off-page connectors** option checks for off-page connectors that are not connected to any other off-page connectors.

3. Check all the options under **P&ID objects**.

Expand **3D Piping**, and you notice the **Disconnected port**, **Placeholder part**, and **Property mismatch** options.

The **Disconnected port** option checks for pipes in the 3D Piping model, which are not properly connected to a component.

The **Placeholder part** option checks for parts, which are placed in a 3D Piping model, which are not available in the selected spec.

The **Property mismatch** option checks for pipe segments that are connected but have different properties.

4. Uncheck all the options under **3D Piping**.

Expand **Base AutoCAD objects** to check for AutoCAD objects. You can check for objects that are not created using P&ID tools. The base AutoCAD objects such as lines, polylines, circles, blocks, annotations do not have any project data attached to them. The options under this node are very helpful in eliminating the unintelligent AutoCAD objects.

5. Uncheck all the options under **Base AutoCAD objects**.

Expand the **3D Model to P&ID checks,** and notice the options to check the coordination between the P&ID objects and 3D Piping components. There are quite a few conditions to test the coordination between the P&ID and 3D Piping components. For example, if you have created a P&ID schematic line, but there is no piping component in the 3D model with the same properties (line tag), then an error appears. You can go through the other error types as they are self-explanatory.

6. Uncheck all the options under the **3D Model to P&ID checks**.
7. Click the **OK** button on the **P&ID Validation Settings** dialog.
8. Click the **Run Validation** button on the **Validate** panel of the **Home** Ribbon; the validation starts, and the **Validation Progress** dialog appears.

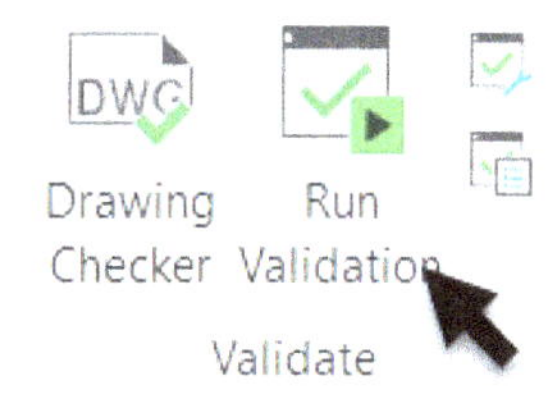

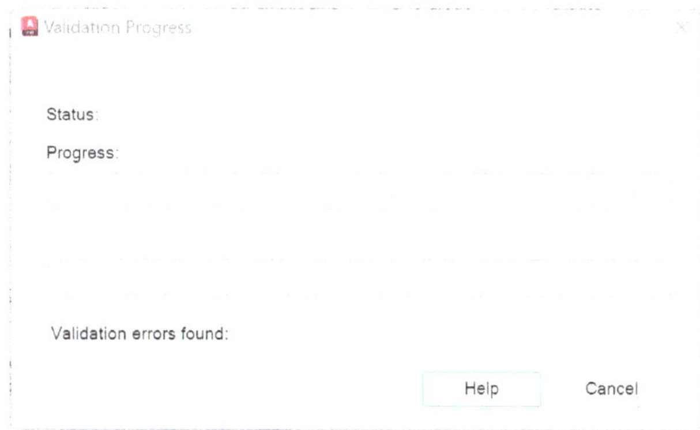

After completing the validation, the **Validation Summary** appears.

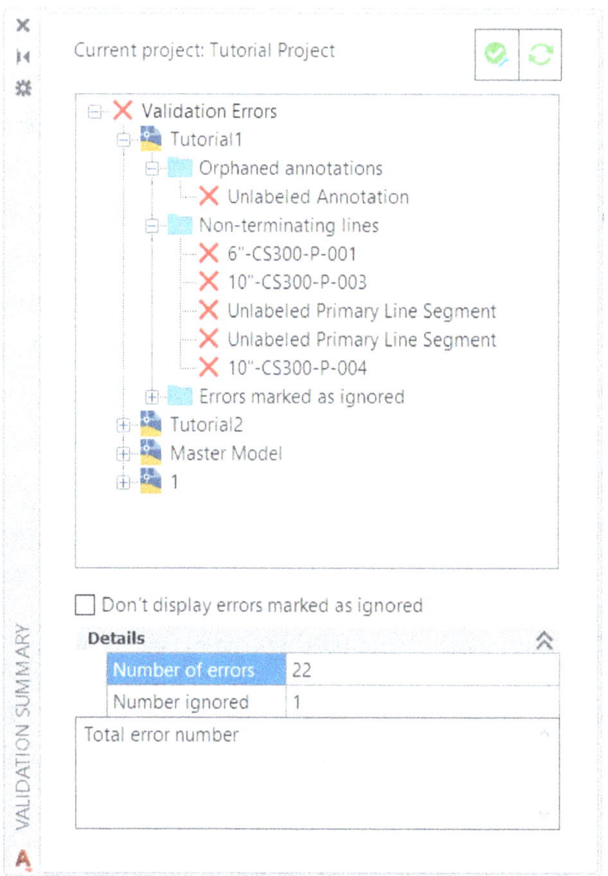

9. On the **Validation Summary** palette, under Tutorial 1, click the first **Unlabeled Annotation**. The orphaned annotation is highlighted in the

drawing. The **Details** section on the **Validation Summary** palette shows the error type and the action to be taken. It also shows the actual and allowed distance between the component and tag.

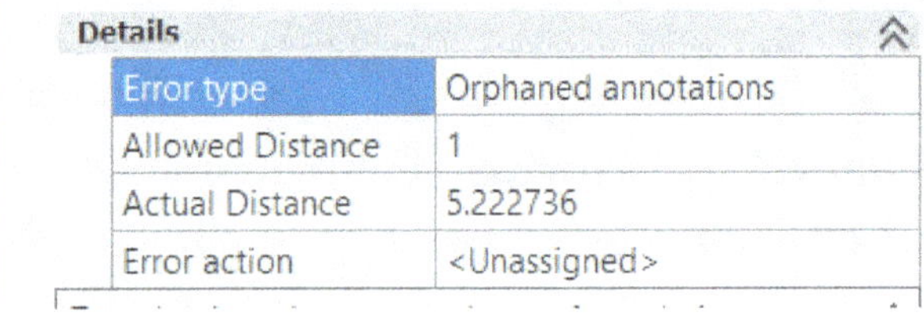

10. Under the **Details** section, click **Error action > Ignore**. The program ignores the selected error.
11. Check the **Do not display errors marked at ignored** option to hide the ignored errors.
12. Click the **Revalidate Selected Node** icon on the **Validation Summary** palette.
13. Close the **Validation Summary** palette.

Validating the 3D model

1. On the **Project Manager**, click the right mouse button on **Tutorial Project** and select **Validation Settings**.

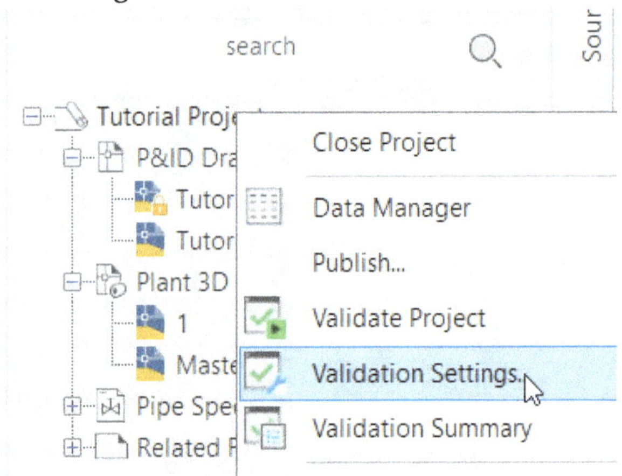

2. On the **Validation Settings** dialog, check all the options under **3D Piping** and **3D Model to P&ID checks** nodes. Uncheck all the options under **P&ID objects,** and **Base AutoCAD objects** nodes, and then click **OK**.
3. Click the right mouse button on **Tutorial Project** and select **Validate Project**. The program performs validation and displays the validation summary.
4. Click **Tutorial 1 > Unmatched P&ID inline assets > HA-105** on the **Validation Summary**

palette. The inline asset in the P&ID is highlighted because the pipe component corresponding to the P&ID asset is not placed in the 3D model. Under the **Details** section, you can find the description related to the error.

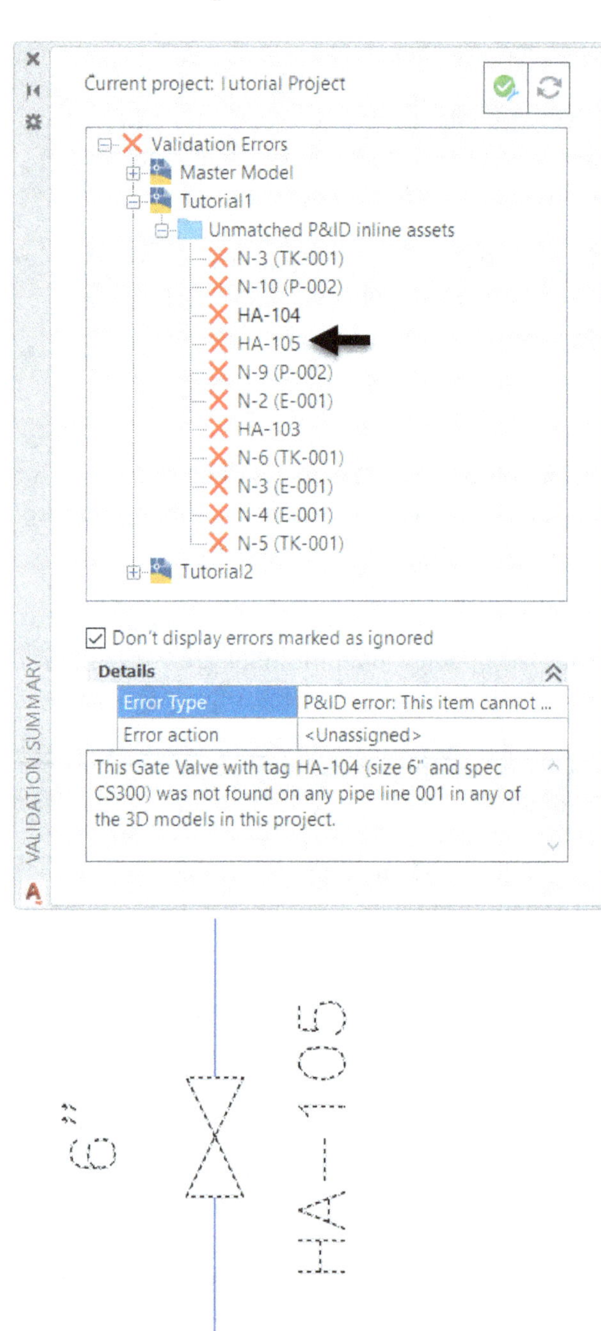

You can solve this error by placing a gate valve in the 3D model. You can use the P&ID Line list to place the gate valve.

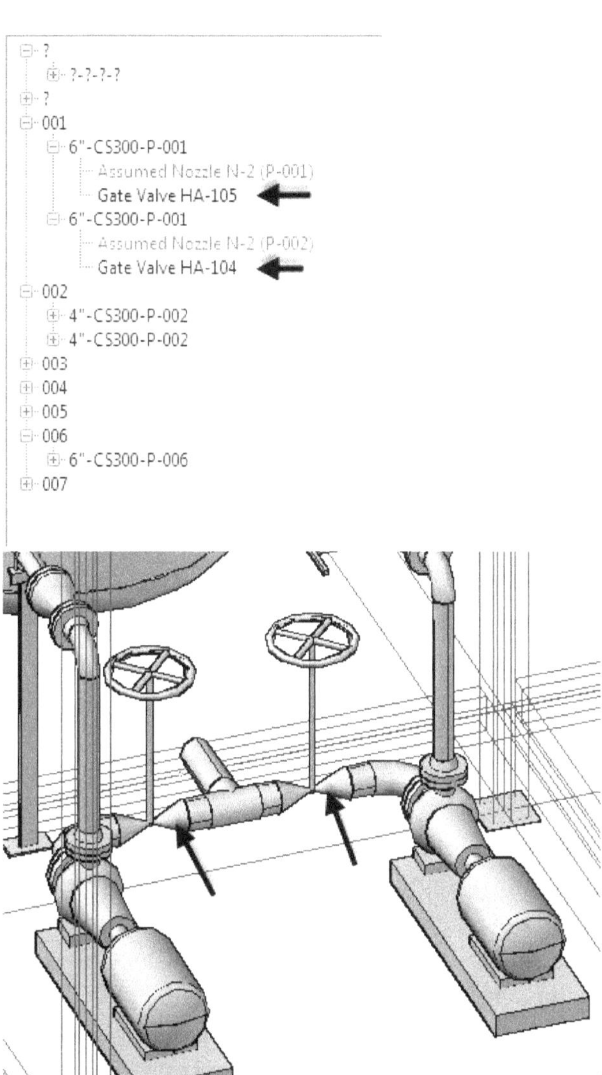

5. Likewise, solve the other errors or ignore them.

Chapter 6: Creating Isometric Drawings

After creating a 3D model, you can create Isometric Drawings, which assist in assembling the pipe components.

Specifying Iso Styles and other settings

In AutoCAD Plant 3D, the Isometric Drawings are created based on the project settings. You need to know about these settings so that you can modify the representation of the isometric drawings.

1. On the ribbon, click **Home > Project > Project Manager > Project Setup**.

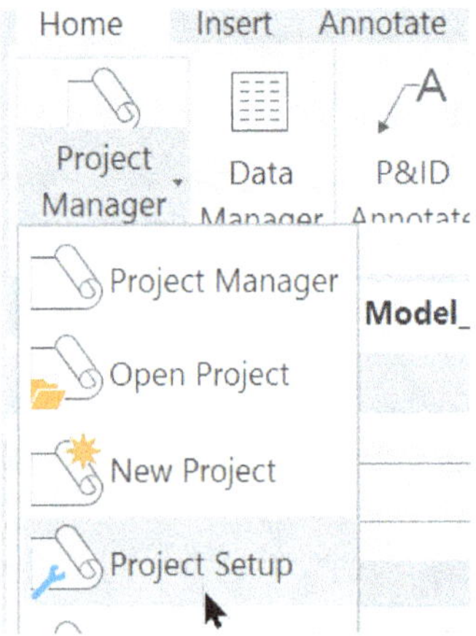

2. On the **Project Setup** dialog, expand **Isometric DWG Settings** and select **Iso Style Setup**.

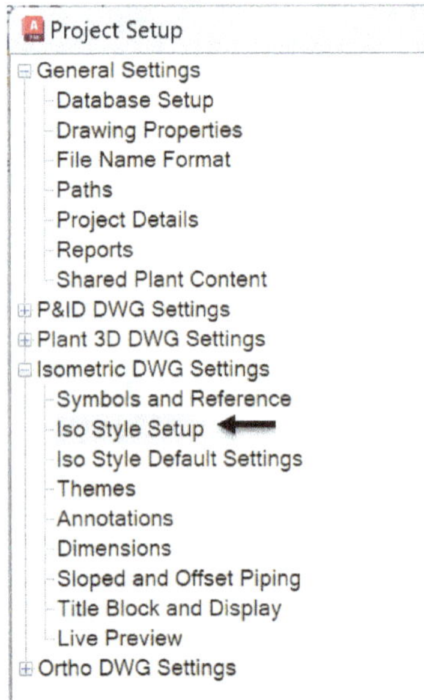

On the **Iso Style Setup** page, the **Iso Style** drop-down lists the Iso styles available. The **Check ANSI-B** Iso style is used to create isometric drawings. However, you can select other Iso styles. Click the + button next to the **Iso Style** drop-down, if you want to create a new Iso style.

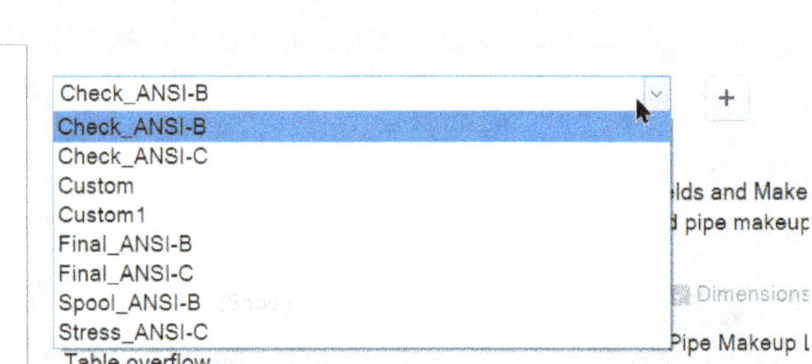

The **Add pipe makeup length to BOM for Field Fit Weld** option adds an extra pipe length to the bill of materials list to provide room for any adjustments in the field. Usually, the makeup length varies from 3" to 1'.

The **Place field welds at maximum pipe lengths** option adds weld points on a long pipe based on the maximum length pipes that are available in the field. For example, if you have created a very long pipe in the model, but the available pipe length in the field is 25' only. Then, you can check the **Place field welds at maximum pipe lengths** option and type-in 25' in the **Maximum pipe length** box. The weld points are added in the isometric drawing at 25' intervals on any pipe longer than 25'.

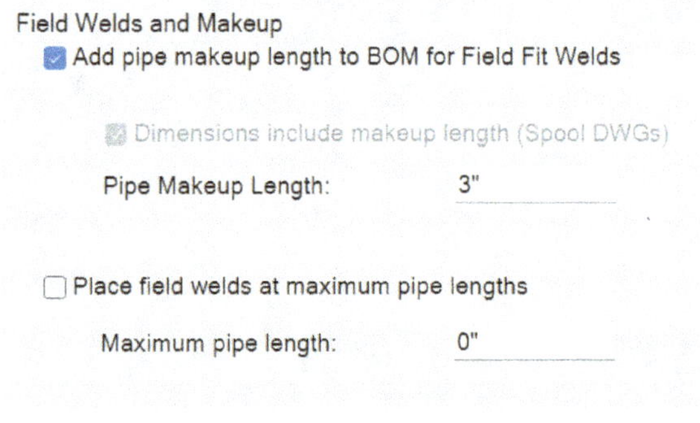

In the **Table overflow** section, specify the action when a piping size is more than the sheet size. Instruct the system to overflow the drawing onto another sheet or split the isometric drawing.

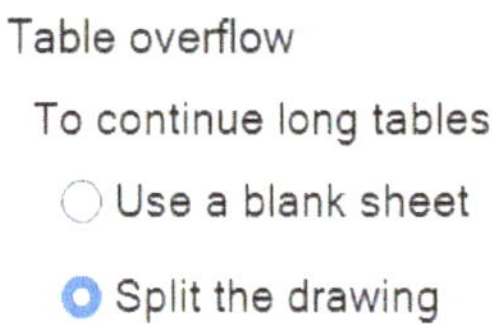

Table overflow

To continue long tables:

◯ Use a blank sheet

🔵 Split the drawing

The **Filename format** section provides options to define the file name format. To define the prefix, click before the **Line Number** tag and then click the **Add** button. This opens the **Add Property** dialog. From there, select a property from the Property section and click the **Add Property** button. The selected property will be added as a prefix before the **Line Number** tag. If needed, you can remove the **Line Number** prefix by simply clicking the '**x**' icon next to the **Line Number** tag.

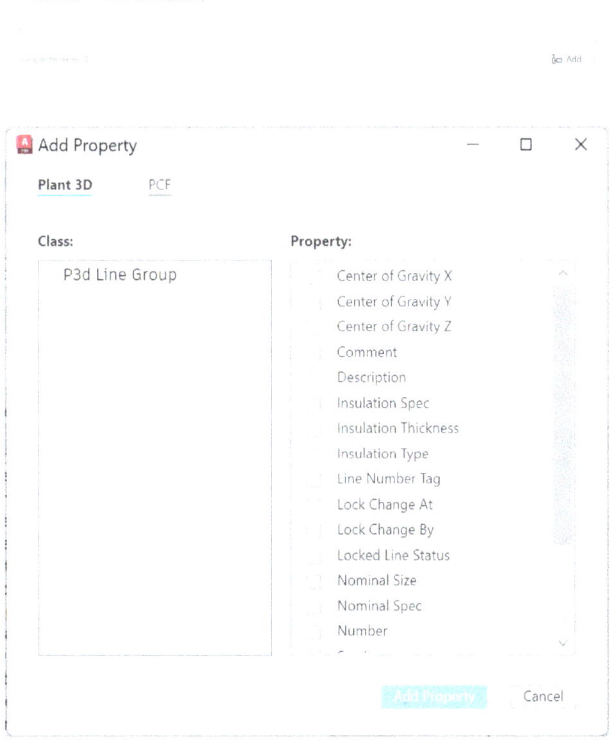

You can enter the delimiter by clicking between the Prefix and Suffix tags and typing any delimiter such as Comma (,), Semicolon (;), Tab (\t), Space (), Colon (:), Dash (-), Underscore (_), Pipe (|), Forward slash (/), Backslash (\).

The **Suffix** drop-down has two options: **Numeric (01, 02, …)** and **Alphabetic (A, B, …)**. These options name the suffix based on the alphabetical or numeric systems. The naming format helps you while sorting drawings inside a folder.

Filename format

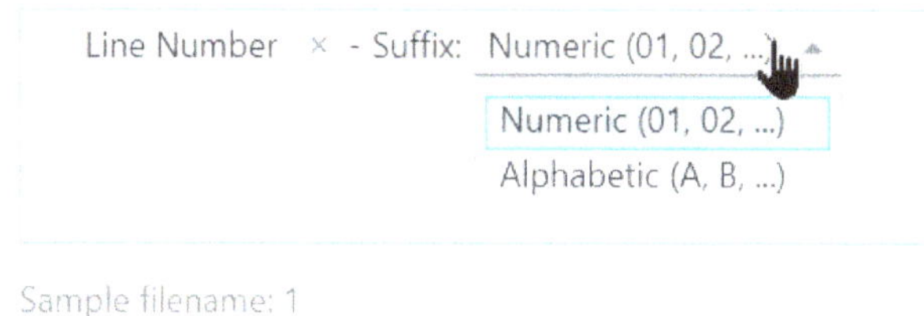

If you want to create a spool drawing, then select the **Spool (Fabrication)**option from the **Drawing Type** section. A spool drawing is created by dividing the piping into sections. It includes all the piping components and labels them. The spool drawing helps in assembling the parts correctly. You can notice that the **Table overflow** and **Filename format** sections are grayed out as the piping is already broken into smaller parts in a spool drawing.

Drawing Type

◯ Isometric

🔵 Spool (Fabrication)

The **Naming method** drop-down in the **Spools** section has five options to define the spooling format: **Numeric, Alphabetic, Line – Numeric, Line – Alphabetic**, and **Use spool number from the model**.

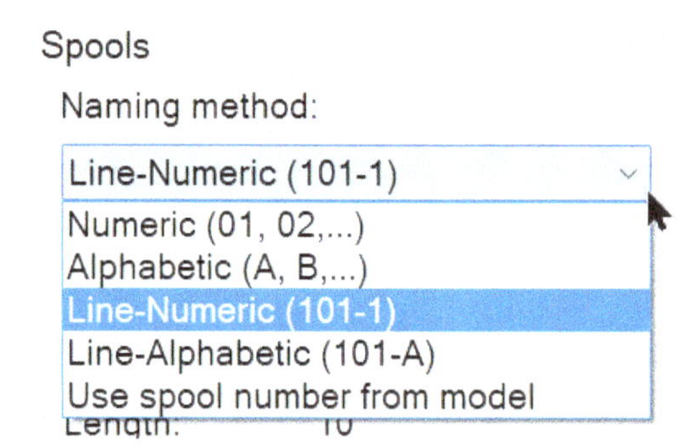

The **Sizing method** drop-down in the **Spools** section has three options. The **Automatic (Max. size)** option checks the lengths of the pipes in the model and generates a spool drawing based on them. The **Automatic (Max. weight)** option creates the spool drawing based on the pipe weight. The **Use spool number from model** option uses the spool number from the model to create the spool drawing.

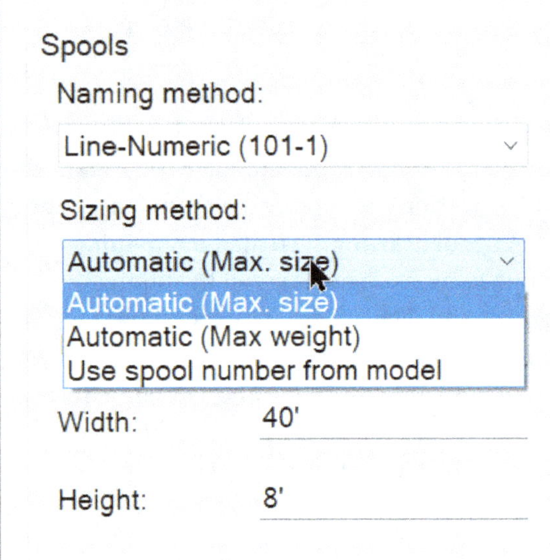

Type-in values in the **Length, Width,** and **Height** boxes to define the area of the spool. The pipe layout is broken into individual sections of a specified area.

The **Content paths** section is used to define the locations for the production and quick isometric drawings. These files are saved at default locations under the project folder.

You can also specify all the above settings for the Iso Style in the XML Editor. To do this, click the **Open Iso Style Editor** icon located at the top-right corner of the **Project Setup** dialog. When the Plant 3D Iso Style Editor message box appears, click "**Save Changes in Project Setup (Recommended)**".

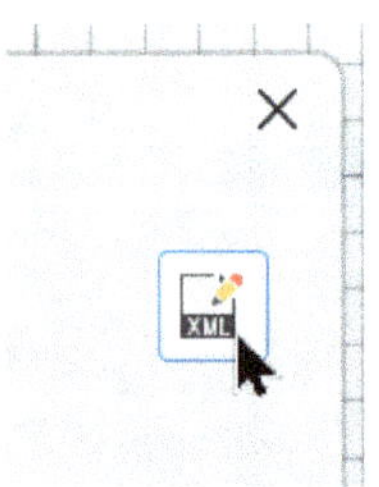

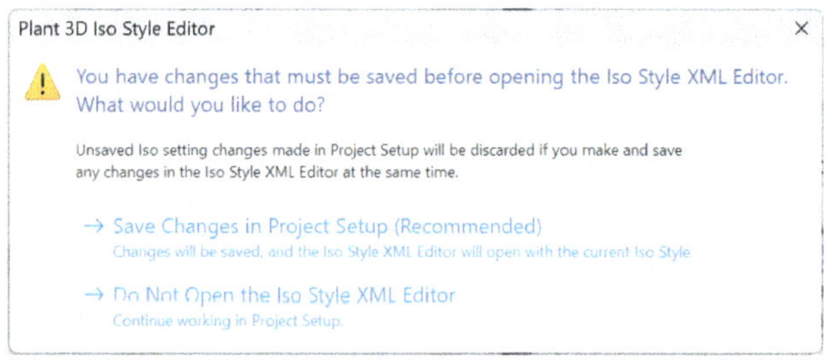

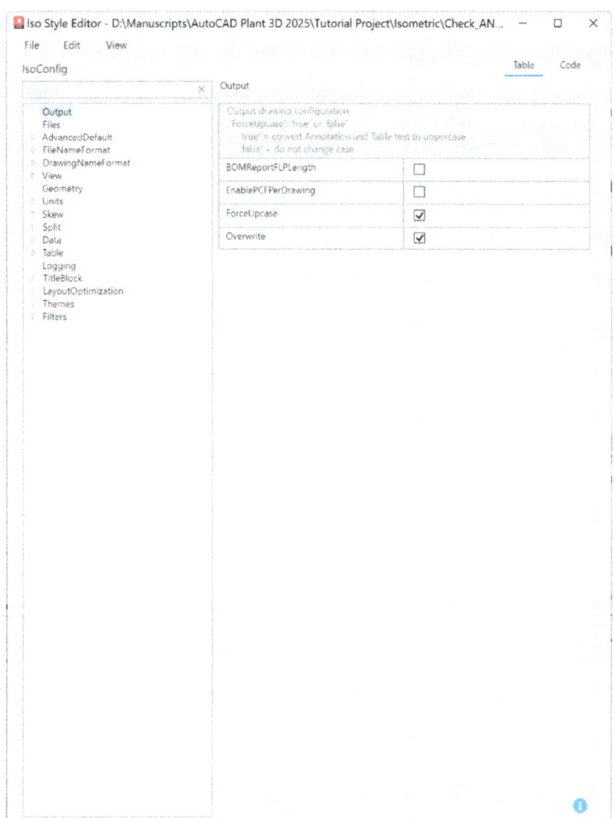

In the **Iso Style Editor** dialog, select the desired option from the tree view on the left side. Then, specify the relevant options for the selected nodes. Finally, close the dialog.

3. Click **Sloped and Offset Piping** under the tree.

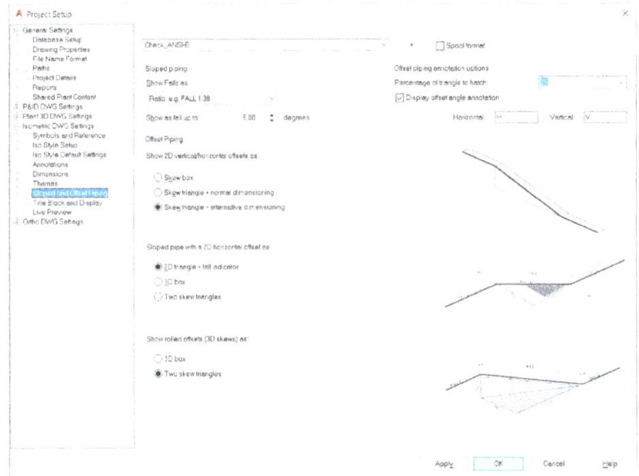

The **Sloped and Offset Piping** page has options to define the display of sloped piping in the Isometric drawings.

The **Show Falls as** drop-down has six options to display the sloped piping: **Ratio**, **Angle**, **Percentage**, **Gradient**, **Imperial incline**, **Metric incline**, and **Suppress falling Line Inclination**. The last option will not show any falling line indication.

The **Offset Piping** section has options to display three types of offsets.

You can show a 2D vertical/ horizontal offset using a skew box.

The **Skew triangle + normal dimensioning** option shows the 2D offset using the triangle and default dimensions.

The **Skew triangle + alternative dimensioning** option shows the 2D offset using the triangle and alternative dimensions.

You can show the sloped piping with a 2D horizontal offset using a 2D triangle + fall indicator, 3D box, or two skewed triangles.

The rolled offset (3D skews) can be shown using a 3D box or two skew triangles.

In the **Offset piping annotations options** section, you can modify the annotation settings, such as the percentage of a triangle to be hatched. The **Display offset angle annotation** option can be used to turn on/off the offset angle annotation.

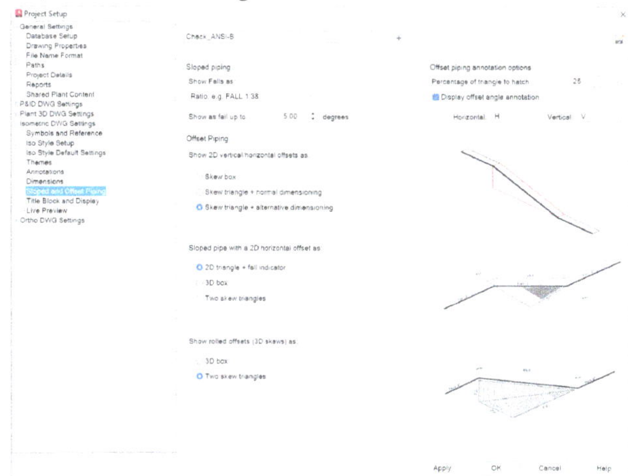

4.   Click **Symbols and Reference** in the tree.

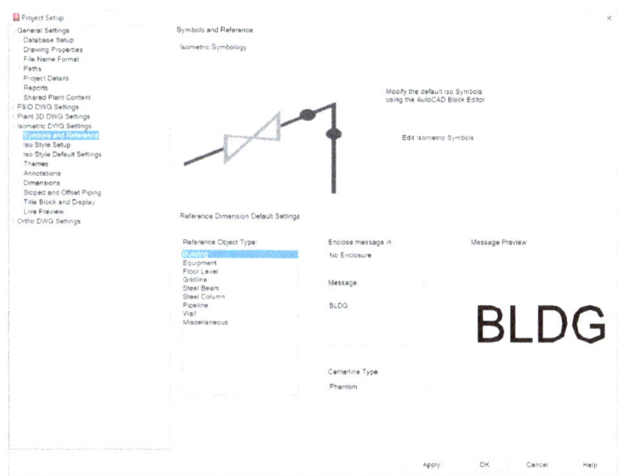

The options in the **Isometric Symbology** section help you to change the display of the default isometric fittings. To do so, click the **Edit Isometric Symbols** button.

On the **Edit Block Definition** dialog, you can select the symbols to edit from the dialog. Click **Cancel** to exit this dialog.

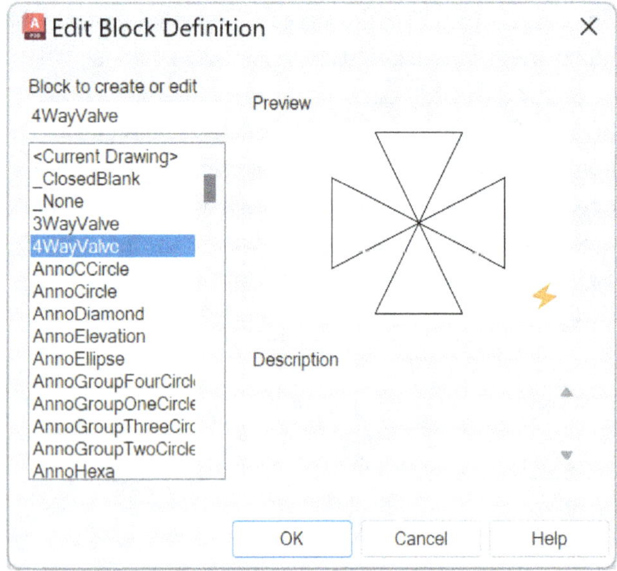

The options in the **Reference Dimension Default Settings** section help you to specify the display of the reference objects in the Isometric Drawing. For example, you can specify the way equipment is displayed in the Isometric drawing. To do so, select **Equipment** from the **Reference Object Type** list.

Next, click the **Select Class Property** icon in the **Message** section. In the **Select Class Property** dialog, select a property from the **Property** list and click **OK**. The selected property will be displayed in the **Message** box. Also, the preview of the equipment message is updated. You can also select an enclosure for the message from the **Enclosure message in** drop-down.

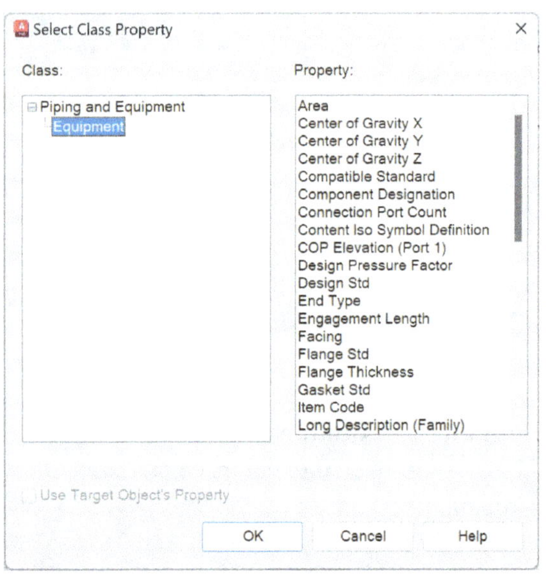

The **Centerline Type** drop-down is used to specify the way a centreline is displayed in the isometric drawing. You can select different line types such as Dashed/Existing, Centerline, Phantom, and so on.

5.   Click **Title Block and Display** in the tree.

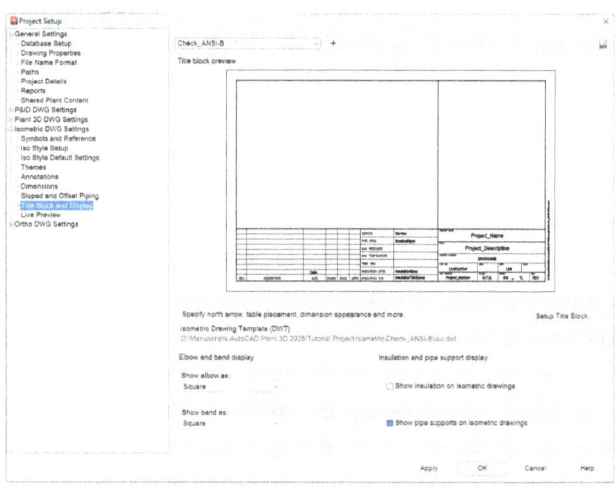

The **Elbow and bend display** section has options to modify the display of elbows and bends. The **Insulation and pipe support display** section has options to show or hide the pipe supports and insulation in the isometric drawing.

Annotation and Dimension settings

Annotations and dimensions settings of an Iso style are two of the most important settings.

1.   Click **Annotations** under the tree.

On the **Annotations** page, has five tabs: **Settings**, **Table ID's**, **Connections**, **Piping**, and **Property Changes**.

On the **Settings** tab, you can configure the **Annotation Settings**, including how **Coordinate Labels** are displayed. In the **Text Options** section, you can specify the annotation text and enclosure height, as well as set the **MText Width Limit** value. Additionally, under the **New Annotation Defaults** section, you can define the default settings for annotations, including settings for **Blocks**, **Leaders**, and **Placement**.

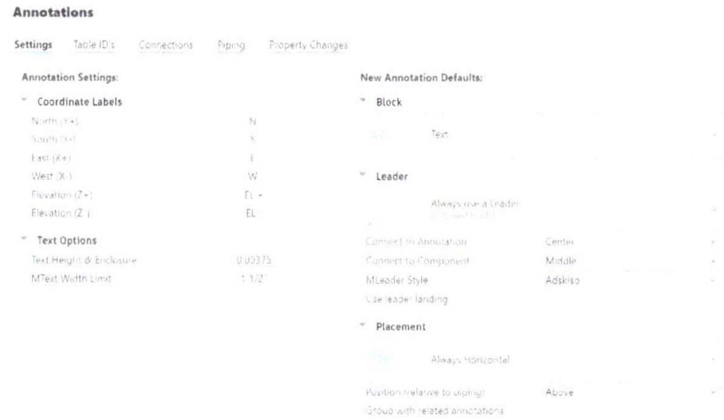

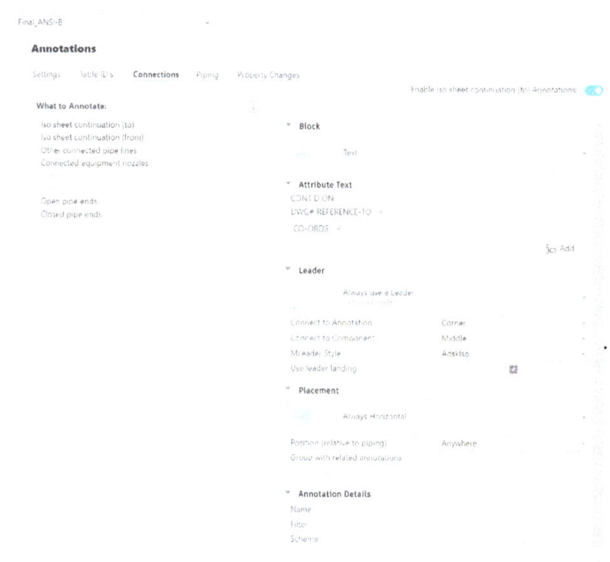

On the **Table IDs** tab, you can choose which table to display by selecting an option from the "**What to Annotate**" section. The available options include **Bill of Material ID (Components)**, **Bill of Material ID (Pipe)**, **Cut Piece ID**, **Spool ID**, **Weld ID (Shop)**, and **Weld (Field)**. Once you select the desired option, turn on the enable button located on the right side. This will reveal the settings related to the selected table type on the right side, including options for **Block**, **Attribute Text**, **Leader**, **Placement**, and **Annotation Details**.

The **Piping** tab offers annotation settings for all the piping objects. Select the piping object from the **What to Annotate** section and modify the settings.

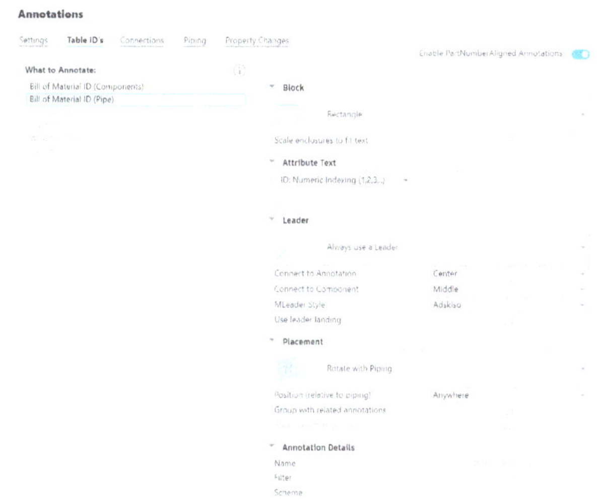

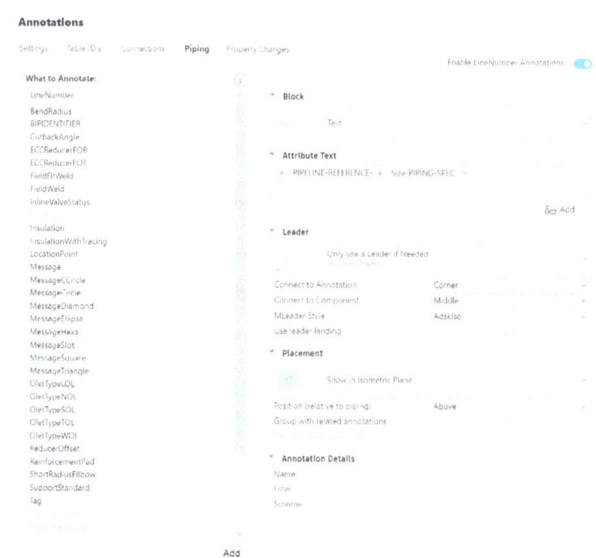

The **Connections** tab offers settings for various end connection annotations, including Iso sheet continuation, connections to other pipelines, drains, vents, open pipe ends, and closed pipe ends. From this tab, you can enter a custom prefix and text for each type of end connection. Please note that these settings are exclusive to the Final Iso drawing and are not available for other drawing types.

The **Property Changes** tab enables you to configure how changes to properties, such as Elevation, Size, and Insulation Limit, are displayed

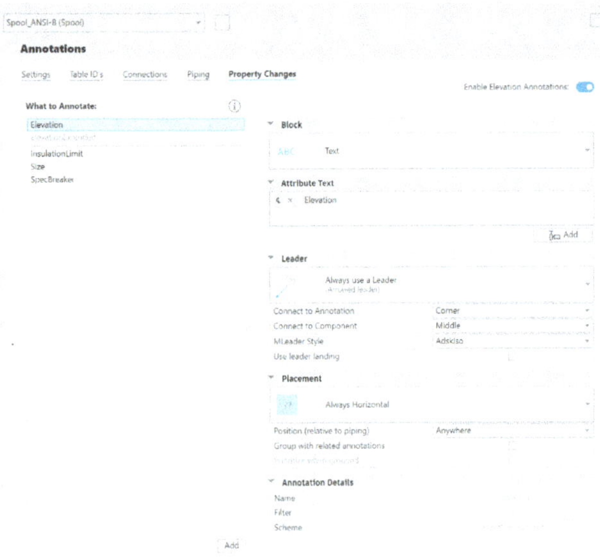

2. Click **Themes** under the tree.

There are three tabs on the Themes page: **Default Piping**, **Override**, and **Branch Piping**.

Isometric drawings have a default theme that can be viewed on the **Default Piping** tab. This tab allows you to customize the appearance of your Isometric drawings by adjusting the symbol scale. Additionally, you can choose to enable or disable annotations and dimensions, giving you control over the level of detail displayed in your drawings.

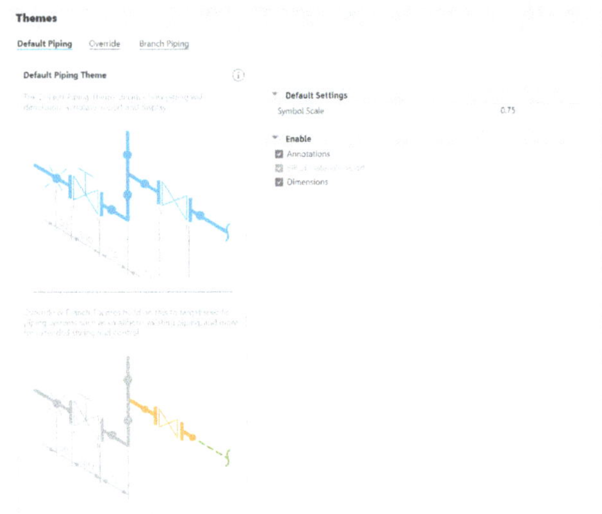

The **Override** tab offers advanced customization options for Isometric drawings, allowing you to modify their themes. Within the **Override Themes**

section, you can select specific components of the Isometric drawing and adjust their settings to suit your requirements.

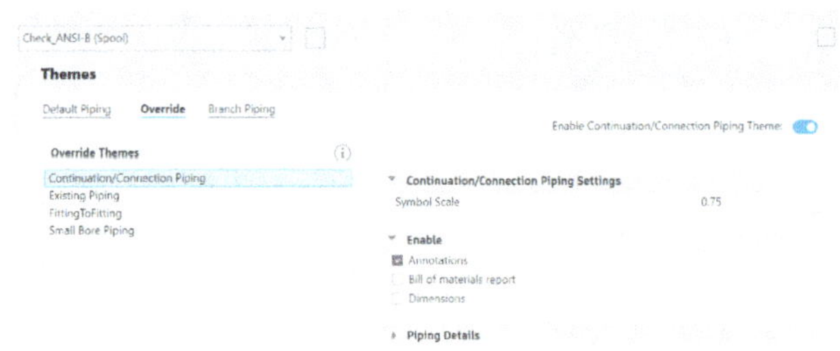

The **Branch Piping** tab offers advanced customization options for the pipes or lines that branch off from the main pipe or line, creating secondary lines that deviate from the primary flow path. This tab allows you to tailor the visual representation of these branch connections, including the **Offline Instrument Connection** and **Vent/Drain Piping**.

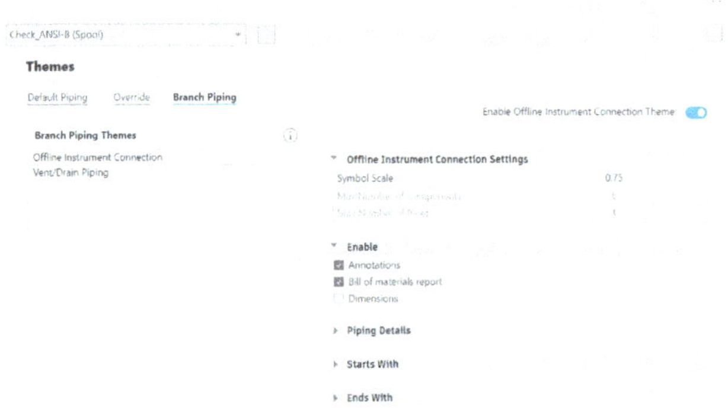

3. Click **Dimensions** under the tree.

There are four tabs available on the **Dimensions** page: **Settings**, **End to End (Overall)**, **String**, and **Locating**.

The **Settings** tab allows you specify the General Settings of the dimension such as text height and other display settings. Check the **Hide last string dimension** option to remove the last string dimension when you have an end to end dimension.

The **Dimension Offset Distances** section has options to specify distances between the pipelines and dimensions. Enter a value in the **Offset** box to specify the distance between the pipeline and dimension. Likewise, enter a value in the **Stacking** box to specify the distance between the stacked dimensions.

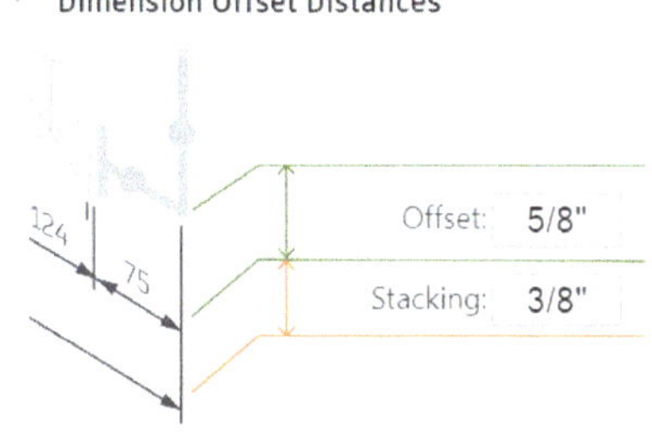

The **Gaskets Dimensioning** drop-down has three options: **Include in component**, **Dimension gaskets**, and **Do not Dimension Gaskets**.

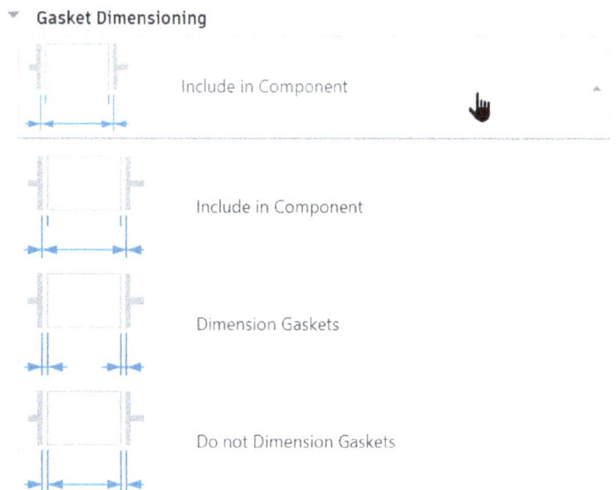

Selecting a theme from the drop-down menu at the top-right corner allows you to display dimensions related to the chosen theme in the **Dimension** section. A dimension theme is a predefined setting that controls which dimensions are displayed.

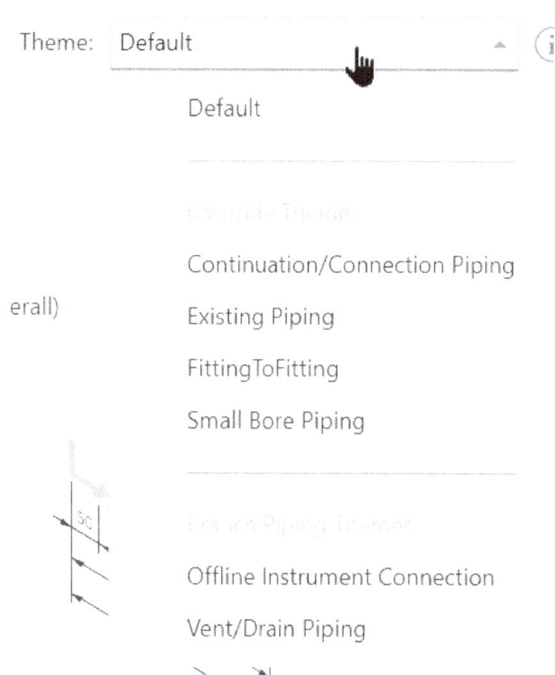

The **End to End (Overall)** type dimensions option displays dimensions of complete pipe run.

The **String** type dimensions option adds dimensions to piping segments, including fittings and inline accessories.

The **Locating** option adds a dimension to define the location of weld points or pipe supports from a specific point, such as the elbow.

As you check the dimension types one-by-one, they are displayed in the preview image. Each dimension type has a table to define the stopping point for different piping components.

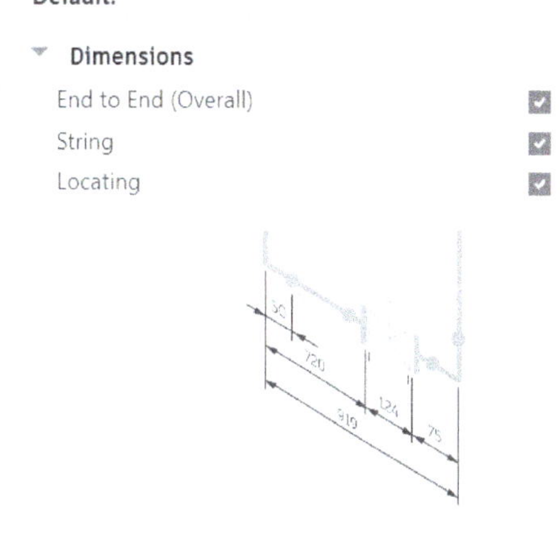

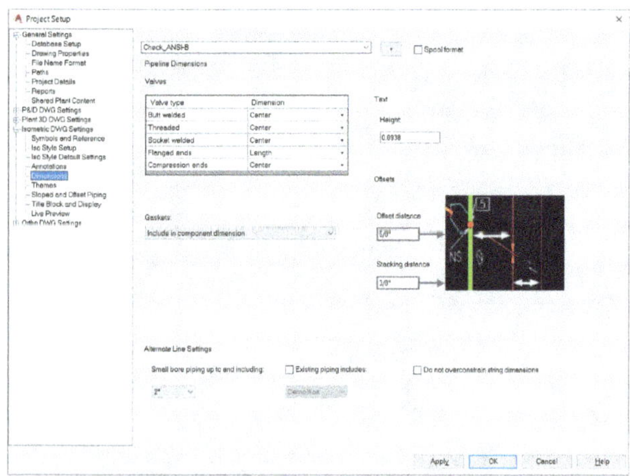

The **End to End (Overall)** tab allows you to specify the end-to-end dimension settings of the individual elements of the Isometric drawing. You can select them from the **What to Dimension (Anchors)** section and select an option from the **How to Dimension (EndPoints)** section.

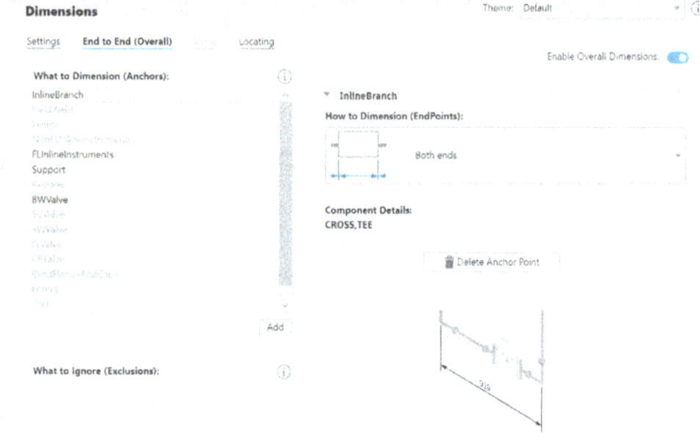

The **String** tab allows to you specify the dimension settings of the fitting along the individual piping segments.

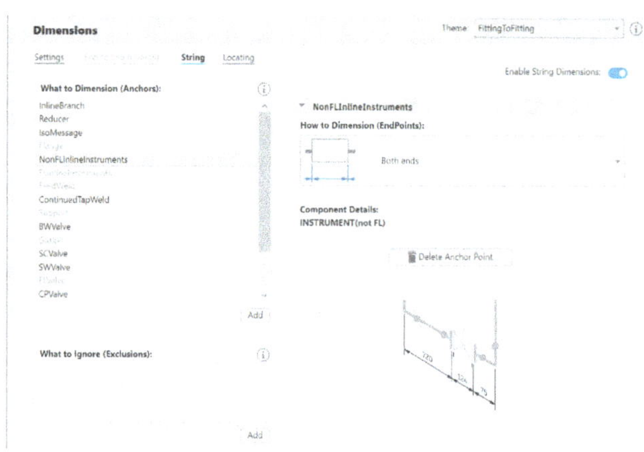

The **Locating** tab allows you specify the settings related to locating dimensions.

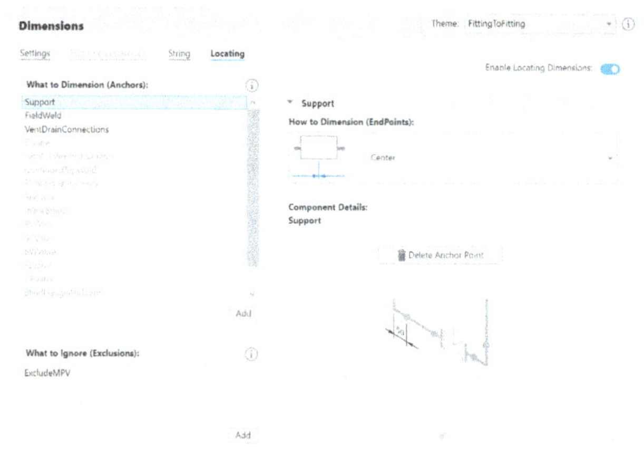

4.   Click **OK** to close the **Project Setup** dialog.

Creating New Iso Styles

Earlier, you have learned about various options of an already existing Iso Style. Now, you will learn to create a new Iso Style.

1.   On the ribbon, click **Home > Project > Project drop-down > Project Setup**.
2.   On the **Project Setup** dialog, expand the tree located at the left side and select **Isometric DWG Settings > Iso Style Setup**.
3.   On the **Iso Style Setup** page, click the plus button located next to the **Iso Style** drop-down.
4.   On the **Create Iso Style** dialog, enter **Custom** in the **Iso Style** name box.
5.   Select **Create new Style**, and then click **Create.**

The **Create Isometric Style** dialog appears. In this dialog, the **Table Layout and Paper Size** page appears. You can get more information about this page at the bottom of the dialog. On this page, notice the arrows available at the bottom. Use these arrows to explore different table layouts and sizes.

6. Click the right arrow located at the bottom to select the ANSI-B 4" layout.

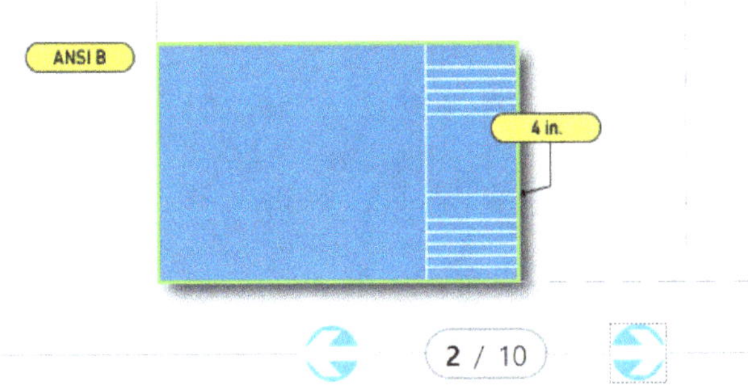

7. Click the right arrow located at the top.

The **Leader lines & Enclosures** page appears. On this page, you select the annotation leader and enclosure settings. Click the arrows located at the bottom to explore the different leader lines and enclosure settings.

8. Use the right arrow located at the bottom to go to the **10/10** leader line and enclosure settings.

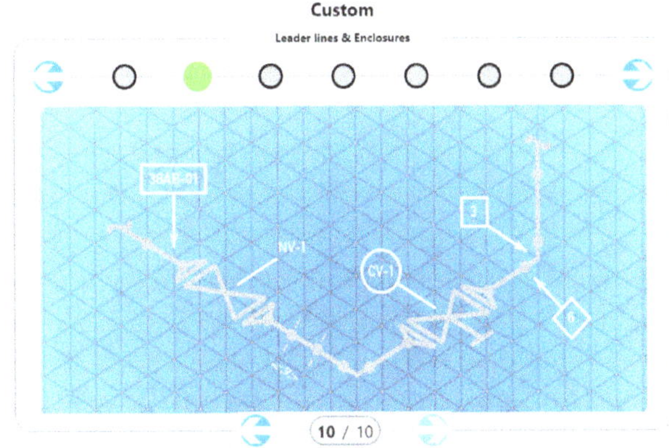

9. Click the right arrow located at the top to move to the next page.

On the **Ribbon planes** page, you can specify the distance between the pipelines and dimensions.

10. Explore the ribbon plane settings using the arrows located at the bottom.

11. Select the **1/3** setting.

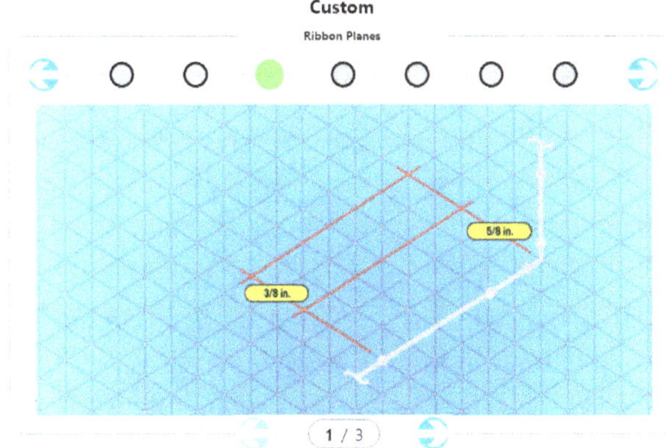

12. Click the right arrow located at the top to move to the **Default piping styles** page.

On the **Default piping styles** page, you can select the predefined dimension styles by clicking the arrows located at the bottom.

13. Select 1/3 setting.

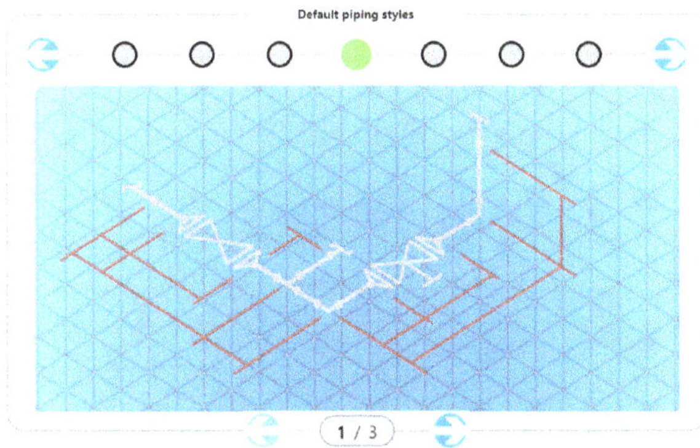

14. Click the right arrow located at the top to move to the **Fitting-to-fitting piping styles** page.

On the **Fitting-to-fitting piping styles** page, you can specify the dimension styles for fitting-to-fitting pipe runs.

15. Select the **2/3** setting.

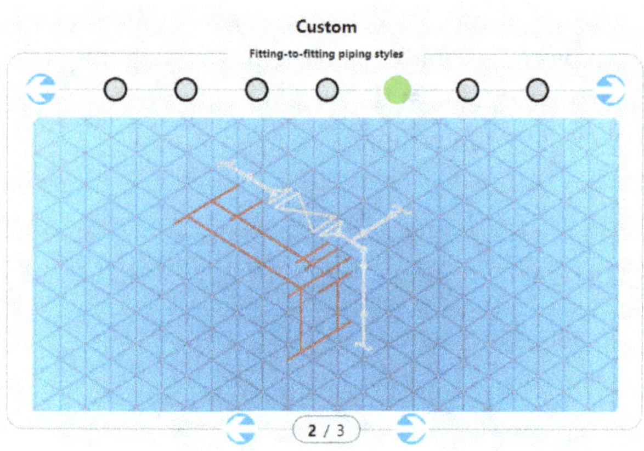

16. Click the right arrow located at the top to move to the **Small bore piping styles** page.
17. Select the 2/2 setting and move on to the next page.
18. On the **Text height & Symbol Scale** page, select the 1/4 setting.
19. Click **Create Style**.
20. Click **OK** to close the **Project Setup** dialog.

Generating a Quick Isometric Drawing

After configuring the Iso style and other project settings, you need to check whether the Isometric Drawing has all the information or not. The Quick Iso helps you to do this.

1. Activate the **3D Piping** workspace.
2. Change the **View Style** to **2D Wireframe**.

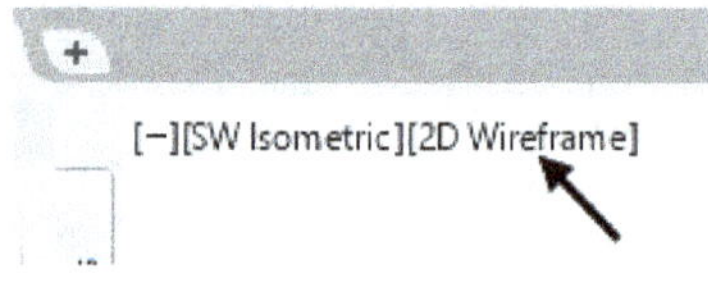

3. On the ribbon, click **Isos > Iso Annotations > Start Point** (!).
4. On the Status bar, click the down arrow next to the **Object Snap** icon and select **Endpoint** from the flyout.
5. Zoom to the left pump.
6. Place the pointer of the vertical pipe connected to the pump.
7. Select the endpoint of the centreline of the pipe.

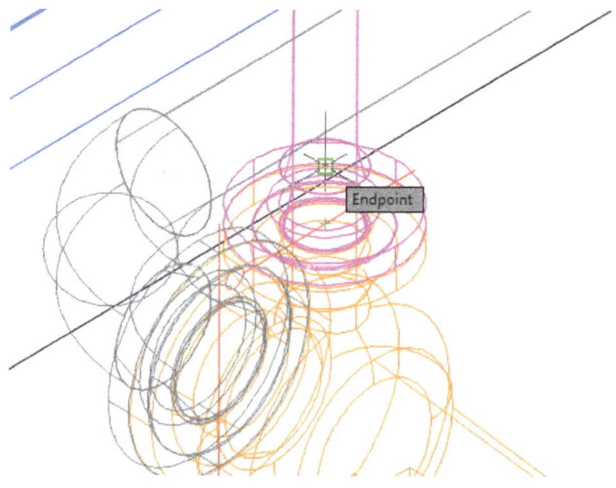

The start point is defined, as shown.

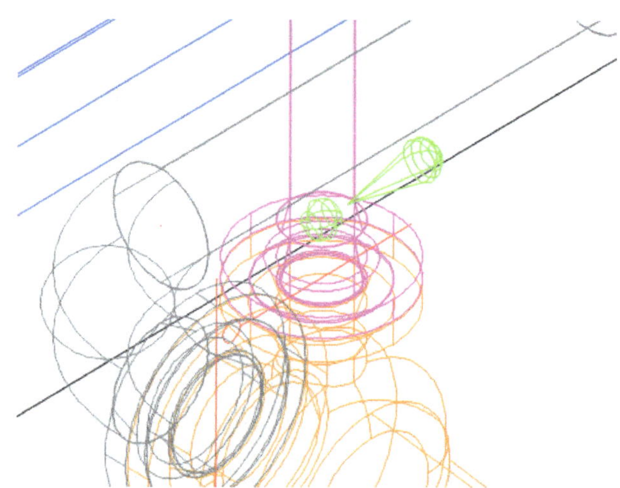

8. Change the **View Style** to **Realistic**.
9. On the ribbon, click **Isos > Iso Creation > Quick Iso**.

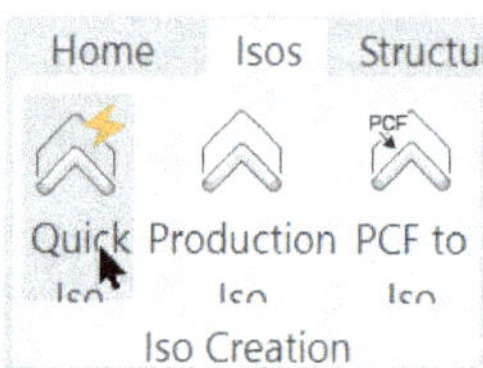

10. Select the pipe connections between the vessel and pumps. Also, select the pipe support and press **Enter**.

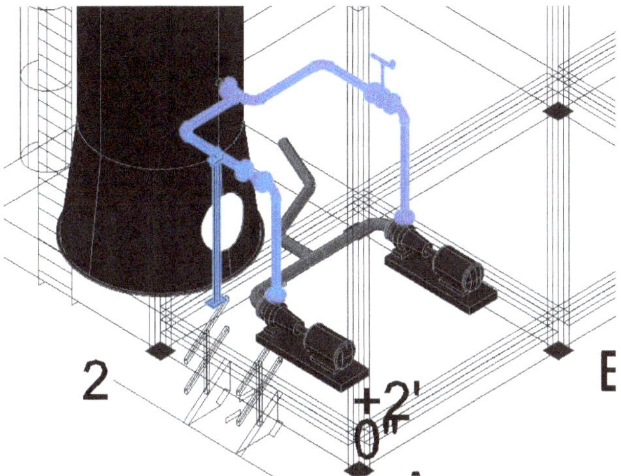

On the **Create Quick Iso** dialog, you can use the **Reselect** button to select the piping components again.

11. Select **Iso Style > Check_ANSI-B** from the dialog.
12. Click **Create** to generate the Quick Iso. The quick Iso is generated in the background. After a few seconds, the **Isometric Creation Complete** balloon appears at the bottom right corner.

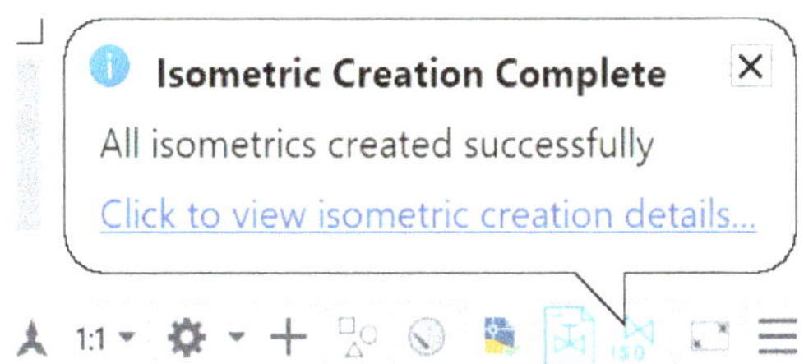

13. Click the link on the balloon to view the isometric creation details. The **Isometric Creation Results** dialog appears showing the warnings and the isometric drawing links.

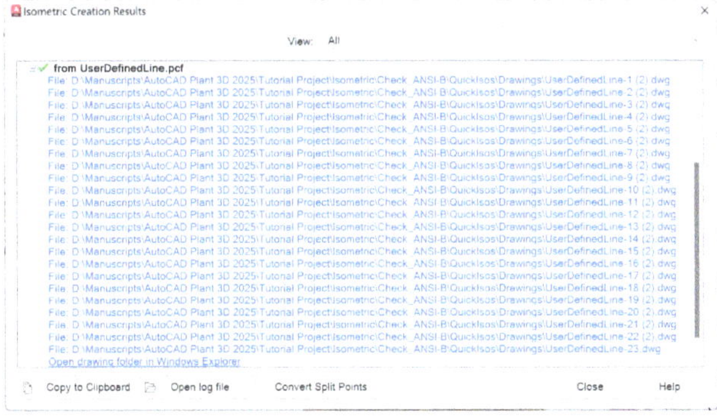

14. Click on any one of the file links to open it. The isometric drawing appears (It may not be the same as that given below).

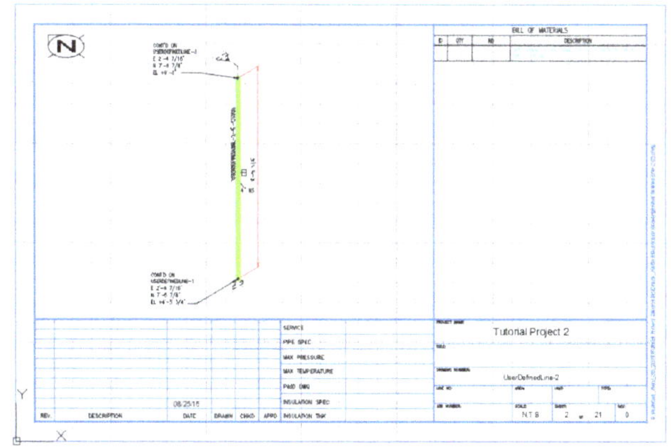

15. Review the Quick Iso and close it.

Creating Reference Dimensions

You can create reference dimensions to show the locations of the components, such as structural members that cannot be documented in the Iso drawings.

1. Open the 3D piping model.
1. Set the view orientation to Top.
2. Change the **View Style** to **2D Wireframe**.
3. On the ribbon, click **Isos** tab > **Iso Annotations** panel > **Reference Dimensions**.

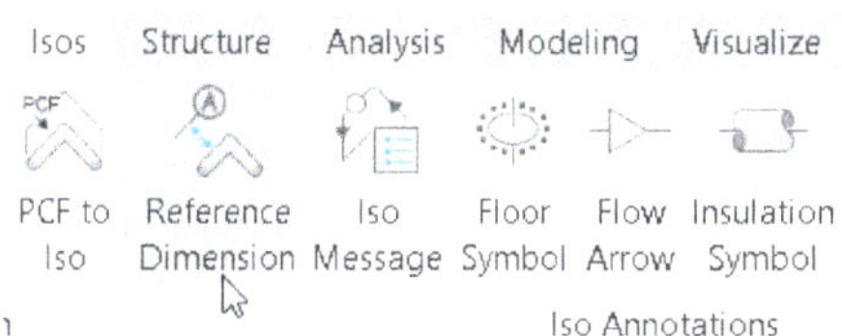

4. Select the horizontal pipe connected to the left pump.
5. Move the pointer horizontally and select a point on the steel beam adjacent to the pump; a dimension appears between the selected points.

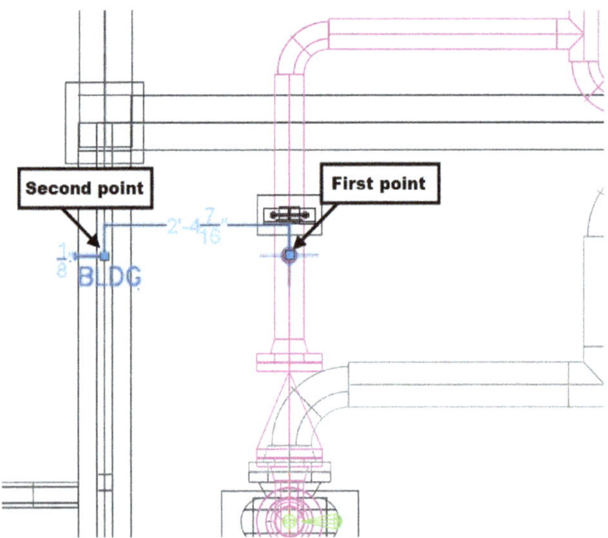

6. On the **Properties** palette, scroll down to the **Reference Object** section.
7. In the **Reference Object** section, select **Steel Beam** from the **Object Type** drop-down.
8. Click in the **Message** field and press Backspace on the keyboard.
9. Type **STR** in the **Message** box.

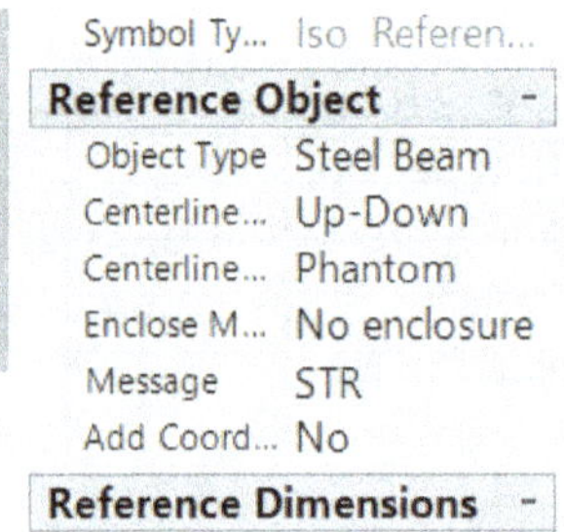

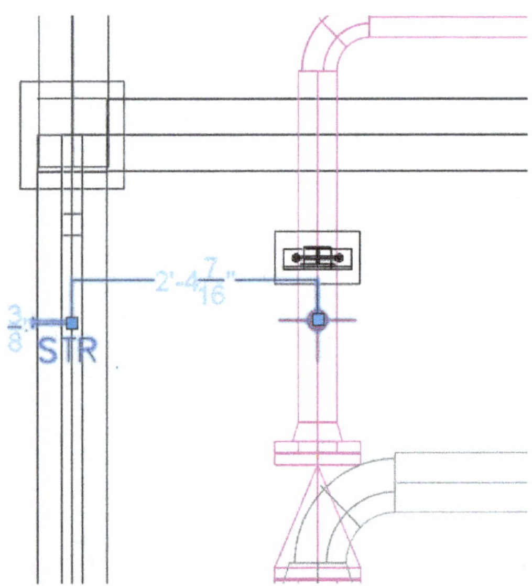

10. Save the 3D piping model file.

Generating Production Isometric Drawings

In AutoCAD Plant 3D, you can create Production Isometric drawings based on the 3D model.

1. On the ribbon, click **Isos > Iso Creation > Production Iso**.
2. On the **Create Production Iso** dialog, check 002 in the **Line numbers** section.
3. Set the **Iso Style** to **Final_ ANSI-B**.

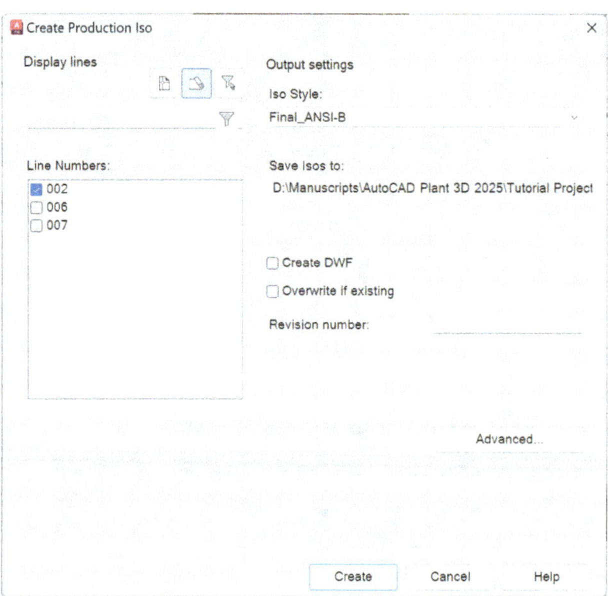

4. Leave the other default settings and click the **Advanced** button.

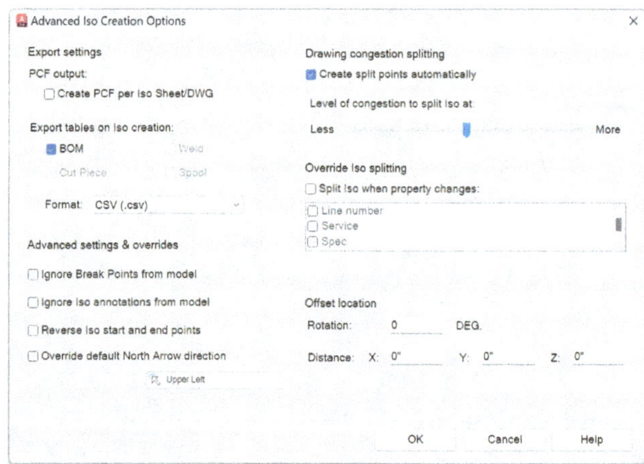

On the **Advanced Iso Creation Options** dialog, the **Export Settings** section has options to export the tables on the isometric drawing.

16. Check the **BOM** option and set the **Export format** to CSV(.csv).

The options in the **Override Iso splitting** section allow you to split a large Isometric drawing into small Isos. You can instruct the program to break the Iso if a property such as Line number or service changes.

17. Check the **Split Iso when property changes** option, and then check the **Line number** property.
18. Review the other settings on the dialog and click **OK**.
19. Click **Create** on the **Create Production Iso** dialog. The **Production Iso** generation runs in the background. A balloon appears after generating the Production Iso.
20. On the balloon, click the link to see the results.
21. Click on the first hyperlink on the **Isometric Creation Results** dialog; the Isometric drawing appears along with the reference dimension.

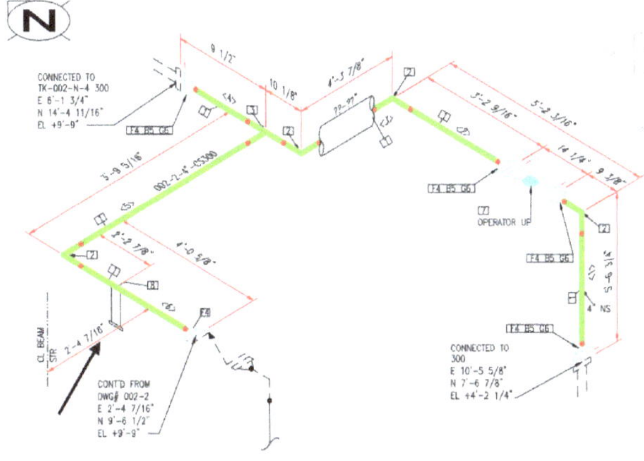

22. Close the isometric drawing.
23. On the ribbon, click **Isos > Iso Creation > Production Iso**.
24. On the **Create Production Iso** dialog, check 002 in the **Line numbers** section.
25. Set the **Iso Style** to **Spool_ ANSI-B**.
26. Click **Create**.
27. On the balloon, click the link displayed to see the results. You notice that there are four hyperlinks,

which means that a separate drawing is created for each pipe.

28. Click on the first hyperlink on the **Isometric Creation Results** dialog.

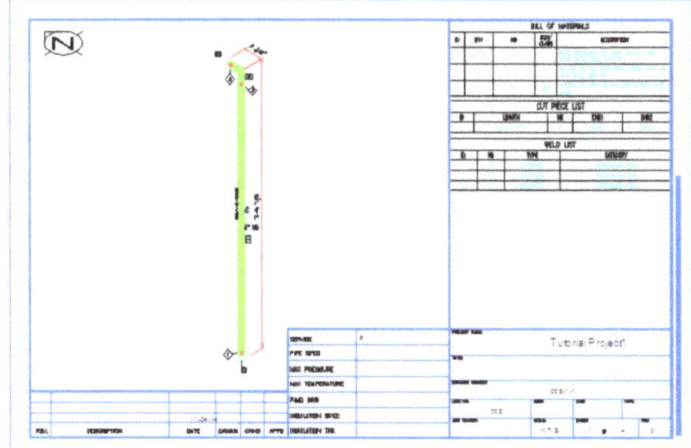

29. Click the **Isometric DWG** tab on the Project Manager, and you notice that the drawings are arranged in folders. You can access the isometric drawings from these folders.

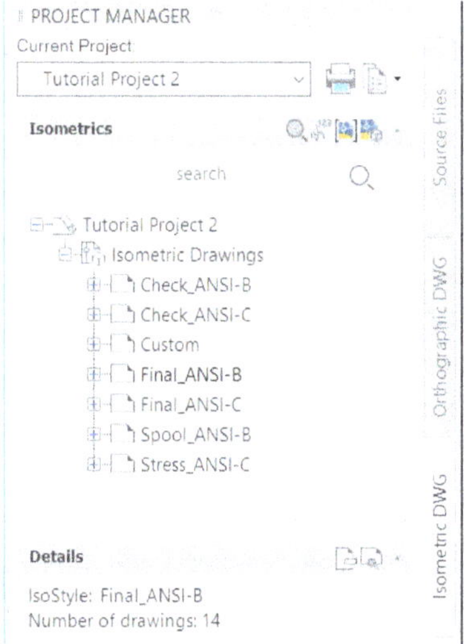

Adding Isometric Messages and Annotations

You can add some additional information to the Isometric drawings using symbols and messages. They are available on the **Iso Annotations** panel. They are inserted in the 3D model and visible in the Isometric drawings.

1. Set the **View Style** to **2D Wireframe**.
2. On the ribbon, click **Isos > Iso Annotations > Iso Message**.
3. On the **Create Iso Message** dialog, select **Box (Diamond end)** from the **Enclose message in** drop-down.
4. Type-in a message in the **Message** box and click **OK**.
5. Click on the pipe connected to the right pump, as shown. A sphere appears at the selected point.

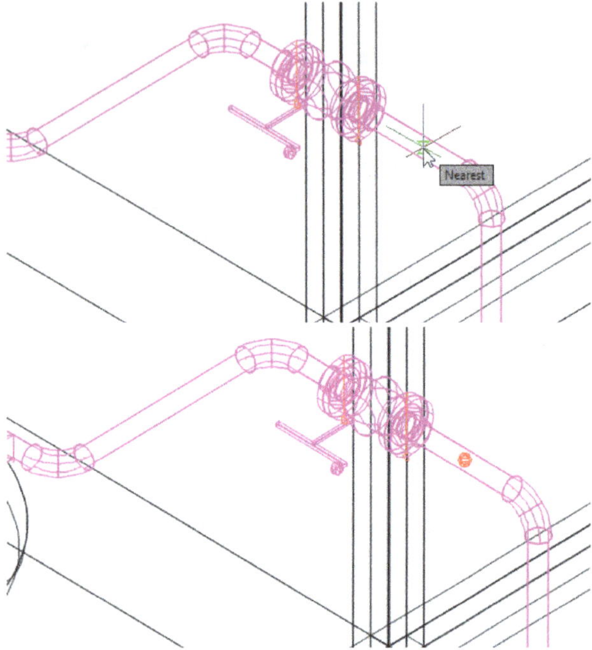

6. On the ribbon, click **Isos > Iso Annotations > Flow Arrow**.
7. Click on the pipe to define the insertion point, as shown.

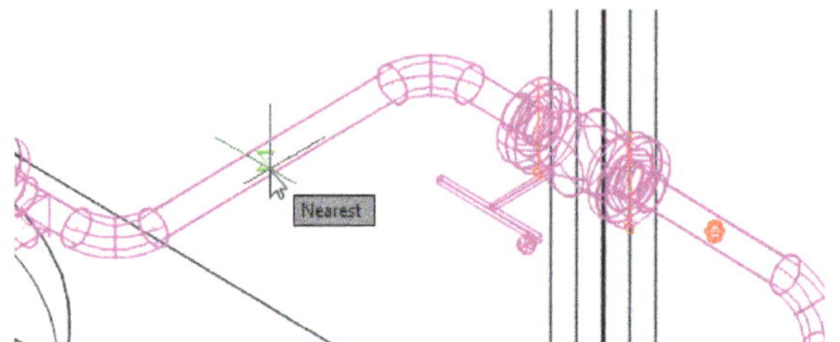

8. Click **Accept** in the command line. You can also click **Reverse** if you want to change the flow direction.
9. On the ribbon, click **Isos > Iso Annotations > Insulation Symbol**.
10. Click on the pipe, as shown.

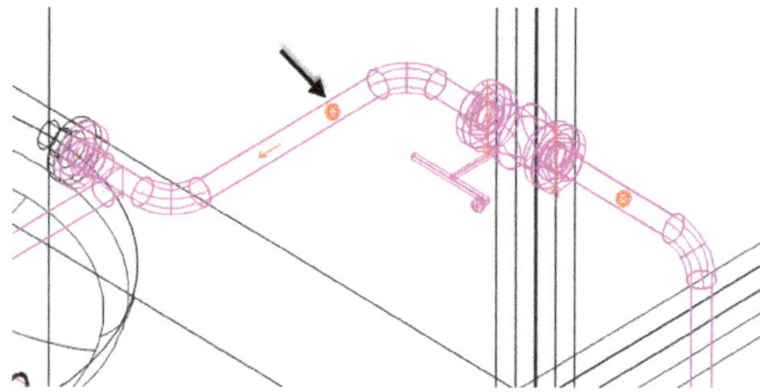

Likewise, you can add other symbols to the Isometric drawing.

11. Create a Quick Iso and view the results.

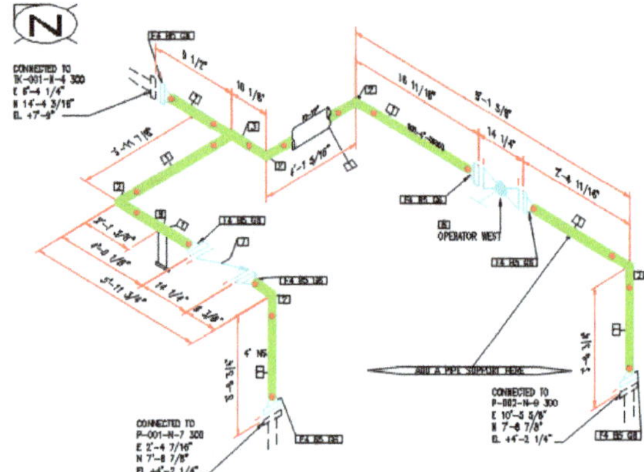

Export the Piping data to PCF format

You can export the piping data to a PCF (pipe component files), which helps you to use the information in other applications.

1. On the ribbon, click **Isos > Export > PCF Export**.
2. On the **Export PCF** dialog, check the 002 under the **Line Numbers** list. You can also define the file location using the **Save PCF files to** option.

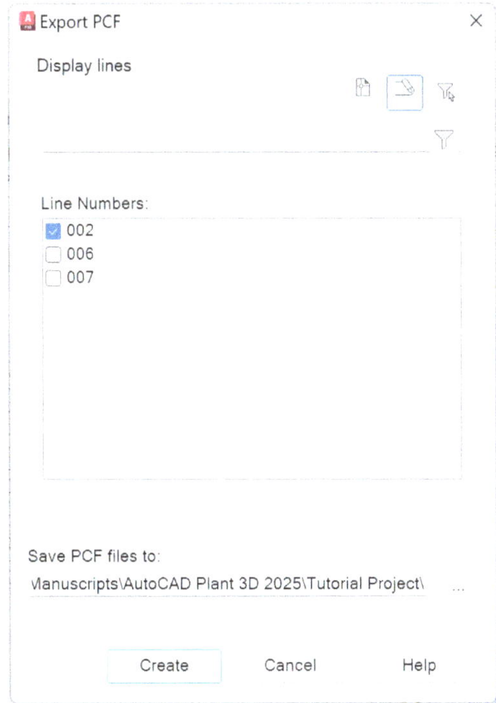

3. Click **Create** to complete the PCF creation.

Now, you can use the PCF file to create an Isometric Drawing.

4. On the ribbon, click **Isos > Iso Creation > PCF to Iso**.
5. On the **Create Iso from PCF** dialog, click the **Add** button.
6. Go to the location of the 002.pcf file.
7. Select the file and click **Open**.
8. On the dialog, select **Iso Type > Final_ ANSI-C**.
9. Click **Create** to create an Isometric Drawing from the PCF.
10. On the balloon, click on the link displayed to see the results
11. Click on the hyperlink on the **Isometric Creation Results** dialog.

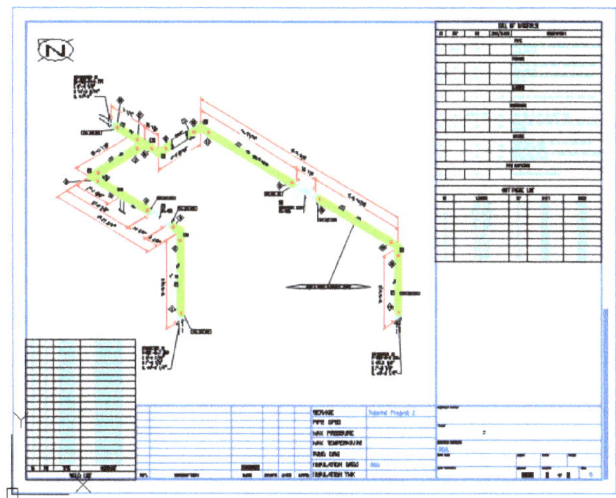

The Isometric drawing created from the PCF is not linked to the project.

12. Close the Isometric drawing.

Importing the PCF file into a 3D Model

In AutoCAD Plant 3D 2025, you can import the PCF file and convert it into a 3D piping model.

1. Create a new Plant 3D drawing using the New Drawing button located on the Project Manager.
2. On the ribbon, click **Home** tab > **Part Insertion** panel > **PCF to Pipe**.
3. Browse to the location of the 002.pcf file.
4. Select the file and click **Open**.
5. Click the **Create Piping** button on the **PCF to Pipe** dialog; the PCF file is converted into the 3D pipe.
6. Click **Close** on the dialog.

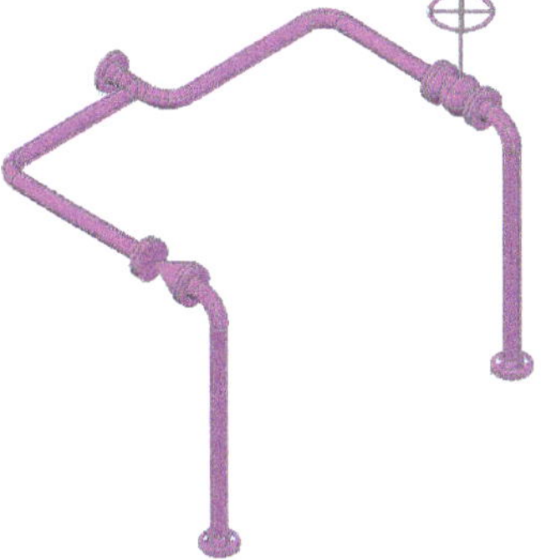

Locking Pipes after creating their Isometric Drawings

AutoCAD Plant 3D provides an option to lock the pipe number after generating its final Isometric

Drawing, which prevents anyone from changing the
piping.

1. On the Project Manager, click the **Isometric DWG**
   tab.
2. Expand the **Final_ANSI-B** folder.
3. Click the right mouse button on 002 line number
   and select **Lock Line and issue**. The program
   locks the line number. If you want to unlock it,
   then click the right mouse button on it and choose
   Unlock Line.

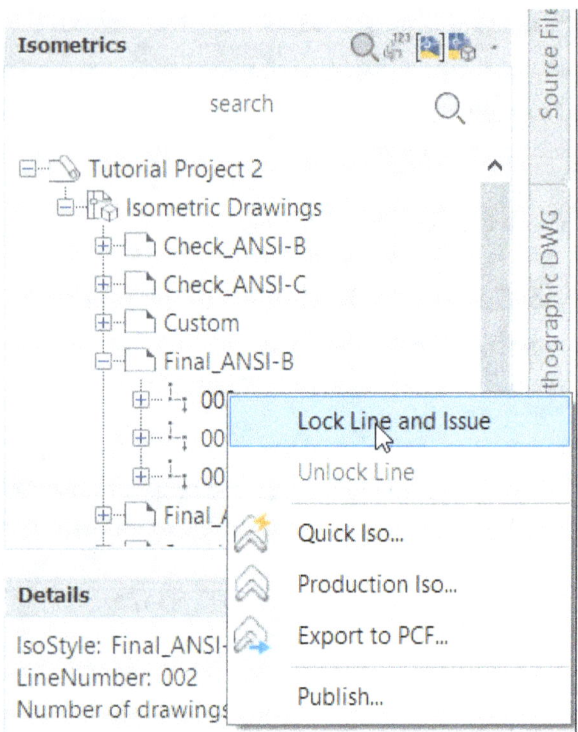

Chapter 7: Creating Orthographic Drawings

AutoCAD Plant 3D allows you to create plan and elevation views using a 3D model. The changes in the 3D model are reflected in the views automatically.

1. On the ribbon, click **Home > Ortho Views > Create Ortho View**.

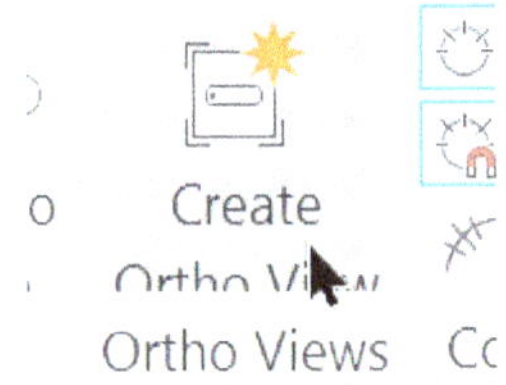

The **Select Orthographic Drawing** dialog displays the already existing orthographic drawings.

2. Click **Create new** on the **Select Orthographic Drawing** dialog.
3. On the **New DWG** dialog, type-in **Plan** in the **File name** box.
4. Click **OK**.

The **Ortho Editor** tab appears on the ribbon.

5. On the **Ortho Editor** tab, click **Ortho Cube > Top** to create the top view of the 3D model.
6. On the **Ortho Editor** tab, click **Select > 3D Model Selection**. The **Select Reference Models** dialog appears. This dialog is used to select the 3D models to include in the orthographic views.
7. Under the **Project models** section, make sure that the **Master Model** is selected. Click **OK**.

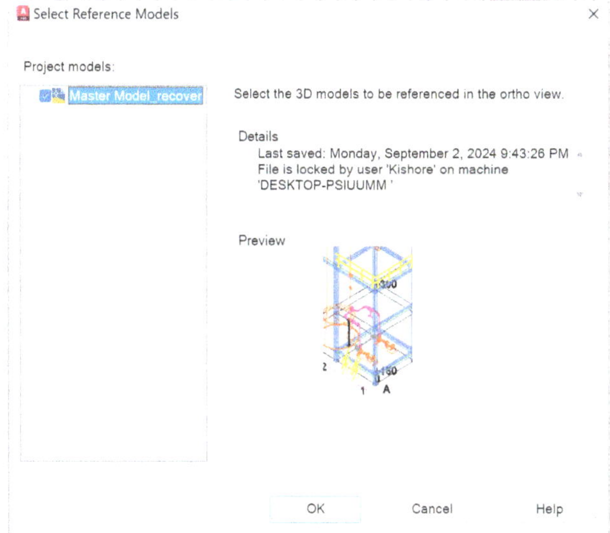

8. On the **Output Appearance** panel, select **Hidden Line Piping** from the drop-down.
9. Make sure that the **Matchlines** and **Cut Pipe Symbol** icons are highlighted. These options turn ON the matchlines and cut pipe symbols.
10. Click the **Paper Check** icon to check the view with the paper size.

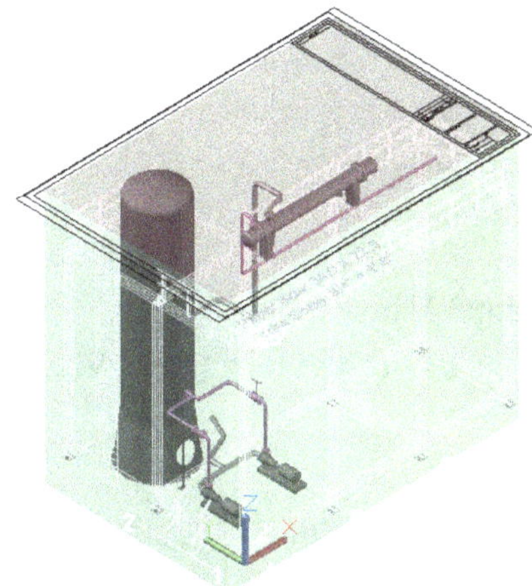

11. Set the **Scale** to ¼"=1'-0".
12. On the **Ortho Editor** tab, click **Library > Save Ortho Cube**.

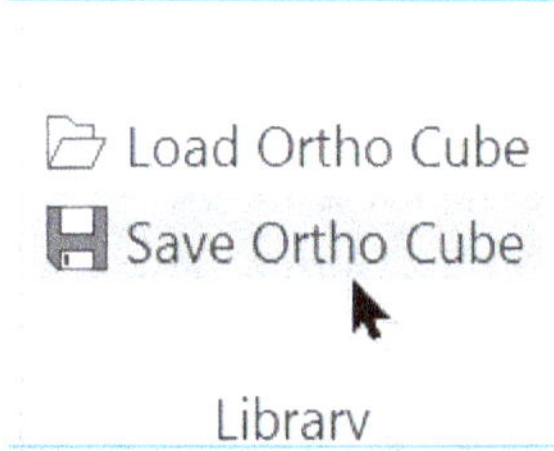

13. On the **Save View** dialog, type-in **First Plan View** in the **View Name** box and click **OK**. The ortho cube settings are saved for future use.
14. On the **Ortho Editor** tab, click **Library > Load Ortho Cube**. On the **Load View** dialog, the **View List** displays the saved ortho cubes. You can select an ortho cube configuration to load it.
15. Close the **Load View** dialog.
16. Click **OK** on the ribbon and position the view on the paper space. The view is placed, and a viewport is created.

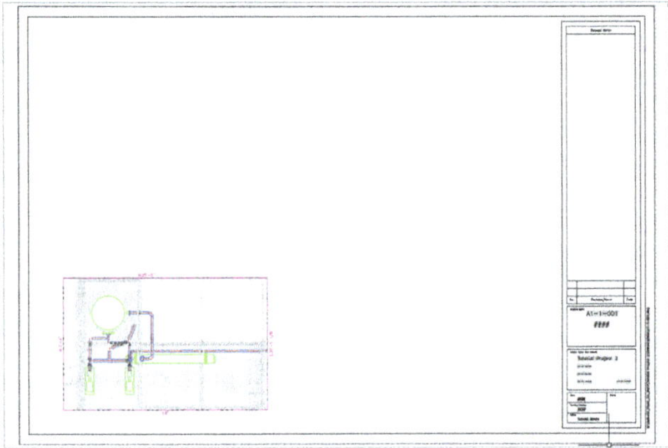

17. Double-click inside the viewport to activate it.
18. Select any one of the objects in the viewport and notice that it is a block. These blocks are arranged in separate layers.

Creating Adjacent Views

1. On the ribbon, click **Ortho View > Ortho Views > Adjacent View**.

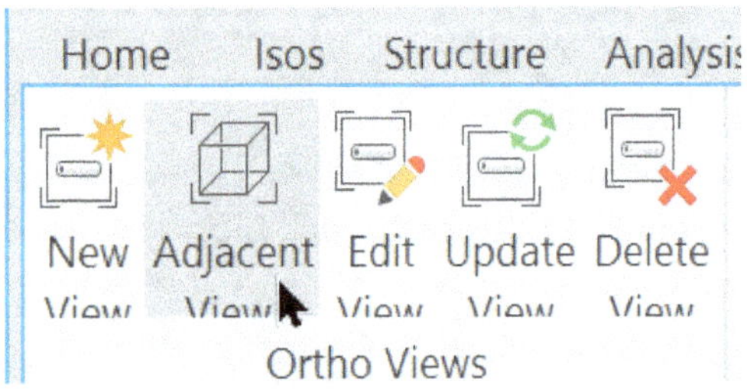

2. Select the viewport.
3. On the **Create an Adjacent View** dialog, select the **Front** view and click **OK**. In the command line, notice the options to scale, rotate, or use the settings of an existing view.

4. Place the pointer on the top-left corner point of the viewport and move it up. A trace line appears.
5. Click to place the front view.

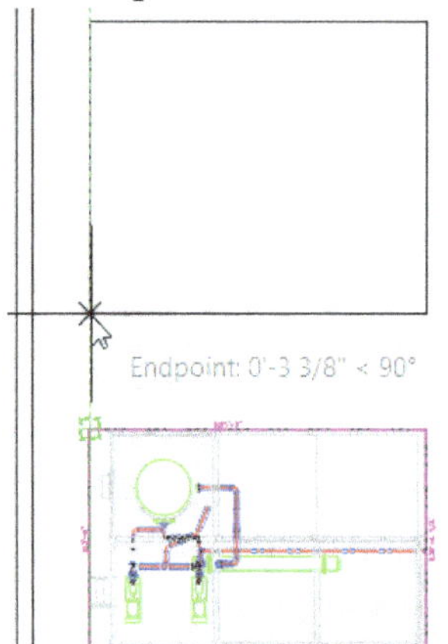

6. Activate the **Adjacent View** command and select the plan view.
7. On the **Create an Adjacent View** dialog, click **SW Isometric** and then click **OK**.
8. Click on the paper space to position the Isometric View.

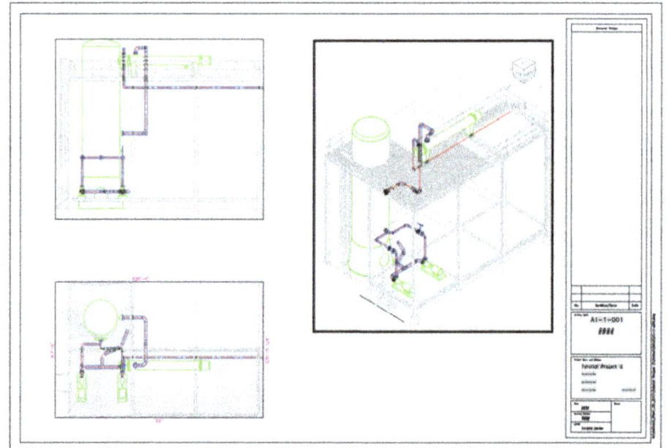

.

Editing Ortho Views

In the real world, there is always a need to modify the drawings. AutoCAD Plant 3D provides the essential tools to modify and update a drawing.

1. On the ribbon, click **Ortho View > Ortho Views > Edit View**.
2. Click on the plan view.
3. Click on the Ortho View cube (transparent enclosure) in the **Orthographic View Selection** window. You notice various grips on the ortho cube. You can use these grips to modify the ortho cube.
4. Change the view orientation to Top.

5. On the ribbon, click **Ortho Editor > Ortho Cube > Add Jog**.

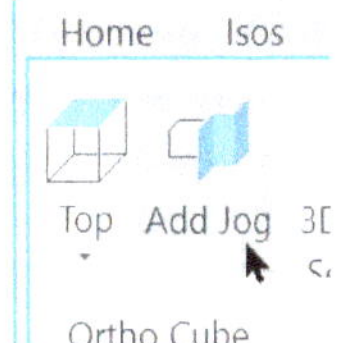

6. Click on the top horizontal edge of the Ortho View cube. A jog is added to it.

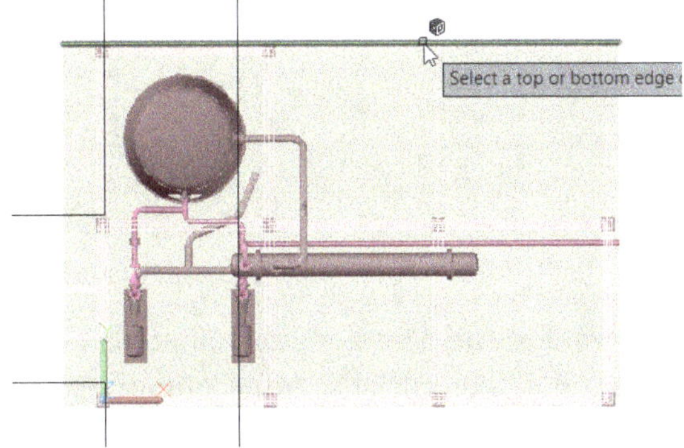

7. Click on the arrow that appears on the vertical edge of the jog.
8. Move it toward left and click to increase the jog width.

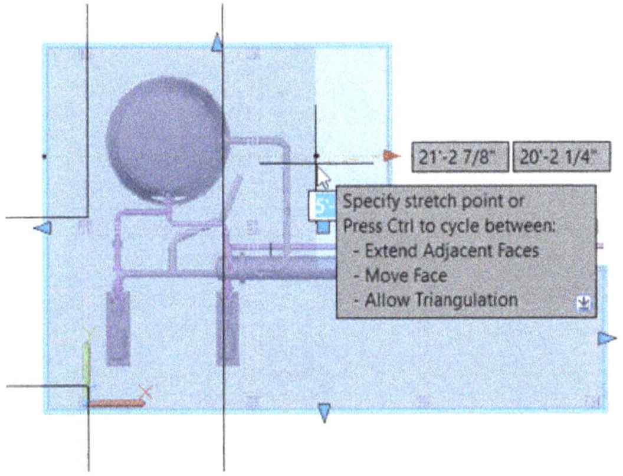

9. Likewise, modify the horizontal edge, as shown.

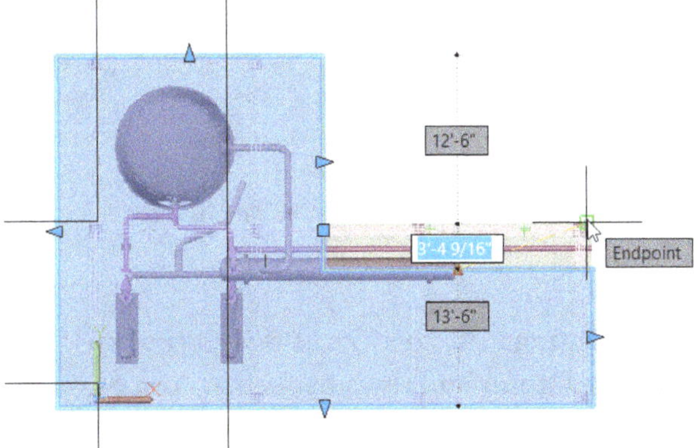

10. Click **OK** on the ribbon. The view is updated in the paper space.

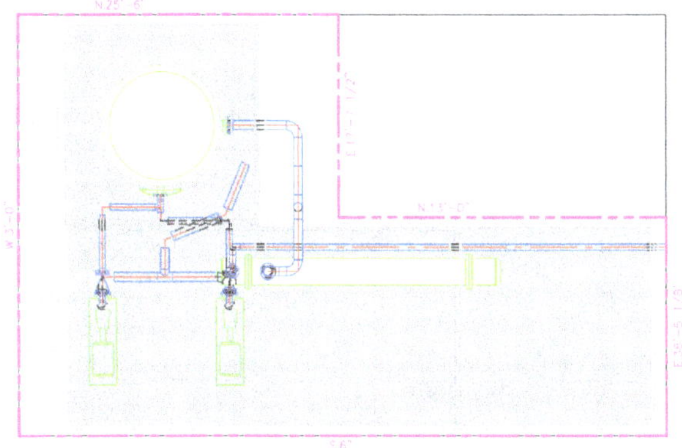

Updating and Deleting Ortho Views

Earlier, you have learned to edit the ortho views. In addition to that, AutoCAD Plant 3D allows you to update the changes made in the 3D model.

1. Switch to the 3D Model file.
2. Click on the horizontal pipe connected to the heat exchanger.
3. Click the Move Part grip that appears in the middle of the pipe.

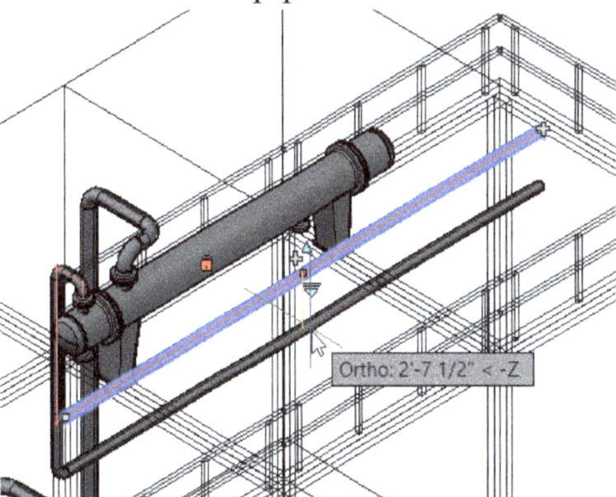

4. Move the pointer down and click to change the length of the vertical pipe connected to it.

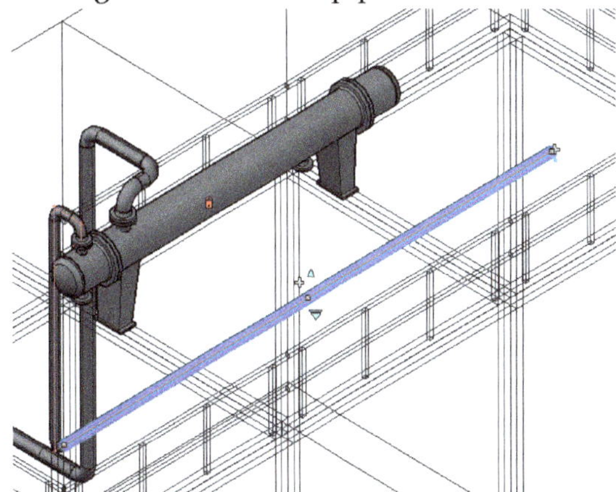

5. Save the 3D model and switch back to the ortho views file.
6. On the ribbon, click **Ortho View > Ortho Views > Update View**.
7. Click on the front view to update it.

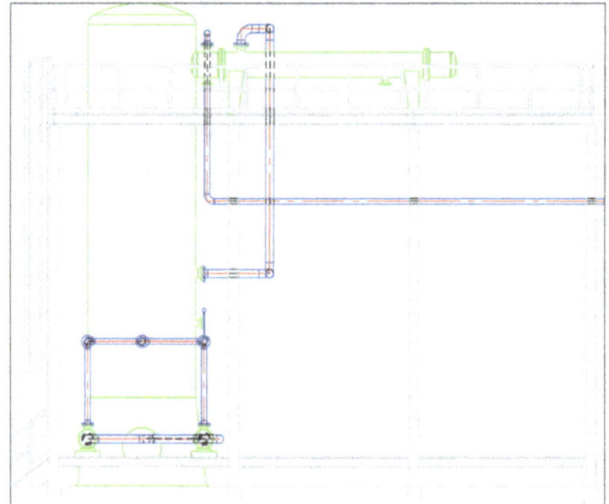

8. On the ribbon, click **Ortho View > Ortho Views > Delete View**.
9. Select the Isometric view to delete it.

Adding Bill of Materials

AutoCAD Plant 3D provides you with a couple of tools to define the BOM format, add and update BOM. These commands are located on the **Table Placement & Setup** panel.

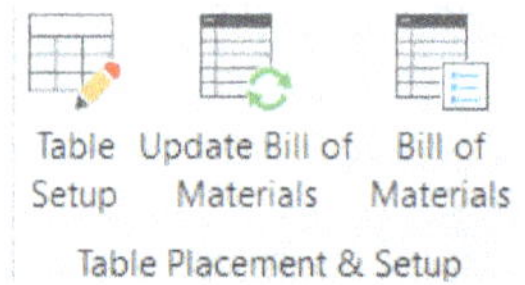

1. On the ribbon, click **Ortho View > Table Placement & Setup > Table Setup**.
2. On the **Ortho Table Setup** dialog, click **Table type > Piping BOM**.

3. Click **BOM layout template > Grouped with category titles**.

The **Simple Layout** option creates a BOM without categorizing the components.

The **Grouped with category titles** option categorizes the BOM based on the component types (Pipes, fittings, and valves).

The **Grouped with independent columns** option divides the BOM into separate categories. Also, you have control over the columns displayed for each category. By default, the BOM displays only four columns (ID, QTY, ND, and DESCRIPTION). For example, if you want to display the Schedule/Class column only for pipes, then check the **SCH/CLASS** option for **Pipe**.

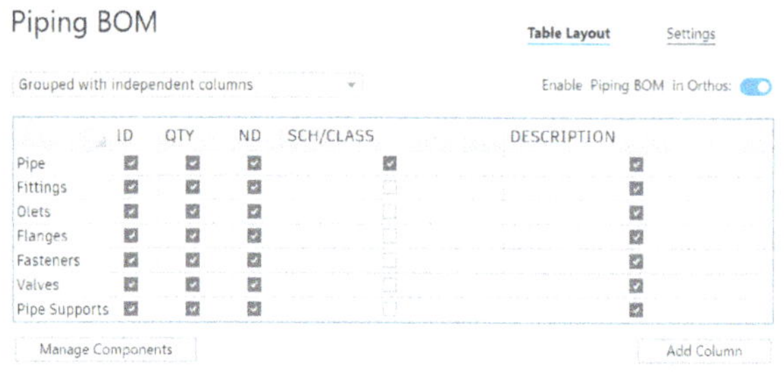

If you want to add a new column other than the existing ones, then click the **Add Column** button on the dialog. On the **Select Class Property** dialog, select the class and its related property.

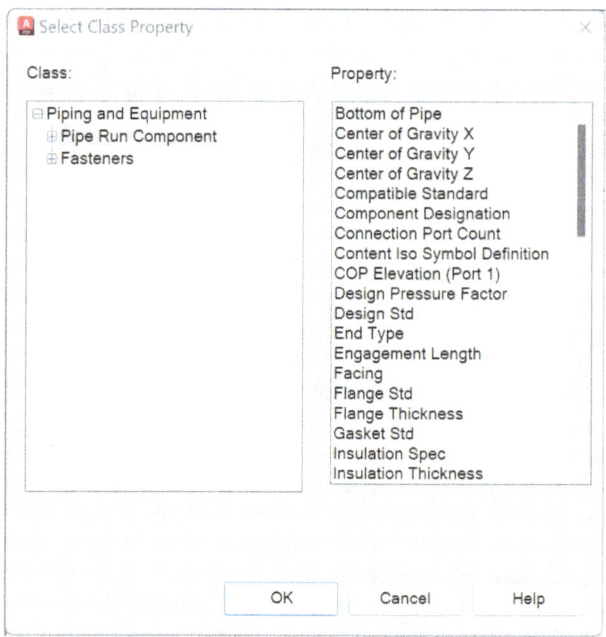

4. Click the **Settings** tab on the **Table Setup** dialog.

On the **Settings** tab, check/uncheck the options under the **Group into rows by** section. You can also add groups to the table by clicking the **Add** button.

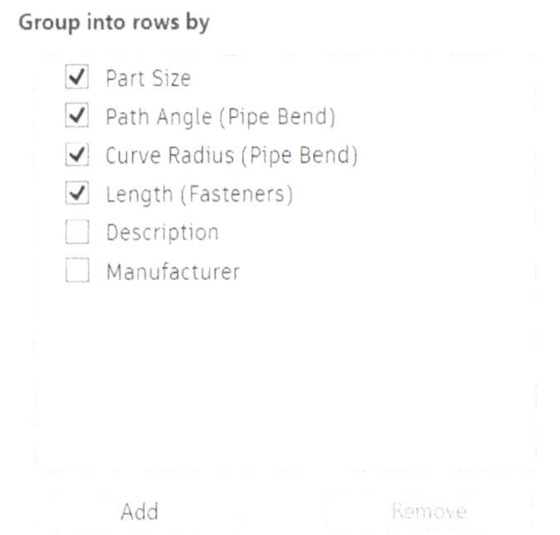

In the **Sort rows by** section, you can select or deselect options to organize the table based on specific properties. To further refine the sorting order, right-click on a property and choose from the following options: Move Up, Move Down, or Reverse. This allows you to rearrange the properties and adjust the sorting sequence to suit your needs.

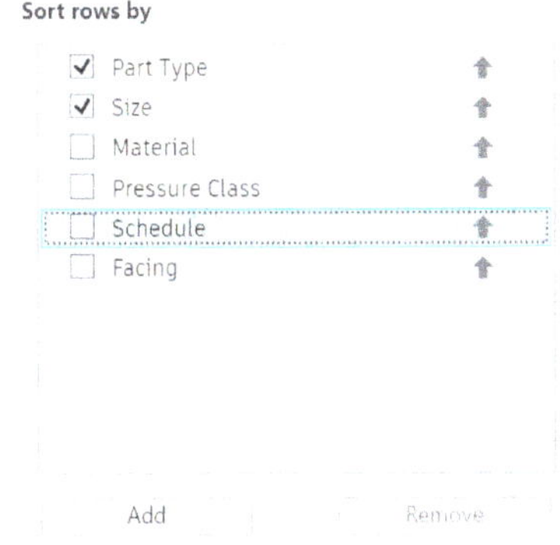

Use the **Descriptions** drop-down to control the way a part description is displayed.

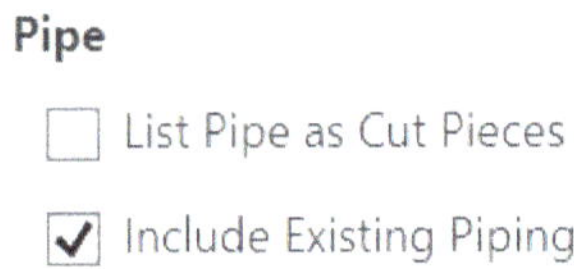

Pipe

When creating a piping Bill of Materials (BOM), you have two important options to consider:

List Pipe as Cut Pieces

Include Existing Piping

List Pipe as Cut Pieces: This option lets you choose how to show pipe lengths in the BOM. You can either report the total length of pipe needed or break it down into individual cut pieces.

Include Existing Piping: This option allows you to decide whether to include already installed piping in the BOM.

Fixed Length Pipes

When working with piping Bill of Materials (BOM), you can manage fixed length pipes by selecting the **Report Quantity** or **Report Length** option.

Show Custom Fixed Length Pipes as Separate Line Items: This option gives you control over how fixed length pipes are displayed in the BOM. If you select this option, each fixed length pipe segment will be shown as a separate line item in the report. This means you'll see a clear and detailed list of each pipe segment, making it easier to track and manage your piping materials.

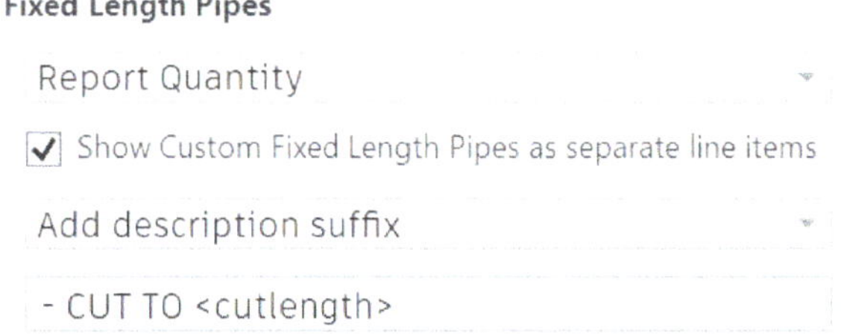

Cutback Elbows

When creating a piping Bill of Materials (BOM), you can choose how to report elbows that have been cut back to fit specific piping needs.

Show Cutback Elbows as Separate Line Items: This option lets you decide how to display cutback elbows in the BOM. If you select this option, cutback elbows will be shown as separate items, rather than being treated as standard 45 or 90-degree elbows.

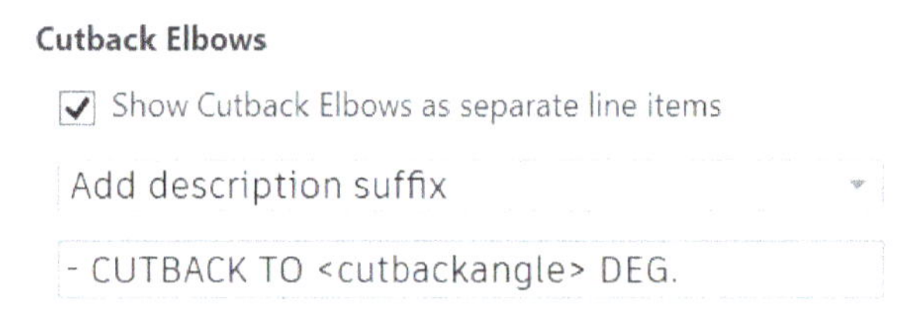

5. Leave the default settings and click **OK**.
6. On the ribbon, click **Ortho View > Table Placement & Setup > Bill of Materials**.

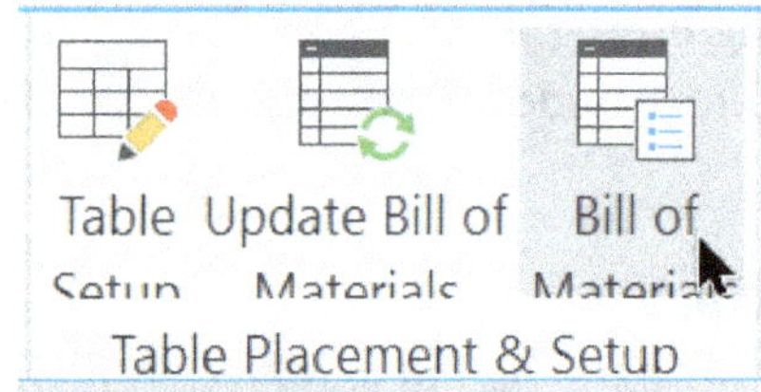

7. Select the plan view.
8. Define the first and second corners of the BOM, as shown. The BOM is created.

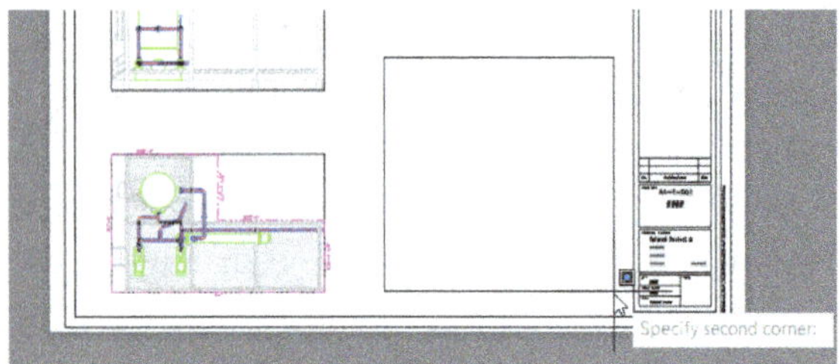

ID	QTY	ND	SCH/GLASS	DESCRIPTION
			PIPE	
1	52'-8 15/16"	4"		PIPE, SEAMLESS, PE, ASME B36.10, ASTM A106 Gr B SMLS, Sch 40
2	39'-9"	6"		PIPE, SEAMLESS, PE, ASME B36.10, ASTM A106 Gr B SMLS, Sch 40
			FITTINGS	
3	8	4"		ELL 90 LR, BW, ASME B16.9, ASTM A234 Gr WPB SMLS, Sch 40
4	1	4"		TEE, BW, ASME B16.9, ASTM A234 Gr WPB SMLS, Sch 40
5	3	6"		ELL 90 LR, BW, ASME B16.9, ASTM A234 Gr WPB SMLS, Sch 40
6	1	6"		TEE, BW, ASME B16.9, ASTM A234 Gr WPB SMLS, Sch 40
			FLANGES	
7	8	4"	300	FLANGE WN, 300 LB, RF, ASME B16.5, ASTM A105
8	4	6"	300	FLANGE WN, 300 LB, RF, ASME B16.5, ASTM A105
			FASTENERS	
9	8	4"	300	BOLT SET, RF, 300 LB, STUD BOLT
10	8	4"	300	GASKET, SWG, 1/8" THK, RF, 300 LB, ASME B16.20, CS/PTFE
11	4	6"	300	BOLT SET, RF, 300 LB, STUD BOLT
12	4	6"	300	GASKET, SWG, 1/8" THK, RF, 300 LB, ASME B16.20, CS/PTFE
			VALVES	
13	1	4"	300	Check Valve, Swing, 300 LB, RF, ASME B16.10, ASTM A216 Gr WPB
14	1	4"	300	Globe Valve, 300 LB, RF, ASME B16.10, ASTM A216 Gr WPB, Hand Wheel
			PIPE SUPPORTS	
15	1	6"		Custom Trunnion/Stanchion

You can change the **Table Setup** anytime and use the **Update Bill of Materials** command to update the BOM.

Adding Annotations and Dimensions

In AutoCAD Plant 3D, annotations and dimensions are added at the final stages of the design. The annotation and dimensions commands are available on the **Annotation** panel.

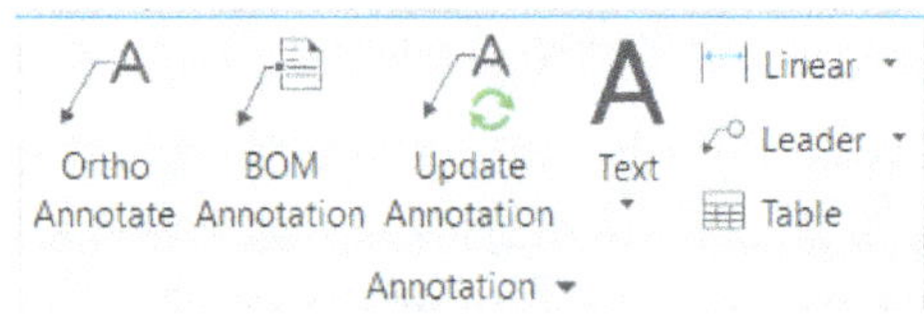

1. On the ribbon, click **Ortho View > Annotation > Ortho Annotate.**

2. Click in the top view and select the heat exchanger.
3. Press Enter to add the Equipment Tag.
4. Place the annotation below the heat exchanger.

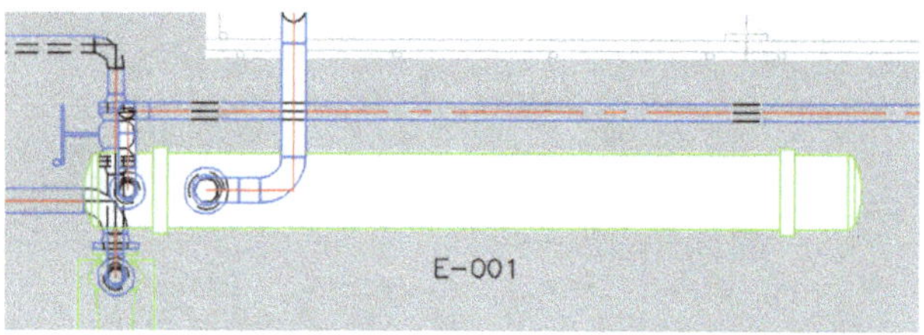

5. On the ribbon, click **Ortho View > Annotation > BOM Annotation.**
6. In the Bill of Materials, select a data element in the first row under the **Pipe** category. The balloon is attached to the pointer.

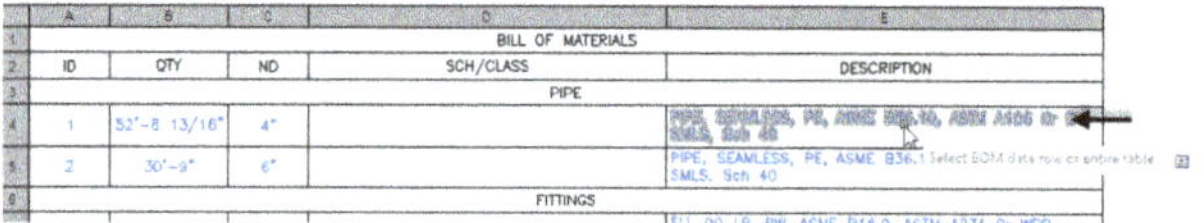

	A	B	C	D	E
1				BILL OF MATERIALS	
2	ID	QTY	ND	SCH/CLASS	DESCRIPTION
3				PIPE	
4	1	52'-8 13/16"	4"		PIPE, SEAMLESS, PE, ASME B36.10, ASTM A106 Gr B SMLS, Sch 40
5	2	30'-9"	6"		PIPE, SEAMLESS, PE, ASME B36.1 SMLS. Sch 40
6				FITTINGS	

7. Position the balloon near the pipe to which it is attached. Another balloon is attached to the pointer as there are many pipes with the same size.

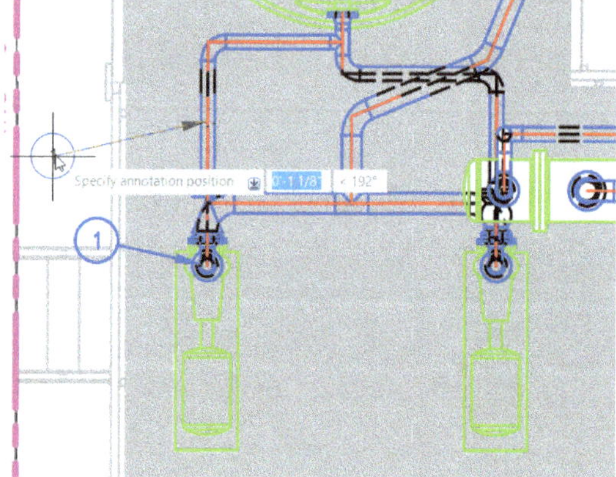

8. Press Esc to exit the balloon creation.
9. On the ribbon, click **Ortho View > Annotation > Linear.**
10. Zoom to the front view.
11. Use the Object Snap and select the endpoints of the horizontal pipe.
12. Move the pointer and position the dimension below the pipe.

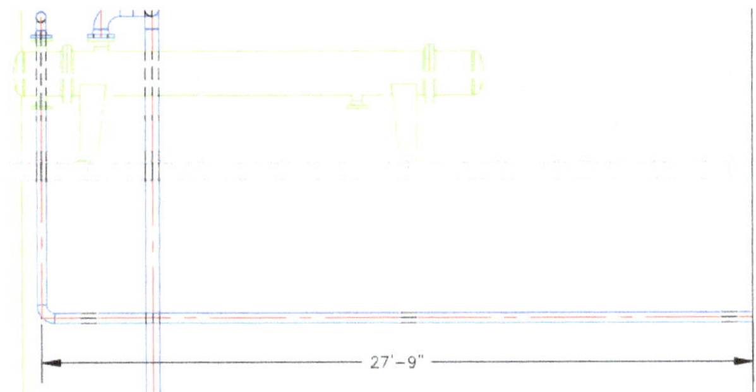

Updating Dimensions

1. Create a selection window across the BOM table.
2. Type M and press ENTER.
3. Click the top left corner point of the BOM table and move it down.
4. Click to position the table.

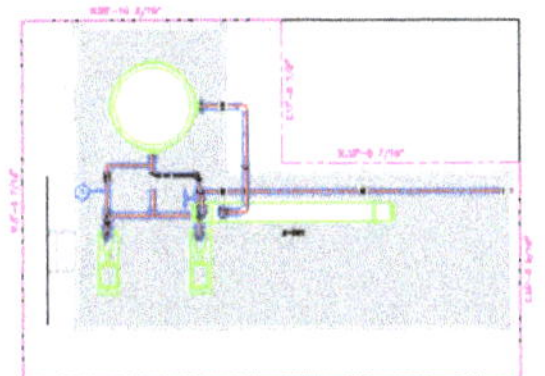 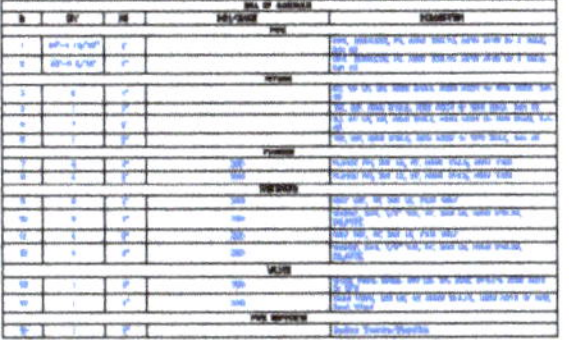

5. On the ribbon, click **Ortho View > Ortho Views > Edit View**.
6. Select the front view.
7. On the **Ortho Editor** tab, set the **Scale** to 3/16" = 1'-0". Click **OK**.

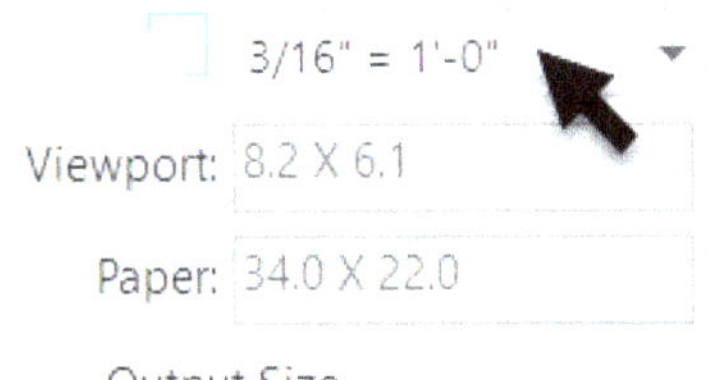

The scale of the front view is changed. You notice that the dimension is not changed. The reason is that the dimensions are created in the paper space but not inside the viewport. You have to update the dimension manually.

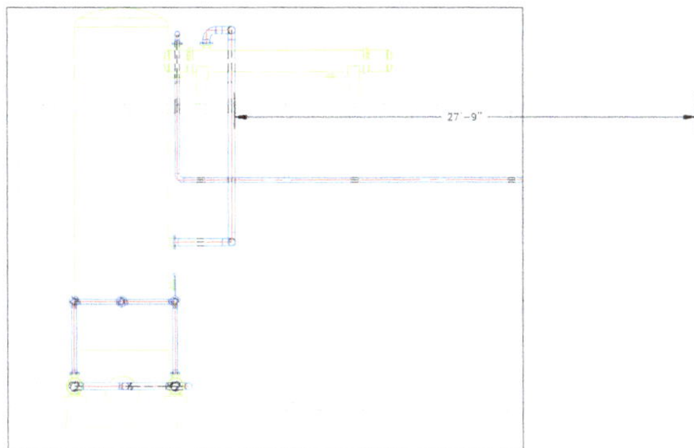

It is recommended that you add dimensions to the view at the final stages as it requires much rework to update them.

8. Select the dimension and press **Delete**.

Using the Locate in 3D Model and Pipe Gap commands

1. On the ribbon, click **Ortho View > Plant Object Tools > Locate in 3D Model**.

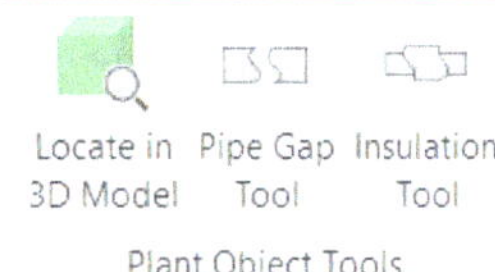

2. Click on the left pump in the Top view. The Pump is highlighted in the model space.

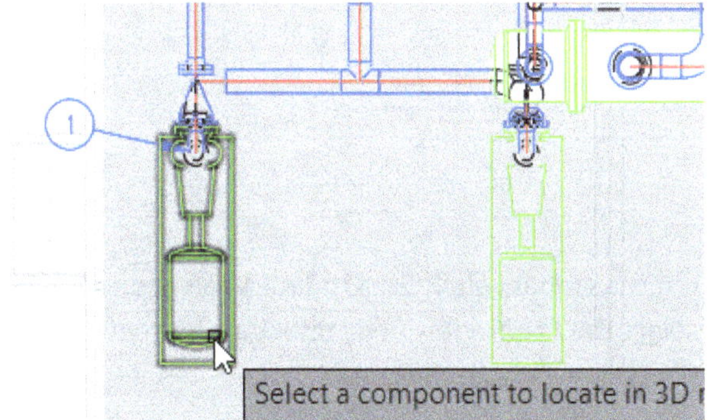

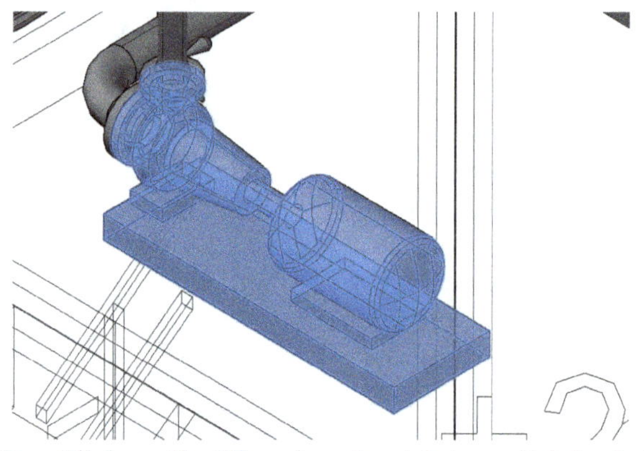

3. Click on the **Plan** drawing tab to switch back to the Plan.dwg file.

4. On the ribbon, click **Ortho View > Plant Object Tools > Pipe Gap Tool**.

5. Zoom to the Front view and select the horizontal pipe. Two break symbols appear on the selected pipe.

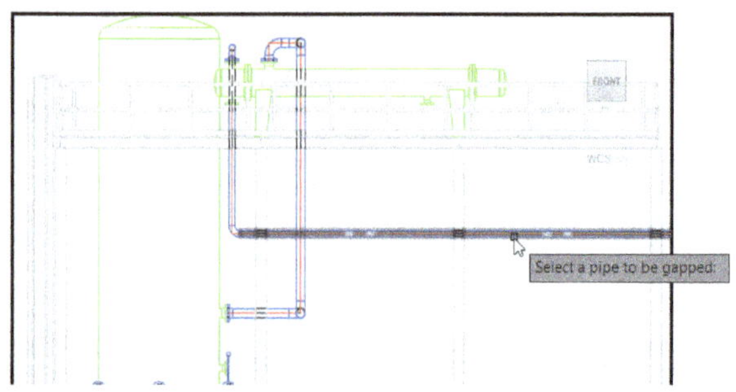

6. Increase the distance between the break symbols by dragging anyone of them. Press Esc.

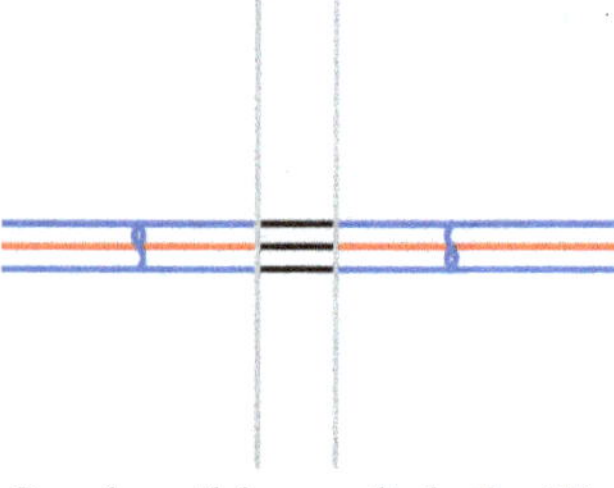

7. On the ribbon, click the **Update View** icon and select the Front view. The pipe gap is created.

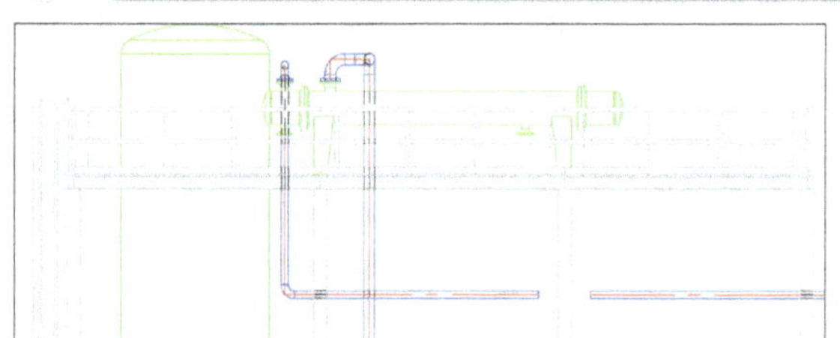

8. On the ribbon, click **Ortho View > Plant Object Tools > Insulation Tool**.

9. Select the vertical pipe connecting the vessel and the heat exchanger.

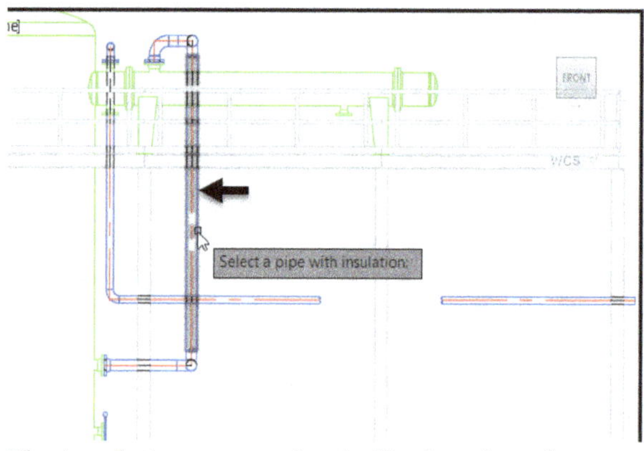

The insulation annotation is displayed on the selected pipe.

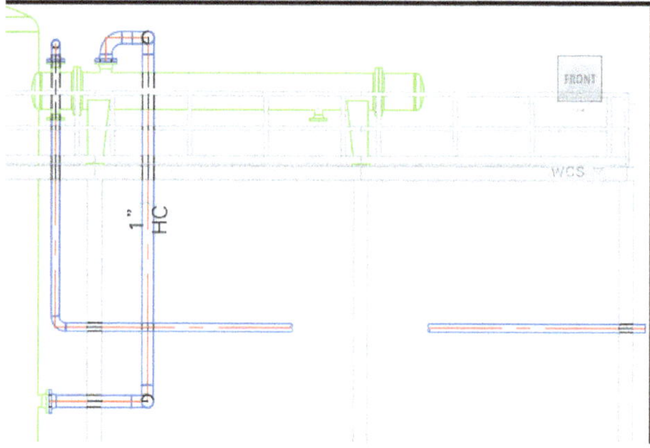

10. On the ribbon, click **Ortho View > Ortho Views > Edit View**.

11. Click on the front view.

12. On the **Ortho Editor** tab of the ribbon, click **Output Appearance > Insulation** drop-down > **Hidden Line Insulation**.

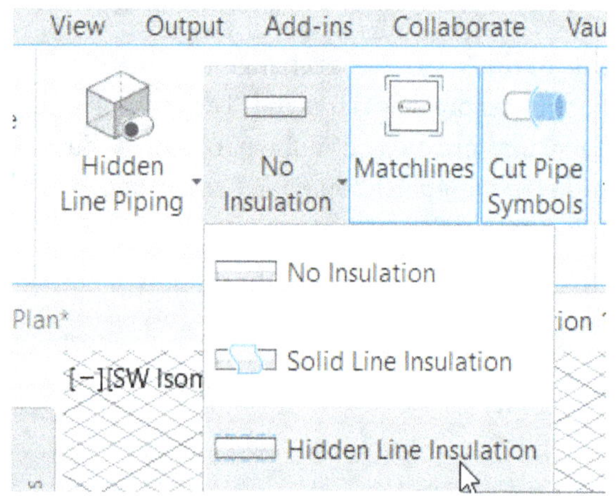

13. Click **OK** on the ribbon. The insulation is added to the pipe, and the view is updated.

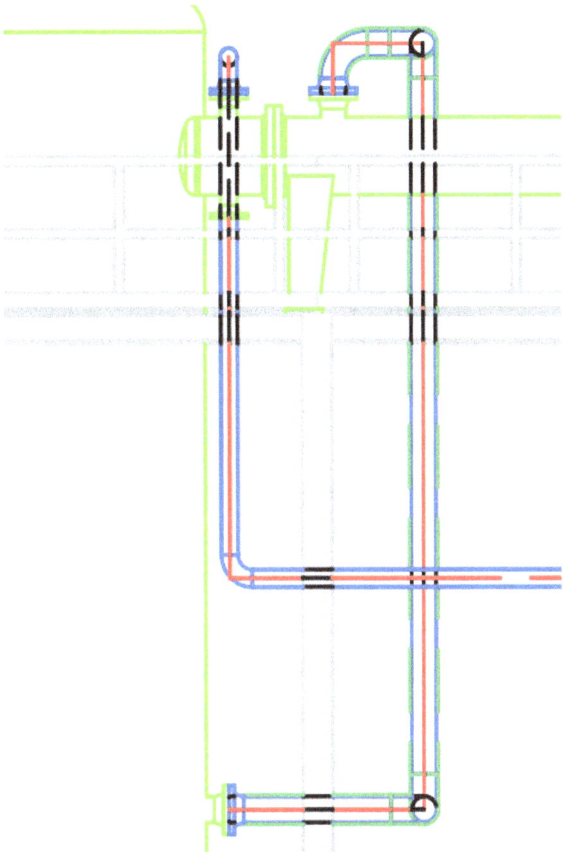

14. Save and close the drawing file.

Chapter 8: Working in a Project

AutoCAD Plant 3D is a project-based application. Every object you create is stored in the project database. Therefore, it is essential to know how to manage a project.

Using the Project Manager

The Project Manager helps you to create, open, add, and remove drawings from the project. The Project Manager appears on the left side of the screen. You can hide, close, or dock it to the application, but everything inside the Project is associated with it. There are quite a few options, which help you to organize files and perform additional operations related to the project. Examine the options on the **Project Manager** as most of them are obvious.

If the **Project Manager** is not displayed, click **Home > Project > Project Manager**.

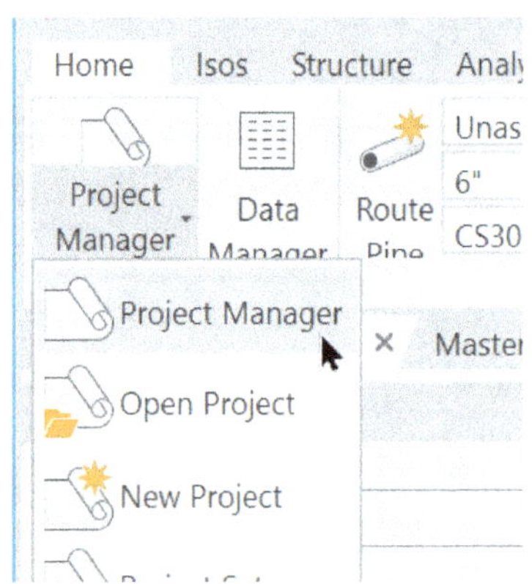

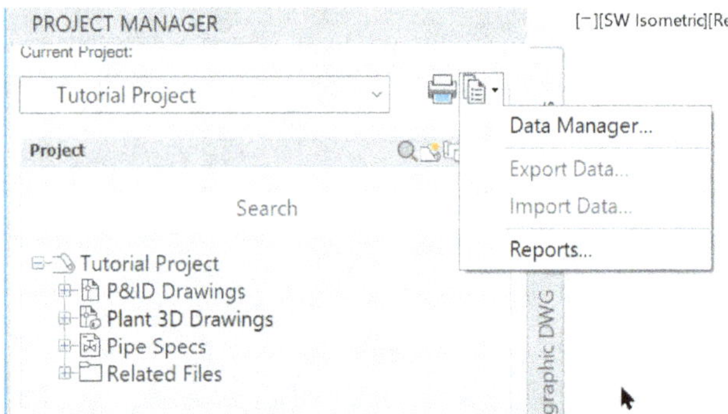

Changing the General Project Settings

The **Project Setup** dialog can be used to define or change the general project settings. It is recommended that you define the project settings while starting a project. However, here it is covered after basics.

1. On the ribbon, click **Home > Project > Project Manager > Project Setup**.
2. On the **Project Setup** dialog, expand **General Settings**. It has seven sub-settings: **Database Setup**, **Drawing Properties**, **File name Format**, **Paths**, **Project Details**, **Reports**, and **Shared Plant Content**.
3. Click **Project Details** under **General Settings**.

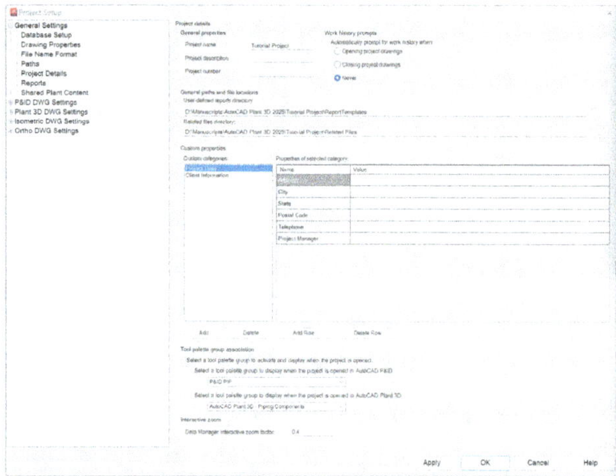

The **General properties** section on the **Project Details** page has **Project name**, **Project Description**, and **Project number** boxes. You can type–in the project description and number but cannot change the project name.

The **Work history prompts** section has **Opening project drawings**, **Closing project drawings,** and **Never** options. If you select the **Closing project drawings** option, the program prompts you to enter the changes made to drawing before closing it.

4. Select **Closing project drawings** from the **Work history prompts** section.

The **General path and file locations** section has options to define the locations of the report files and other related files such as spreadsheets and text documents.

The **Custom properties** section has options to enter data related to different categories such as project and client. You can add a new category in addition to **Project data** and **Client Information** using the **Add** button.

There is a table showing properties such as Address, City, and State. You can add a new property to the table using the **Add row** button.

The **Tool palette group association** section helps you to set the P&ID and Piping tool palettes to be loaded when you open a file.

The **Interactive Zoom** section helps to set the zoom factor when you use the **Data Manager** to identify the components in the file.

5. Click the **Add** button in the **Custom properties** section.
6. Type **Contractor** in the **New category name** box and click **OK**.
7. Click the **Add Row** button to add a new field to the table.
8. On the **Add Row** dialog, type-in **Name** in the **Name** box and click **OK**. The **Name** property is added to the table.
9. Likewise, add the **Address** and **Telephone** properties to the table.
10. Click **Database Setup** under **General Settings** node.

The **Database Setup** page has two types of databases: **SQLite local database** and **SQL server database**. The database settings are defined while starting a project. If you want to change the database, then click the **Learn More** link on the dialog.

11. Click **Drawing Properties** in the **General Settings** node. On the **Drawing Properties** page, you can use the **Add** button to add custom properties to a drawing.
12. Click the **Add** button and type-in **Custom Properties** in the **New category name** box. Click **OK**.
13. Click the **Add Row** button.

14. On the **Add Row** dialog, type-in **Job Name** in the **Name** box and click **OK**.
15. Likewise, add the **Job Number** property.

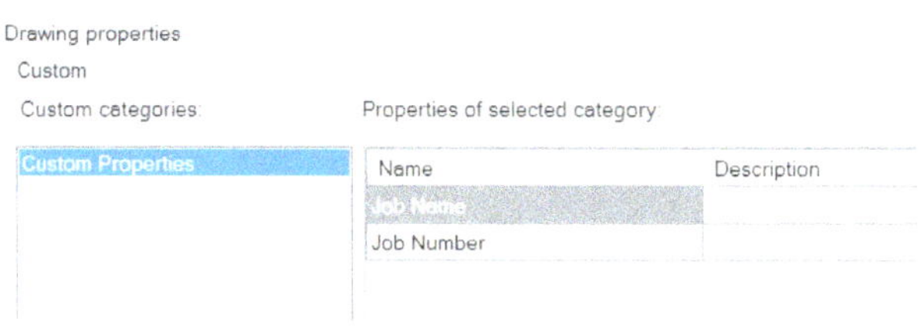

16. Click **Reports** under **General Settings**. On the **Project reports** page, you can add, delete, or modify a project report type.
17. Click **File name format** under **General Settings**.
18. Click the **Add** button on the **File name format** page.
19. Type-in **Discipline** in the **Name** box.
20. Set the **Type**, **Length**, and **Delimiter** to **String**, **2**, and **-**, respectively.
21. Likewise, add two more fields, as shown. Do not type any value in the **Delimiter** box of the **Sheet Sequence** property.

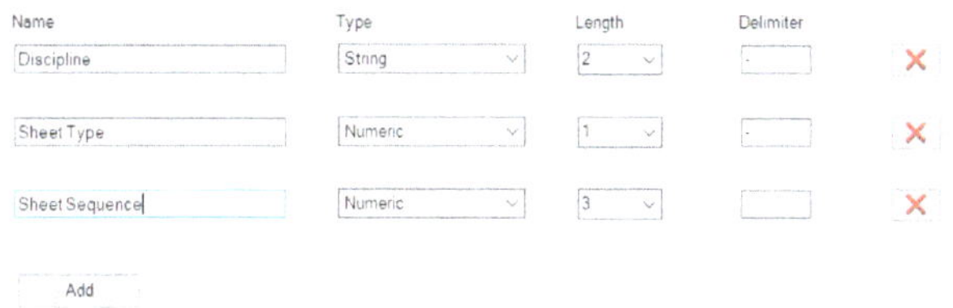

22. Click **OK** on the **Project Setup** dialog.
23. Select the **P&ID Drawings** folder in the **Project Manager** and click the **New Drawing** icon. The **New DWG** dialog appears with three fields that you have created. You can check the **Override** option if you want to create a file without any naming format.

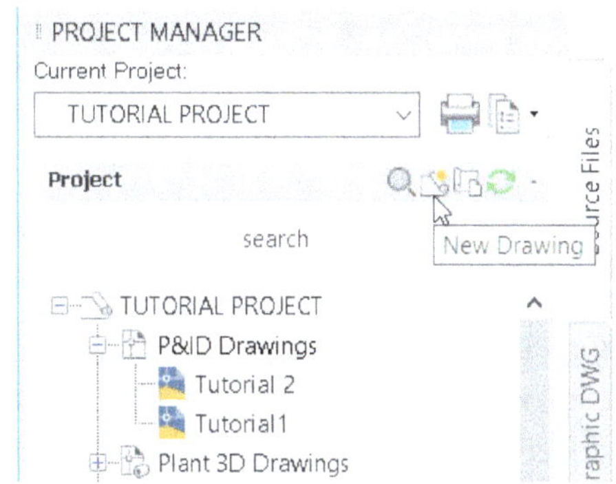

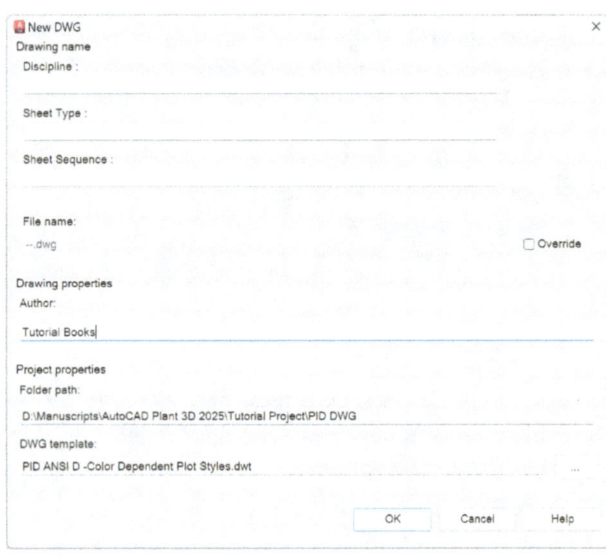

24. Type-in D, 6, and 001 in the **Discipline**, **Sheet Type,** and **Sheet Sequence**, respectively. Click **OK**.

25. The D-6-001.dwg file is added to the **P&ID Drawing** folder.

26. In the Project Manager, click the right mouse button on D-6-001 and select **Properties**. On the **Properties** dialog, notice the **Custom Properties** section. It has the **Job Name** and **Job Number** properties.

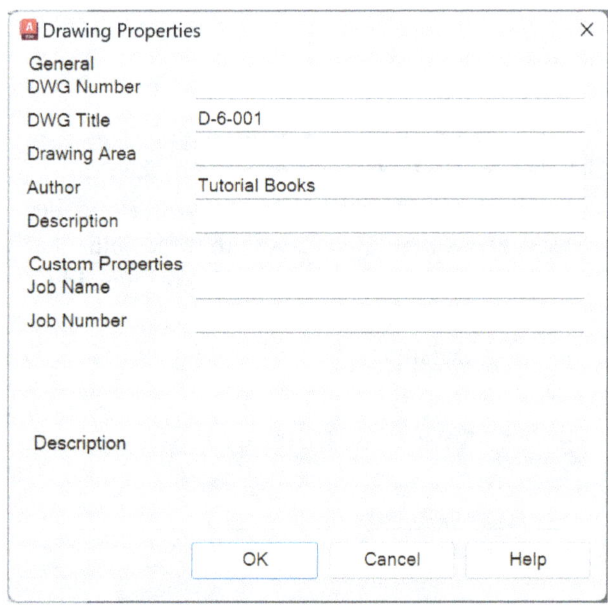

27. Click **OK** on the **Drawing Properties** dialog.

28. Double-click in the title block of the drawing sheet to deactivate the viewport.

29. Type-in **FIELD** in the command line and press Enter.

30. On the **Field** dialog, click **Field category > Project**.

31. Select **Project** from the **Field names** section.

32. Set **Format** to **Uppercase** and choose **ContractorName** from the **Property** list.

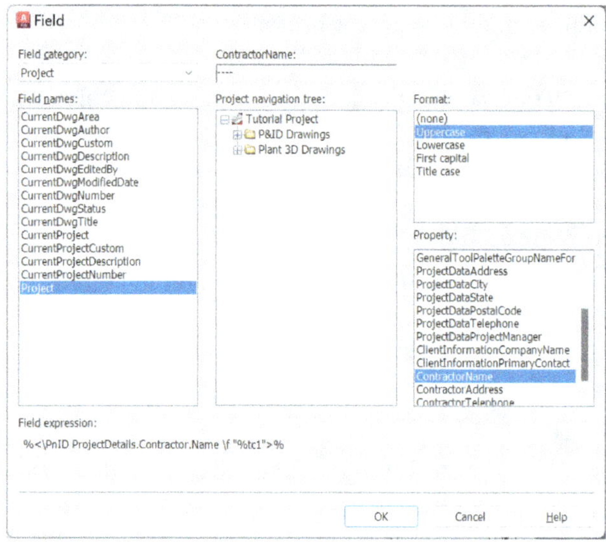

33. Click **OK** and place the property text on the **Title block**, as shown.

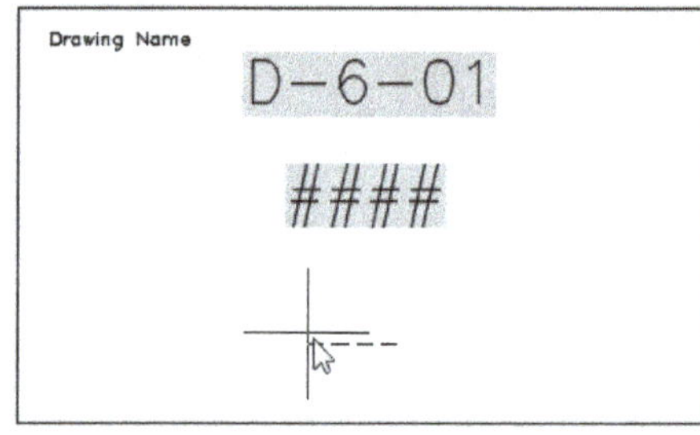

34. To enter a value for the property, click the right mouse button on **Tutorial Project** in the Project Manager and select **Project Setup**.

35. On the **Project Setup** dialog, click **Project Details** in the **General Settings** node.

36. Under the **Custom properties** section, select **Contractor** from the **Custom categories** list and type-in **Matt** in the **Name** box.

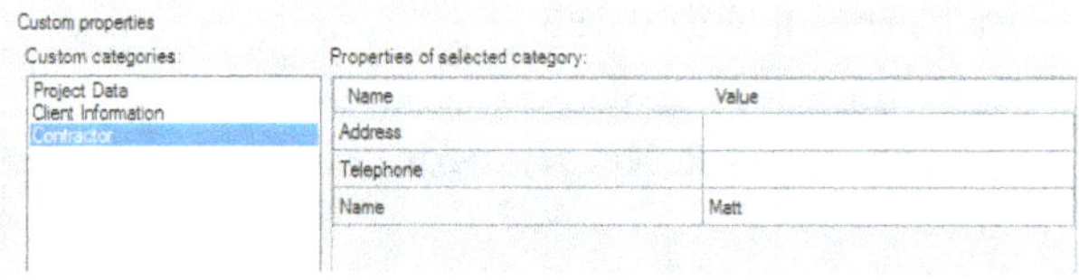

37. Click **OK** and type-in **REGEN** in the command line. Press Enter to see the property value.

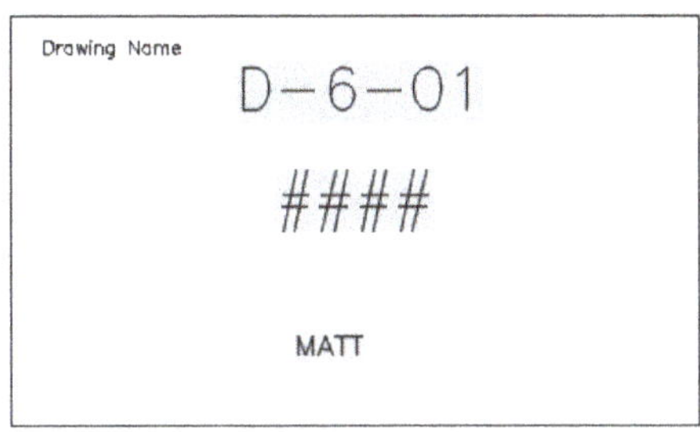

38. Click inside the viewport of the drawing sheet.
39. Add two pumps to the drawing, save and close it. The **Work History** dialog appears.
40. On the **Works History** dialog, set the **Status** to **In progress** and type **Added two pumps** in the **Notes** box. Click **OK**.

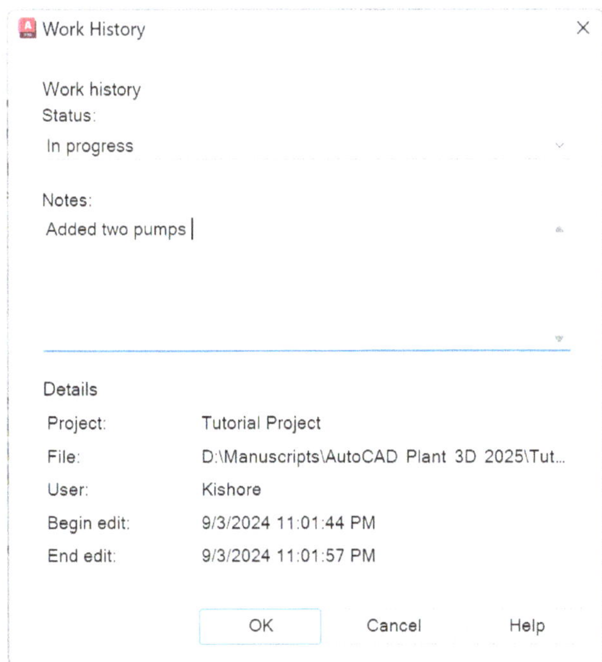

Using the Export to AutoCAD option

As the name says, the **Export to AutoCAD** option can be used to export the drawing files to AutoCAD format.

1. Open the **Tutorial 1** file from the **Project Manager**.
2. Click the right mouse button on Tutorial 1 and select **Export to AutoCAD**. The **Export to AutoCAD** dialog appears.

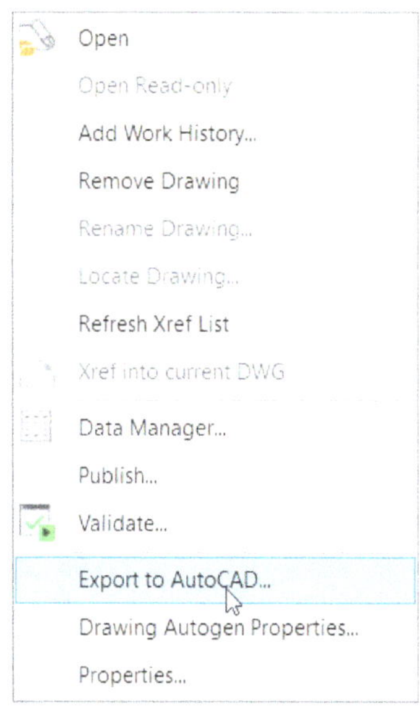

3. Go to the **Tutorial Project** folder.
4. Type **Tutorial1-exported** in the **File name** box.
5. Click **Save** to export the file.
6. On the **Quick Access Toolbar**, click the **Open** icon.
7. Open the exported drawing file.
8. Click the right mouse button on the vessel and select **Properties**. On the **Properties** palette, you can notice that the object is converted into a block reference. The P&ID properties of the object are not available, as it is no more linked to the project database.

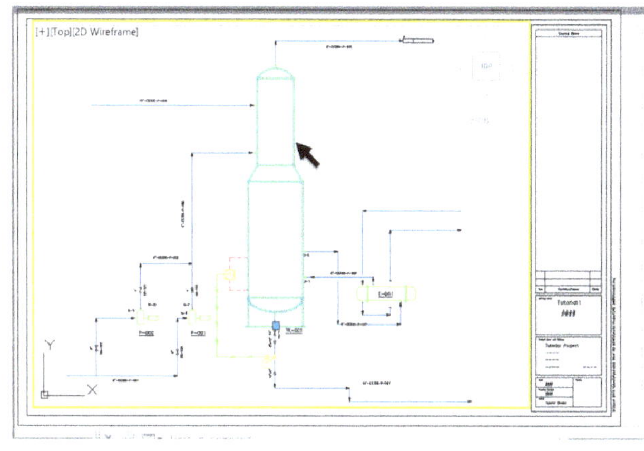

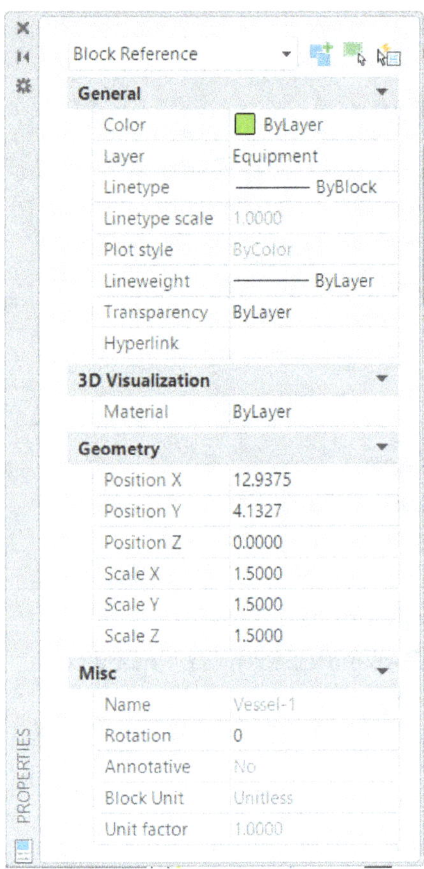

9. Likewise, you can export the Plant 3D drawings as well.

You can also export the project files into another format. To do this, click the **Application** icon located at the top left corner and select **Export > Other Formats**. On the **Export Data** dialog, select the format from the **Files of type** drop-down.

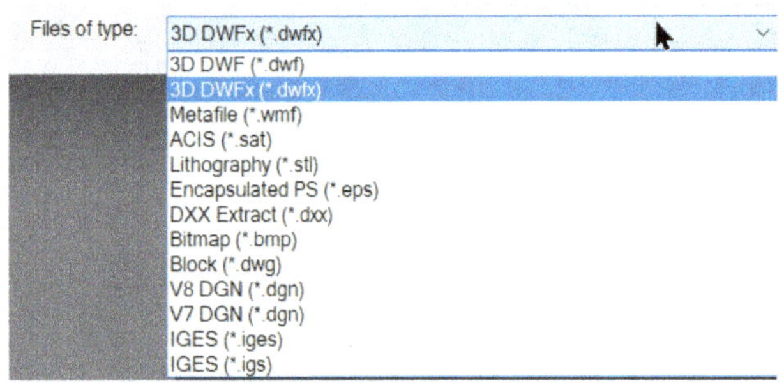

Chapter 9: Publishing and Printing

You can produce a physical copy of a drawing or publish it in electronic forms such as DWF, DWFx, or PDF.

Publishing a Drawing to DWF format

1. On the **Project Manager**, click the right mouse button on the **P&ID Drawings** folder and select **Publish**.

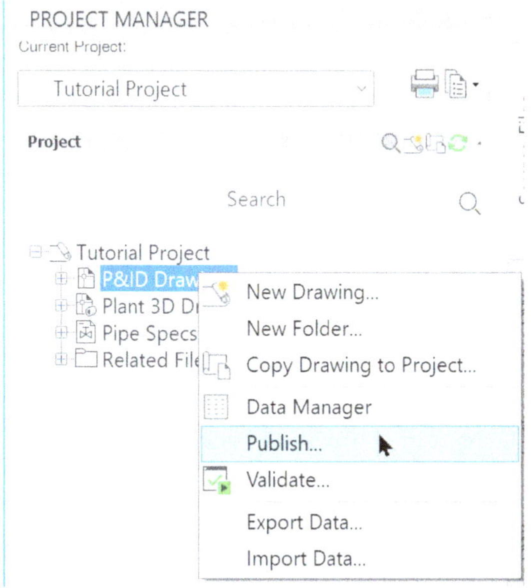

2. On the **Publish** dialog, click the **Publish Options** button.
3. On the **Project Publish Options** dialog, under the **P&ID DWF Options** section, click the icon next to the **P&ID Information** drop-down.

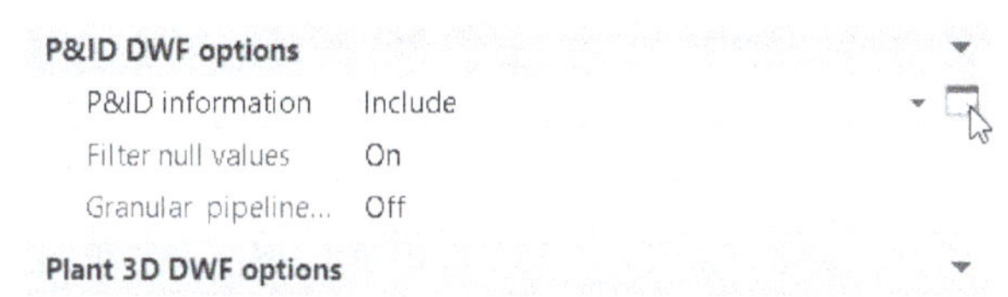

The program opens the **P&ID DWF Output Settings** dialog. The **Object Properties** tab helps you to control the symbol properties to be published. For example, select **Engineering Items > Equipment > Heat Exchangers > TEMA type BEM Exchanger**. The properties of the heat exchanger appear in the **TEMA type BEM Exchanger Properties** section. By default, all the properties are checked. You can uncheck the properties to be excluded from the output.

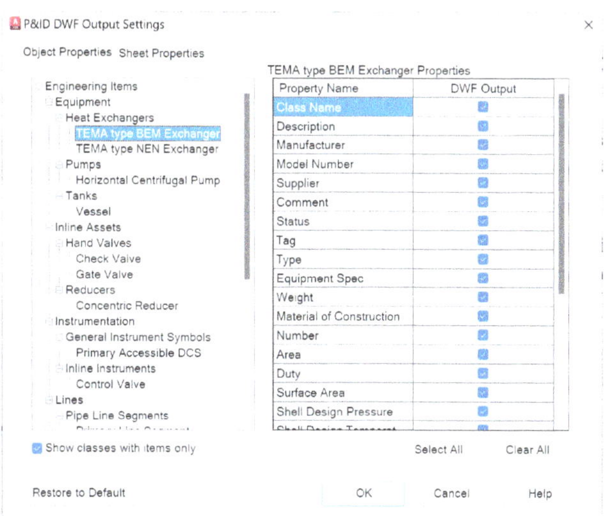

The **Sheet Properties** tab helps you to control the project details and drawing properties to be published.

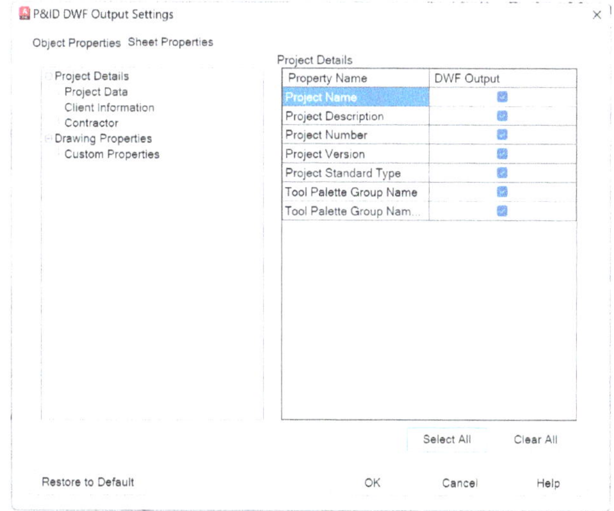

4. Click **OK** on the **P&ID DWF Output Settings** dialog.
5. Set the **P&ID Information** to **Include**. The program publishes the **P&ID information** along with the drawing.
6. Set the **Filter null values** to **On** to exclude the P&ID properties without any value.
7. Leave **Granular pipeline output** to **Off** to publish the pipe segments as a single output.

8. Leave the **Plant 3D DWF options** as default. These options are self-explanatory.
9. Under the **Default output location (plot to file)** section, click the icon next to the **Location** drop-down.
10. Go to the project folder location and click **Select**.
11. Under the **General DWF/PDF options** section, set the type to **Multi-sheet file**. The program creates a multi-sheet file.
12. Set **Naming** to **Prompt for name**. The program prompts you to provide the name while publishing the drawing.
13. Set **Layer information** to **Include** to publish the drawing along with layer information.
14. Likewise, examine the other options on this dialog. Place the pointer on each option to get a brief explanation of it.

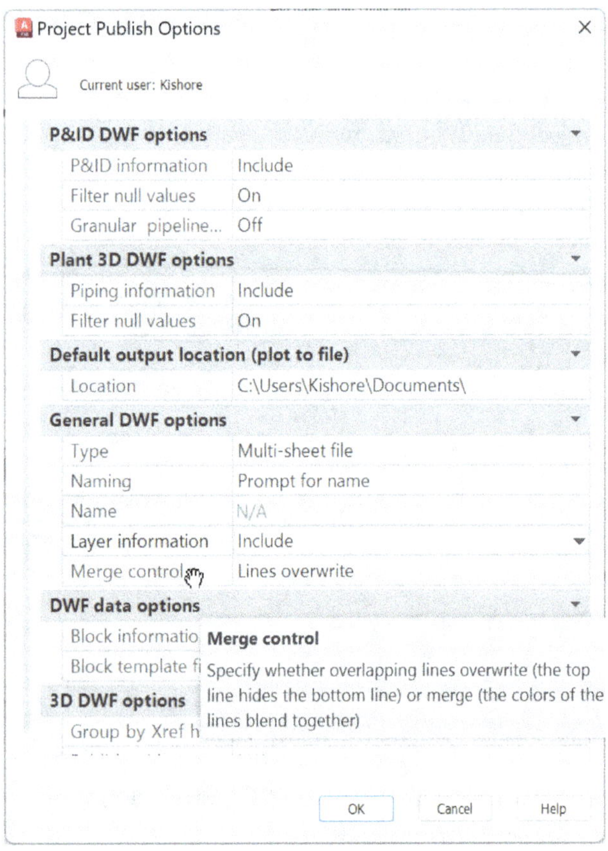

The options under the **3D DWF Options** section are available only while publishing drawings with 3D objects.

15. Click **OK** to close the dialog.

16. Select **D-6-01** from the sheet list and click the **Remove Sheets** icon. Likewise, you can add sheets to the list using the **Add Sheets** icon.
17. Select **Tutorial 2-Model** from the sheet list and click **Move Sheet Down** . This action moves down the selected drawing.

On the **Publish** dialog, the **Sheet List** drop-down shows a sheet set. You can also create a sheet set using the **Save Sheet List** icon next to the drop-down.

18. Click the **Save Sheet List** icon next to the **Sheet List** drop-down.
19. Save the sheet list as **PID Drawing.dsd**. The P&ID drawings listed on the **Publish** dialog are saved as a list.
20. Select **DWF** from the **Publish to** drop-down.
21. Select **Precision > For Civil Engineering**. You can also choose **Manufacturing** or **Architecture** (or) create custom precision. It depends on the precision that is required.
22. Uncheck the **Publish in background** option and check **Open in viewer when done** option.
23. Click **Publish** and save the file as **Tutorial Project.dwf**.

Publish a Drawing using Page setup

1. Open the **Tutorial 1** file.
2. Click the **Application Menu** icon at the top left corner and click **Print > Page Setup**.

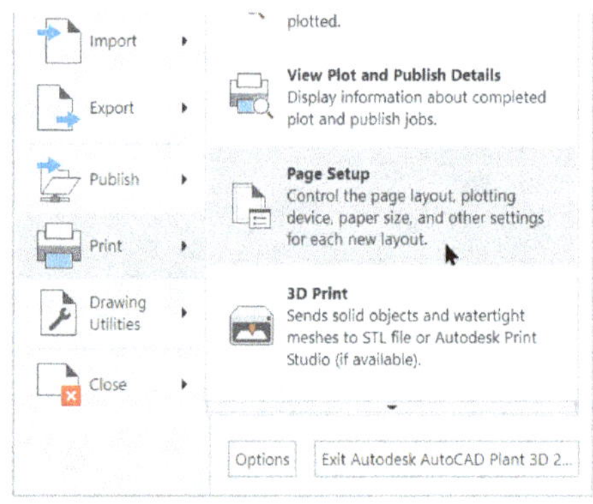

3. On the **Page Setup Manager** dialog, click the **New** button.

4. Type-in **Project Print Setup** in the **New page setup name** box and click **OK**.
5. Select a printer from the **Name** drop-down.
6. Set the **Paper Size** to **ANSI D (34.00 x 22.00 Inches)**.
7. Set the **Plot area** to **Layout**.
8. Make sure that the **Plot Style** is set to **PID.ctb**. The program prints the drawing using the P&ID color-dependent lineweights.
9. Set the **Scale** to **1:1** and check the **Scale lineweights** option.
10. Leave the other default options and click **OK**.
11. Click **Set Current** and close the **Page Setup Manager** dialog.
12. Save the drawing.
13. Click the **Application Menu** icon and select **Publish**.
14. On the **Publish** dialog, select **Plotter named in page setup** option from the **Publish to** drop-down.
15. Select **Tutorial 1-Model** from the sheet list and click **Remove Sheets** .
16. Select **Project Print Setup** from the **Page Setup** drop-down.

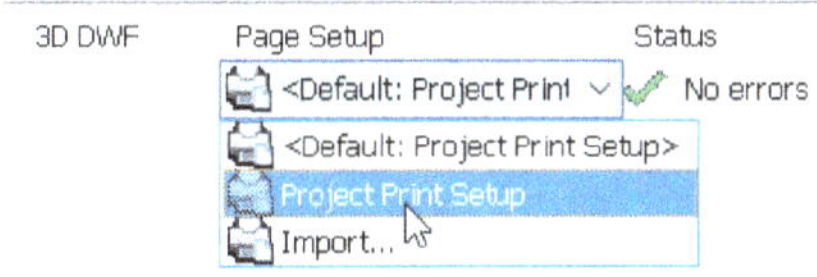

17. Click **Publish** to publish the document.
18. Likewise, you can print or publish Isometric, orthographic, or Plant 3D drawings.

www.ingramcontent.com/pod-product-compliance
Lightning Source LLC
Chambersburg PA
CBHW081252130726
47998CB00010B/2772